Towards a Local Tribal Church

Towards a Local Tribal Church

An Anthropological and Missiological Exploration of the Jesuits among the Santals

Vadappuram Mathew Jose SJ
(VM Jose SJ)

Jnana-Deepa Vidyapeeth

&

Christian World Imprints

First Published in 2021 by

Jnana-Deepa Vidyapeeth
Ramwadi, Nagar Road, Pune-411014
jdvoffice@jdv.edu.in
www.jdv.edu.in
Phone: +91 20 41036111

&

Christian World Imprints
Christian Publishing & Books from India
C-3, Wazirpur Industrial Area
Delhi-110052
cwidelhi2017@gmail.com
www.ChristianWorldImprints.com
Phone: +91 11 41526079

ISBN: 978-93-5148-514-8

Printed in India.

Dedicated to all the Missionaries who have given their
Blood and Life for the Tribal people.

Contents

Foreword

We human beings live in a time of great insecurity where humanity is faced with many grave threats and challenges; from climate change to political instability, de-culturation of cultures or even their extinction (as is happening in the Indian tribal culture), from species extinction to poverty, financial crisis and warfare. Fear has eaten its way into the human psyche. The rise of fear is more intense today than ever before in history. From this perspective, we human beings are in great crisis. Although this crisis can mean danger, change and transformation are also possible. Thus, we human beings are at a crossroad; our future depends on how we choose and deal with the situations in which we are.

Tribal societies have seldom recorded their own history. They usually relied on oral transmission of events, which raises definite difficulties for mainstream historians who have seldom given serious thought to tribal struggles or movements. The author has tried to bring out the situation of the Santals as historically and factually as possible. The tragic life of the tribal people is very vividly explicated. He has also suggested ways and means of solving some of the problems prevalent among the tribal people.

The early work of the missionaries is highly commendable. Though some of their ways and methods may not be very appropriate seen from today's perspective, their hard work and struggle with the people are to be highly appreciated. It is worth noting that there is an emphasis on the changing scenario of the people and how we can try to prevent the changes that will do harm to the tribal set up.

We experience God as someone who is actively involved in the life and struggle of people and this God constantly cares for his people in their need, though at times we may not feel his presence. The faith dimension from the perspective of the Bible is highlighted meaningfully. He as a Jesuit has seen to it that adequate importance is given to the Spiritual Exercises and General Congregation and how they can influence and help us do our ministry effectively.

I appreciate the optimistic note that he explicates. We should never become discouraged. We are about a holy purpose in building up the Kingdom to redeem all humanity; or, at least those people within our regions. If the whole Church would take more seriously the high calling, we might come closer to fulfilling

Jesus' great commission to reach all people everywhere with the Gospel of the Cross. If the churches everywhere would somehow open our doors to all seekers, then people everywhere would stop a minute to consider the message of the Cross.

I recommend this book as an attempt to know the Santals, their church history and mission. It can be a great help to find some ways of proper missionary activity in order to be effective, efficient and relevant missionaries today for the Tribal people.

Rev Fr Varghese Puthuserry, SJ
Former Provincial
Dumaka-Raiganj Province

November 14, 2020

Acknowledgement

My studies in Innsbruck were made possible first and foremost because of the Society of Jesus (the Religious Order I belong to) and my then Provincial Superior (of Dumka-Raiganj Jesuit Province, India) Fr. Varghese Puthuserry SJ. I appreciate the initiative and support he rendered to me. I am greatly indebted to the Austrian Jesuit Province for their generous support, hospitality and encouragement to study here. Without their generosity my studies in Innsbruck would not have been possible. I cannot but mention the Rector of Jesuitenkolleg, Innsbruck, Fr. Josef Thorer SJ and all the other community members who personally and constantly helped and supported me.

It goes without saying that the continuous support, encouragement and technical advice given by my guide has contributed significantly to the writing of this research work. I sincerely thank Prof. Dr. Franz Weber, MCCJ, for his scholarly and personal guidance all through my studies. He kept telling me that he was keenly interested in knowing the world of the Santals and I could sense that feeling every time we met for discussion. That was definitely a boost for my work as my own interest in my theme was maintained. He has supported this study by his wisdom and expertise. His personal experiences of the third world have inspired and supported my views and understanding of my own world better. I cannot forget Dr. Anni Findl-Ludescher, in particular and the students of the Research Seminar Group in general, who always had challenging and valuable observations for me.

I am very deeply indebted to Fr. Paul Aquilina SJ (Dumka-Raiganj Province) for his timely and prompt replies to my requests for documents from the Province. He knew the archive of the Jesuit Province and sent me the needed documents without delay. I am also grateful to Fr. John Scicluna, SJ (who was once my superior, now residing in Malta) who sent me the required documents I requested. I would like to thank the Klaunzer-Gomig family in Osttirol where I had easy access to computer and internet during my summer vacation so I could continue my research work then. I appreciate their hospitality and generosity. Another important person who has helped me generously is Mrs Sylvia Baumgartner. She had the patience to read through my dissertation and correct it with her own comments and suggestions. I am very personally grateful to her.

I am indeed grateful to the Papal Seminary community in general and to the Rector, Fr. Bhausaheb Sansare, SJ, in particular, for the encouragement and support they rendered to me during the last few years. I am also indebted to Fr Francis Gonsalves, SJ, President and Staff of JDV faculty for the academic help and support I received. I am also indebted to Rev Vincent Crasta, SJ and Rev Jose Thayil SJ, administers of both sister-institutions, to which I owe a lot.

I am immensely grateful to Dumka Raiganj Province of the Society of Jesus and all its members, who have made this research possible. Particularly, I am grateful to Rev Fr Varghese Pallipalakatt, SJ, the Provincial.

I place on record my deep sense of appreciation and gratitude for the Santals with whom I have spent several days, months and years. To honour those who are worthy of honour is the highest blessing. The Santals are worthy of honour and respect. No matter how illiterate or oppressed they may be. My best way of expressing my gratitude to them may be by being compassionate to them in their need. It is their life that has been the inspiration for this work. Many of them may not even know or hear about what I have written about them. I ask the Lord to bless them all and hope to give support that I can render them.

As a way of gratitude to what others have done to me, I need to do something for them. If I develop the sublime state of loving-kindness, compassion, sympathetic joy and equanimity then I would be an ideal person for everyone who has been part of my life in some way. While thanking God, my parents and family members for all that they have been to me and done for me all these years, I also thank one and all for all that they have done for me. To the Lord, I owe everything. For the Lord, I have nothing. Nothing but a heart of thanks. He gave me that too. Take it, Lord.

Dr Vadappuram Mathew Jose SJ

Abbreviation

AG	Ad Gentis
AISWACS	All India Santal Welfare and Cultural Society
AsIPA	Asian Integral Pastoral Approach
BCC	Basic Christian Communities
BHC	Basic Human Communities
CBCI	Catholic Bishops Conference of India
CRS	Catholic Relief Service
CTC	Catechists Training Centre
DV	Dei Verbum
EN	Evangelium Nuntiandi
EP	Evangelii Praecone
FABC	Federation of Asian Bishops' Conference
GC	General Congregation
GS	Gaudium et Spes
IBVM	Institute of the Blessed Virgin Mary
ICSE	Indian Certificate of Secondary Education
ISC	Indian School Certificate
LG	Lumen Gentium
MCCJ	Missionarii Comboniani Cordis Jesu
Mgr	Monsignor
MP	Member of Parliament
NGO	Non-Governmental Organisation
NS	Nostra Aetate
OL	Orientale Lumen
OMI	Oblates of Mary Immaculate
OP	Order of Preachers (Dominicans)
PIME	Pontificio Instituto Missioni Estere (The Pontifical Institute for Foreign Missions
PME	Pretres de Missions Etrangeres (Fathers of the Foreign Mission Society)
PT	Pacem in Terris

RM	Redemptoris Missio
RN	Rerum Novarum
SA	Slavorum Apostoli
SCC	Small Christian Communities
SCN	Sisters of Charity of Nazareth
SD	Sublimus Dei
SDB	Salesians of Don Bosco
SDO	Sub Divisional Officer
SJ	Society of Jesus
SpEx	Spiritual Exercises
SVA	Sampradayikta Virodhi Andholan
TOR	Third Order Regular
WCC	World Council of Churches

General Introduction

The Point of Departure: Experience and Context

One day, during the year 1988, when I was doing my regency in a village of the Santals, a man came to meet us (me and another priest with whom I stayed). He wanted us to visit his house and pray for his only son who was seriously sick, on the verge of death, (the family was Christian). He had taken him to a doctor living about 10 kilometres away. But the doctor could not heal him as he was not equipped with all the facilities to treat such serious cases. The patient was advised to be taken to another hospital where he could be properly treated. But the parents were helpless as they did not have enough money nor a conveyance to take him to a faraway hospital. We visited the family immediately and prayed for him. But without much delay, the boy breathed his last, (he was only 20 years old). However, the family was grateful that we prayed for him. Almost with horror I watched the scene which becomes all the more shocking especially when I realize that it is the real thing and not some Hollywood scripted scene. The true tragedy of the event only hit home after I saw parents looking for their lost child. I realized then that when nature takes its toll, it is serious because there are several other similar cases in the village. It saddens me to hear similar reports; the despair in the eyes of the people who have lost their family members or mourning those that lost their lives in sicknesses due to lack of facilities. Sometimes nature can act with brutal force, without warning and without cause, taking its toll; and adding to that we lack facilities, proper medicine, transport, etc. I am unable to forget that moment in my life though several years have gone by.

I was deeply moved by this incident and it made me reflect a lot and think of the plight of these people, the Santals. I was very upset because we could not do anything for this patient in spite of our ardent desire to help him in his dire need. I need to say that we had no vehicle at hand and so we could not take him to the hospital. In a way it was an eye opener to the reality of these people living in such remote villages. This is only one of the many incidents that occur in the Santal villages almost every day of their lives. I decided that I should do something in a situation of this kind. This personal experience has made me reflect on the life of the people in the light of faith so that I am able to find meaning and hope in such a situation. God is alive and active in such situations as these, although it is difficult to experience the presence of God so clearly. But as a believer I reflect that God has to be definitely present in this situation and so I want to understand God as someone very close to humanity, someone who is attuned to the cries and joys of people. If I understand God in this perspective then theology has to be also close to the people. It cannot be aloof from the ordinary situations of people. Thus theology becomes a science of interpretation, interpretation of human experience in the light of the interpretation of the Word of God and human experience becomes the starting point. Human experience provides questions and at the same time it is shaped by the light of the Word of God.

Purpose and Goal

The Santals, who have become Christians, have to a great extent lost their identity as the Santal tribe. Many of the Christian Santals live with non-Christian Santals in the same village. They face difficulties because of two types of religions, namely, Christianity and tribal religion. I want to try to make the Church more effective and functional for both the groups, namely non-Christian Santals and Christian Santals. Here I should admit that with the process of evangelisation and Christianisation the Christian Santals have lost their tribal identity to a great extent. My goal or attempt is to find out how the Santals can keep their identity as Santals and remain Christians as well. That is a challenge for me/us to understand and settle the issues that are at stake.

Some people argue that the conversion effort is part of service to humanity, that the missionary is motivated by love of humanity. This is also questionable. If you are motivated by love of humanity you will help people regardless of their religious background. You will try to help people in a practical way rather than aim at getting them to embrace your religious belief. You will also love their religion, even if it is an aborigine worshipping a stone. You will not condemn any person to hell for not following your particular belief. You will not interfere with that person's religious motivation and seek to convert him to your belief. You will honour the divine in that person and in his belief. Such social work born of love is hardly to be found in missionary Christianity, though it likes to pretend that this is the motivation. If one were truly motivated by love of humanity and the need to serve humanity, one would not promote massive conversion agendas. In fact, one would regard such practices as inhumane, which they are.

I have lived with these people (Santals) in their villages. I have tried to help them in some situations. I have talked with illiterate and poor people from the villages; I have also talked with literate, educated and reasonably rich people. I have heard from them about their myths, legends and history. I have also heard their sad stories of oppression by the British people, money lenders and landlords. At times I have shared my views with them and tried to help them during meetings or seminars in their villages. I have gone from village to village collecting information, statistics; I have, with the help of others, made surveys and reports in order to help them. I have celebrated the holy Eucharist with them in their villages, and have baptized them, blessed their marriages, and have buried the dead. I have sat by their side and heard their everyday existential problems of hunger and thirst. I have witnessed some of their feasts and festivals. I have even participated in some of their (non-Christian) festivals, sacred celebrations, marriages and funeral services.

My life among the Santals has made me know more about them and study their reality more systematically and scientifically. I know that I should be equipped with sufficient knowledge of the people to deal with the life of the people. We need to have also the knowledge of how to upgrade their standard of living. The tragic economic situation of these people is really very cruel and painful to see. I earnestly desire that these people have sufficient to eat and drink, rather than grovelling in the dirt. I feel I am indebted as a Jesuit and Christian to help them eliminate their poverty. My life in their midst has raised several questions in me and I thought it would be a good idea that I write something about them so that I can understand and know them a little better.

I have taught theology for two years in the regional theologate (Santiniketan, West Bengal) and to continue teaching theology in the tribal context with the perspective of the tribal reality I need to be supported with a proper understanding, reflection and analysis of the tribal reality. For a contextual theologizing, the reality and experience of the people are essential. I hope that my study may help me to be more effective and efficient to work with and for the Santals.

The desire to help people in terms of social uplift and the desire to change their religion are clearly not the same and can be contradictory. Changing a person's religion may not help them in terms of health, education, or economics. This study investigates the reality of Santals from their different perspectives so as to experience total liberation for the Santals.

Method and Procedure

As a methodology for the dissertation we make use of what is called "the pastoral circle." "The pastoral circle is just a more detailed description of the hermeneutic circle.[1] There are four major moments that constitute the pastoral circle: insertion,

1 Hermeneutic circle refers to the circle of interpretation necessarily involved when understanding some work of art. According to this theory, it is not possible to really understand any one part of a work until you understand the whole, but it also is not possible to understand the whole without also understanding all of the parts. This means instead, a way of explaining and expressing how understanding and interpreting a work of art is an ongoing process which takes time. Those who argue that no attempt at interpretation can ever reach any sort of closure will refer to this as a hermeneutic spiral, because it simply goes around and around forever (available from: http://atheism.about.com/library/glossary/aesthetics/bldef_hermeneuticcircle.htm, accessed on 10.03.2009).

social analysis, theological reflection and pastoral planning for action. However the circle would be better called a "spiral" and not hermeneutic circle because it never comes back to the same starting point; after the evaluation of the planned pastoral action a new process, starting from the insertion in a new human situation, will begin."[2] I am trying to follow this methodology.

The classical task of theology is understood as "wisdom and rational knowledge." It was related to spiritual perfection because of the dichotomy between body and soul, sacred and profane, and secular and divine. This understanding of theology was founded on metaphysics and stressed the existence of a higher world, the transcendence of an absolute and so this world is not valued. Theology as rational knowledge is "meeting between faith and reason." "The traditional method in scholastic theology proceeded by way of deduction that is, deducing from the Biblical text the guidelines for faith and morals."[3] Biblical texts are quoted to support a particular truth. Sometimes this methodology has to invent its own questions, even if not necessarily connected with human life. Many theologians were accused of providing responses to questions they themselves had invented. With the rapid changes in society, this method became more obsolete. So "induction", the role of human experience in scientific research, pervaded not only science but also theology. A text becomes alive only when the reader approaches it with his or her own cultural background and from his or her own personal experience.[4]

The intrinsic interrelation between the reader of the Bible and the Bible as a book is described as the "hermeneutic circle", that is, the circle of interpretation whereby the reader understands the text according to his or her own experience, and the biblical text on the other hand affects and shapes the human experience of the reader.[5]

The shift came with the new understanding of theology as "liberation theology." Here theology is understood as "critical reflection on historical praxis." I understand liberation theology as an integral theology, treating faith from a particular perspective, the perspective of the poor and their liberation. It develops the meaning of the gospel as historically liberative. The hermeneutic circle becomes effective in this context.

I find that the methodology of pastoral circle suits my theme well. I follow the procedure in four steps. The first step is contact or immersion. The important factor here is to know, what is happening to the poor in their situation. This option for the poor places a priority on the experiences, views, needs, feelings, and stance

2 Mejia, Rodrigo, SJ, Pastoral Theology and the Pastoral Circle, This paper is an extract from IMBISA OCCASIONAL PAPER, No. 5 entitled "The Pastoral Circle. Harare-Zimbabwe, 2000, 125.

3 Mejia, Rodrigo, SJ, Pastoral Theology and the Pastoral Circle, 122 – 23.

4 Mejia, Rodrigo, SJ, Pastoral Theology and the Pastoral Circle, 123.

5 Mejia, Rodrigo, SJ, Pastoral Theology and the Pastoral Circle.

of the poor, and what is most vulnerable in a community. The second step is social analysis. The question of why such conditions exist will be guided by those whose rights are being violated and whose responsibilities are called upon to change the situation. Here the rights and responsibilities, human dignity of each person in community are taken into consideration. Their economic, social, political and cultural causes are also dealt with. The next step is theological reflection: When we come to ask what it means to our faith to evaluate this situation and what is really most at stake in this situation, we can be guided by the church's social teaching about human dignity and solidarity. Every person is made in the image of God. Therefore, all have equal dignity in this world. Finally, we come to the culmination of this phase of the process. Based on our analysis and reflections we now move towards the appropriate response. This step is very important because without it everything will be mere theory without any significance to all the other prior steps. This orients towards planning, action, and evaluation.[6]

I know that all these are not sufficient knowledge for a comprehensive understanding of a tribal group. However, I venture into a challenge that may enlighten me to learn more and understand them better in order to find some ways that can be of help to enhance the life standard of the Santals. Adding to my life experience among the Santals, I have books about them which should help me to delve deeper into their reality. All these things may help me to understand and better my knowledge.

Significance of this Book

The immediate challenge for the tribal people at the moment is to save their tribal identity. The tribal people are being ruled by non-tribal people. Consequently, no tribal system is being effectively observed in many tribal communities. As in the past, so also in the present, the tribal people are being looked down upon, are being labelled as backward, uncivilized and stupid. They are unable to keep abreast with the progress of civilization. They seem to be at the crossroads of civilization, unable to decide whether to hold on to their age-old traditions or follow the main stream of civilization. The Society of Jesus of my Jesuit Province (Dumka-Raiganj Province) wants to work together with them, the Santals, so that they have an identity of their own by establishing a true local church.

Tribal societies have seldom recorded their own history. They usually relied on oral transmission of events, which raises definite difficulties for mainstream historians who have seldom given serious thought to tribal struggles or movements. We should keep in mind that most of the books about tribal people are written by non-tribal people. It is expected that there are views and perspectives held by the authors inherent in the writings. We have no other option other than accept these writings but we can perceive them and understand the people from our own experiences of these people. This will not be, however, without prejudice.

6 Mejia, Rodrigo, SJ, Pastoral Theology and the Pastoral Circle, 140-41.

The legend of the Santals to account for the origin of their race is told with many variations and additions, excusable among a people of vivid imagination and unblessed with a written history, but always adhering to the main points of interest, whether it is told on the banks of the Ganges or elsewhere in Bangladesh. In a legend so vague and mythical there is little idea of locality. The Santals have no knowledge of where the earliest ancestors of their race first made their home. The place of residence according to tradition is Hihiri Pipiri. Many attempts have been made to find out the place but no exact place has been found yet. Different theories have been stipulated.

There are two different perspectives in the understanding of the tribal (*Adivasi*) or indigenous people. One is the **tribal self-understanding** and the other the ruling **elite's understanding**. It is quite obvious that one view does not usually agree with the other. Policies and laws are made by the elite class and are thrust upon tribal peoples. So, it is natural that the idea of the ruling class will prevail over the ruled class. The history of the tribal people against all types of oppressive groups testifies to their determination to assert their distinct identity.

The history of the tribal people is preserved in their oral traditions. These traditions are in their own language. There are works which have made attempts to trace the history of the tribes from the Hindu Scriptures and the kingly dynastic histories. These attempts are from the ruling class. The tribes have however kept a separate identity from the other groups till today, which is seen in their religious and social institutions, beliefs, practices and relationships, economic and political structures. The past of the tribal people is kept alive in their *oral tradition.*[7]

The oral tradition is found in the form of myths and the history preserved in their family trees, sayings, songs and burial grounds. The oral tradition reveals two main ideas. 1. How the tribes have been driven out of their homelands by latecomers who were more cunning and had the latest know-how, and 2. How the tribes loved to struggle in order to preserve their identity and homeland.[8] The following translation of a Santali song thus speaks of the story: "for just one span of stomach (just to get a little food), just to stay alive, I have wandered from country to country, I have travelled twelve (i.e. a great number) countries."[9]

The influence of the church among the Santals is another factor to be dealt with. What does it mean to be a 'fully Indian and authentically Christian' church? What does it mean to be a true Church in India? How should the church understand itself in the multi-cultural-religious context of India? The task of this research is to attempt to answer the above questions from the perspective of communion ecclesiology. In current ecclesiology there is a tension between the classical and the progressive features, one that comes from above and one

7 Mundu, John, Tribal and Indigenous Peoples in India, Media House, Delhi: 2003, 13.

8 Mundu, John,Tribal and Indigenous Peoples in India, 14.

9 Areeparambil, Mathew, Struggle for Swaraj: A History of Adivasi Movements in Jharkhand, Tribal Training Centre: Chaibasa, 2002, 242.

that grows from below. Such tension is engaging and enriching. Neither can the church of God exclude any. So, I need to focus my research work in the right perspective and understanding.

Plan of this Book

The research work is divided into five parts with a personal epilogue at the end. The first chapter deals with an introduction of the Santals. How Santals are placed in the context of Indian reality and the reality of the Santals. For this analysis the starting point is a society (in our context, the Santal society) which is always complex, because it contains several interrelated factors. The foundation for a societal analysis is an attempt to investigate a situation or existing social problem as objectively as possible by discovering the cause of the problem and establishing the relationship of the factors. To analyse the reality of Santals we need to know the myth, legends, politics, economy and socio-culture as well as geography and history. This analysis is to help us find or offer alternatives to political decisions or practical actions. In our context we need to orient our goal for changing the status quo. We demand an immediate end to the particular abuse of human life among the Santals by oppressive forces (government machinery and local machinery). We recognize that this abuse has always included subjugation and injustice by the *mahajans* (money lenders) and landlords. We demand an end to this degradation, as well as other forms of oppression among the Santals and other tribal people of India. We believe in the absolute equivocal, political, social, cultural, religious and economic equality of all people of India. We demand the elevation of tribal people to their rightful place as equal partners and leaders in forward motion of the development of Santals as leaders, makers and shapers of their own human history.

Once we know the people in general, we can move onto the next chapter which deals with the mission of the Church among the Santals. It is a historical analysis of Christianity among the Santals. The missionaries and their challenges; success and failures must be dealt with so as to understand what is right and what is wrong. The context of our missionary endeavours among the Santals fits very well into the context described by the Lord in Matthew 10, which contrasts the challenges, dangers and hazards of the missionary enterprise with the blessings, securities and insurances provided by the Lord of the Harvest Himself. Most of our mission stations are located in the highly conflict-prone areas where landlords and *mahajans* oppress them. Our missionaries have been operating in the face of dangers and in environments and situations fraught with hazards. In spite of such situations of conflict, the missionaries had the enthusiasm to work for the Lord in His vineyard. The other side of the picture is a little different. Christianity in India is considered a 'foreign religion' even after many centuries of its existence in India. This has happened because the missionaries did not give importance to the customs and culture of the people. It is impossible to forget the sufferings and injustices inflicted by colonisers on the indigenous peoples, who often had their basic human rights trampled. People often understood that missionaries worked with the colonisers though they were not directly responsible for the oppression of the tribal people.

Social structures are changing all the time and Christianity will certainly influence those changes. In the past (and even in the present), for most Catholics evangelisation was perceived to be the work of a special group within the Church, e.g., those with a special vocation, missionaries or priests. Conversion to Christianity did not raise the country economically. Central and South America, which are much more staunchly Catholic and religious are also much poorer and have a lower level of education. Educated people in the West are less likely to be staunch Christians, and many of them look to Eastern religions for spiritual guidance.

Today we need to understand evangelisation as the call to the entire people of God. In the past few decades, there has been a theological quest to 'incarnate' the church in India, i.e., in the culture and context of India, especially inspired by the renewal of theology of Vatican II. There is an ever-growing, ever-strengthening plea to make the church 'fully Indian and authentically Christian.' The multi-religious, multi-cultural and multi-caste context of Indian society and the Indian church call for an ever-renewed ecclesiological reflection so that the church in India can be the salt of the earth in India, a true witness of Jesus and his Gospel. This is a remarkable shift in emphasis; one that I believe necessitates a pastoral plan by the bishops of the Church for helping the faithful to share in the responsibility of evangelisation and the mission. All the Christian faithful should participate in the calling to the new evangelization of the life-changing, gospel message to be experienced as "Good News" in each of their lives. The message of the gospel must be heard, understood, embraced, lived and shared by all members of the Church.

Therefore, in the next chapter I concentrate on inculturation and point out how essential it is to be inculturated so as to have "a new way of being Church." Inculturation is a term designating the process by which the Gospel takes root in local values and cultures, discovering and using their richness, as well as purifying their deficiencies. The Church has existed throughout the centuries in varying circumstances and has utilized the resources of different cultures in its preaching to spread and explain the message of Christ. Faithful to its own tradition and at the same time conscious of its universal mission, it can enter into communion with different forms of culture, thereby enriching both itself and the cultures. Jesus who was born, who died and who has risen from the dead, who is living among us, who comes, not to destroy but to bring to perfection, is the one who inspires us to be inculturated. It can be truthfully said what is inculturated is Jesus Christ himself. He is the subject matter of inculturation. Inculturation is a further and definitive step by which Jesus Christ enters into a living relationship with a cultural tradition. Proper inculturation can lead us to have a theology that is contextual.

The fourth chapter deals with contextual theology which is necessary for the reality of Santals today. I remember reading once the quotation from Marx, "philosophers have explained the world; our task is to change it." Therefore, we cannot conclude that theologians are mere theoreticians; they should also be practitioners. Contextual theology should deal with the struggle to bring about society's transformation. That is the reason why we need to employ a Marxist-style class analysis, which divides the culture between oppressors and oppressed. This conflicting sociological analysis is meant to identify the injustices and exploitation within the historical situation. Marxism and the theology that we want to do, condemn religion for supporting the status quo and legitimating the power of the oppressor. In the context of India, both on the theoretical and the practical level many Christian groups have come in contact with non-Christians involved in the struggle for liberation. The Bible and Christian tradition as a whole do not address themselves directly to us in our present situation. They stand as a basic point of reference for us and indicate to us how God speaks to human beings in widely divergent contexts. Such a context can help us see how God might be speaking to us in our present context. Therefore, it is a type of Christian reflection that corresponds with their own practical experience of the faith in the context of political praxis. This praxis aims at bringing about liberation. Thus, a theology derived from such praxis leads us to concrete action.

Therefore, I deal with pastoral planning in the fifth chapter. Marx failed to see the emotive, symbolic, and sociological force the Church could be in the struggle for justice. Liberation theologians claim that they are not departing from the ancient Christian tradition when they use Marxist thought as a tool for social analysis. They do not claim to use Marxism as a philosophical world view or a comprehensive plan for political action. Human liberation may begin with the economic infrastructure, but it does not end there. A comprehensive analysis of the situation in the light of faith can lead us to proper liberative action. We need to plan effectively and efficiently to have a pastoral vision for the Santals. In the last chapter I have to conclude with this idea of a new vision of humanity for Santals to live a meaningful happy life. Our own experience has shown that the activities of new humanity, while enhancing the spirit of mutual understanding, lead to social actions that value the contribution of all tribal people and inspire hope for a united tribal society.

Limitations of the Work

I would say that my first experience when I stayed with a Santal family was to some extent similar. Life of a Santal family is a life of struggle in the real world. This is how most of the Santals live in the world today. It is often a hand to mouth existence for many and for many others still worse. Many families manage with one meal a day. I have spent a few years working with the Santals. I have tried to learn their language and culture. Still I should confess that my understanding of these people is limited. I am not a Santal. I have not experienced the poverty the Santals experience. My language and culture are different. As anyone would understand, my ability to comprehend the reality of Santals is limited because I am an outsider to the Santal world. I have to admit that there may be inherent prejudices and misunderstandings about the Santals as I write about them. I can assure that this is not done deliberately, but the way I understand their reality. On many occasions I have used the term "non-Christian" due to the unavailability of another term which might be more appropriate. I hope that the people are not disturbed by such a terminology.

I should admit that there are not many authors who have written about the history of the church among the Santals as that history is only about 80 years old. Only one person (Fr. Yves Steenhault SJ) has so far written elaborately about it. The other writer who has written about the Santal church history is Fr. John Scicluna SJ. I have to largely rely on these two authors. The other writers have limited themselves to short narrations of places and incidents. I have not left them out. However, I have managed to get all possible letters related to the Santal church history from the archive of my Jesuit Province (Dumka-Raiganj).

Another limitation I cannot avoid is that I am unable to plan the project with them as I write the dissertation. In fact, a proper planning for pastoral action can be done only with the cooperation of people. I have no option but to suggest some ways based on my own personal experience which probably will help the people. With all the shortcomings and limitations my attempt is oriented towards the welfare of Santals, that they too may live in peace and harmony in a just world where they have their rightful place as persons and as Santals.

1

The Santals and Their World

1.1. Introduction

In a country as diverse and complex as India, it is not surprising to find that people here reflect the rich glories of the past, the culture, traditions and values relative to geographic locations and numerous distinctive manners, habits and food that will always remain truly Indian. According to five thousand years of recorded history, India has been invaded by armies, traders and immigrants who brought with them their own habits, faiths, practices and observances which have all contributed to the rich texture of Indian life and living. With all these the history of India is shrouded in antiquity. The country has been thought of as a nation of philosophers with a well-developed and even idyllic society. Excavations of sites belonging to the Harappan and Mohenjo Daro era (c. 3000 – 1500 B.C) show that the people lived in brick houses in towns with excellent drainage. One of the oldest scriptures in the world is the four volume Vedas (The Vedas (knowledge) are a large corpus of texts originating in ancient India written by the Aryan Civilization) that many regard them as the repository of national thoughts that anticipated some modern scientific discoveries. Despite formidable barriers in the form of the mighty Himalayas and oceans, India also received a succession of foreigners, many of them carrying swords and guns. But, nearly all of them stayed on. Out of these waves of immigration has emerged the composite culture of India and made it a land of unity in diversity. India became a land of assimilation and learning, a land of change and continuity. The Aryans were among the first to arrive in India, which was inhabited by the Dravidians. Others who came here included Greeks, Persians, Mughals, British, Portuguese and French. Over the years there have been many major ruling dynasties like the Shakas (ca. 180

B.C.-A.D. 15), the Kushans (ca105–250 B.C), the Mauryas (ca. 326-184 B.C) and Guptas (ca. A.D. 320-550). Nearly every major world religion (Christianity, Hinduism, Islam, Buddhism, Jainism, and Sikhism) is represented in India. It is also the land of Lord Buddha, Lord Mahavira and Guru Nanak Dev, the founders of Buddhism, Jainism and Sikhism.

In this land of India, the Santals made their home. My attempt in this chapter is to give an overall explanation about the Santals. This basic section of my dissertation deals with the theme of Santals' life and context. One needs to know the history and background of the people to know the people well. We may be able to know their church history in the right perspective only if we know the people, their culture and their religious beliefs and world view. So, I try to describe their socio-political, religious and cultural background.

We should know that the Santals had no written tradition in the earlier days. They have kept their tradition orally. For the so-called civilized and educated society the oral tradition may not hold much truth. The written history of the Santals that we have is only from the 19th century. I must add a clause here; that history too is written by foreigners and non-Santals. Santals themselves had not written any of their own history till recently.

1.2. The Tribal People in Indian History

Tribal people comprise a substantial minority of the population of India. They are about 8.08 percent of the nation's total population, nearly 67.8 million people according to the 1991 census. One concentration lives in the belt along the Himalayas stretching through Jammu and Kashmir, Himachal Pradesh and Uttaranchal in the west, to Assam, Meghalaya, Tripura, Arunachal Pradesh, Mizoram, Manipur and Nagaland in the northeast. In the north-eastern states of Arunachal Pradesh, Meghalaya, Mizoram and Nagaland, more than 90 percent of the population is tribal. Another concentration lives in the hilly areas of central India, Chhattisgarh, Madhya Pradesh, and Orissa. The Santals are found mainly in Jharkhand, West Bengal and Orissa. Central Indian states have the country's largest tribes, roughly around 75 percent of the tribal population live there, although that amounts to only 10 percent of the region's total population.[1]

Tribal people in India originate from the following language families. They are: Andamanese, Austro-Asiatic, Dravidian, and Tibeto-Burman. It is believed that some of the Austro-Asiatic group have been living there for the last 60,000 years. It is also important to point out that those tribal people who belong to different language families live in distinct geographic settings. For example, in South Orissa there are languages that originate from the Central Dravidian family, Austro-Asiatic (Munda) family and the Indo-Aryan. In the Jharkhand area, languages are from the Indo-Aryan, North Dravidian and Austro-Asiatic.

1 Mammen, Mathew (ed), Manorama Yearbook 2008, Kottayam: Malayala Manorama Press, 2008, 563.

These people in India live in the following five territories. 1. The Himalayan belt: (Assam, Meghalaya, Arunachal Pradesh, Nagaland, Manipur, Mizoram, Tripura, hills of Uttar Pradesh and Himachal Pradesh). 2. Central India: Bihar, West Bengal, Orissa, and Madhya Pradesh. 55% of the total tribal population of India lives in this belt. 3. Western India: Rajasthan, Maharashtra, Gujarat, Goa, Dadra and Nagar Haveli. 4. The Dravidian region: Karnataka, Andhra Pradesh, Kerala and Tamil Nadu. 5. Andaman, Nicobar and Lakshadweep Islands.[2]

In the history of India, we find that the tribal people are an integral part of Indian civilization. Various elements in the ancient civilization of India were contributed by the tribal people. It is believed that they were the earliest among the present inhabitants of the country. They seem to have lived harmoniously with the other races. "In the ancient literature of India, the Vedas, the Puranas, the Ramayanaand the Mahabharata present good accounts about the people of India. When the Aryan immigrants entered the country, they found in the land non-Aryan people and called them *dasyus*" (servants). A reference has been found in the travel accounts of HiuenTsiang, the Chinese Pilgrim, who visited India about 645 AD. From the record of his travels it is learnt that he visited the kingdom of Champa, the northern boundary of which extended along the Ganges. To the east of Champa lay the kingdom in which Santal Parganas was part. According to Paul Olaf Bodding before the Santals arrived in this area of Santal Parganas, two very primitive tribes, Sauria Paharia and Mal Paharia had already been living on the hills of Rajmahal.

The co-existence of fundamentally different culture patterns and styles of living has always been a characteristic feature of the Indian stage. Unlike most parts of the world, in India, the arrival of new immigrants and the spread of their way of life did not necessarily cause the disappearance of earlier and materially less-advanced ethnic groups. The old and the new co-existed. Such a consequence was partly due to the great size of the sub-continent and dearth of communication. More important than this was an attitude basic to Indian ideology, which accepted a variety of cultural forms as natural and immutable, and did not consider their assimilation to one dominant pattern in any way desirable.

1.2.1 The Situation of the Tribal People

"The tribal India used to live in forest hills and naturally isolated regions known as a rule by different names meaning either the people of forest and hill or the original inhabitants."[3] The popular names are: *Vanyajati* (castes of forest), *Vanavasi* (inhabitants of forest), *Pahari* (hill dwellers), *Adimjati* (primitive people), *Adivasi* (original settlers), *Janjati* (folk people) and so on. Among these terms, *Adivasi*

2 Biswas, Probhas Chandra, Santals of Santal Parganas, Delhi, Bharatiya Adimjati Seva Sangh, 1956, 220.

3 Biswas, Probhas Chandra, Santals of Santal Parganas, 25.

is best known. Today according to the Constitution of India they are called *Anusuchit Janjati* (ST or scheduled tribes).[4]

The Tribal people have suffered the indignity of caste discrimination for centuries. It was Mahatma Gandhi who fought hard to recognize them as free citizens of India and called them *Girijans* or the *Children of the Forest God.* Upon independence of India in 1947, the Indian Government spent a lot of resources to improve the life of the native Indians or scheduled tribes (ST), as they are known in India today. In practice, it has been the assimilation approach (explained in 1. 2. 2) of the upper caste and upper class combine of the majority community. The perception of the Constitution is basically juridical and protective in nature, but from the perspective of the rulers and not the people.[5]

1.2.2. Criteria of Tribalness

The problem of determining which groups and individuals are tribal is difficult and complex. A number of traits have customarily been seen as establishing tribal rather than caste identity. These include language, social organization, religious affiliation, economic patterns, geographic location and self-identification. Recognised tribes typically live in hilly regions somewhat remote from caste settlements. They speak a language recognised as tribal. They tend to form self-sufficient economic units. They often practice swidden farming (shifting cultivation) rather than the intensive farming typical of most of rural India. Land use rights traditionally derive simply from tribal membership. Tribal society tends to be egalitarian, its leadership being based on ties of kinship and personality rather than on hereditary status. Tribal religion recognises no authority outside the tribe.[6]

After the independence of India for writing the Constitution of the country, there was hardly anybody to represent the interests of the tribal peoples. The ruling class was faced with the existence of these people spread out in all parts of the country. Three main theories were proposed to address the question of the tribal people. The theories are: 1. Isolation: In many areas tribal people were unable to resist the gradual alienation of their ancestral land, either they withdrew further into hills and tracts of marginal land, or accepted the economic status of tenants or agricultural labourers on the land their forefathers had owned. In most areas encroachment on land held by tribes continued even in the face of protective legislation. Thus, the tribal people could be isolated, leaving them to remain as they are. 2. Assimilation: Acceptance or denial of the necessity for assimilation with Hindu society is ultimately a question of values.In the past, Hindu society had

4 Biswas, Probhas Chandra, Santals of Santal Parganas.

5 Kamat, Krishnanand. Laxman., The Tribes of India, (available from: http://www.culturopedia.com/, accessed on 09.05.2008).

6 Adivasi, Library of Congress Studies, (available from: www.wikipediaencyclopedia.com, accessed on 09.05.2008).

been tolerant of groups that would not conform to the standards set by the higher castes. It is true such groups were denied equal ritual status; but no efforts were made to deflect them from their chosen style of living. Vigorous tribal populations which resist assimilation as well as inclusion within Hindu caste system live all along India's northern and north-eastern frontier. 3. Integration: Integration may be understood in this way, namely, the Indian ruling class wanting to assimilate the tribal societies into the mainstream of Indian society. The Constituent Assembly chose the third theory. Accordingly, two constitutional arrangements were made. First a state-wide list of tribes was drawn up and it was left to the Parliament to officially determine the list of the scheduled tribes from time to time. Secondly, provisions for the administration and control of scheduled areas and scheduled tribes were made and were incorporated in the Constitution of India for further governance.[7]

The aim of the government of India was at least clear in its ideology; the policy was to help and safeguard tribal people. The government adopted a policy of integration of tribal people with the mainstream aiming at developing a creative adjustment between the tribes and non-tribes leading to responsible partnership. By adopting the policy of integration the government thought that the foundation was laid for the uninhibited march of tribal people towards equality, upward mobility, and economic viability, thus reaching the national mainstream. The constitution has committed the nation to give protection to the distinct tribal way of life and protect them from social injustice and all forms of exploitation and discrimination.[8] The different Articles of the Constitution of India clearly state the following elements: Educational safeguards (15, iv) and 29; safeguards for employment (16, iv, 320, iv and 333); Economic safeguards (19); Abolition of bonded labour (23); Protection from social injustice and all forms of exploitation (46).[9]

1.2.3. The Santals in the Tribal (Indian) Context

The Santals also belong to the group of tribe or Adivasi. The Santals are the most numerous of the Indian tribes. They are generally settled in West Bengal, Bihar, Orissa and Jharkhand as well as in Bangladesh. The general theory is that they belong to the Proto-Australoid stock. However there are other theories which state that they belong to the group of Pre-Dravidians, Lolarians, Mongoloids,

7 Areeparambil, Mathew, Tribals of Jharkhand: Victims of Development, New Delhi: Indian Social Institute, 1998, 242.

8 Areeparambil, Mathew, Tribals of Jharkhand: Victims of Development, New Delhi: Indian Social Institute, 1998, 243.

9 Constitution of India, (available from: http://indiacode.nic.in/coiweb/welcome.html, accessed on 09.05.2008).

Austrics, etc.[10] According to A. B. Chaudhury, Santal is a large pre-Dravidian tribe, belonging to the Austro-Asiatic family and linguistically they have been classed as Kolarian. Santal is a corruption of the word *Saontar* and was the name given to them because of their sojourn in the Saont or Samantabhumi (modern Midnapore district in West Bengal).[11] Their language has survived in the Kol or Mundari (Munda) in eastern and Central India.[12] Santali, the language spoken by the Santals, fall in the family of Munda language. Since different authors have different views I leave these theories as they are.

1.2.4. The Santals: A General Description

As already mentioned, the name Santal is a corruption of *Saontar*. There are different terms used by different authors. *Saont* is another name given to the community around Saont, near Burdwan district in West Bengal.[13] According to O`Malley[14] Santal is an English word adapted from Hindi Language. This corresponds to the form *Santar* used by Bengali speaking people. Thus, various names were used to designate the people who are now known generally as Santals. But this term is generally used by non-Santals. Many anthropologists agree that the name is given by non-Santals. Among themselves the Santals use the term, *hor*, meaning man in the sense of human as in English.[15]

The Santals are found mainly in Jharkhand, West Bengal and Orissa. The main concentration is in "Jharkhand" which literally means "forest tract." It is a land with forest and rich minerals.[16] The Santals are a non-Hindu people. In fact, they make a clear distinction based on race between themselves and Hindus and are classified as a pre-Dravidian tribe. "The Santals are the largest tribal group in India. They had a population of about 2,500,000 according to the census of 1931 and their estimated population in 1950 was about 3,000,000."[17] According

10 Cf. Ray, Prafulla Chandra, Socio-Cultural Process and Psychological Adaptation of the Santal, Calcutta: M7s Reliance Printing Works, 1975, 3.

11 Chaudhury, Arnab, The Santals: Religion and Rituals, New Delhi: Ashish Publishing House, 1987, 15.

12 Tribes of India – The Origin of Races in India, (available from: www.culturopedia.com, accessed on 09.05.2005

13 Troisi, Joseph, Tribal Religion: Religious Beliefs and Practices among the Santals, New Delhi: Manohar, 1978, 23

14 O'Malley, Lewis Sydney Steward, was an English Author who wrote extensively on Santals. He is considered an authority on Santals.

15 Troisi, Joseph, Tribal Religion: Religious Beliefs and Practices among the Santals, 26.

16 Lakra, Christopher S.J., Theologizing in the Jharkhand context, taken from: Sevartham Vol 22, 1997, 4.

17 Biswas, Probhas Chandra, Santals of Santal Parganas, 236.

to the Library of Congress, they numbered about 4,200,000 at the 1991 census of India.[18]

1.3. The Santal Creation Myth

It is in our nature to wonder about the unknown and search for answers. At the foundation of nearly every culture is a creation myth that explains how the wonders of the earth came to be. These myths have an immense influence on people's outlook on life. They influence the way people think about the world, and their place in relation to their surroundings. Despite being separated by numerous geographical barriers many cultures have developed creation myths with the same basic elements.

Many creation myths begin with the theme of birth. This may be because birth represents new life and the beginning of life on earth may have been imagined as being similar to the beginning of a child's life. This is closely related to the idea of a mother and father existing in the creation of the world. The mother and father are not always the figures who create life on earth. Sometimes creation doesn't occur until the first god comes into being. As I know, a Supreme Being appears in almost every myth. He or she triggers the chain of events that create the world. The Santal myth is no different from this perspective. The Santals, though they cannot give a clear narrative of their wanderings, have preserved the traditions of their origin and early doings of their race. Steeped in myth and legendary lore, they have obviously invented stories to account for their origins, customs and practices. The story of their genesis that has been handed down through countless generations is implicitly accepted and unquestioningly believed by the Santals.

1.3.1. The Santal Creation Myth: The Genesis

In the beginning, the world was a waste of waters and there was no dry land. Only Thakur (the Supreme Being), and Marang Buru (the Great Spirit, literally means, Great Mountain) and the Council of Spirits reigned over the desolate kingdom. Then it occurred to one of the lesser divinities that it would be well to create human beings and he proposed the plan to Thakur. The Supreme Being consented and one of the attendant spirits, known as Malin Budhi (some sources say the name is Lita) was chosen to prepare suitable bodies into which, when ready, he might breathe the breath of life. Malin Budhi at once set to work, and labouring all day, finished her task towards sunset. The two forms that she made out of froth that floated on the face of the waters, being not yet dry, were laid out to dry to catch the warmth of the last rays of the setting sun. But at that time *Sin*

18 Troisi, Joseph, Tribal Religion: Religious Beliefs and Practices among the Santals, 26.

Sadom (the day horse) came down to drink water and not noticing, trampled the new made bodies under foot and they were completely destroyed.[19]

Malin Budhi (Lita), in great distress hastened to Thakhur bitterly complaining of what *Sin Sadom* had done and accusing him of carelessness and actual malice and ill-will. Thakur however pacified her and ordered her to remodel them, severely reprimanding *Sin Sadom* and commanding him to interfere no more with the fulfilment of his orders. She prepared the forms and this time managed to get them ready without disruption. Once finished, she went to Thakhur and besought him to give the crowning touch to her handiwork by giving life to them. He and his attendant went to see the work and were satisfied, whereupon he ordered her to go to his house and bring the spirit of life that they might live. He had warned her before she went to his house, to follow his instructions carefully, or dire consequences might follow. Above the door frame of his house was the Bird Spirit; that, she was not supposed to touch. Higher up among the rafters was the Human Spirit. She was supposed to bring the Human Spirit. But unfortunately Malin Budhi was short of stature, and when she reached the house, she found that she could not reach up as high as the rafters. There was none near to help her and she was at a loss what to do. Then temptation came to her and she took the bird spirit from above the door, disobeying the strict injunctions of the Supreme Being, but thinking to deceive him. She returned to the place where the gods awaited her, and saying nothing, handed the bird spirit to the Supreme Being who apparently did not recognise the deception. He solemnly imparted the spirit to the two lifeless forms, and they became birds and flew away. *Malin Budhi*'s punishment was swift. The Supreme Being turned upon her in wrath and condemned her for her faithlessness, to become a *Bhut* (evil spirit) and have her dwelling only in the loneliest of rocks and caves in the forest.[20]

1.3.2. Creation of the Earth

After a period of twelve years, the birds flew back to Thakur with the request that he would give them a place to build their nest. The Santals describe the situation thus:

> *Hai hai Jalapuri re, haihai Manmi Janamlen,*
> *Hai hai Poyrani Sakamcetan, haihai Poyrani Sakom ho Udul-dubul,*
> *Hai hai Céldo Menai Te, hai hai nukin Manawa,*
> *Hai hai okareng doho kin, hai hai Manmi Hopon jalapuri re,*
> *Hai hai Manmi Hopon okareng doho kin.*[21]

19 Guru Kolean (dictated), Horkoren Mare Haprakko reak' Katha (The Traditions and Institutions of the Santals – English translation), Benagraia (West Bengal): Benegaria Mission Press, 2000, 1.

20 Bradley-Birt, Francis, The Story of an Indian Upland, London: Smith, Elder & Co, 1905, 133 – 36.

21 Guru Kolean (dictated), Horkoren Mare Haprakko reak' Katha, 4.

(What a tragedy! The human children are born on the lotus leaf on water.
There is no soil, no land;
They are on the back of geese in the sky.
They are crying to alight on the land.
But alas there is no land).

This situation of landlessness was something the divinities had not thought of. So they assembled together to discuss a plan. A fish, *Sole hako*, was the first to be called upon to try his plan. All his efforts to raise dry land up above the waste of waters were in vain. He had to accept his failure. The next to come forward was, the crab *(katkom)*. He managed to bring a little earth but could not manage to keep it. Next the earthworm took up the task. He placed himself with his head resting on the land at the bottom of the water, so that the earth which he ate might pass through him and fall on the surface, thus forming dry land. But the earth did not remain long enough; everything fell back into the water. He admitted that the work was greater than he could accomplish.[22]

The assembled divinities were completely desperate. At the last moment came the centipede with a proposal that gave them hope. In the water lived the tortoise and his back was broad and strong. By chaining him to the bottom of the water, it might be possible to heap earth upon his back until dry ground appeared. He was promptly chained with four iron chains to a particular spot. The earthworm and centipede began working and at last dry land appeared. On the land the Supreme Being planted a tree and grass. It is on this same island the people live today. Earthquakes are caused because the tortoise moves now and then to let himself free. The end of the world will come when the tortoise finally shifts the burden from his back and the land will sink again back into the water.[23]

1.3.3. Creation of the First Human Beings

On this land the birds, *has* (he-goose) and *hasin* (she-goose), made their home. Building a nest among the *siron* (coarse grass), the female bird laid two eggs. In the fullness of time two human beings, a boy and a girl, the progenitors of the human race were born from these eggs. These two persons are known among the Santals as *Pilchu Haram* (first old man) and *Pilchu Budhi* (first old woman). As soon as Thakur heard that they were born he ordered Marang Buru to bring them before him. They had no clothes and he gave them two pieces of clothes made of leaves and showed them how to make clothes made of leaves. Marang Buru was supposed to look after them as human beings. He taught *Pilchu Haram* how to plough the land and cultivate. Thus, they realized that the harvest yielded its bountiful return. Once their barn was full, he proceeded to teach them how to

22 Guru Kolean (dictated), Horkoren Mare Haprakko reak' Katha. 4.

23 Nita, Mathur, Santal Worldview, New Delhi: Concept Publishing Company, 2001, 118.

brew rice beer (*Handi*) that they might enjoy life to the full. They were told to drink it when it was ready after pouring the libation to the gods. Marang Buru had shown them how to pour out the libation to the gods. It took four days for the rice beer to be ready. They made leaf-cups to drink the rice beer. They both drank the rice beer and finding it good they drank plenty of it. They became intoxicated and indulged in sexual pleasure. Since then they began to live like husband and wife.[24]

Eventually seven handsome sons and seven beautiful daughters were born to *Pilchu Haram* and *Pilchu Budhi*. The sons were skilful with the bow and arrow, and the daughters were gentle and good. Unfortunately, when the children were still quite young the peace of the family was broken by the quarrels of the parents. Finally, in a fit of temper they separated. *Pilchu Budhi*, with her daughters, went to the forest; while *Pilchu Haram* with his sons took the opposite direction. It was only after many years they met again.[25]

1.3.4. The Children and their Marriage

Meanwhile the sons grew into manhood and became great warriors. They often wandered in search of game. One day during their hunt in the forest they came across the seven sisters who went daily to the forest to collect firewood and herbs. The sisters had meanwhile grown up and had learned everything women in a family should have learned. Naturally they were attracted to each other and gradually they paired off and settled down in different places as man and wife. Meanwhile *Pilchu Haram* and *Pilchu Budhi* awaited the return of their children but they never came back. *Pilchu Haram* set out in search of his sons. Several days he spent searching for his sons but in vain. At last he came upon *Pilchu Budhi* in the forest and they recognised each other and decided to live again together.[26] There is another version of their reunion: *Pilchu Budhi* was very upset over the disappearance of her daughters. Seeing her grief, *Marang Buru* came to her and asked her the cause of her grief. He assured her that there was nothing to worry about and that the daughters and sons were safe and well settled. *Marang Buru* then told her to make up with her husband and live together. So, he took her to *Pilchu Haram* and they lived together again.[27]

Later the sons were told by their parents that they had married their sisters. At this the sons were very angry and they almost killed their parents, had Marang Buru not come in the nick of time. He had to take them to the cave to protect them. It is said that they never emerged from their cave again. To avoid incest *Pilchu Haram* and *Pilchu Budhi* divided them into seven exogamous clans, so

24 Bradley-Birt, Francis, The Story of an Indian Upland, 140.

25 Bradley-Birt, Francis, The Story of an Indian Upland, 140-41.

26 Bradley-Birt, Francis, The Story of an Indian Upland, 142.

27 Nita, Mathur, Santal Worldview, 118.

that a brother may not marry a sister. The clans were Hasdak, Murmu, Kisku, Hembrom, Marandi, Soren and Tudu.[28]

1.3.5. Sin and Punishment

It is said that after some years they went to live in another place called Khoj Kaman where they became very bad – *kadabitkille kaenako* – (acting sexually like buffaloes and buffalo cows). (It is not said from where they came. One part of their narration states that they were living in Hihiri Pipiri). Seeing their bad behaviour Thakhur became very angry and told them that he would destroy humankind if they did not change their way of living. But, they did not pay heed to him and continued their life in the same wicked manner. So Thakhur rained down fire for seven days and nights destroying all humankind except a couple whom he had chosen and sent to a cave at Harata Mountain. Here the Santals once again increased and multiplied. Then they migrated to Sasanbeda and once more they divided themselves. Besides the seven clans, five more were formed; Baskey, Besra, Pauria, Core and Bedea; the last of which disappeared long ago.

From Khoj Kaman they moved from one country to another till they reached Champa. Here they stayed for a long time, as already mentioned. To defend themselves against their enemies they built forts, each clan having its own fort.[29]

1.3.6. The Clans and Their Professions

In Champa it is said that each clan was occupational and there were social distinctions or divisions between them. The Kisku became the Royal tribe under the cognomen of the Kisku Raj (Raj means kingdom). The Murmus became the princely tribe and were named Murmu Thakur. The Soren became the soldier tribe and were named Soren Sipahi (soldier). The Marandis were appointed the king's treasurers and stewards and named Marandi Kipisar. The Tudus took to music and received the title of Tudu Mandariya. There is no record of the offices conferred upon the others.[30]

These occupational distinctions, however, rapidly disappeared. At present though certain clan members still bear the occupational appellation, there is no trace of occupational specialisation. The clans enjoy the same social status. They are scattered all over the Santal territory, and every Santal village includes members of different clans. It is said that earlier, the members of the other clans avoided marriage with members of the Besra and Core clans since these were considered as somewhat inferior. A Santal is not allowed to marry a member

28 Troisi, Joseph, Tribal Religions: Religious Beliefs and Practices among the Santals, 29.

29 Bodding, P. O., Traditions and Institutions of the Santals, Gyan Publishing House, New Delhi, 2001, 23.

30 Culshaw, Wesley J, Tribal Heritage: A Study of the Santals, London: Lutterworth Press, 1949, 12.

of his own clan. If he does so, then he is an outcaste and is cast out of the tribe through a process called *Bitlaha*.[31] The main function of the clan organisation is to regulate marriage relationships within the tribe. The prohibition was more rigid in the case of intra-sub clan marriage. A Santal is prohibited from marrying a girl belonging to his mother's sub-clan. The reason for this is linked up with the worship of the *abge bongas* or sub-clan spirits. This is expressed in the Santal saying, "*mitkhutrenkanale, mitkhondrele,* meaning we are of one stock, we perform sacrifices in the same circle."[32] Because of the religious significance involved in this convention it is strictly observed.

1.3.7. Conflict with the Non-Santal

After a long sojourn in Champa, the Santals had to flee out of fear of having their daughters ravished by the powerful tyrant Madhao Singh. Madhao Singh's story goes like this: In that country there lived many Birhors (another tribal group who live in the forest) who were at the service of the royal house of Kiskus. They had to provide the ropes with which to tie the elephants and cattle belonging to the king. It so happened that on one occasion they neglected their duty, and no new ropes were provided. One night the elephants and cattle broke loose and created havoc in the village, destroying crops and houses. The Birhors, hearing what had happened as a result of the neglect of duty, were overcome with fear at the thought of the rigorous punishment that would befall them. Hastily they left the place taking with them a few personal belongings and went to the forest. The news reached the ears of the king and he was determined to get revenge. The king with his followers chased them. As the Birhors were fleeing, one of the women gave birth to a child on the way. But because of the fear of the king, she was forced to leave the child behind, covering the child with a few large leaves. As the pursuers passed by, they heard the cry of the child. The king inquired and was eager to know what the matter was. So, his people took the child to him. It was a male child, strong and good looking and the king took compassion on the child. The day was already drawing to a close and abandoning the chase they returned home, taking the child with them. The child was reared in the king's house as his own son. The child was given the name Madhao Singh.[33]

He became presumptuous and forgot that he was sprung from the Birhors, who were the servants of the Santals. Many things were however forgiven him until at last he announced his desire to marry one of the ladies of the Raja's family. That was one aspect which none of the Santals could bear, for the Santal marriage law is strict that no one may marry or be given in marriage to one of another race. He threatened to go against the custom by applying *sindur* (vermillion; applying vermillion on the head is like wearing the wedding ring; this form of marrying is

31 Campbell, Alexander, Santal Folktales, West Bengal: Pokhuria Santal Mission Press, 1891. 28.

32 Troisi, Joseph, Tribal Religions: Religious Beliefs and Practices among the Santals, 31.

33 Bodding, Paul.Olaf., Santal Folk Tales, New Delhi: Gyan Publishing House, 1997, 57.

called *Itut* in Santali) on the forehead of the girl he loved. This threat so enraged the Santals that they had a consultation of the wise men to devise plans to prevent such an act by Madhao Singh. No one had ever done such a thing in their life and so they had to think a lot. He was the first one to take advantage of a Santal custom to defy a Santal law. Either the tribe must alter the marriage law or abolish forced marriage if men of another race were not to be admitted within its limits. But, the Santals hated to do either of these things. To admit a stranger within the tribe was altogether repugnant to the first principles of their tribal organisation. There was nothing that the wise men found fit to do. So, they decided to flee from the evil rather than suffer disgrace. They had to leave behind a prosperous land and find a new home where they might safely maintain the integrity of the immemorial customs of the tribe.[34] They did not want to take any risk. They were not strong enough to challenge the powerful tyrant. It was important to keep the tradition intact.

1.3.8. Departure from the Homeland, Champa

The hasty and secret flight from Champa is described in the legend. Unknown to Madhao Singh, the Santals left the place at night taking with them their essential belongings. But after some distance they met with an obstruction on the way. It was called the Singh door. They found that the whole area was closed by a mass of stone covering the whole face of the hillside. They tried their level best to go through somehow, but to no avail. In despair they sat down before it and wept. Then two men appeared before them and inquired after their distress. They told the grieved people to call upon their *bongas* (spirits). At first, they refused to call on strange gods but having no other option they relented. Then the two men with arrows struck the stone door and gradually it fell into fragments. Thus they escaped from that place, impressed with the power of the strange gods. They faced similar difficulty again on their way. So again they called upon the spirits and were successful. They were told to be grateful to the gods and thus they were introduced to the mysteries of worship. Sacrifices were offered by the way side, a black cock for one spirit and a brown cock for another spirit and *sindur* (vermillion) was applied on stones at various stages on their way as a mark of respect.[35]

1.3.9. Arrival in Santal Parganas

Meanwhile Madhao Singh had discovered their flight and pursued them. He had no difficulty crossing the door as it was already open. Then he saw the places where Santals had offered sacrifices and realized that they had abandoned the old worship and gone after other gods. He returned to his kingdom and lived among

34 Bradley-Birt, Francis, The Story of an Indian Upland, 152.

35 Bradley-Birt, Francis, The Story of an Indian Upland, 152.

the Birhors. So, the Santals reached a new country unmolested, and followed after the strange gods who so miraculously assisted their escape.[36]

With this, the Santal traditions of their wanderings practically cease. It is said that they reached the place called Chotanagpur which the Mundas had already occupied. They preferred to go away rather than settle down there though both the tribes are said to have the same origin. They went further and reached the place called Saont where they seemed to have got the name Santal, as mentioned earlier. But, they did not stay long here as the *Raja* (King) of the place wanted to marry a Santal maiden. Naturally the Santals fled from there. After many wanderings through Manbhum and Hazaribagh, they finally reached Santal Parganas, where they still live.

1.3.10. Understanding the Myth

As I understand a myth is not just a folktale; it's not just a piece of fiction or a made-up story. Our lives are shaped and guided by myth. Creation myths often invoke primal gods and animals, titanic struggles between opposing forces or the death and/or dismemberment of these gods or animals as the means whereby the universe and its components were created. The Santals believe that they foster a shared set of perspectives, values, history and literature, in the stories themselves. Through these communal tales, they feel they are connected to one another, to their ancestors, to the natural world surrounding them, and to society.

Myths present guidelines for living. When myths tell about the activities and attitudes of deities, the moral tone implies society's expectations for their own behaviours and standards. In the Santal myths they find justification for their cultural activities. Through their authoritativeness and the respected characters within them, myths establish a culture's customs, rituals, religious tenets, laws, social structures, power hierarchies, territorial claims, arts and crafts, holidays and other recurring events, and even tips for hunting, warfare, and other endeavours.

Myths give meaning to life. They are able to transcend their ordinary, common lives into a world in which deities interact with humans, and they can believe that their daily actions are part of the deities' grand schemes. In their difficulties, the pain is more bearable because they believe that the trials have meaning; we are suffering for a bigger cause rather than being battered randomly. Problems and difficulties are associated with punishment for the people's bad behaviour. Myths explain the unexplainable. They reveal the reasons for crises or miracles and yet they retain and even encourage an aura of mystery. Myths also satisfy our need to understand the natural world; for example, they might state that a drought is caused by an angry deity. Myths offer role models and even explain why men should do certain work and women certain other work.

In order to fully understand, the world the Santals live in and the world they are in the process of creating, we need to at least try to understand their

36 Cf. Bradley-Birt, Francis, The Story of an Indian Upland, 153-55.

mythologies and how they have shaped the course of their history. This myth is a story that carries meaning for the culture in which it arises. The Santal myths tell us deep truths about themselves, either as they are or as they would like to be. I may say that the Santal myth can support multiple, sometimes contradictory interpretations, and continue to be meaningful even after the culture from which it comes has died.

1.4. Santals' Legend and History about their Origin

The origin of the Santals is a matter of some dispute. The myth does give some inkling into their origin and history. What is certain is that they came from an area which was extremely hilly and forest covered, as such, they had practiced shifting cultivation well before they reached Chotanagpur.[37] There is evidence of Santals inhabiting this area since very early times. "During the long period of Indian history, the years between 800 and 600 B.C., we have only a few scattered references to the tribal people. Historical anthropology which includes the popular beliefs, legends, myths, tales, etc., of the folk people can help us know about the unrecorded past."[38] There has been such continuous migration in these areas, even during the historic period, that it is not possible to locate the original places in the absence of records. Still their wandering conditions explain their history of retreats being pushed by a stronger section of the Indian people.

The traditions of the Mundas as well as of their companions and kinsmen, the Santals, speak of a struggle with another tribe, Kharwar, before they left Rohtasgarh (in present Bihar state) and retreated to the wilder recesses of the Vindhyas.[39] Between 1790 and 1810, due to overpopulation in this area, the Santals moved north into the area known as Damin-i-Koh,[40] which comprised the hilly portions of what would become the Santal Parganas. Then they crossed the river Sone (in Bihar, Jharkhand states), and reached Chotanagpur. It is believed that the tribe migrated from north-east India following the sacred river Damodar, found their way up to Chotanagpur plateau and scattered to the adjoining highlands. After some time, the Santals and the Mundas parted company. The Santals then went to Hazaribagh (now a district in Jharkhand) and then to Santal Parganas.[41] "But according to W. G. Archer, the last British District Commissioner of the Santal Parganas, Santals are the original inhabitants of this land."[42] According to me that

---

37 Chotanagpur: The district where the majority of the population is tribal and majority among them Christians. The major tribes living here are, Oraons, Kharias and Mundas.

38 Vidyarthi, Lalita Prasad, & Rai, Brajesh Kumar, The Tribal Culture of India, 30.

39 Vindhyas: hill region of middle India.

40 Damin-i-koh: It is a Persian word which word means "Skirts of the hills." This was the name given by the Mughals to the place Santal Parganas which is today divided into 4 districts called, Sahibganj, Dumka, Pakur and Godda.

41 Vidyarthi, Lalita Prasad & Rai, Brajesh Kumar, The Tribal Culture of India, 31.

42 Holiday (newspaper, Bangladesh), Holiday Publications limited, Dhaka, Friday, March, 2005.

is not a very reliable account because the Paharias had already existed here much before the Santals arrived. This view is held by even the people living in Santal Parganas. It is said that the Paharias had lived here without being disturbed by the Mughal Government till the middle of the 18th Century. They (Santals) failed to penetrate into this area as it was a vast hill tract covered by deep forest. Thus,, they (Paharias) remained cut off from the outside world.[43]

1.4.1. The Fascinating Land of Legend and Tradition

F. B. Bradley-Birt has vividly described the area where the Santals settled down:

> It is a fascinating land of legend and mystery, this strip of country in the Central Bengal now designated by the picturesque name of the Santal Parganas. Set apart from the rest of the province, with its own laws and its own peoples, its rugged range of hills, where a race of hill-men has doggedly held possession, as they believe, since time began. Stands like a barrier to turn the (river) Ganges from its course. Its primitiveness untouched by the stir of passing events, it has looked down with unresponsive gaze upon all that was best and highest and furthest advanced in the India of the day.[44]

It is a land of sharp and vivid contrasts. Except for the Valley of Barhait[45] there is no wide stretch of level country anywhere. On all sides rise precipitous tree-clad hills and rocks. Steep, rocky and inaccessible, clothed in a dense shrub jungle, it stood untouched till the beginning of the 20th century, as when the earliest of the hill-men (Paharias) first took possession of the land.[46]

The second stretch of country, almost equal in extent, presents a far different aspect. Here nature has adopted a milder mood. It is a land full of gentle undulations which the Santals eagerly seized upon, and where they found their labour well repaid. It is here that the Santals made their home, joyfully settling to the work of intake and slowly reclaiming step by step the fertile lands that had so long awaited the touch of their awakening hand.[47]

What do the tribal people say about themselves? In this land of hill and jungle hangs a veil of impenetrable mystery. To a people ignorant of written records, and with no calendar save the moon and the changing seasons, time is vague and memory fails of all except the oral traditions of their race faithfully handed down from generation to generation. Fragments of their history remain buried in the records of other races with whom they have come in contact. To piece together these fragments with the help of legend and tradition, and to bridge the long gaps

43 District Commissioner, National Informatics Centre, District Profile.

44 Bradley-Birt, Francis, The Story of an Indian Upland, 1-2.

45 Barhait: at present a small little town in Sahibganj District.

46 Bradley-Birt, Francis, The Story of an Indian Upland, 2.

47 Bradley-Birt, Francis, The Story of an Indian Upland, 5.

where all is silent, is to raise probability to the region of historical certainty and fact. In order to give answers to this enquiry, we need to differentiate a-historical (mythical) and historical consciousness. One is not to be preferred over the other in this context when we deal with the tribe because each of them is on a different plane. Ahistorical consciousness highlights that there is a reality beyond history. Historical consciousness emphasizes the historical conditioning of reality and tends to limit itself to history.[48]

The tribal and indigenous people overstress ahistorical consciousness in their understanding of reality. The self-identification of the historically conscious tribal communities indeed use the term Adivasi. But the particular tribes among themselves do not use the term Adivasi, instead, the Santals use the term "Hor" for themselves and the Mundas call themselves "Horo." The self-identification as Adivasi corresponds to the modern concept of indigenous peoples.[49] They affirm that they are people with distinct historical, political and cultural identities. They are united by their histories as distinct societies, by their languages, laws, traditions and unique spiritual and economic relationships with their lands and territories.

1.4.2. People with Oral Tradition and History

In a legend so vague and mythical there is little idea of locality. Where these earliest ancestors of their race first made their home, the Santals have no knowledge. The Santals have no recorded history and so they say; "the mouth is our printed book."[50] The traditional history of migration, the details of which the tribes still hand on today, is now in the written form. Peoples remain peoples in their memory of the history of their ancestors. Some factual details may not be important according to them because they stress the meaning of the history. The traditional history of the Santals wandering for a homeland is summarised in the following lines:

> Hihiri Pipiri rebon janam len, Khojkaman rebon khoj len,
> Haratrebon hara len, Sasan Beda rebonjatena ho.[51]
> (We were born in Hihiri Pipiri, we were called to the Promised Kaman,
> We grew and multiplied at Harata, we were divided into clans at
> Sasan Beda).

To reach Sasanbeda, the Santals, according to their traditions, had to pass through several countries. Then from Sasanbeda they went to Champa and from there, after a long sojourn, had to flee out of fear of having their daughters ravished by the powerful tyrant Madhao Singh, as already mentioned above. On the basis of their tradition several theories have been advanced regarding their origin. Many scholars have tried to identify the countries, rivers, forests the Santals mention in

48 Bradley-Birt, Francis, The Story of an Indian Upland, 6.

49 Mundu, B. John, Tribal and Indigenous Peoples in India, Media House, Delhi: 2003, 8.

50 Troisi, Joseph, Tribal Religions: Religious Beliefs and Practices among the Santals, 31.

51 Troisi, Joseph, Tribal Religions: Religious Beliefs and Practices among the Santals, 32.

their tradition. Very little supporting evidence was found to locate them exactly. Inferences have been made to trace the Origin of the Santal institutions. There is some historical verification here. From Khojkaman they moved to Chae, and then to Champa, both situated in the north-west corner of the Hazaribagh District. At Chae they had built a fort. It was in the possession of Jaura, a Santal Raja, who was unable to hold it against the advancing Muslim army, destroying himself and his family rather than fall into the enemy′s hands. The victorious troops are said to have been commanded by one Sayyed Ibrahim Ali. This is a definite historical period in Santal history. Sayyed Ibrahim was the General of Mohammed Tughluk who died in the year 1353 A.D.[52]

Champa seems to have been the name vaguely given to a stretch of country in the north-west corner of Hazaribagh. Their stay here was the time of the Santals' greatest prosperity, which their descendents still love to recall today. The tribe seemed to have lived in peace, with broad land at their disposal and with no hated foreigner to interfere. It was the golden age when for the Santals there was no law, save the rules and precepts of the tribe, which it was their nature by custom and tradition to revere and obey. The land was theirs for the taking. Those days of freedom in Champa impressed the Santals so much that even today they fail to understand how any power, any law, or any authority can rob them of their immemorial right to the land and to cut as much timber as they desire. But, even into the peaceful land of Champa the oppressor came, and the Santals preferred to pack up his goods and trek for pastures new rather than submit to the slightest sign of domination from the *diku* or foreigner (*diku* or foreigner meant a non-tribal person). Whatever their original habitat might have been, there is no doubt that by about the middle of the eighteenth century, at the beginning of British rule in India, large numbers of Santals were found in Chotanagpur, especially in the districts of Hazaribagh, Palamau and Singhbhum (in Jharkhand State) and in the neighbouring districts of Midnapore and Birbhum (in West Bengal State).[53]

1.4.3. Santals and Their New Home

Towards the end of the eighteenth century, the Santals who were expert in clearing forests and bringing them into cultivation began to migrate to the Rajmahal hills situated on the north-eastern side of the Chotanagpur plateau. In 1883, the British government in India demarcated an area surrounding the Rajmahal hills. The idea behind this move was to declare this hill tract occupied by the tribal people the property of the government. The Santals were now encouraged to settle in this area. Damin-i-Koh (literally means skirts of the hills) became the centre of Santal life.[54] Thus it was said "in the 'Skirts of the Hills' dwell the

---

52 Culshaw, Wesley J. Tribal Heritage: A Study of the Santals, London: Lutterworth Press, 1949, 24.

53 Troisi, Joseph, Tribal Religions: Religious Beliefs and Practices among the Santals, 31.

54 Troisi, Joseph, Tribal Religions: Religious Beliefs and Practices among the Santals, 34.

Santals. "Here again Nature seems to have stepped in to provide for a people in need a home and the means of subsistence best suited to the manner of people they were. At the foot of the hills had lain, undisturbed for centuries, a fertile land waiting only the touch of the plough to yield a grateful and abundant return."[55] They lived happily here for a short period of time and then began to feel the pinch of the enemy intruder oppressing them. Initially everything was apparently hail and hearty but the Santals realized the gravity of the situation. The land they had taken possession of was gradually drifting away from them as the others had more control and power. Finally, they had no option but strongly resist the oppression, the oppressors.

1.5. The Important Historical Event: Santal *Hul* (Rebellion)

Sir William Wilson Hunter, a great British statistician and historian, wrote in the Annals of Rural Bengal, "What we (British Army) fought was not a war. So cling as their (Santal) drum went beating, they went on fighting to the last man. There was not a single *Sepoy* (soldier) in the British Army who did not feel ashamed."[56]

Santal Rebellion (or *hul* in Santali) is a very important event in the history of the Santals. Every grown-up Santal knows about this historical event, in which a very large number of Santals took part to fight against their enemies first time in their history. This event is narrated on certain occasions by the Santals so that the coming generations also know about it. I have heard from different people about the event during my stay among the Santals. There are different opinions about the number of Santals who took part in the movement. I think it is quite believable to think that there were about 20,000 Santals[57] who shed their blood. This event has a tremendous effect on their present life situation. In fact the Santals say that without this event there is no modern history for them.

1.5.1. Reasons for the *Hul:* Colonisers, *Mahajans and Zamindars*

With the capture of political power of India by the East India Company, the natural habitats of the *Adivasi* (indigenous) people including the Santals began to be shattered by intruders like moneylenders. Traders and revenue farmers descended upon them in large numbers under patronage of the Company. I have heard from the Santals that the rate of interest on loan to the poor and illiterate Santals varied from 50% to 500%. In fact we have even confronted some similar exploiters in this area in 1986. These intruders had crucial links in the chain of ruthless exploitation under colonial rule. They were the instruments through which the indigenous groups and tribes were brought within the influence and

55 Bradley-Birt, Francis, The Story of an Indian Upland, 9.

56 Bradley-Birt, Francis, The Story of an Indian Upland. 9.

57 O`Malley, L Lewis Sydney Steward, Bengal District Gazetteers: Santal Parganas, Calcutta: The Bengal Secretariat, Book Department, 1910, 53.

control of the colonial economy. Thus they realized that they had no option other than fight the enemy.

"The Skirts of the Hills was a land such as the Santals loved. It offered to them the labour and the recreation that centuries of custom had made characteristic of their race. What the Santals perhaps valued most of all - they could still preserve their nationality intact."[58] But, the situation was not going to be the same any more and the population of the Santals increased and multiplied and it was no longer easy for them to move from place to place as they had done before, in order to preserve the heritage. Now they came in conflict with the enemies, the *mahajans* (money lenders) and *zamindars* (landlords) who were Hindus and Muslims. Suspicious of interference and restless of control, the Santals have always entertained a peculiar aversion to the entire Hindu race. The hatred and contempt on either side have been equal. The Hindus regarded the Santals as the meanest of the races. The Santals looked on them as weak-kneed people who fed on vegetables and rice (they did not eat meat). So, the Santals had the humiliation of being despised and oppressed by a race for which they had nothing but contempt. The *mahajans* and the *zamindars* exploited the Santals, by taking possession of their land through illegal means. In fact the Santals were working on their own land as meanly paid workers. They could not go to court for an appeal or to the police to file a complaint. Ignorant and dazed amidst all the legal forms, it was necessary for the Santals to pay again in bribes in both the places. The *mahajan* and the *zamindar* had better access to these places because they worked hand in glove with one another. Maddened by the sharp contrast between his oppressed status and that of the free man, a wild desire for release from the oppressor's yoke sprang up in the Santals' mind. It grew and they were no more willing to suffer in silence as they had done before. And so at last the end came to challenge the enemies.[59]

The causes of the Rebellion were several. The Santals themselves declared that their chief grievances were the prevalence of falsehood, the negligence of the officers, the extortion of the *mahajans*, the corrupt and oppressive police. This was the first armed struggle against the exploitation and oppression perpetuated by the British rulers and their local agents. The movement was masterminded by Sido Murmu and Kanhu Murmu, hailing from the village Bagnadih in Sahibganj district.

The winter of the year 1854 was a time of unrest. All through the Santal tribe, from one end of the land to the other, into the remotest villages passed one of those strange waves of feeling, deep, mysterious, real and intense that made the people restless. So it happened at length after years of patient endurance that the out break came. The Santals knew that there was no one to help them, and that their salvation was the work of their own hands. To the waiting Santals, mystic

58 Bradley-Birt, Francis, The Story of an Indian Upland, 160.

59 Bradley-Birt, Francis, The Story of an Indian Upland, 183.

and superstitious, came news that had the most power to stir their imagination – the news of a sign from heaven. Marang Buru, the Great Spirit, had appeared and spoken, and a thrill of awe passed through the race as the rumour spread. With unquestioning faith they accepted the rumour. The emergence of Sido, Kanhu, Chand and Bairat (four brothers from Bagnadih, now Sahibganj district), youthful, dynamic and charismatic, provided a rallying point for the Santals to revolt against the oppressors.[60]

Marang Buru had appeared to these brothers seven times, each time in a different guise, so they claimed. First he came in the form of a cloud descending from the skies, then as a tongue of fire, thirdly as a hooded figure with the face veiled in mist, fourthly as a shadow in full sunlight where no earthly shadow fell, fifthly as a mountain rising suddenly out of the earth, sixthly as a *Sal* tree (*Sarjom*/Shorearobusta in Santali) springing up where no trees grew. The last apparition was like a white man clothed as a Santal. At this last appearance the divinity gave the brothers a sacred book wherein no words were written but the pages were supposed to be distributed as a sign to prepare for the great events to come and by which all their wrongs would be redressed and the Santals become once more a free people. The paper passed from village to village, apparently meaningless and vague but it stirred the race to the depths, by its mysteriousness. The *Sal* tree branch, the Santal national emblem of war, was sent like a fiery cross through every village in the land, speaking its eloquent message of revolt. From every hill and valley, came the youth unquestioningly obedient to its call.[61]

On 30th June 1855, a large number of Santals (about 10,000) assembled in a field in Bagnadih village of Santal Parganas. Two of the four brothers, Sido and Kanhu, were the recognised leaders. Among them passed the bolder spirits, dwelling in eloquent words upon their wrongs and inflaming the passions of retaliation and revenge. Then came the unanimous deep-voiced cry from all the vast assembly, and the cry was death to the *mahajan*, the *zamindar*, the police and all the British rulers who did not hear their plea for justice. There was another influence at work, namely, the Santals' yearning for independence and for recognition as lords of the soil – a motive which inspired them with the idea of establishing a kingdom for themselves under their own chiefs.[62]

They declared themselves as free and took an oath under the leadership of Sido and Kanhu to fight unto the last against the British rulers as well as their agents. The militant mood of the Santals frightened the authority. The police officer at the nearby police station (Borio) heard of the gathering of the Santals, he set out to arrest the four brothers with a false charge of dacoity. He reached the place of assembly, ordered the Santals to disperse and ordered the arrest of

60 O`Malley, Lewis Sydney Steward, Bengal District Gazetteers: Santal Parganas, Calcutta: The Bengal Secretariat, Book Department, 1910, 46.

61 Bradley-Birt, Francis, The Story of an Indian Upland, 185-86.

62 O`Malley, Lewis Sydney Steward. Bengal District Gazetteers: Santal Parganas, 44.

the four brothers. The angry crowd reacted violently and killed the police agent and his companions. The event sparked a series of confrontations with the British Company's Army and subsequently reached the scale of a full-fledged war. After this killing the Santals set out on the war trail. They were now masters of the country and ravaged it from one end of the district to the other, in Bengal and Bihar States. The first move against the Santals was made by a detachment of 400 men of the Native Infantry on the 11th July by the magistrate of Murshidabad (District in West Bengal). On some occasions the Santals brutally killed their enemies.[63]

The ruling British government was unaware of the happenings in the state. Though rumours came in, the authorities were reluctant to accept that there was anything wrong with the government and its rule. They did not in fact want to admit that something was wrong with the government machinery. When the people, who had fled before the Santals' wrath, came in telling how village after village had been burned to the ground, the young crops destroyed, *mahajans* and *zamindars* put to the sword, and English men and women killed, the gravity of the situation could no longer be ignored. Government at last woke to the fact that an actual rebellion was in progress. The British army hastily despatched soldiers to suppress the revolt of the Santals. The *zamindars* were happy to see the English soldiers because then they were confident that the Santal army would be suppressed.[64]

The Santals had no strategy in military fighting. They were not organised to fight against a mighty well-armed force which had trained soldiers and enough arms and ammunition. The Santals had only bows and arrows and the knowledge of the country and they could suddenly have surprises in ambush. On a few occasions the British army was overwhelmed at the wild onslaught of the Santals. The Santals could only have an occasional ambush against the British army. The British army had difficulties in marching through the unknown country and lacked provisions as they went along. The inclemency of the weather too impeded the British army and gave the Santals a temporary advantage.[65]

The first brief success of the Santals was turned into utter and irretrievable defeat. The Santals, driven to bay, but fighting to the last, were mown down like corn before the reaper's sickle. They carried on the revolt with untiring determination. The Santals showed great bravery and incredible courage in the struggle against the military. Marvellous stories of their courage and absolute insensibility to danger remained. But in front of the well-armed British soldiers the Santals with bows and arrows could not have the smallest chance. When they were called to surrender, their only answer was a shower of arrows. There was no

63 O`Malley, Lewis Sydney Steward. Bengal District Gazetteers: Santal Parganas, 50.

64 Bradley-Birt, Francis, The Story of an Indian Upland, 196.

65 Bradley-Birt, Francis, The Story of an Indian Upland, 197.

sign of yielding. The courage, chivalry and sacrifice of the Santals were countered by the rulers with veritable butchery.[66]

1.5.2. The Tragic Conclusion of the Hul

Of course, the enemy attacked the Santals brutally, defeating them. In the face of attacks, they stood firm, their drums beating with a note of determination and defiance. The defiant challenge of the drums ceased only as the drummers fell at their posts and music of the flutes ended only in the wail of death. No one fled and only the wounded fell into the hands of the attackers. Out of the 50,000 Santal rebels, about 15 to 20,000 were killed by the British Indian army. Sido was captured by the British forces through an encounter *(It is said that he was betrayed by some of his own men)* and subsequently killed, and Kanhu was caught in another encounter and killed later. The company was finally able to suppress the rebellion in 1856, though some outbreaks continued till 1857, when the Indian struggle for Independence or *Sepoy Mutiny* (as the British called it) began.[67]

Santal *hul* was one of the fiercest battles in the history of Indian freedom struggles causing greatest number of loss of lives in any battles during that time. The number of casualties of Santal *hul* was about 20,000 (mentioned above). The Santal *hul* of 1855-57 was a heroic episode in India's prolonged struggle for freedom. It was, in all probability, the fiercest liberation movement in India next to the Great Indian Independence Struggle (*Sepoy Mutiny*) in 1857.

We should know that the British army was able to win over the Santals because the so called British army used Indian soldiers to kill the Indians. When people are poor and they are totally suppressed they have no option but oblige the needs of the dominant class. That is what happened to the Indians as long as the British Government ruled India, using the Indians to fight against the Indians, as if they were doing the Indians a favour by ruling India. It is difficult to understand the meaning of such a government and their mean attitude towards the Indians. In such a context it is difficult to understand the religion they practised, or their ethic of life. The majority of the Indians thought that all the British people were Christians. They could not believe that Christianity would teach such a way of life as the British people lived and ruled in India.

The sad part of it is that in spite of or because of the hul the social, political, economic situation of the Santals did not change for the better. The authorities did not remain mere spectators of the situation of the Santals but they began to further interfere with the social, political, economic life of the Santals. We need to know that they have their own particular and organized way of life, quite different from the administration of other people. It is good to know a little about their way of life and world view so that we know how they are affected by outside forces.

---

66 Bradley-Birt, Francis, The Story of an Indian Upland, 199.

67 O`Malley, Lewis Sydney Steward, Bengal District Gazetteers: Santal Parganas, 53.

1.6. The Socio-Political Structure and Administration of Santal Society

Paul Olaf Bodding, who had studied Santali language extensively and spent most of his life to understand the life and culture of Santals, observed in the preface of Santali Dictionary. "If their (Santals′) traditions are to be believed, their ancestors – or at all events, some of them – at one time were of a much higher civilization than the Santals of today and they themselves administered a country of their own."[68]

A human life exists within the framework of social, political, and economic situation. To have a holistic view of a people one needs to know the infrastructure that is present within any society without which no community can exist. In this part I want to deal with a very important change that has taken place in the course of Santals' life in terms of their social as well as political life and how that affects their culture and religion too.

Santals are normally a carefree people who enjoy music and dance; hunting, fishing and drinking are other entertainments. It is their way of relaxing and celebrating life. But as the situation changed some of these elements have become rare things in their life as outside elements have distorted the social life and exploited the people. They are unable to view their social life in the same way as they had viewed it earlier. Systems of kinship and descent have organized human life for most of our history and until recently it was vitally important in everyday life in all societies. Thus, it has become an essential part of anthropology because of its importance to the people from whom we learn.

It is difficult to differentiate the Santal social, political and economic systems. It is to be noted that they used to have a very well-organised democratic system of functioning combining all these aspects of life. As years passed by and they were caught up in the so called mainstream of life of the country, they lost quite a lot of their administrative tactics. In fact they are unable to maintain their democracy as the local government authorities interfere with their system.

1.6.1. The Social Structure

Traditionally the Santals possess a well organised socio-political structure to ensure discipline in the whole community. The people-based governance is more than an idea; it is also a concept that needs to be practiced at different levels. The tribal world view of democracy is a broad concept that includes the symbolic triad of human beings, animals and forest. The functioning of a vibrant democracy demands not only a proper ecological balance but also due respect for one another. A holistic view of the tribal lifestyle, customs and culture underscores the critical role played by natural resources in establishing a thriving democracy.[69]

---

68 Bodding, Paul Olaf, *A Santali dictionary (5 volumes).* Oslo: I Kommisjon Hos Jacob Dybwab (Norwegian Academy of Science and Letters), 1936, 3.

69 Kumar, Arbind, Tribal Participation, Jharkhand: Lok Jagriti Kendra, 2002, 5.

In a village the head person of the village is called *manjhi* (headman). A number of villages form part of one local administrative unit, administered locally by a *parganait.* He is the custodian of all social functions of these villages. Kinship is the tie that binds human beings together. A society is organized in such a way in order to perform functions necessary for the well-being and maintenance of the society. Santal social organization is characterized by a lack of the caste cleavages so prominent in Hindu society, a patrilineal kinship system, and a relatively low level of political integration. The basic family unit is the extended patrilocal (relating to residence with a husband's kin group or clan) family. Each village is usually composed of a number of lineages as the ancestors are very important for the family and village.[70]

It is important to note that the concept of family in the tribal community goes beyond the circle of one's own household and encompasses the entire village. Further the surrounding forest, water, land, animals, river and so on constitute an inseparable part of the village community. Although the term "democracy" is not part of tribal vocabulary, they very much practice the spirit of democracy. Unfortunately, over the years, this relationship has considerably weakened due to external influences.[71]

The Village Set-up

The basic unit of the Santal communal system was the village. For the efficient running of the village administration they elected a village headman and his assistants from among the leading members of the group. A full-fledged village council consisted of seven village officials, namely *manjhi* (village headman), *paranik* (assistant headman), *naeke* (village priest), *kudamnaeke* (the priest worshipping local spirits), *jog manjhi* (guardian of morals), *jog paranik* (assistant of the *paranik*), and *godet* (messenger of the village). Succession to these posts was hereditary. However, any official could be removed for incompetency, by the people of the village.[72]

Ordinarily the social authority in the villages is exercised by the headman, *manjhi,* with the help of the above-mentioned village officials. He conducts meetings in the village and makes decisions. Problems are brought to the meetings and at times a fine may be imposed depending on the case and the *manjhi* has to give the final decision on the case. *Jog manjhi* has an interesting office. He is responsible for arranging feasts, and acts as a censor of village morals. He has to instruct the people sometimes. *Godet* is actually to help the *manjhi* to announce to the villagers the forth-coming events.[73] Although, these functionaries have

70 Singh, Sunil Kumar, Inside Jharkhand, Ranchi: Crown Publications, 2003, 196.

71 Kumar, Arbind, Tribal Participation, 5.

72 Ray, Praful Chandra, Socio-Cultural Process and Psychological Adaptation of the Santal, Calcutta: Reliance Printing Works, 1975, 7-8.

73 Mukherjea, Charulal, The Santals, Calcutta: A. Mukherjee & Co. Pr. Ltd, 1980, 152.

distinct responsibilities, decisions could be taken only through the collective consensus of the community in a *kulhidurup* or village meeting in which all the adult members of the village participate. Most decisions on social, cultural and political issues are taken at the village level.[74]

The social authority in the villages is exercised ordinarily by the headman, *manjhi,* with a batch of village officials to assist him. He collects rents from the people (to be paid to the government). All abandoned holdings and waste land are in his charge. He is the custodian of the village property – the communal wells, streets and grazing grounds. He has to maintain the *manjhithan* (founder's shrine) and the *jaherthan* (sacred grove). He has to also see to it that the yearly festivals are duly held and every householder contributes for the feasts. He requests all the people of the village to participate in the ceremonies of birth, marriage and death. If a sickness breaks out in the village, he must summon a meeting and arrange for special sacrifices. His position is that of a disciplinarian and a communal custodian. Because of his role in the village, he commands respect. The Santals regard him as the father of the village.[75]

The Council of Five People (*Mone Hor*)

Social authority in the village is exercised by the headman but always in consultation with the *monehor* (five people council: *manjhi* (headman), *paranik* (assistant headman), *jog manjhi* overseer of morals), *godet* (announcer), *naeke* (priest) and *kudamnaeke* (assistant priest). Though there are six people or at times seven people it is called *monehor* because five people are important. All the villagers are members of the village council. Village council is the institution that settles all the disputes of the villages. Santal community as a whole maintains certain uniform customs and laws with relation to marriage, divorce, birth, etc. *Manjhi*presides over the village council meetings when they are held to discuss matters related to village. In the event of disputes with other villages he acts as the representative of the village. *Paranik* is the principal assistant to *manjhi* and representative of *manjhi.* If *manjhi* dies without any male issues or brothers, then *paranik* will get the office. No public sacrifice, no festival, no ceremony such as marriage can be done without *manjhi* taking initiative. *Jog manjhi* serves as the supernatant of the youth of the village and he is the link between younger generations and older generations. Equally important is the religious headman called *naeke* and his assistant *kudamnaeke.*[76]

The People's Assembly (*Disom Hor*)

The highest authority in Santal society is known as *DisomHor* or assembly of the people of the region. Even the *pargana* or *parganait* and the assembly do not

74 Sahu, Chaturbhay, The Santal Women: A Social Profile, New Delhi: Sarup & Sons, 1996, 72.

75 Archer, W. G., Tribal Law and Justice, New Delhi: Concept Publishing Company, 1985, 4.

76 Choudhury, Sahu, The Santhal Women: A Social Profile, New Delhi: Sarup & Sons, 1996, 73.

exercise final authority. This is vested in the people of a number of villages. The final authority is exercised once every year through the medium of the *Lo Bir* or hunt council. If there is an inter-village dispute, the matter is taken up with the *parganait* and not with the *manjhi*. He is expected to settle the problem. In case he fails to come to a decision, the matter is taken up by the Hunt Council (*Lo bir*). In such a case the head of the group is the hunt priest (*dihri*). In this case usually the people themselves make the decision and the hunt priest and other officials are only to assist in making the decision. Punishment for serious breaches of discipline may be as serious as *bitlaha* (excommunication) which may be decided by the hunt council. It is the administration of the people, conducted by the people, for the benefit of the people. There is no appeal against this judgement.[77]

The assembly meets during the annual hunt (*lo birsindra)*. In the *lo bir* all Santals, with or without an official position, have equal status. Any matter may be raised by anyone and is fully discussed. As the highest court of appeal, the decisions of the *lo bir* are binding to all. The decision about excommunicating (*bitlaha*) a person from Santal society can be taken and executed only by *lo bir*. *Bitlaha* or social ostracism is the most severe form of punishment known to the Santal and is imposed for a violation of the rules of sib exogamy (Santals having the same surname/clan cannot get married) and tribal endogamy (marriage is not allowed outside the Santal tribe). Social ostracism has two forms, temporary and permanent. Temporary *bitlaha,* because of the violation of the rule of sib exogamy, can be lifted by the performance of *jamjati*, which is an expensive ceremony (because of the expenses to be paid for it is more than an ordinary Santal can afford). Permanent *bitlaha*, deals with grave cases like serious break down of morals and beliefs, murder and so on. Such punishment is also given to a woman who indulges in sexual relation to any *diku* (non tribal) or accepts herself to be a concubine. It consists in formally expelling him or her from the tribe for good.[78]

The Code of Behaviour and Taboos and Restrictions

There are no written laws and patterns of behaviour codes. Ethical principles have guided social behaviour for centuries. There are many traditions and customs that have come down through oral tradition and they are strictly followed. There are several taboos and prohibitions which regulate and control behaviour.

Santal code of behaviour is rooted in early tradition, based in their religion. The Santals have respect for their elders. They are generally a very hospitable people. Though the parents generally do not punish the children, they are expected to follow the norms and practices of daily life. Children are told not to steal, quarrel and mix with *dikus* (non-Santals who exploit them). The idea

77 Ray, Praful Chandra, Socio-Cultural Process and Psychological Adaptation of the Santal, 8.

78 Datta-Majumdar, The Santal: A Study in Culture – Change, Delhi: Dept. of Anthropology, Govt. of India, 1956, 47.

of personal sin as understood in Christianity does not exist. But the idea of sin does exist and so does the idea of punishment. When a person commits a sin, the whole community is affected and the Supreme Being may punish the whole community. That is to say that any breach of discipline is against the community and against God. Disobedience to God's law can lead to punishment as it had happened in the primordial punishment of the rain fire (mentioned in the myth, 1. 3. 5).

All Santals are expected to observe certain restrictions in daily life. These restrictions are to preserve the society in good stead as they believe. Through these taboos the spirits remain pleased. The *manjhithan* (founder's shrine) and *jaherthan* (sacred grove) are considered sacred. Therefore, all should respect these places. No one should plough this area or cut the trees from here. Women must never climb the trees in this area nor cut their branches. The village street *(kulhi)* is also considered sacred as it is the abode of the *manjhithan* and meetings are held on the street. No one should plough this area. It is also the place where village meetings are held. The priest has to abstain from sexual relation on the eve of offering sacrifices to the spirits.[79]

Santal women must avoid a number of actions which men are permitted or even expected to do. Women are barred from ploughing the field; it is even inauspicious for a Santal woman to touch a plough. They are not supposed to thatch the roof of a house, strike with an axe, shoot an arrow, play a flute or even to wear male clothes. They are not expected to go for the hunt. A pregnant woman must not sit on the narrow ledge surrounding the house with her legs dangling or her hair loose or any portion of her clothing hanging loosely from her body. She may not look upon a dead body. She must not weep when a death occurs. If there is an eclipse of the moon she should remain inside the house; she should not look at it. Such breaches would be regarded as symbolic perversions by the *bongas* (spirits) and at the same time safeguard the mother so that the child is born well.[80]

It is taboo to marry outside the tribe or inside one's own clan. Having sexual relations with them is also taboo. Adultery and homosexuality are also prohibited. Such breaches are believed to incur the wrath of the spirits and to bring immediate punishment. The relation between a Santal and his younger brother's wife is marked by taboo. They are not supposed to have any physical contact; they cannot be alone in the same room or in a courtyard; they must never sit near each other. They are also expected not to mention the names of these persons. When they have to be referred to, they are referred to in terms of their children.[81] (E.g. mother or father of Maria or Joseph (children). Although, some taboos can be traced to evident risks to health and safety, there is no generally

79 Troisi, Tribal Religions: Religious Beliefs and Practices among the Santals, 227.

80 Culshaw, Wesley J., Tribal Heritage: A Study on the Santals, 122.

81 Troisi, Tribal Religions: Religious Beliefs and Practices among the Santals, 230.

accepted explanation of most others. I may say that they tend to relate to objects and actions that are significant for the maintenance of social order.

Bitlaha (Ostracism)

As already mentioned, *Bitlaha* is imposed on someone in a very grave situation. Clan and kin incest, sexual intercourse with *diku* (non-tribal), eating with forbidden relatives, are some of the reasons for being ostracised. The village *bongas* (spirits) are deemed to be polluted and in many cases the offenders are liable to full and immediate out casting followed by the ceremony known as *bitlaha.* On rare occasions an offence may be punished with a fine; that is when the crime is not as serious as incest.[82]

The first step for holding a *bitlaha* is to obtain regional approval. The village headman must first inform the local *pargana.* He has to tell him of the village decision and ask him to consult the headmen from the nearby villages. These village headmen should approve of the case and confirm the village decision. Once they have confirmed a date is fixed for the *bitlaha.*[83]

If the *bitlaha* is declared it is announced in the market place a few days before the actual date of the event. On the day of *bitlaha*, the male members from the nearby villages including the village of the culprit, with flutes and drums, bows and arrows meet in the street where the culprit lives. Drumming is kept high so that it can be heard from a long distance. When most of the people have reached the village, they tie a short charred bit of firewood, a worn out broom and some used leaf plates on a bamboo pole and fix at the entrance of the courtyard. Then the room of the culprit is desecrated by throwing away the things from the house. He or she is not allowed to take food with the others and they cannot give or take children in marriage within the Santal community. Thus, he or she is cast away from the village and Santal society.[84]

Jamjati (Re-admittance)

By performing *jamjati*, an out-casted Santal is accepted back into the society. It is done in the following manner. However, if the crime is serious as mentioned above there is no re-admittance possible. When both the parties are ready to pay the necessary amount of money for the performance of the ceremony they inform the headman. The headman in turn has to inform the *parganait* and the neighbouring villages as it had been done earlier in the case of *bitlaha.* Then they fix a day to perform the ceremony. The person who is to be re-admitted has to prepare a big feast. On that day the out-casted man and woman go to the village street with twisted cloth around their necks and water in a small pot. Before the

---

82 Archer, William Gorge, The Hill of the Flutes, London: George Allen & Unwin Ltd, 1946, 90.

83 Archer, William Gorge, The Hill of the Flutes, 93.

84 Biswas, Prabhat Chandra, Santals of the Santal Parganas, Delhi: Bharatiya Adimjati Sevak Sangh, 1956, 95.

headman and his assistants, the offenders acknowledge their offence and agree to pay the fine for it. Then they wash their faces with water from the pot and give the water to the leading men who will repeat the same. After this ceremony, the feet of the headman and other leaders are washed by the female culprit. Once this is over they all sit down to eat and on the plate of the *parganait* some money is kept. The other headmen also receive some money though not a big amount.[85]

Significance and Problems of Bitlaha

Usually when an incident of *bitlaha* takes place a huge crowd gather. If the number of people is very small then the effect of *bitlaha* is also less significant; the Santals say like wise. That is the reason why so many nearby villages are informed to show the seriousness and enormity of the problem. A *bitlaha* is considered like a hunt in which the offenders are like the prey. 'They must be tracked and hunted down.' For this reason, the men carry the sticks of hunters and a hunt-master presides. They dance, beat drums and play flutes, all similar to the annual hunt.[86]

A *bitlaha* demonstrates the beast like behaviour of the culprits. The headman says on this occasion, "We have made them like cattle. They have acted like the early ancestors whose conduct ruined the world. They have rutted like buffaloes." For this reason, also the songs dwell constantly on bestiality. It conveys the meaning that such behaviour is not becoming of the tribe.[87]

In the mocking song here, we see how abominable such behaviour of the culprit is.

> Across the river, Barsa, you are always at a sheep.
> I shall tell your father, but my father goes to girls.[88]

Bitlaha is considered as an *"atobapla"* (wedding of the village). The crowd is a wedding party. But they say that the family did not marry them but the individuals did. The village puts the two offenders together, exposes their secret relationship and broadcasts it over the area. Another song that shows the crime,

> The Street is filling, with men from the country
> What a wrong you did me, but you flirted, Sonodi (name of a girl)
> You flirted with me, and we are both to blame.[89]

Bitlaha is a tribal (Santal) punishment. In a Santal society the sole wish of individuals is to remain anonymous to lead their lives quietly, not to attract the attention of others. *Bitlaha* reverses all this and makes the offender public which he/she most dislikes. It pulls him out of the obscure settings and dangles

85 Biswas, Prabhat Chandra, Santals of the Santal Parganas, 96.

86 Archer, W. G., The Hill of the Flutes, 96.

87 Archer, W. G., The Hill of the Flutes, 96.

88 Archer, W. G., The Hill of the Flutes, 97.

89 Archer, W. G., The Hill of the Flutes, 97.

him before the whole region. This is to create shame for the deed. It also reveals the tribe's sense of defilement. Even the use of the worn-out broom implies the degradation of the act and the burnt piece of wood suggests the sexual ruin which the wilful breach of rule has caused.

What is unacceptable today during *bitlaha* is some of these cases land in courts and then there are unending problems not only for one family but several of them. At times the Santals are so infuriated that they commit *bitlaha* on non-Santals. But Santal customary law suggests that the non-Santals are beyond their jurisdiction. However, when they are passionately angry nothing can control their anger. The problem comes later because the others may go to court and file petitions against the Santals. Such cases are prevalent today.[90]

Social Evils: Magic and Witchcraft

Witchcraft as sorcery has existed since humans first banded together in groups. Prehistoric art depicts magical rites to ensure successful hunting. Western beliefs about witchcraft such as sorcery grew out of the mythologies and folklore of ancient peoples, especially the Greeks and Romans. Roman law made distinctions between good magic and harmful magic, and harmful magic was punishable by law. When Christianity began to spread, the distinctions vanished. Witchcraft came to be linked with worship of the Devil. Today, most historians agree that all the victims were falsely accused. Magical practices and witchcraft are very prevalent among the Santals and other tribal people. It has been considered as a cultural/religious practice.[91]

The Witch-Finder

The Santal village is organised to secure the greatest possible degree of co-operation not only in temporal affairs but also in dealing with the spirit world. A good relationship is established between Santal society and the spirit world. A representative called *naeke* (village priest) maintains the right relationship with the tribal spirits. He is a man apart and is conscious of his separation from his people. He is not appointed by the fellow villagers but by the *bonga*, the spirits that are worshipped. Investing of a new priest occurs after the death of his predecessor. The spirits take possession of the individual and so establish the identity of the priest. The process takes place in the following manner.[92]

The marks of possession, the result of the process known to the Santals as *rum*, are quiet familiar. *Rum* is the regular method by which the spirits reveal their wishes, convey comfort or warning, and assure the warning, and assure the living of their fellowship with the spirits of the tribe and with their ancestors. The

90 Mukherjea, Charulal, The Santals, Calcutta: A. Mukherjee & Co. Pr. Ltd, 1980, 164.

91 Orans, Martin, The Santal: A Tribe in Search of a Great Tradition, Detroit: Wayne State University Press, 1965, 54.

92 Culshaw, W. J., Tribal Heritage: A Study on the Santals, 78.

behaviour of a person possessed is similar to that of one who has suffered a sudden onslaught of insanity, and he speaks in the character of the spirit who has for the time being taken possession of his personality.[93]

For practical reasons it is normal that the eldest son of the *naeke* assumes office after his death. Failing him they may appoint a brother of the deceased. The son is expected to know the activities, rules and regulations of the *naeke.* Secondly when the distribution of land was made, the first *naeke* received a portion of the land by his profession. This land is not expected to pass out of the possession of the particular clan.[94]

Santals believe that apart from the various benevolent spirits there are also malevolent spirits which have to be scared away through exorcism or magic. The Santals have to cope with a number of inexplicable supra-natural phenomena.[95] For this reason there are also magicians (*ojhas* or medicine men) as they are known, to protect Santal society. Many of these *ojhas* are non-Santals. There are also Santals now among them. *Ojhas* are needed because diseases are seen as something unnatural, ascribing to the agency of evil spirits, witches and evil eye. Natural medicines are used by people or medicines given by *ojhas* are also used; but when they fail, they need to call upon a *Jan Guru* or witch finder.

The Witchcraft: Detection

To find out the witch (*dan* = as said in Santali)) a person named *jan* or *jan guru*[96] is called. "To name the individual is the business of the *jan.* He is the man who knows, viz., by revelation. The *jans* are our High Court in witchcraft matters. Those which the *jans* pronounce to be witches, we deem witches."[97] He consults the oracles in order to determine the cause of the disease or fatality. He has to discover whether it is due to natural causes or due to a witch. He sits down in the courtyard and waits until two Sal leaves and some mustard oil are brought to him.

Holding one of the leaves in his left hand, he dips his right index finger in the oil and sprinkles some drops on the ground as an offering to the spirits. While doing so he asks for guidance in determining the correct cause of illness or fatality. He then puts a drop of oil into each of the compartments of the leaf that he is holding, one drop representing one possible agency of evil. There is one for natural causes, three or four for different *bongas*, and other drops represent households in which there may be a witch, including the sick man's house, his father-in-law's house, the houses on the other side of the village street, and so

93 Culshaw, W. J., Tribal Heritage: A Study on the Santals, 78.

94 Culshaw, W. J., Tribal Heritage: A Study on the Santals, 79.

95 Troisi, Joseph, Tribal Religion: Religious Beliefs and Practices among the Santals, 204.

96 Jan Guru: A witch finder. When a man is ill the *jan* is consulted as to what witch is responsible. The *jan* usually divines by gazing at an oiled leaf.

97 Bodding, Paul Olaf, Studies in Santal Medicine and Connected Folklore Parts I, II & III, Kolkata: The Asiatic Society, 2001, 41.

on. When the drops are in position the *jan* rubs the two leaves together and then holds the first leaf up to the light to discern the shapes that have been taken by the oil. He pronounces the cause of the disease in accordance with the pattern that he sees. If he decided that the *bongas* are displeased, he performs the ceremony known as *bulmayam* (literally means bad blood) in much the same manner as the village co-priest does during the festivals. The blood which he draws from his arm, chest or thigh is mixed with some sundried rice until the whole is saturated. The *jan* then proceeds to scatter the rice on the ground and prays to the spirits to spare the sick man from further interference. He confirms his diagnosis by oracle by examining the patient and in particular by feeling his pulse, and apart from his power with the spirit he has stock-in-trade that includes many remedies, spells and also powers of exorcism. This is resorted to at once in certain cases such as snake bite. The *jan* squats down beside the sick person and takes in his left hand a peacock feather or sometimes one or two twigs from an old broom, and these he passes along the patient's body without touching it, moving from head to feet and chanting the correct spells as he does so.[98]

He warns his clients that there may be a possibility of error in his diagnosis, for it is the common belief that witches can interfere with the process of divinisation in order to draw attention away from them. When the illness persists in spite of all attempts at a cure, the suspicion of witchcraft arises and a second divinisation reveals that a witch is at work. Then the villagers are expected to cooperate in identifying the witch because the villagers know all the houses and people living there. But everyone has fear whether a witch is there in his own house. Underlying this activity is the conviction that the welfare of society and of the individual depends on establishing a balance between the human being, nature and the spirit world, and they witness to a faith that can achieve such a balance. At times frivolous accusations of witchcraft are made in order to pay off an old grudge.[99]

Once it is established that a witch is at work and that she lives in a certain house or village, the villagers of the sick person proceed to the *jan guru* who must give precise information about the individual who is a witch. The *jan gurus* are so clever that they try to get all possible details before hand by hook or by crook. Once the witch is found out she is severely beaten, the household may be fined for keeping a witch, and she may be ostracised or even killed. Unfortunately, the woman is not consulted or interrogated; she is simply judged. She has no opportunity to speak of her innocence.[100]

98 Culshaw, W. J., Tribal Heritage: A Study on the Santals, 97-98.

99 Culshaw, W. J., Tribal Heritage: A Study on the Santals, 98.

100 Culshaw, W. J., Tribal Heritage: A Study on the Santals, 98.

Personal Experience: "Witch" to be Killed

During the year 1986 a friend of mine and I were having a walk in the afternoon around 2.30. From the village where we were staying, we had walked a distance of about two kilometres towards the nearby town. As we were going along, we could hear loud shouting and screaming from a distance. We were curious to know what was amiss. We came closer to the place of incident, and saw that a big crowd had gathered, both men and women. As we reached the spot, we found that the men were mere spectators and the women, well-armed with sickles, knives and sticks, were attacking a young woman. We asked some of the men about the cause of that incident. Although, we were strangers to them because of our language and appearance, they told us that she was a witch and must be put to death.

I said to myself that it was no light matter to deal with. All the same I felt that there could not be much truth in what they said that she was a witch. The next moment I was in the middle of the group of women who were attacking the lady. I shouted at them in all the possible languages I could speak. In those days my Santali was not sufficiently good to convey the message; I spoke Hindi, English and Santali. It had a substantial effect. The women suddenly stopped beating the so-called witch. All of them moved back and I was in the middle of the crowd talking a very strange language to them. Many of them went away and two three other women came to help the afflicted woman.

I get frightened even today when I think of the incident and the consequences involved. I feel that they could have even killed me. That day I did not make too much reasoning and so I was able to help a poor, afflicted woman in her helplessness. Our further inquiries revealed that she was accused of being a witch (*dan*) who was the cause of the death of another woman.

These days there is a lot of corruption associated with the so-called witch finding. In many cases the woman is a widow, living alone and possessing some land. The *jan guru* is taken into confidence by a family and then he can name a widow as a witch and then both the persons manage to inherit the wealth. The *jan guru's* charge for witchcraft is often very high. Though there are fewer instances of witchcraft now, there are cases even among the Christian Santals, practiced without the knowledge of the parish priest or diocese.

1.6.2. Religious (Cultural) Heritage

Santals do not consider themselves to be Hindus. They have a religion of their own which is completely different from Hinduism or Christianity. It is called *Sarna Dhorom*. A yearly round of rituals connected with the agricultural cycle, along with life-cycle rituals for birth, marriage and burial, involve petitions to the spirits and offerings that include food articles and sacrifice of animals and birds. Religious leaders are male specialists in medical cures who practice also divination and witchcraft. In every village there is a *jaherthan* or sacred grove. Usually the *jaherthan* is found at the boundary of every village, with a number of *Sal* trees

(*Shorearobusta)*, and the sacrifices are offered in this particular place by the *naeke* (priest). It is believed that many spirits dwell in the sacred grove and many festivals are held during the year. For all the festivals there is a *puja* (Sacrifice) held here.[101]

Santals are a joyous community; *raska* meaning joy, pleasure, happiness as a motto in life. They are happy and contented even in the worst situation of utter poverty. Thus, there are numerous seasonal rites and festivals by the Santals to keep them happy. Their behaviour during these festivals is characterised by a carefree, uninhibited attitude and a joyous frame of mind. I am dealing with this particular section because for the Santals all these feasts and festivals are also religious ceremonies. I shall also show later how these celebrations can alienate or unify the Santals because some of them have become Christians. We need to find ways and means of remedying the situation so that the non-Christian Santals and Christian Santals can live in peace in the same village.

The Santal Life-Cycle

Our human life has basically four important stages, birth, initiation, marriage and death. The Santals have very special rites/ceremonies on these occasions. All these different stages of transition are significant moments in their life and they make these occasions important through various symbolic activities. Santals consider these rites of passage as religiously significant. These rites and ceremonies are mainly concerned with securing active help of benevolent spirits and passive forbearance of the malignant ones. This is to ensure the safety and well-being of the individual. They are also collective occasions to emphasise the mutual harmony and solidarity between the individual and society. I explain briefly these aspects because to know a people we need to know their life-cycle too. It is good to know who they are, what they are, and how they form and organise their life.

Birth and Purification (Janam Chatiar)

"One of the greatest things a Santal married couple dreads is to have no offspring. They will secure adult respect only when they beget a child. So important is a child, especially a son, that a husband can lawfully divorce a wife if she is found to be barren and a wife can divorce her husband if he is found to be sterile. In some cases, the husband is persuaded to take a second wife. This however, is done only with the consent of the first wife."[102]

The birth of a child is announced by saying, "The new relation has arrived." Children are spoken of as the gift of the Supreme Being and so they are a blessing to the family. It is true that every family likes to have a male child at first because they want to keep the family clan and inherit the father's lands. It is also important that he needs to assist at his father's funeral ceremonies and perpetuate the worship of his own ancestors. Girls are welcome but not in the same priority. The first girl

101 Sahu, Chaturbhay, The Santal Women: A Social Profile, 74.

102 Troisi, Tribal Religion: Religious Beliefs and Practices among the Santals, 156.

is not considered as a curse as seen by many Hindus. A villager on hearing the birth asks, "What is it? Does it carry on the shoulder (a boy) or does it carry on the head (a girl). Or he may say, is it a hunter or is it a water carrier?"[103]

Once the child is born the message is announced to the people in the house. Later the whole village is notified about the birth. All the villagers are expected to know this because of the impurity involved as well as the happy message of the new member. The next important ceremony is the ritual purification (*janamchatiar*). The ceremonial uncleanness resulting from birth is shared by the whole village. There are three reasons for this ceremony. First there is the purification of the house and village from the defilement caused by child birth. The second is giving the child a name and admitting the child into the father's clan and giving the child protection of the father's spirits. The third is incorporating the child into the tribe. For this ceremony the relatives are invited. The removal of defilement consists in shaving and bathing. A barber shaves all the men of the village, starting from the *naeke* (priest). A few locks of hair are also cut from the child's head. Once this is complete all the men folk go to the river and bathe themselves. After they return the women folk bathe.[104]

Once the people have returned to the house after their bath, the child's mother is made to sit on the veranda of the house with the child in her lap. The midwife sprinkles cow-dung water on the mother and child. Then the child is given a name and thus the child receives a definite status in the family and village. In order to be united with the ancestors the boy child receives the name of his grandfather and the girl child the name of the grandmother. The ceremony is complete when all are given rice boiled with *neem* tree (Azadirachta indica, a medicinal tree) leaves (*neem dak mandi*). Part of the boiled rice is offered to the spirits for the protection of the child.[105]

Initiation (*Caco-Chatiar*)

The second important period in the life of the Santal is initiation or *caco-chatiar*. This ceremony may be observed any time before marriage and no Santal boy or girl may be permitted to be married before the initiation is performed. Once this is done, they become full-fledged members of the tribe with all the responsibilities and privileges. The members enter into a new relationship with the *bongas* (spirits) who can now be approached with sacrificial offerings and also share in the sacrificial meal.[106]

On the fixed day the villagers are summoned to the house where the ceremony is to take place. At times there may be more than one member to undergo initiation. The midwife who presided at the birth may be present. She or

103 Culshaw, W. J., Tribal Heritage: A Study on the Santals, 120.

104 Troisi, Joseph, Tribal Religion: Religious Beliefs and Practices among the Santals, 160.

105 Culshaw, W. J., Tribal Heritage: A Study on the Santals, 128-29.

106 Troisi, Joseph, Tribal Religion: Religious Beliefs and Practices among the Santals, 164.

some other elderly woman bathes the children by pouring water over them. After that the midwife or a girl from the village anoints all the people present with oil and turmeric, starting with the *naeke* (priest). Rice beer brewed for the occasion is served to all present and after that they sing and dance. At this juncture an old man comes to narrate the story of creation, and the wanderings of the Santals as narrated in the myth. It is important that they know their tribal tradition. It also helps to transmit the tribal lore, ensuring certain continuity in the tradition.[107]

The practices of tattooing (*Khoda*) the girls and cicatrisation (*Sika*) of boys are also associated with initiation. Many Santals say that these marks are very important for them to reveal their identity. The boys are branded on the hand/arm (in odd numbers) and girls are tattooed on the arms, shoulders and breasts. These marks are a guarantee for life in the next world to prove that they are Santals.[108]

Marriage (Bapla)

"The Santals cannot simply understand the proposition as to how a man can go on in a state of single blessedness. So both sexes despise the unhappy wretch and do not hesitate to call the solitary one, 'a thief, a witch, or a no man.'"[109] Even today bachelors and old maids are few among the Santal tribe. Marriage (*bapla*) is the most important stage in the Santal life cycle because they want to protect the solidarity of the tribe. Tribal endogamy and clan exogamy are practised very strictly by the Santals. These people enjoy abundant freedom in social contacts and they find their own partners although it is not always the case; marriages may be arranged by the parents. It is common among the Santals to marry quite young, many of the girls get married just after reaching puberty; many boys get married before they are twenty. They do not practice polygamy unless the wife is barren.

Bride Purchase (Kirin Bahu Bapla)

Though there are various forms of marriage (traditionally seven) the usual form is called *kirin bahu bapla* (bride purchase). It means the wife is bought by the bridegroom by paying a price to the bride's father. This is usually arranged by the elders. The would-be-relatives meet each other and a day is arranged to visit the boy in his house. On this occasion the bride price (*gonon*) is fixed as well as other matters related to the marriage. This ceremony is called *nepel* (meeting each other). It is the same as betrothal. Later the bride is visited at her place. On both the occasions sacrifices are offered to the village spirits and to the ancestral spirits for the protection of the couple.[110]

---

107 Mukherje, Charulal, The Santals, Calcutta: A Mukherjee & Co. Pr. Ltd, 1939, 190.

108 Mukherje, Charulal, The Santals, 192-93.

109 Mukherje, Charulal, The Santals, 195.

110 Troisi, Joseph, Tribal Religion: Religious Beliefs and Practices among the Santals, 174-75.

The preparations for the marriage are very important and many people of both the villages (bride's and bridegroom's) take part. The houses and the streets (*kulhi*) are decorated. The bridegroom bathes and then oil and turmeric are applied on his body. After this the procession starts with drums and cymbals beat to the accompaniment of merry music. When the groom's party enters the bride's village they are received with traditional ceremonies. The best-man carries the groom on his shoulder and the bride is carried in a palanquin. Both are sprinkled with water. The bride's face is uncovered and the groom applies *sindur* (vermilion) on her forehead. (This is equal to putting the rings on each other's fingers). This is accompanied by loud shouting, drumming and cheering. Then the couple enter the house. The priest offers sacrifice to the village spirits at the *jaherthan* (sacred grove) for the welfare of the couple. After these rituals are over, they begin the meal.[111]

Other Types of Marriage

The other forms of marriage are for convenience and at times due to the prevailing situation. *Kirinjawaebapla*: when a husband is acquired/bought for a girl who is made pregnant by a man who, either does not want to marry her, or cannot marry her because he belongs to her clan. In such a case the cost of acquiring/ buying (*kirin*) a husband (*jawae)* is borne by the offender. *Tunki Dipil Bapla*: This is observed by people who are poor who cannot bear the expenses of a regular marriage. No bride price is paid. The bride gathers all her belongings in a small bamboo basket (*tunki*) and she is brought to the groom's house with the basket on her head (*dipil*). *Sanga Bapla*: This is contracted by a widow or a divorced woman, a widower or a divorced man. In this case the bride price is half of the normal rate. The reason for this is because it is believed that after death the woman will rejoin her first husband. *Ghardi Jawae Bapla*: This is resorted to by the parents who have only daughters and no sons. So a man is brought in to help in the work of the household. All marriage expenses are borne by the girl's party. The groom pays no bride price either. Normally only boys from poor families agree to this kind of marriage. He is obliged to stay in the bride's house for five years. After this period he may go back to his house. In the case of *Ghar Jawae Bapla* he stays permanently in his in-law's house. However he continues to retain his rights on his father's land and property. He cannot make sacrifices to his father-in-law's *bongas* but he keeps his father's *bongas*. Two other types of marriages (*Itut Bapla, Nir Bolok Bapla*) are rare because there is force involved. In the case of *Itut* (to mark with paint) *Bapla* the boy takes the initiative because he does not know if the parents agree to the marriage. So in a public place he forcibly applies vermilion (*sindur*) on her forehead claiming her as his wife. In *Nir Bolok* (intruding) *Bapla* it is the girl who takes the initiative. She intrudes into the house of the boy because he

111 Orans, Martin, The Santal: A Tribe in Search of a Great Tradition, 61-63.

has had sexual relations with her and refuses to marry her. So she forces him into marriage.[112]

Marriage is understood as a relationship not merely between two persons but between two families and villages. The following words indicate the union of two villages, "From now on our villages have become as one. Formerly you were strangers and you used to pass by our village. Now if any of your people is passing this way he must stop and ask for a drink."[113]

Death (Gujuk) & Funeral Rites

The Santals do not recognise the possibility of natural death. They attribute death to the malignancy of certain *bongas* (spirits). Though one has to fight against these *bongas* all through life, finally the *bongas* put an end to human life. When a death takes place in the tribe, the village headman and the villagers flock together in mourning. They anoint the body with oil and turmeric. The corpse is then taken out of the house in a cot and is kept on the courtyard. Without much delay, when most of the villagers are present, they carry the dead body to the outskirts of the village and bury it. Usually women do not go to the burial place.[114]

A grave is dug at the outskirts of the village facing north south. The body is buried there with the head facing south. It is buried with the cot and above it dry branches or bamboo sticks are placed so that mud does not fall directly on the corpse. They then cover the grave with earth and place some stones above it. After this the chief mourner, usually the eldest son, has his head shaved completely. Then all go for their purificatory bath because the Santals believe that after the death of a person the whole village is polluted. The next important ceremony after the funeral is known as '*telnahan*` (oil washing). It is also known as *umulader* (bringing in the shadow). Until this ceremony is performed the dead person will remain in the clutches of the hostile agency.[115]

The *telnahan* ceremony takes place five days after the death of the person. The ceremony is important because of the double effect; one is for the redemption of the dead person and the other for the purification of the village.

The village men gather at the dead man's house. After all have been shaved, some male relatives of the deceased accompanied by other villagers go to the grave. Here, the chief mourner collects a handful of earth which he burns and puts into a new earthenware pot. On returning to the end of the village *kulhi,* where they are met by womenfolk, the pot is smashed to pieces and the burnt earth is sprinkled with water and turmeric. Then everyone goes for his purificatory bath. The chief mourner carrying the burnt earth keeps it on a leaf plate. After taking bath and rubbing themselves with oil given by the deceased's family, the chief mourner,

---

112 Troisi, Joseph, Tribal Religion: Religious Beliefs and Practices among the Santals, 170-72.

113 Troisi, Joseph, Tribal Religion: Religious Beliefs and Practices among the Santals, 184.

114 Mukherje, Charulal, The Santals, 220-21.

115 Troisi, Joseph, Tribal Religion: Religious Beliefs and Practices among the Santals, 192.

surrounded by his male relatives and villagers, makes offerings of oil cakes and sal twigs to Maran Buru (Supreme God), Pilchu Haram and Pilchu Budhi, and to the departed soul. He implores Maran Buru to lodge the deceased's soul in the shadow of the house till he reaches his final rest.[116]

Though with the *telnahan* ceremony the departed spirit is said to have been released from the underworld, he has not reached his final abode. The last funeral ceremony, *bhandan* (meal after the death of a person) is what joins the spirit of the dead with the realm of the ancestors. Several relatives and villagers are invited for this celebration. They bring along goats and chicken and rice beer to be offered to the spirit. After the sacrifices are offered the people's mourning comes to an end. The meal is cooked with the meat offered to the spirits. All eat and drink and celebrate the occasion because they know that the dead has joined the world of the ancestors.[117]

Santals believe that death is essentially an interruption of the normal process of living. They in fact speak of *hormo* and *jion* (body and life or soul). The body remains here on this world (*noa puri*) and soul (*jion*) goes to the other world or sky or heaven country (*hanapuri or sermadisom*). Life in the other world depends on the type of life one has lead here in this world. If one has led a good life on this earth one is rewarded with a happy life in the other world; if one has led a bad life on this earth one will receive punishment and will remain in hell which is known as *ich kund* (excrement heap).[118]

In all societies, major events in the life cycle (as mentioned above) are subject to ritualized forms of recognition. Across the world, such events are celebrated in diverse and sometimes elaborate ways, with different cultures singling out different stages of life for attention. Because rites of passage appear around the world and concern deeply human transitions, it is easy to lapse into universal claims: When there is a death, you should grieve; everyone rejoices at a birth; weddings are dramatizations of love. The point in examining other people's rites and ceremonies is not to steal or even borrow them but to evoke more appreciation and understanding towards them. Each tribe or race has its own unique customs and practices. These are elements that make a tribe rich and worthy of attention.

Santal Cultural (Religious) Festivals

Religious and secular festivals and feasts have many uses and values beyond the public enjoyment of a celebration. In the Santal society, festivals provide an opportunity for the elders to pass on folk knowledge and the meaning of tribal lore to younger generations. Their festivals and feasts focusing on the customs of their traditional or ethnic group enrich understanding of their heritage. Communal feasts are also occasions for eating, drinking, and merrymaking for the Santals.

116 Troisi, Joseph, Tribal Religion: Religious Beliefs and Practices among the Santals, 193-94.

117 Troisi, Joseph, Tribal Religion: Religious Beliefs and Practices among the Santals, 194.

118 Culshaw, W. J., Tribal Heritage: A Study on the Santals, 158.

Sohrae (Harvest Festival)

Sohrae is the principal and the most important festival and public event of the Santals. *Sohrae* is usually celebrated in the month of *Push* (December – January) when the paddy has been harvested and stored. This is a festival for affinity between people and cattle. Ancestors, deities and other spirits are worshipped on this occasion. New clothes are purchased for everybody. The house has to be cleaned before the festival and new earthen pots are bought for the celebration. *Handi* (rice beer) has to be prepared for the festival. It is celebrated for about six days, and the dates are fixed by the community according to the convenience of the people of the particular village. So, the celebration is held at different times in different villages, but always within December – January. It is also a time for blessing the cattle and fishing expeditions. *Sohrae* is the biggest event for the Santals to relax and enjoy life. The married daughters return to their houses for this celebration. Other people from other villages also come with gifts.[119] They eat, drink, sing and dance together. All are participators in the songs and dances. There are no spectators and performers; all are equally involved in the celebration. It is considered as the occasion for the great communion whereby all the relatives along with the ancestors and the spirits come together. The song below explains the importance of the feast:

> Elder sister, I will catch it by hand, I will catch it by leg,
> The festival like elephant is going away.
> A leaf cup of meat, a bowl for rice beer.
> You have invited your daughter and sister.[120]

Baha Porob (Flowering Festival)

Baha Porob is the flower festival celebrated only after the flowering of the *matkom* tree (*mahua, (*Madhucalongfolia). It is celebrated with the aim of obtaining good rain, good harvest and general prosperity during the whole agricultural year in the month of Phagun (February – March). No one is allowed to collect or eat the fallen flowers from the *matkom*[121] till the festival is celebrated. This is the spring festival and has great significance not only for the Santals but also for the other tribes. The central point of the feast is the *jaherthan* deity (*jaher era*); she is the guardian spirit of the village, children and cattle as well.[122] God gives land but land itself cannot produce anything and so God helps humanity in many ways. During this feast, prayers are offered to the deity who is responsible for good monsoon and good crops. She shares in the joys and sorrows of the people of the

---

119 AISWACS, Santal Festival, New Delhi: AISWACS, 2004, 2.

120 Sahu, Chaturbhay, The Santal Women: A Social Profile, 78.

121 Matkom flower: It is used for distilling the drink called Paura. They also boil this flower and eat.

122 Tirky, Agapit S. J., *Tribal Land: A Theological Reflection,* in "Sevartham Vol. 30", 2005. 25.

village. So it is not only the worship of nature but also to make union with nature. Singing and dancing are part of this festival.[123]

Erok′Sim (Sowing Festival)

Erok ′sim is another of the agricultural festivals and is celebrated in the month of *Asar* (June – July), just before the winter paddy is sown. The community decides upon the day of the celebration. The materials required for the celebration are collected from different families by the *godet* (messenger). After the purificatory bath, the *naeke* (priest) goes to the *jaherthan.* He is accompanied by the *kudamnaeke, godet* and some villagers. The *naeke* sacrifices fowls, one each to propitiate the *Marn Buru* (the Great Spirit*), moreko-turuiko* (spirit of the five people council), and *jaher era* (lady of the sacred grove). Another fowl is sacrificed in honour of *manjhi haram* (headman). Through these sacrifices spirits are implored to keep the village free from disease and to bring rain and festivity to the land thus enabling them to have a successful crop. The spirits are also implored to keep the cattle healthy enabling them to increase in number. After the sacrificial offering, the fowls are cooked with rice, and all the people present eat of the *sura-jel* (meal cooked with rice and meat). However it is noteworthy, the fowls offered to *jaher era* and *moreko-turuiko* are cooked separately and eaten only by the *naeke.* After the ceremony, the villagers sing and dance in the *kulhi* (village street or path). The following day each household in the village sacrifices fowls in honour of *Marang Buru, abge bongas* (sub-clan spirits) *and orak ′bongas* (household spirits). After the completion of this ceremony, the sowing of the winter paddy begins.[124]

Karam Festival

Karam is the most important festival of many of the tribal people all over India. Karam[125] is the name of a tree (Naucleaparvifolia). The Santals celebrate this festival during the month of Asin (September – October). The feast is meant to ensure protection of standing crops, and is the feast of unmarried girls who have been recently engaged. They pray for the blessing of healthy children.[126]

There is a story about karam *puja* (sacrifice). There were seven brothers in a family who used to live with their wives and children. The elder brother Karma and the younger brother Karma did not perform the *puja.* Moreover they threw the karam tree which was planted at the place of worship, into the river. It is said that they became the victims of diseases, economic hardship and many other problems. Then they became repentant and went out in search of King Karam. At

123 Sahu, Chaturbhay, The Santal Women: A Social Profile, 77.

124 AISWACS, Santal Festival, 3.

125 Karam: According to legend, in an ancient war, only a young couple that hid in the hollow trunk of this tree was left alive, and ever since then this tree has been regarded as sacred, (Information from Santals).

126 AISWACS, Santal Festival, 4.

last they found King Karam and started offering *puja*. They got relieved of their problems and started living peacefully.[127]

The exceptional feature of this festival is that no sacrifices are offered but only rice beer libations are offered to *manjhi-haram bonga* and *Marang Buru*. *Karam* celebration usually begins in the evening when it gets dark. After they have bathed two unmarried men go to the nearby forest to bring two branches of *karam* tree. The village folk accompany them to and fro, singing and dancing. The branches are then planted in the *kulhi* (village street) and the people continue singing and dancing. One of the elder men sprinkles water and a small light is lit in front of the branch. He then puts *sindur* (vermillion) on the branches and offers rice beer libation in front of the branch and invokes *Marang Buru* and *manjhi-haram bonga* to give prosperity and wealth. Then the villagers drink rice beer and recite the creation story (creation of the world and Santals) and the division of the clans and sub-clans among the Santals. After that they sing and dance till sunrise. Then the branches are taken out and immersed into the village pond.[128]

These festivals and feasts are not only occasions for eating, drinking, and merrymaking, but also have many uses and values beyond the public enjoyment of a celebration. These occasions provide an opportunity for the elders to pass on folk knowledge and the meaning of tribal lore to younger generations. They also enrich understanding of their heritage and fulfil an informal educational function.

1.6.3. Economic Structure: Heritage and Deprivation

The Santal village communities had collectively controlled and used vital resources like land, water and forests for centuries. They ensured the sustainable use of these renewable resources. They had learned to remain on the land and nourish themselves from it. This perspective is highlighted here: "Our land is more valuable than the money. It will last forever. It will not even perish by flames and fires. As long as the sun shines and water flows this land will be here to give life to people and animals. We cannot sell the life of people and animals. Therefore, we cannot sell this land. It was put here for us by the Great Spirit and we cannot sell it because it does not belong to us. As a present to you we will give you anything we have that you can take with you, but our land, never."[129]

The greatest culture of the aborigines is agriculture and it will be so for many years. The prosperity in this and having good rains are signs of God′s blessings. That is the reason they say that land is not individual property; it belongs to all the living and the dead. Land is a gift from the Supreme Being and so it is sacred. Therefore no one can sell it or misuse it as he desires. Once a Red Indian said, "every part of the earth is sacred to my people. We are part of the earth and

127 Sahu, Chaturbhay, The Santal Women: A Social Profile, 77.

128 AISWACS, Santal Festival, 7.

129 W.C.C. (World Council of Churches), Land Rights for Indigenous People, Geneva: W.C.C., 1983, 14.

the earth is part of us. If land is sold then human being would die from great loneliness of spirit."[130] The land for the Santals is not only an economic factor but an inalienable inheritance.

Land: Significance for Santals

The creation myth depicts that the Supreme Being is the creator of earth, land. Some creatures that collaborate in the creative action of God are, the earthworm, tortoise, etc. Ultimately, He is the giver of land, nature, crops, children, clans and tribes. He taught humanity (the first couple) how to find things for sustenance. He taught them how to work in the field, how to plough and cultivate as well as how to offer sacrifices to God. Humanity is entrusted with the task of taking care of the land. It is the land that unites all the tribal people with one Creator and the ancestral world. Land is the place where the Supreme Being manifests. It is the altar to offer sacrifice to the Supreme Being. The land is where the ancestors are resting in peace. For the tribal people the ultimate goal or salvation is to enter into the ancestral community. They see a symbiotic relationship with everything in nature and so they are in contact and communion with the ecosystem. The land becomes central to these people's lives, their history, their culture, their identity, their spirituality, their economy and to their very survival. In order to be in communion with their ancestors, the tribe depends very much on their land. To attain this goal they have to fulfil some sacred duties in this world, such as giving food and drink to the ancestors. These food and drink can be given from the product of their ancestral land alone. Before starting any work, the tribal people offer sacrifices on the land. Therefore, land is at the core of tribal life and spirituality, which gives Santals a distinct religious and cultural identity.[131]

Settlement in Damin-i-koh

The first few years in the Damin-i-koh (already mentioned in the sub-title ***Santals and Their New Home****1. 4. 3)* were years of strange peace and quiet. The Santals, almost part of a wandering tribe, had found a home at last. Here for the first time in all the history of their race they felt secure. To them the land was a haven of rest such as the people had never known whence Hindu and *mahajan* (moneylender), Musalman and *zamindar* (landlord) might oust him at will. So, long as he kept the peace, the land was his. The Skirts of the Hills (Damin-i-koh) was a land such as the Santals loved. It offered escape from contact with the hated race and so to them it was a veritable land of Canaan. Here, without fear of being merged in a so-called higher but repugnant civilization, they could maintain their old tribal life and time-honoured customs intact. To settle on some tract of land and to turn the virgin soil and force subsistence from a hitherto unproductive land was labour that appealed to the Santals. Here at last they seemed to have found a

130 Ibid, 15.

131 Tirkey, Agapit, S.J., *Tribal Land: A Theological Reflection*, 24.

home where change need never come. So greatly content and seemingly secure, the Santals tilled the rich soil and gathered in their first abundant crops. In their newfoundjoy, they did not dream of the dark days that were soon to follow.[132]

They could preserve their nationality intact as well. With jealous exclusiveness, they had shrunk from mixing with people of another race. "Time and again, as their legends have recorded, this passionate desire to preserve the tribe from contamination had led them to forsake their homes and wander forth in search of new lands rather than admit a stranger within their ranks. It was this national spirit, this clannish sentiment that united the Santals in one unbroken front against the foreigners. But, they had long since learned the danger that beset the integrity of the tribe from constant contact with the stranger at their gates."[133]

Insufficiency of Land

The times had changed (the days of prosperity and plenty) and they could no longer wander on as they had done in their legends, wandering from Champa to Chotanagpur along the banks of Saont river, ever finding new lands to claim. The old conditions of movement and unrest were coming to an end and order and stability were the watchwords of the new powers. The tribe had already multiplied and grown beyond its old tribal limits; it was no longer possible for them to move as one united family like in former patriarchal days. There was a real danger that they might split up into smaller scattered groups and gradually lose their nationality and become absorbed in the lowest classes among the Hindus. The whole Santal nature rebelled against such a fate. For the Santals life among the Hindus was doubly galling.[134]

Settlement in Jharkhand

The land (present Jharkhand) of the Santal tribe is one of the richest areas in the whole country; rich in minerals with huge reserves of coal, iron, mica, copper, china-clay, uranium, etc. Adding to these are the lush green forest, and the fertile soil which is conducive for cultivation. They had more than enough food in the earlier days when they were by themselves. Historically, the economy of most tribes was subsistence agriculture or hunting and gathering.[135] They did not have to depend on others as they were masters of their own land.

The Santals settled down in the valleys and jungles of Jharkhand. The whole area was practically a virgin forest. Each family of settlers made its own clearing and together became a village. The forest was abounding in live game, edible roots and fruits. Here the land was cultivable and offered extensive pasturage for their cattle. Later they cherished the idea of common ownership of the families. "Within the

132 Bradley-Birt, Francis, The Story of an Indian Upland, 159.

133 Bradley-Birt, Francis, The Story of an Indian Upland, 160.

134 Bradley-Birt, Francis, The Story of an Indian Upland. 161.

135 Areeparambil, Mathew, S.J., Tribals of Jharkhand: Victims of Development, 3.

limits of the village thus demarcated all the land, cultivable as well as waste, all the hills, jungle, and streams – everything above ground and underground became the common property of the village. A portion of primitive forest was consecrated to the more important amongst them and named the *jaher* or *sarna* (sacred grove). Here to this day, the village offers sacrifices not only to the principal village deities but also to the whole host of general spirits that are of any account."[136]

Land: Its Alienation

As early as in the year 1676 Hindus began snatching away the land of the tribal people of Chotanagpur. Gradually the problem was spreading to other tribal areas. By the 19th century the Santals were in Santal Parganas. The new policy of the *mahajans* and the British administration was against the Santals. Cornwallis, the then Viceroy introduced a new economic policy which favoured the *mahajans*. The British administration was interested in collecting revenue and not in the welfare of the tribe. The division of land and removing common ownership of land facilitated the administration's, the *mahajans*' and the traders' action against the Santals.[137] Thus, the situation began to change from what they had lived through for some years.

According to Marx, in a capitalist society an alienated man lives in alienated nature and he performs estranged labour and the product of his labour becomes alien to him. Alienation as a concept is used by many social scientists in India, merely as a sociological phenomenon. Since land alienation is the crux of the de-peasantisation of the tribal people, the concept assumes utmost importance in the analysis of tribal rights as a part of the human rights discourse. The problem of land alienation is a deeply rooted problem full of contradictions related to the existing socio-economic order. The separation of land from the tribal communities can be understood only if we are able to understand the psyche of tribal people.[138]

There are different ways of manipulating and alienating the tribal people from their land. Primarily there is the manipulation of land records. The unsatisfactory state of land records contributed a lot to the problem of land alienation. The tribal people were never legally recognised as owners of the lands though they cultivated it. The second form of land alienation is reported to have taken place due to '*benami*' transfers (Fictitious transfer of land or other property) in which land remains in the names of the original owners who are reduced to the level of share croppers. Another form of land alienation is related to the leasing or mortgaging of the land. To raise loans for various needs, the tribal people have to give their land as mortgage to the local moneylenders or to the rich farmers. Encroachment

---

136 Tirkey, Agapit, S.J, *Tribal Land: A Theological Reflection,* 37.

137 Prasad, Narmadeshwan, Land and People of Tribal Bihar, Ranchi: Bihar Tribal Research Institute, 1961, 48.

138 Prasad, Narmadeshwan, Land and People of Tribal Bihar, 49.

is another form of dispossessing the tribal people of their lands and this is done by the new entrants in all the places where there were no proper land records. Bribing the local *patwari* (local revenue officer) for manipulating the date of settlement of land disputes, antedating etc., are resorted to in order to claim the tribal lands.[139]

Agents of Alienation

Landlords were waiting with covetous eyes to reap the harvest they had not sown. Here was a field ready to hand over to the rapacious *zamindars* and *mahajan*. The Santals, carried away by the wondrous fertility, were wishing to sell stores of grains for the smallest sum of money. The astute traders, not content with legitimate trade, resorted to deceit and fraud. The trader, having fleeced the Santal of his stock of grains by fair means and foul, let the *mahajans* step in. The Santal took a loan executing a bond of whose contents he was blissfully ignorant. One advance of money led to another. When at last the Santal was safely in his power the *mahajan* began to reap the fruits of the well-laid plan. The debtor's flocks and herds were taken from him merely to pay the interest of the debt. Thus, the unfortunate Santal saw his possessions go one by one. Anxiety and despair succeeded peace and plenty. The landlords called the Santals to work with a promise of higher wage. Those who went to work became tenants. Neither could they go back to the hills from where they came, nor did they receive higher wages. However, some people disappeared and went out to seek the inhospitable recesses of the jungle rather than remain slaves of the taskmasters.[140]

Another way of exploiting the Santals was through collecting revenues. The British appointed intermediaries who had power over vast areas to collect revenues. Though legislation controlled their power, they manipulated the situation to exploit the people. They managed to evict the Santals from their land by foul means; many of them were made tenants who would work for the *mahajans*.[141]

New Regulations and Further Deprivation

The Bengal/Bihar Tenancy Act of 1885 brought about some changes. A tenant need not hold a piece of land for twelve years for occupancy right (before the Tenancy Act, he had to); if he held any land for twelve years in a village he was entitled to occupy right of the land he held in the same village. Rent could not be enhanced for the next five years. If a tenant refused to pay the rent, the court would decide about the rent. If the tenant was evicted he had to be given compensation.[142]

139 Areeparambil, Mathew, S.J., Tribals of Jharkhand: Victims of Development, 4.

140 Bradley Birt, Francis, The Story of an Indian Upland, 168-69.

141 Dubey, S. N. & Mirdha, Rahia (Ed), Land Alienation and Restoration in Tribal Communities in India, Bombay: Himalaya Publishing House, 1977, 36.

142 Dubey, S. N. & Mirdha, Rahia (Ed), Land Alienation and Restoration in Tribal Communities in India, 38.

In the year 1894 the land acquisition act was passed. It was an act to amend the law for the acquisition of land for public purposes and for companies. Later in 1927 the Indian forest act was passed. It was to consolidate the law relating to forest, and the duty taxable on timber and other forest products. Both these acts only added misery to the Santals as more and more land and forest were being lost by them.[143]

In 1949 the Santal Parganas Tenancy Act came into existence to facilitate the tribal people. But the tribal people did not benefit from this Tenancy Act. This regulation prohibited transfer of land from tribal to non-tribal. If the land was transferred in contraventions, there should be punishment with imprisonment up to 3 years or a fine of 1000 rupees or both. In the case of continuing of offence, a further fine of fifty rupees per day had to be given. Legislature loopholes and administrative apathy led to the same and even worse kind of exploitations. *mahajans* and landlords prospered by these acts. Santals themselves were too innocent and illiterate to know the intricacies of the problems. There was a wide cultural barrier which separated them on very different levels. The Santals were unfamiliar dealing in trade and wealth.[144]

Bound down by custom and tradition and mindless of the future, the Santal thought only how to celebrate each event as it occurred. Yet again he found the *mahajan* near at hand, complacent still and ready to lend, for there was one thing more the Santal had that the *mahajan* coveted. His land and all his possessions gone, the wretched peasant had no further degree of degradation to which he might fall; but the *mahajan*, with his keener instinct, saw into the future and demanded of the Santal the last thing he had to give – himself. Degraded, landless and penniless as they were, they might set out again blindly in search of a new land, as they had done on occasions before. That would mean the undoing of all the *mahajan's* work. If the Santal left, there would be no one to cultivate and so the *mahajan* planned out ways to lose his right to go away. This explained the *mahajan's* willingness to lend. "Having nothing tangible to give, the Santal pledged himself to work off the debts, little dreaming even then in his simplicity and guilelessness to what a life of slavery he was dooming himself and his family. Work as the Santal might, he would never even so much as pay off the exorbitant interest that would mount up by leaps and bounds until the original sum was but a trifle in the huge burden of indebtedness."[145] The *mahajan* took care that the Santal had no time to work elsewhere, no leisure from his slavery to earn the wherewithal to pay off his debt. Look where he might, the Santal could find no escape from the oppressor.

143 Dubey, S. N. & Mirdha, Rahia (Ed), Land Alienation and Restoration in Tribal Communities in India, 38.

144 Singh, Virendra, The Indian Forest Act – 1927, Allahabad (India): Law Publishers, 1976. 36.

145 Bradley-Birt, Francis, The Story of an Indian Upland, 175.

Development and Oppression

The tribal belt has the largest mineral deposits in India. The important coalfields are Jharia, Bokaro, Ramgarh, Giridih and Santal Parganas (Districts in Jharkhand). Iron ore and copper are found in Singhbhum. Ranchi and Palamau possess bauxite. In Hazaribagh, mica is available. "Jharkhand receives a fifth of the total public sector investments in industrial pursuit."[146]

The rapid industrialisation in Jharkhand was accompanied by fast urban growth and by a steady increase in the rate of immigration. Despite this fast growth, a very small group of tribal people enjoy the facilities. Since the tribal people are not accustomed to factory work and are used to agriculture, they are not employed as skilled labourers. Therefore, they do not enjoy the privileges and facilities, which the others enjoy. This type of development has led to the intrusion of outsiders to the tribal area. The effect on the lives of the Santals has been one of tragic note. Loss of tribal rights over land and forest is a result of this. Even those who own a little land are unable to cultivate due to various reasons. They lack sufficient amount of money to buy the seeds needed; there may not be enough rains and they are unable to pump water into the fields due to the unavailability of pump sets and so on, to mention just two reasons.

With dried-up water resources and ill-implemented irrigation projects, they have only one harvest a year and eagerly await a good monsoon. During the rest of the year, the adivasis, including women and children, are forced into daily wage labour in mines, stone quarries and sanitary works where conditions of work are hazardous and there are grave violations of human rights. Seasonal migration in search of occupation has become rampant. The situation becomes particularly acute during drought. As a result, the tribal people are alienated from their own land and their unique identity stands eroded. Land alienation has led to migration. They go to tea plantations, mines and factories as daily labourers. These people are exposed to an alien culture and they come back to the village with values alien to the community and thus finding themselves alien and poor in their own land. The negative effect can be seen in their villages.

According to my personal knowledge, the large-scale industrialization of the region is aimed at exploiting its rich mineral resources. The setting up of coalmines and steel plants, and various development projects has led to extensive environmental degradation, widespread industrial pollution and depletion of forest and water resources. Furthermore, it has unleashed corrupt commerce and politics, unbridled exploitation of the tribal communities and haphazard urbanization. Thousands have been forced to give up their habitat with paltry compensation for displacement.

146 Devalle, Susanna, Discourses of Ethnicity, New Delhi: Sage Publications: 1982, 82.

Sanskritization: Its Negative Impact on Santals

Due to contact with other people, situations and cultures, the tribal culture is undergoing a revolutionary change. The tribal people are imitating western culture in different aspects of their social life and leaving their own culture. It has led to degeneration of tribal life and tribal arts such as dance, music and different types of craft. This change is called sanskritization. It indicates a process of cultural mobility that is taking place in the traditional social system of India. Many tribal people adopted some customs and practices of the Brahmins in order to raise their position in the caste hierarchy and gave up some of their own which were considered impure by the higher castes. There are cases of tribal people who gave up eating meat, drinking liquor and animal sacrifice to their deities. They imitated Brahmins and other urban people in matters of dress, food and rituals. By this, they could claim higher positions in the hierarchy of castes within a generation. The reference group in this process is not always Brahmins but may be the dominant caste of the locality. The process of sanskritization is an endogenous source of social change. Sanskritic rites are often added on to non-sanskritic rites without replacing them. Often the motive force behind sanskritization is not of cultural imitation per se but an expression of challenge and revolt against the socioeconomic deprivations. I am a witness to several cases of this expression in the Santal villages.

Conclusion

In the first chapter, I have described the life, situation, worldview, and their socio-politico-economic and cultural context. I have described their creation myth, legend and history. Their feasts and festivals and their important life cycle are explained. By these, I want to convey the message that all these factors are important to know the type of people that they are, the Santals. I have described their wanderings from place to place to their final settlement in Santal Parganas. They have had their happy situations and sad and painful ones. But of late it has been a constant struggle for survival because they have been constantly oppressed and exploited by outsiders whom they call *dikus*. During their life time in the 19th century they even revolted against the oppressors but many of them were brutally killed and their revolt was inhumanly put down; still they did not get justice. This is the situation they are in today.

The Indian Tribal Communities in general and Santals in particular today are passing through a critical phase in their history. Unrest and discontentment is sweeping through tribal India. Tribal belts in the country are the richest in natural resources but ironically, the tribal people are among the poorest of India. In spite of several schemes and projects by the Constitution of India[147] for the tribal people, they have become victims of exploitation and negligence. I have tried

147 Constitution of India: Fifth Schedule deals with Tribal people and the Provisions for them.

to understand the problem in historical perspective, and attempt to answer the questions like: why did the economic condition of the Santals deteriorate? What was the impact of migration of non-tribes into the tribal area? Why is tribal land being still alienated despite the existence of land transfer regulations? What types of cleavages exist within the tribal communities? There are also problems and anti-values which are in themselves harmful to any society. For example, one cannot tolerate the practice of witchcraft. Often women are killed without prior enquiry and proper process. Just because the *ojha* or *jan guru* (witch finder, magician) says that there should be a witch who caused the problem or sickness, it may not be true. Such evil practices have to be questioned, challenged and opposed so as to create a society that is more conducive for good living. I have tried to analyse the society of Santals with the goal that we may be able to understand the people better in their context so that our efforts to improve the situation of the Santals are not futile; instead, we reach the right goal. I need to know these people in order to deal with them and to continue the mission of Christ among them. For this purpose, it is good to know the history of the Church among the Santals. What has happened to the Santals who became Christians or who were converted to Christianity?

2

History and Spread of the Church Among the Santals

2.1. Introduction

Church history, today, seems irrelevant to 21st century Christianity. However, Christianity is deeply rooted in history. Central to the Christian faith is the fact that God came to earth as a man - Jesus Christ. He lived, loved and taught among humanity about 2000 years ago. The historical reality of His life, sacrifice, burial and resurrection is the cornerstone of the Christian faith and the Bible is all about that. The Bible is not a fairy tale, but a divinely inspired record of God's plan of redemption for a hurting world. To study church history is to see the hand of God at work amidst the strife, transgression and glory of human ways. Church history is vital to our understanding of the institution of the Christian church. Much is to be gleaned from the events between the time of the apostles and the present. Like the history of ancient Israel, we can learn and remember from the history of the Christian church.[148]

Church history has two sides, a divine and a human. On the part of God, it is his revelation in the order of time (as the creation is his revelation in the order of space), and the successive unfolding of a plan of infinite wisdom, justice, and mercy, looking to his glory and the eternal happiness of humankind. On the part of human, history is the biography of the human race, and the gradual development, both normal and abnormal, of all its physical, intellectual, and

148 Schaff, Philip, *History of the Christian Church*, accessed on 22.02.2008, available from: http://www.ccel.org/s/schaff/history/1__gen.htm.

moral forces to the final consummation at the general judgment, with its eternal rewards and punishments.[149]

History is often described only as the history of kings, queens and the powerful and their invasions and victories. The history of the Church too is associated mainly with popes, bishops and the hierarchy. That is a history from above where the ordinary people do not matter; they are non-persons, having no voice in history. But the church had a very humble beginning and the initial stages of the church had many insignificant people who played very significant roles for its growth. That is the reason that today many people say we need to write history from below. The experience, life and struggles of ordinary people, who have contributed to the victory of the so-called people who do not matter in the world, should not be forgotten. These people are important and we need to recognize them as persons who hold their place in history.

The history of the church in Santal Parganas is a history of struggle, difficulties and pain mixed with a lot of joy, satisfaction and gratitude to God. Deep faith in and commitment to God are aspects of this history. I have heard from some senior priests that there were times of frustration, hopelessness together with lack of luxury, inconveniences and situations of being let down. In such situations tremendous faith in God and hope, hope for a new dawn was needed. Moreover, to survive and to live on in a foreign land with a strange culture, language and people was not very easy. Who can be the inspiration for these people other than Christ!

I try to include in my reflections as many people as possible who contributed to the growth and spread of Christianity among the Santals. I have to rely on two main authors for the history of the church among the Santals, namely, Fr. Yves de Steenhault SJ and Fr. John Scicluna. I also describe my own experiences and knowledge and the experiences of people I have met in order to have a better understanding of the places and people. However, I have to say that I am unable to pen all their names of people I have dealt with, because it is impossible to get the names of all the people who have played important roles in the history of the church here. I emphasise the mission and history of a few missionaries more than the others because they were pioneers or have done significant work. I have lived with people in the Santal villages and in parishes. I have talked with them and asked them about the church they belong to. This is an important part of the research paper because my paper is centred on the church among the Santals. Without knowing the history, we are unable to understand the situation of the people today.

I should also say something very important here about the process of evangelization that had taken place. Many of the missionaries with all their good intentions of doing good to the people, and the type of theology that they had learned, probably did not foresee the deculturation that was taking place. In the

149 Cf. Schaff, Philip, *History of the Christian Church.*

process, the Santals lost a lot of their culture and tradition. The missionaries were very clear in their perspective that if the Santals wanted to become Christians they had to renounce their culture and religion completely. The Santals were ready to sacrifice their culture, probably because they did not realize what the eventual consequences would be.

2.2. Christianity among the Tribals of North India

Christianity came to India in two main periods: According to tradition and legend, *(unfortunately, there is no exact recorded history of this time; that is why I have mentioned according to legend and tradition. The Syro-Malabar Christians believe strongly that St. Thomas came to Kerala)*, the first Christians in India, were converted by Saint Thomas the Apostle, who arrived on the Malabar Coast of India in A.D. 52. He died as a Martyr in a place called Mylapore near the present town of Chennai (Madras). His tomb is still venerated there. This church, as believed, is founded by St. Thomas and is known as the Syro-Malabar church. These Christians are known as St. Thomas Christians. Therefore, it is believed that there have been Christians in India since the time of the Apostles.[150] The second period deals with the western missionary activity from 1500, mainly related to St. Francis Xavier who preached and converted people on the coastal areas of India, mainly in South India. However, the tribal belt of Chotanagpur and Santal Parganas attracted the attention of Christian missionaries only in the middle of the 19th Century. Out of three main tribal belts in India, the major impact of Christianity has been more deeply felt in the north-eastern and central tribal belts.[151] In the latter case, the impact is more tremendous among the tribes of Chotanagpur plateau in the state of Jharkhand.[152] The Santals live also in this state and they have many things in common with the other tribes of Chotanagpur (Mundas, Oraons, Kharias, Hos and Paharias). But, each group has its own distinct features and culture.

2.2.1. The Advent of Christianity in Chotanagpur

In Chotanagpur, the advent of Christianity goes back to 19thcentury with the Lutheran Missionaries sent by Johannes Evangelista Gossner of Berlin. They arrived at Ranchi in 1845. The conversion of the first tribal families was made in 1850. Since 1860, great importance was given to Chotanagpur by the Catholic Church, the most promising part of the Calcutta Archdiocese. The missionaries

150 History of the Syro-Malabar Church, The Syro-Malabar Major Archiepiscopal Curia, Kerala, India, 2008.

151 Sahay, K. N., Dynamics and Democracies of Tribal Societies: Regional and Indian Perspectives, New Delhi: Commonwealth Publishers, 1998, 309.

152 Sahay, K. N., Dynamics and Democracies of Tribal Societies: Regional and Indian Perspectives, 309.

found that Chotanagpur was a good place for evangelization and all the efforts of the Belgian Fathers were directed to Ranchi.[153]

Thus, the Roman Catholic missionaries were late comers to this region. The first organized attempt towards mass conversion and proselytisation began with the advent of Fr. Constant Lievens, SJ from Belgium in the year 1885. Although, a few missionaries had come here earlier they had met with little success.[154] Fr. Lievens spent six and a half years in Chotanagpur (1885-1892). This was a time of extraordinary signs of divine power at work. There developed such a movement of grace that people began to speak about the miracle of Chotanagpur. The Lievens' mission caught the attention of the world.[155] "The Jesuit Mission, better known as 'Lievens' Mission' in Chotanagpur tribal stronghold of the present Jharkhand, is one of the successful missionary enterprises of the Indian Church as the growth of the conversion movement under Lievens was phenomenal. Lievens' missionary work accomplished a century ago, has great relevance for us in the present day when integral liberation is declared to be the mission of the church."[156]

At the time these missionaries came to Chotanagpur, its tribal population was groaning under the clutches of landlords, money-lenders, traders and police officials who exploited them in several ways. The missionaries helped them regain their land which had been illegally taken away by the landlords and money lenders. The missionaries helped the tribal people with regard to legal problems and disputes. So, the major factor responsible for their conversion was because these people received legal protection against their exploiters, and various other temporal benefits generally known as "*works of mercy*" which the missionaries offered them. In some cases, the tribal people were genuinely moved by the preaching of Christianity or accepted it as it promised to them emancipation from the worship and fear of spirits or witchcraft. Christian converts felt obliged to the missionaries for giving them the "true religion" and saving them from groping in the darkness. Fear of indigenous spirits and deities and their propitiation ceased. The Christian God was considered to be the powerful God. The former was considered to be the manifestations of the devil.[157]

This is the context in which Christianity took root in the Chotanagpur tribal belt and later named as Ranchi diocese. "The history of the Church is the story of the active intervention of Gracious Providence in her success, trials and expansion. Thus in May, 1927, Ranchi was detached from the Archdiocese of Calcutta and it appeared that the Archdiocese had lost its most flourishing area

153 Scicluna, John SJ, Can You face a Challenge? Madras: St. Joseph's Technical School, 1961, 15.

154 Sahay, K. N., Dynamics and Democracies of Tribal Societies: Regional and Indian Perspectives, 309.

155 Toppo, Telephore P. (Archbishop, Ranchi), in the Forward of the book, "The Missionary Approach of Fr. Lievens" by Aril, James SJ, Ranchi: Catholic Press, 2001, ix.

156 Aril, James S. J, The Missionary Approach of Fr. Lievens, Ranchi: Catholic Press, 2001, xi.

157 Sahay, K. N., Dynamics and Democracies of Tribal Societies: 311.

of Catholic life, Gracious Providence threw open to the Calcutta Archdiocese the still untilled fields of the Santal Parganas."[158] In July 1929, hardly a year after Ranchi was separated from Calcutta Archbishop Ferdinand Perier, SJ thought of sending priests to the Santal Parganas. The beginning of this work was a very great act of trust in Divine Providence because there was no shelter, no house and no land. The Maltese fathers, some of whom were already working in the Calcutta Archdiocese, were entrusted with this new promising field by Archbishop Perier.[159]

2.3. The Advent of Christianity among the Santals

Catholic priests made several attempts to establish a mission among the Santals who are the most numerous aboriginal tribes in India. From 1826, Capuchin fathers, and from 1887 Jesuit fathers ministered to the European and Anglo-Indian inhabitants of Purnea district and town, (now in Bihar) then famous for its indigo plantations, where a church was built and blessed in 1849. It was not very easy for the Belgian missionaries to access the Santals as they were far away from the region of the Santals.[160] In other words, some of the priests had to come to India with the colonisers to meet the so-called spiritual needs of the invaders. The priests could not do anythingelse other than meet the needs of the colonisers.

2.3.1. Initial Missionary Attempts in Santal Parganas

In the year 1879, Fr. Charles Schiff, a Belgian Jesuit missionary, attempted to visit Santal Parganas which was then an unknown territory to the missionaries of Bengal. He travelled by train to a place called Pakur (at present a district in Jharkhand) and from there tried to contact the headman of the Santal village. The headman was not very sympathetic to the foreigner and the missionary did not reveal his identity. After touring some villages, he returned to the railway station where he had to reveal his identity to receive a letter from the police. This information was reported to the headman and the people were told not to show him any hospitality. He had to leave the place without success at his first attempt. But, he did not give up his desire to visit this region again. Fr. Schiff made another attempt in December 1886 to visit Dumka, then capital town of Santal Parganas district. He was supposed to examine the locality and find a place to begin a mission station. A public security officer named Mr. Charles Fabre-Tonnere (a catholic) welcomed the missionary. Fr. Schiff lived here for ten months and he was happy to tour the whole of Santal Parganas in the company of this honest and virtuous man. After ten months Fr. Schiff returned to Calcutta and submitted the report of his observations and indicated the place

---

158 Dyer, Vivian A (Archbishop, Calcutta), from the Forward of "Can you face a Challenge?", by Scicluna, John, SJ, Madras: St. Joseph's Technical School, 1961, v.

159 Dyer, Vivian A (Archbishop, Calcutta), from the Forward of "Can you face a Challenge?"

160 Scicluna, John SJ, Can You face a Challenge? 16.

where he could begin his mission. However, the reply from the superior was a shock to him. The plan was to postpone the evangelization in Santal Parganas as Rome wanted to start a college in Darjeeling, West Bengal. Therefore, the priests from Asansol (another district in West Bengal) were responsible for the evangelisation of this area. All they could do was to visit the Santals when possible. In the year 1908, Fr. Martin Jacques, SJ built a church at Madhupur, in the western tip of Santal Parganas.[161]

In 1887 the Jesuit, Fr. Thomas MacGonagall arrived at Purnea (another district in Bihar; Santal Parganas and Purnea are separated by the river Ganges) from Calcutta to replace the Capuchin Fr. Heliodore (usually the Capuchin fathers do not use their surname), who had been ministering to the people of the locality for five years. Fr. MacGonagall often crossed the river Ganges and visited the people in Sahibganj, in Santal Parganas. Fr. Leopold Knockaert, SJ (from Belgium born in 1850) stayed there from 1900 until 1925, except for three years. In 1900, Fr. Knockaert took charge in Purnea and worked in the region until 1921 except for a gap of three years, when he was in another district, Mayurbhanj, in Orissa. He pioneered the work among the Santals of the Purnea district. His work led to the opening of Majlispur. Fr. Knockaert was admired for his missionary work and is said, "He was crowned with great success."[162]

Records show that as early as 1773 Purnea district was already forming part of the Vicariate of the Great Mughal, which was served by the Jesuits and later by the Carmelites. Subsequently, Rome attached Purnea to the neighbouring Prefecture of Tibet under the Capuchins, with Patna (present capital town of Bihar State) as its headquarters. In 1820, it became part of the Agra Vicariate. By then the Capuchin fathers had been regularly visiting Purnea from different places. In January 1836, Mgr. Anthony Pezzoni (Carmelite) visited Purnea accompanied by Fr. Florian Toposkia, a Polish Capuchin. The latter was appointed as the first resident priest of Purnea to serve the scattered community of European indigo planters who had started settling down in and around Purnea as soon as British rule was established in the district way before the 1770s. When Patna Vicariate was created on February 7, 1845, Purnea became part of it under the Capuchins. On August 1, 1886 the Indian Hierarchy was established and the Patna Vicariate was suppressed and its territory joined to the Allahabad diocese. Then on 7th of June 1887 Pope Leo XIII transferred Purnea district to Calcutta Archdiocese, mainly to provide a territorial link between Calcutta and Darjeeling. Fr. McGonagall, SJ took over at Purnea on December 1, 1888 from Fr. Heliodore. At this point, the parish priest of Purnea was also in charge of the railway colonies from Sahibganj to Burdwan, and used to visit also Rampurhat, Nalhati (towns in West Bengal) and even Naya Dumka (Jharkhand). During this time the Loreto Sisters (Institute of the Blessed Virgin

161 Scicluna, John SJ, Can You face a Challenge? 17.

162 Scicluna, John SJ, Can You face a Challenge? 18.

Mary, IBVM) from Ireland also came to Purnea. They arrived on December 15, 1882 and opened a school, working there until they left for Darjeeling on November 7, 1887.[163]

Later Purnea was the proto-parish of the Santal Mission. Many Jesuits served here as parish priests from 1887 until 1978. In 1978 when Fr. Joseph Schembri, SJ was parish priest, the parish was handed over to the diocesan priests. It was a wide area with Christians spread all over but with fewer priests and parishes. In 1934, the church of Purnea was destroyed in an earthquake. Although, a new church was duly built, it was too small to accommodate the growing number of Catholics. Later Fr. Anthony Sammut, SJ enlarged the church.[164]

2.3.2. Fr. Leopold Knockaert: Leader and Champion

During the First World War, the conversion movement among the Santals developed largely. The number rose from 52 of the 1911 census to 3892 in 1920. In 1912 a number of Santals from another diocese in West Bengal, Krishnagar, migrated to Purnea town because they were in search of land. They were lost in the new surroundings and were left to the mercy of the Muslim masters. Fr. Leopold Knockaert came in contact with these people as he was already informed by a priest in Krishnagar. The Santals welcomed Fr. Knockaert. The Muslim landlords who lived here at first did not appear to be disturbed by the conversions. "But towards the end of 1913, after the harvest of the crops, extortions and quarrels began, and became so violent that Fr. Knockaert finally resolved to transfer the Santals to the neighbourhood of Purnea town. On 28th January, 1914, the "exodus" as it was called, was made during the night in grand silence, without drawing the attention of the Mohammedans."[165]

After this incident, the Santals considered Fr. Knockaert as their leader and champion. In July 1914, he was instrumental in releasing ten Santals from imprisonment. This encouraged the Santals to convert to Christianity. In 1918 Fr. Ferdinand Perier, SJ, the Superior of the mission asked Fr. Leopold Knockaert to go to Santal Parganas. He requested the Superior to excuse him as he was too old (68) for such a difficult and strenuous mission. However, nobody doubted his honesty and love for the Santals. In 1925, he retired and was replaced by Fr. Alphonse de la Croix, SJ, a Belgian Jesuit who had been helping him since 1921. On April 16th 1923, Fr. John Baptist Anselmo, of the Foreign Mission of Milan, entered Santal Parganas. In the course of his visits, he converted many to Christianity. Nevertheless, unfortunately for the Santal Mission he was recalled

163 CBCI Report, Purnea Diocese, New Delhi: CBCI Office, 2004.

164 De Steenhault, Yves SJ, History of the Jesuits in West Bengal Part II, Ranchi: Catholic Press, 2003, 192.

165 Scicluna, John SJ, Can You face a Challenge? 19.

to Italy. A few years later, he came back as Bishop to Dinajpur (now a district in West Bengal).[166] Yves de Steenhault, SJ quotes John Baptist Anselmo:

To begin with – we ought to describe briefly the persons and narrate the events that led to the so called "Santal Mission" of 1920. In 1921, when our own history begins, Fr. Knockaert was still alive, and was residing at Purnea with Fr. A. de la Croix as companion. Fr. Leopold was at the time 71 years old. His must have been a rich personality. He had pioneered in the Jhargram Mission (in Bengal) from 1885 to 1895, where he had succeeded another pioneer, the Belgian Jesuit, Fr. Schiff. There starting from a group of converts belonging to the Hari caste – untouchables whose caste duty was to prepare and to trade in hides, he had initiated a mass movement among other semi-Hinduized Adivasis, Mahatos, Bhumij, Kurmis and also Santals whose 2000 names (approximately) are recorded in the first baptism Register of the Sacred Heart Church, Kharagpur (Bengal). He had made an impression on the people, for in 1949 some old people of Jhargram still spoke of him, although they were but children in Knockaert's days.[167]

Meanwhile Providence was preparing people like Archbishop Ferdinand Perier to intervene and send missionaries to Santal Parganas. It is to the credit of Belgian fathers that the Ranchi mission developed so well and in such a short time. The missionary work started there (Ranchi) by Fr. Constant Lievens, SJ, required more personnel as there were many conversions. The Belgian fathers could not meet the needs of the place as they were engaged also in another Mission in the Belgian Congo. Hence, help from other Provinces of the Society of Jesus was required and so the Superior General of the Society of Jesus, Wlodimir Ledockowski invited the Sicilian Province to help the Belgian fathers in the Archdiocese of Calcutta.[168]

2.3.3. Sicilian Jesuit Province: The New Missionaries

In 1924, the Island of Malta, together with Greece, formed part of the Sicilian Jesuit Province. Therefore, the responsibility of sending missionaries to India fell to Sicily as well as Malta. They gladly accepted the challenge of leaving their home countries to be missionaries in India. Three Jesuits from the Sicilian Province, two Maltese and one Sicilian (Fr. Anthony Debono and Scholastics Bernard Bugeja and Joseph Cordaro) were the first to set sail for India. On October 4th, 1924, they landed in India. Fr. Debono remained in Calcutta and prepared himself as best as he could for his first missionary assignment.[169]

166 Scicluna, John SJ, Can You face a Challenge? 20.

167 De Steenhault, Yves SJ, History of the Jesuits in West Bengal Part I, Ranchi: Catholic Press, 2003, 58.

168 Scicluna, John SJ, Can You face a Challenge? 21.

169 Scicluna, John SJ, Can You face a Challenge? 21.

As Fr. Anthony Debono arrived in Majlispur quite a number of converts of Purnea District went over to the village of Kishanganj sub-division called Majlispur.

Round about Majlispur (a village in Bengal), a group of Santal Catholics had settled around a mud chapel and there was also something of a hut where the missionary could stay while visiting his sheep. There were many other families, far and wide with little instruction besides the Sign of the Cross. This was the long and the short of the Santal Mission when the Maltese Jesuit, Anthony Debono, recently arrived in India, did the right and heroic thing, namely he settled down in the mud hut of Majlispur to live in the midst of his people and share their lives.[170]

It was in the year 1925, on 9th March. The hut where Debono stayed had already been used by Fr. Knockaert. He visited the villages here whose population wanted to come over to Christianity. There were enough problems related to their life and situation. The Santals who came from other places had no land of their own and they roamed about the country in search of work. Fr. Debono soon realized that if he had to do any work he had to win the confidence of the Santals. Besides zeal and courage, he had the mettle of which great missionaries are made. He realized that the only way to do this was to release them from the subservience of the moneylenders. It was no easy task for the missionary. Where was he going to get the money which the Santals could not pay back to the money lenders! As they could not pay back the loans taken from the moneylenders in time they had to give them all their belongings and were obliged to work for them without being paid.[171]

Fr. Debono and His Missionary Attempts

In order to help the Santals Fr. Debono approached the officials to take action against the moneylenders and remedy the situation. The moneylenders realized that the missionary was gaining popularity among the Santals and that would work against them. On 8th October, 1925, Fr. Debono and two Santals went to a village (Katalbari) to settle some dispute among Santals. The next day he hired a bullock cart to reach Islampur railway station from where he would catch a train to return to Majlispur. But on the way while passing through a village, the bullock cart was stopped by two Muslims (agents of a wealthy Muslim) and a crowd of Muslims from the village joined them. The Muslims were annoyed because the missionary was taking away tenants who owed him rents. The moneylenders were quick to act and decided to put an end to the plans of the missionary. The Muslims made up a story about two Santals who moved around with him that they had to pay the Muslim landlord an amount of fifty-three rupees. The fact was that the Santals had borrowed 3 or 4 rupees. Therefore, this wealthy Mohammedan

170 De Steenhault, Yves SJ, History of the Jesuits in West Bengal Part I, 60.

171 Scicluna, John SJ, Can You face a Challenge? 22.

entrapped Fr. Debono, and locked him up in a hut in his village and was told to pay the money (fifty-three rupees) there and then. As he had no money to pay, he was forced to remain there as a culprit.[172]

He had no way of contacting the police. God opened a window for him when all the doors were closed. There was a small piece of paper in his breviary and he wrote a small note to the police official saying that he was imprisoned in the village. But how was he to send the message! A kind man passing by undertook the responsibility of delivering the message to the police. The police were soon on the spot to release Fr. Debono. The police then arrested the Mohammedan. A lawsuit was filed against him. The moneylenders tried their best not to have justice take its course because they knew the eventual consequences, namely, the moneylenders would not get back the money from the Santals and the Santals would not go again to the Muslims to work as tenants. They tried to convince Fr. Debono to withdraw the case, because they knew well that they would lose the case and lose the Santals from their clutches.[173] Fr. Debono won the lawsuit and the "Santals looked upon him as their hero, their father and their protector."[174]

Besides zeal and courage, Fr. Debono had the ability to rough it and to stand opposition. What he wrote is quoted by Yves de Steenhault thus,

Meanwhile, I am living in a hut that lets in the water except for a tiny spot. It is here that I spend the day, but at night – stay in a place given by the headman of the village, where he keeps his hens, his rice and all the rubbish of his house. Besides physical hardships, another drawback was the lack of trustworthy catechists: among them, one is a drunkard, the second a dunce; the third one turned a Protestant, only the fourth one promises to be good when he is out of his teens.[175]

One problem led to another. The Majlispur Santals had obtained from their landlord some land on perpetual lease against a yearly rental of Rs. 204/- for which they received no receipt. As soon as he heard that a missionary was going to stay there in their midst, he demanded four years rent plus interest, which amounted to Rs. 965/-. The landlord did not expect them to pay the amount and was planning to obtain a court decision against the Santals, and he decided to raise the rent and give the land to other tenants, also preventing the missionary from settling down there. Fr. Debono decided to buy the land paying the amount. The next problem was to put up a house. Here again the landlord persuaded the local contractors not to work for the missionary. He had to employ people from far away to get the house constructed. It was a simple house with thatched roof.

172 Scicluna, John SJ, "The Pioneer of the Santal Mission" in Jesuit Profiles (Some Eminent Jesuits of South Asia), Sundaram, Lawrence V (Ed), Gujarat: Gujarat Sahitya Prakash, 1991, 114.

173 De Steenhault, Yves S.J., History of the Jesuits in West Bengal Part I, 61.

174 Scicluna, John SJ, Can You face a Challenge? 22-23.

175 De Steenhault, Yves SJ, History of the Jesuits in West Bengal Part I, 60-61.

He had to build a better and more stable house gradually as he had decided to stay on there.[176]

For nearly four years, Fr. Debono lived in a grass and mud hut, until a bungalow was built for the fathers. Soon after that, a convent for the sisters and church were already in the plan. They were ready in a year and Sisters of St. Capitanio (Sisters of Charity as they are generally known) were invited to work in the mission. For the first two years, Fr. Debono was alone. In 1926, the second group of missionaries landed in India, consisting of three Maltese Jesuits, Fr. Benjamin Cauchi and Scholastics John Milanes and Joseph Portelli and the Sicilian Coadjutor Bro. Rosario Milito. Fr. Benjamin Cauchi was sent to Majlispur to help Fr. Debono. By the year 1929 two other Jesuit Fathers, John Grech Cumbo and Joseph Cordaro joined them.[177]

Progress in Majlispur through Debono

Fr. Anthony Debono continued to stay in Majlispur and gradually there was substantial progress in the missionary activities. As Majlispur mission developed, Fr. Debono introduced some traditional Christian practices. On 7 June 1931, the first Eucharistic procession was held in Majlispur and four days later the titular feast, feast of the Sacred Heart was celebrated with an hour of Adoration for the first time. He also started the Sodality of Our Lady. In the year 1933, the first Santal girl went to join the Congregation of the Sisters of Charity (Sisters of St. Capitanio).[178]

The growth and progress of the Santal Mission inevitably stirred up envy among the landlords who unleashed a persecution of the Santal and other converts. The politicians also went round villages making propaganda against conversions. One landlord threatened the Santals if they became Christians he would induce the money lenders to refuse them loans. "The simple, unsuspecting and illiterate Santals were asked to put their thumb impressions on blank paper which the landlord could use to harass and put them in trouble."[179] On such occasions, Fr. Debono came to the rescue of the people. He was convinced that he should take up such cases and show the people that the church was with them in their need, to take care of them. On various occasions, Fr. Debono was called to give witness on behalf of the Christians against whom false cases were filed in different courts. He told the Archbishop, that he helped and defended many people and hoped that justice would be given to them.[180] This meant also helping the people to redeem the mortgaged lands. However, some Santals ran away as they were persecuted by

176 De Steenhault, Yves SJ, History of the Jesuits in West Bengal Part I, 61.

177 Scicluna, John SJ, Can You face a Challenge? 23.

178 Scicluna, John SJ, "The Pioneer of the Santal Mission", 120.

179 Scicluna, John SJ, "The Pioneer of the Santal Mission", 120.

180 Scicluna, John SJ, "The Pioneer of the Santal Mission", 121.

the landlords. He managed to save some of them because he was able to get some funds but the funds were not enough to help all the villagers.

The difficulties had become unbearable in 1933 and Fr. Debono wrote a letter almost everyday to the Archbishop. He shared with the Archbishop the financial difficulties he was facing and expressed his worry about the financial condition. On one occasion, he did not have money to travel. When his denture broke, he did not have money to repair it and he had to subsist on a liquid diet until his companion became aware of the problem and obtained help from the Archbishop. He was more upset because his companions also had to suffer because of financial difficulties. However, within his ability the Archbishop helped the missionaries in their needs. The Archbishop and even the government officials had confidence in his abilities. Therefore, his name was proposed to be a member of the District Board and of the Education Commission. From all these engagements,the Santals benefited.[181]

Fr. Debono wanted to do more than what he was doing. He did not confine himself to the Santals. He also reached out to the Bengalis though he did not speak Bengali language. Another Jesuit priest from Calcutta, Fr. Remy Louwyck, SJ, helped Debono in his mission among the Bengalis. His mission particularly with the group called Pulis or Puliyas, a low caste group among the Bengalis, was opposed by the high caste people and he was threatened to be beaten up. He was tied to a tree to be beaten up. But the people (Puliyas) came forward in support of him. Therefore, he was released. Soon after this incident, some of them received baptism.[182]

After Fr. Louwyck was transferred and another Belgian Jesuit priest who knew Bengali, Fr. Joseph Sas, came to help Fr. Debono with the Bengali apostolate. But, he did not stay long. Fr. Debono went ahead with his mission. His work among the Santals was not so consoling. His experience during this time was not so satisfactory. Several assistants, Fr. Bertand Tolley, SJ and Fr. Julius Delange, SJ, stayed for a short time with him. After them Fr. Joseph Portelli came who was meant to stay for a longer time. During this time, there were 53 families under instruction to be baptized. Six months later, when they were supposed to be baptized they absconded. That was a sad story for Fr. Joseph Portelli to remember.[183]

Fr. Anthony Debono in Islampur

Islampur was a railway station and police station on the way to Siliguri, a big township of Bengal. Fr. Debono was aware of this place and was open to visit this place to see the possibility of evangelisation. He bought some land there with the intention of opening a mission station later for Bengali speaking people.

181 Scicluna, John SJ, "The Pioneer of the Santal Mission", 123.

182 De Steenhault, Yves S.J., History of the Jesuits in West Bengal Part I, 127.

183 De Steenhault, Yves S.J., History of the Jesuits in West Bengal Part I, 127.

From Majlispur, Fr. Yvo Laferla SJ, another Maltese priest, paid regular visits to Islampur. Soon he was entrusted with founding a new mission station there. So he moved to Islampur where he spent the first week under a tree. Then he built a small hut and later a good house for the fathers.

The main inhabitants of Islampur (as the name suggests) were Muslims. Fr. Laferla was very friendly with them and some of them were good benefactors. The Santals around this area were scattered far and wide and Fr. Laferla had good contact with them and converted many of them to Christianity. Islampur was then made a parish separated from Majlispur at the beginning of 1952. Until then there was only a small chapel there and so he started building a church.[184]

In 1953, Fr. Laferla already had a case filed against him. The case was about forced conversion. It was said that he had converted six children against the desire of the children and their parents and gave them medals and even burnt tribal pictures held sacred by them. The incident seemed to have taken place on 23 March 1953, while it was recorded in the police diary only on the 2nd April. In this situation, a Mohammedan friend of Fr. Laferla stood bail for him. The judgement was given thus, that the report was made to the police only on the initiative of the Inspector of Police. Further, the children themselves stated that they had been Christians, some for three and some for four to five years. The children confirmed that they went to the fathers only of their own accord. With such evidence on record, the magistrate found Fr. Laferla not guilty and acquitted him.[185]

Fr. Anthony Debono: The Meek Lamb

In 1935, Fr. Debono wrote to the Archbishop as quoted by Yves de Steenhault, "I do not have the fighting spirit I had ten years ago."[186] There was no response from the Archbishop in relation to his letter. In August 1936, he wrote again saying that he was tired of his mission in Majlispur and it was part of his fate that he had to stay on there. It is said that he had a very sad experience in Majlispur and after that, he was a broken man. However he never wrote about it. All that is known is narrated by one of his contemporaries. Other fathers who had been to the same parish later heard of this incident from parishioners who were eyewitnesses. When I worked there in the school and hostel as a scholastic in 1986-87, I also heard of this same incident. I narrate the incident as written by Yves de Steenhault:

One morning the sisters reported to Fr. Debono that during the previous night some boy or boys had entered the convent compound with the intention, perhaps, of teasing the hostel girls. Enquiries established that one of the night intruders was a certain Vitus, an orphan boy whom Fr. Debono had found in a village during one of his tours and brought to Majlispur. The missionary loved and cared for the boy as his own son. So, the loving Father called the young man

184 Scicluna, John SJ, Can You face a Challenge? 45.

185 Scicluna, John SJ, Can You face a Challenge? 45.

186 Scicluna, John SJ, Can You face a Challenge? 45.

to admonish him. But, when the boy was confronted with irrefutable facts he offered lame excuses and denials. This seemed to have been too much for the tired Pioneer who slapped the boy. Later in the day Vitus reported the incident to the village elders and told them that Fr. Debono had beaten him. It must be pointed out that it is extremely rare for Santal parents to punish or beat their erring children. Therefore, a village court was convened to deliberate about the accusation. Fr. Debono was found guilty and punishment was imposed: Vitus, the orphan boy, was to tie a rope around the neck of Fr. Debono, his loving benefactor, and take him around the parish house three times. The sentence was duly carried out. Fr. Debono never opened his mouth. His indomitable spirit was however, extinguished! But he was a broken man. Years later Vitus died of throat cancer.[187]

Fr. Debono was later transferred to Kiderpore parish in Calcutta and Fr. Joseph Portelli, a young Jesuit of 33 years took his place and became one of the pillars of Santal Mission. Fr. Debono was later in Asansol where he managed to get sanction from the steel company to build a big church in the Steel Township (Asansol). Fr. Charles Poncelet who succeeded him in 1948 actually built the church. Fr. Debono was transferred to Cilimpur, in West Bengal but among the Santals.[188]

Fr. Anthony Debono and His New Venture

In 1947, Fr. Debono was sent by his Superior to Malta for a rest because he was seriously sick. He was warmly welcomed and several young Jesuits flocked around him to hear about India and all his missionary activities. Many young Jesuits were influenced by him and came to India as missionaries. Fr. Debono himself did not stay in Malta too long taking rest. After he was well, in 1948 together with two new missionaries, Scholastic Franz Wirth and Brother Joseph Fenech he came back to India. He had to found the new mission station of Cilimpur.[189]

In Cilimpur, the Archdiocese of Calcutta had some plot of land bought in June 1938, by Fr. Debono. A small chapel had been built there, but it was dilapidated. There were 20 Catholic families around Cilimpur area and nearly as many had fallen away because of lack of contact by the fathers and because they lived in uncongenial, non-Christian surroundings. Fr. Debono was once again the pioneer here; he had to start everything almost from the scratch. In fact, when he arrived at Cilimpur he had to hire a hut to stay. The pioneer heroically accepted the situation. In 1949, Fr. Debono was back in Santal Mission, Cilimpur, a few metres away from the Santal Parganas Border, after spending some years in Kiderpore, Bowbazar and Asansol. There were twenty Catholic families. His

187 Scicluna, John SJ, "The Pioneer of the Santal Mission" in Jesuit Profiles, 127.

188 De Steenhault, Yves SJ, History of the Jesuits in West Bengal Part I, 128.

189 Scicluna, John SJ, Can You face a Challenge? 42.

priority was clear for him, to visit the Catholics and be in touch with them as much as possible. Although he lacked many things, he was filled with great zeal.[190]

In 1948, Fr. Debono started to build a mud-hut to be used as a chapel and residence. When the walls had hardly risen 5 ft. an untimely shower of rain destroyed the work. Although work was immediately begun, there could not be much progress. The workers were not regular and the required materials were not easily available. Only by 1949, he managed to shift to the incomplete mud hut.[191]

For the first time in 1949, Christmas Eve was celebrated at Cilimpur at 8 p.m. The few Catholics in Cilimpur and from the nearby villages together with some non-Christian friends gathered at Cilimpur and Fr. Anthony Debono led them to the new chapel. He was anxious as to how to keep them busy till the Vigil service at midnight. Luckily, some had brought a broken harmonium and they began to sing Christmas carols to the accompaniment of that cracked and wheezing instrument. The singing was interspersed with rosary, catechetical explanation and a short sermon by Fr. Debono. Meanwhile the headman of the village, a non-Christian, walked into the chapel drunk. He had a one-stringed violin and insisted on playing it. Fr. Debono allowed him to sit by the side of the harmonium. In a short time, the man slept throughout the mass and beyond it. That sleep near the crib had its effect. He and his wife began to come for mass on Sundays and later he began bringing his relatives and neighbours who were later baptized.[192]

The foundations were laid for a church in 1953 and work progressed very slowly because of lack of funds and workers. Adding to that they also took up the task of constructing a road of about two kilometres. The road was part of the tribal development project given through the intervention of the S.D.O (Sub-Divisional Officer). The Community Development Department opened a Social Development Centre in Cilimpur. A night, school and recreation centre were opened and Christian teachers were appointed to teach in the night school.[193]

On the occasion of Fr. Debono's Golden Jubilee as a Jesuit in September 1954, the Jesuit General as well as the Provincials of Malta and Belgium together with the Calcutta Superior gave substantial donations for Cilimpur church. The work was soon begun but Fr. Anthony Debono was not privileged to see the completed church building which had by now an ever-increasing Christian community. Besides working among the Santals, he also contacted the Muslims in the neighbourhood. He asked his Superiors to send a Bengali speaking priest to instruct the Muslims. His desire was to see these Muslims receiving Baptism. Because of the problems they faced at the hands of other Muslims, many fell back to Islam. However, it is narrated that about 12 families remained Catholic. It is

190 Scicluna, John SJ, "The Pioneer of the Santal Mission" in Jesuit Profiles, 129.

191 Scicluna, John SJ, "The Pioneer of the Santal Mission" in Jesuit Profiles, 130.

192 Scicluna, John SJ, "The Pioneer of the Santal Mission" in Jesuit Profiles, 130.

193 Scicluna, John SJ, "The Pioneer of the Santal Mission" in Jesuit Profiles, 131.

also mentioned that they were attracted by the great charity and kindness of Fr. Debono.[194]

Fr. Anthony Debono: Departure from the Mission and Death

In April 1956, Fr. Debono had to go to Patna (present capital of Bihar state) about 350 kilometres away from Cilimpur to undergo an operation. Afterwards he suffered a set back and suffered from cough. He was given some tablets which caused a bad side effect and his leg was almost paralysed. He wanted to go back to his people (the Santals in the parish) but was told that going back to his place was out of question. But, his determination and will power to be with his people urged him on and his health improved to an extent of being able to barely walk. Fr. Debono's sense of duty and responsibility towards his flock convinced him that he could no longer shoulder the post of parish priest. Therefore, Fr. Michael Galea, SJ (another Maltese) succeeded him as Pastor of Cilimpur. Even when he (Fr. Debono) was unable to move by himself, he wished to visit the villages. During one of his visits he suffered a stroke and had to be carried to Cilimpur and then to Calcutta Jesuit Community of St. Xavier's College. As he was being carried to the railway station several people came to kiss his hands and they begged him to return to them.[195]

During the next three weeks, the college infirmarian, Bro. Joseph Fenech, SJ (from Malta), looked after him. "On Saturday, 14 July 1956, the Jesuit community of the college gathered in Fr. Debono's room when he received the last sacraments. Afterwards he thanked all *"very very much"*. Then he turned to Bro. Fenech and in Maltese and told him not to forget to put rosary beads in the coffin. In a few moments the valiant soldier of Christ went to his eternal reward."[196]

2.3.4. Further Missionary Advancement

After two years of the missionary work among the Santals, there was a lull in their work. Fr. Benjamin Cauchi was planning to leave Majlispur to venture into the area of Damin-i.koh. During this period low caste Bengalis desired to join Christianity. As Fr. Debono was not at ease with Bengali language, he called Fr. Louwyck, who had worked with Bengalis. His first mission in Majlispur was to minister to the needs of the new Catholics who had changed over from Protestantism and another group from Hinduism. Gradually a number of other low caste Hindus (about 700) received baptism. The Puliyas, about 200 people, showed interest in becoming Christians as they were oppressed by high caste Hindus and Muslim landlords. Fr. Louwyck was not permanent and a new assistant, Fr. Joseph Cordaro, came to Majlispur. "During his first missionary

194 Scicluna, John SJ, "The Pioneer of the Santal Mission" in Jesuit Profiles, 131.

195 Scicluna, John SJ, "The Pioneer of the Santal Mission" in Jesuit Profiles, 132.

196 Scicluna, John SJ, "The Pioneer of the Santal Mission" in Jesuit Profiles, 132.

tour he had baptized 102 Santals and that he has been approached by a group of Puliyas, who strangely enough addressed him in Santali"[197]

By the end of 1930, in Majlispur there was already a church blessed on the 2nd of December and a convent too for the Sisters of Charity (Sisters of St. Capitanio). "These sisters deserve a special mention for the heroism they have displayed whenever they have been in the mission field. While touring the villages, they made it a feature of their style of proceeding to settle down among the villagers for days and weeks on end, to instruct women and children in the rudiments of the faith. Much of the attractiveness which has brought and kept the Santals in the church is due to them."[198] The sisters opened a school for the girls of the area and they proved to be of great assistance to the missionary when he went touring the villages. It was not an easy task touring the villages those days and particularly for the sisters. Transport facilities were limited or almost nothing at all except for bullock carts. There were no hotels or restaurants on the way. One should take along whatever (food, drinks and other necessary items) one needs for the way. Even today travelling in these areas is an adventure.[199]

Fr. Benjamin Cauchi and the Inhospitable Damin-i-koh

Fr. Benjamin Cauchi, who was in Majlispur, was venturing into the inhospitable jungle of Damin-i-koh, which had an area of about 4,215 sq. miles. The American Jesuits of Patna diocese had already begun with great success the work of evangelization in the western sub-division of Godda and Deoghar which also form part of the Santal Parganas District. "The population of this area of Fr. Cauchi was 1,147,552 of whom 598,000 were animists, 435,000 Hindus, 105,000 Muslims and 9,552 Christians, nearly all of whom were Protestants."[200]

Two major difficulties that Fr. Cauchi had to face were: the difficulty of obtaining land to settle down; and the fact of having come long after the Protestants. Santal Parganas has special laws to protect the tribal people from outsiders. "The regulations divide the district into Damin-i-koh and zamindari land. The former belongs to the Government and the latter is the property of the landlords. In neither of these areas are the Santals the sole proprietors of the land they cultivate. They are not allowed to sell or to make a gift of it to anyone. It passes from father to son. It is lost either through eviction or through the extinction of heirs; the headman of the village can settle it with any Ryot[201] of the same village, or failing this, with a neighbouring one."[202]

197 De Steenhault, Yves SJ, History of the Jesuits in West Bengal Part I, 62.

198 De Steenhault, Yves SJ, History of the Jesuits in West Bengal Part I, 62.

199 Scicluna, John SJ, Can You face a Challenge? 24.

200 Scicluna, John SJ, Can You face a Challenge? 24.

201 Ryot: A peasant or cultivator of the soil, accessed on 29.05.2008, available from: http://www.thefreedictionary.com/Ryot.

202 Scicluna John SJ, Can you face a Challenge? 25.

Fr. Benjamin Cauchiand his Mission

Fr. Cauchi received a very encouraging letter from Archbishop Ferdinand Perier. His letter is quoted by John Scicluna:

> I wish you to be well provided before you start on your expedition. Do not be afraid to tell me what you want. I shall try my best to meet your requirements. I must ask you to go about prudently, especially as regards your health. You have to decide where to establish your headquarters, where you can rest. You must have received your appointment already. I can only congratulate you on having been singled out for this beautiful career and I bless you with my whole heart. I shall certainly not fail to pray for you and the success of your work. I hope that Fr. Grech Cumbo will soon be able to give you help and assistance. Although, I cannot as yet install you as a full-blown parish priest, I grant you hereby the faculties given on the sheet of faculties of regular parish priests. With kindness, regards to all.[203]

Thus, Fr. Cauchi was ready for the adventurous mission. He was filled with joy and happiness to work for the lord, "to win souls for Christ", meaning, converting people to Christianity. He landed on the other side of the Ganges, Damin-i-koh or Santal Parganas. Fr. Cauchi was seriously handicapped with the lack of knowledge of the land and people and there was no one to help him. He could neither get land nor a hut to stay. He was already 67 years of age when he reported that he had walked 42 miles on his old legs the previous years, and mentioned that a promising movement had begun in the Damin-i-koh. It would take courage to settle down in such a remote place with no facilities of life. But this bold step he took. He was the guest of a Santal who could ask him any time to clear out and he would have no option but go away.[204]

Fr. Cauchi made contacts with the Catholics baptized by Fr. John Baptist Anselmo of the congregation of PIME (Pontificio Istituto Missione Estere) and converted others and trained catechists, who were very inefficient at first. By this time, people began to realize that the missionary had come to stay and so many people from near and far flocked to him. On 25 February 1930, Archbishop Perier visited Santal Parganas for the first time officially. There was not much to be seen but his visit encouraged the pioneer. This was a further impetus for the people to think that Fr. Cauchi would remain with the people in the village.[205]

With the monsoon fast approaching it was difficult for Fr. Cauchi to stay in the same tent where he was. Four government officials were kind to give him shelter. But he wanted a mission station of his own. The village, Kasturi, had only

203 Scicluna John SJ, Can you face a Challenge? 25.

204 De Steenhault, Yves S.J., History of the Jesuits in West Bengal Part I, 63.

205 Scicluna, John SJ, Can You face a Challenge? 27.

non-Catholics but he borrowed a hut, 10 ft. by 8 ft., from the village schoolmaster. Such a hut did not serve the purpose and so he tried to get another place. After many disappointments he came across Mr. Megrae Murmu, an Anglican, (he was the father of Anthony Murmu who became a Jesuit later) who introduced Fr. Cauchi to Mr. Sudhu Tudu, a Methodist, at Kasturi. He gave Fr. Cauchi a roofless hut which after four days, on April 12th, became the first mission station. This hut was father's office, chapel, refectory and dormitory, all in one. After six months of his pioneering work, Fr. John Grech Combo from Majlispur joined him in the same hut. Thus, the work was in great earnest and the chapel was crowded when they had the Eucharistic celebration. The other achievement was the starting of a small primary school. The fathers by their charity and medical help saved many Santals' lives. Soon the fathers were well known in the surrounding area. They managed to get a nearby house and converted that into a school for catechists. Young men were invited to come to join the school. Thirty people came including, non-Christians, Protestants and Catholics. They had daily religious classes and showed great enthusiasm. Later some of them were given temporary jobs and some became catechists.[206]

2.3.5. A Brief Report of the Mission

The annual letters of 1930 have an interesting item entitled *Missio Santalica*. The gist of which is as follows as quoted by Yves de Steenhault:

1. The Patna Mission Fathers will care for the Santals in Godda Sub-division (now a district) and the Districts of Deoghar and Sarawan (in present Jharkhand state).
2. The Sicilian fathers to the Bengal Mission will care for the other Santals of the Santal Parganas.
3. According to Law, no Santal can alienate his land in favour of a non-Santal.
4. On 6 July 1930, Fr. John Grech Combo joined Fr. Benjamin Cauchi.
5. A mud chapel was built in Kasturi. By 1930 Kasturi had sufficiently risen to justify a visit from the Archbishop. The Catholic population of Kasturi had risen to 580 of which 300 are converts from the Lutheran Mission.[207]

In the year 1931, Archbishop Ferdinand Perier, paid another visit to the missions and this time he administered Confirmation to several people who had been baptised earlier. He visited several places during this time. He received a warm welcome in Kasturi where he confirmed eight Santals at the Railway Institute.[208]

206 Scicluna, John SJ, Can You face a Challenge? 27.

207 De Steenhault, Yves SJ, History of the Jesuits in West Bengal Part I, 64.

208 De Steenhault, Yves SJ, History of the Jesuits in West Bengal Part I, 64.

There were five mission stations in the Santal Mission in the beginning of 1938. In Majlispur Fr. Bernard Bugeja, a Maltese priest, was in-charge. In Damin-i-koh there were four mission stations. The advantage for the Santals here was that they had the arable land. The stalwarts of these mission stations were Frs. Cauchi, Cordaro, Grech Cumbo and Portelli who had by this time converted several Santals to Christianity. In 1938 Fr. Benjamin Cauchi was in-charge of Dudhani, the suburb of Dumka, the headquarters of Santal Parganas. There was a parish with 1324 Catholics and 54 catechumens. At Guhiajori there were 2085 Catholics and 156 catechumens. At Torai, near Pakur, there were 3039 Catholics and 400 catechumens. At Tinpahar too the progress had been substantial. There were a boarding house for the boys, a school and a church. The Catholics numbered 3285 and 500 catechumens. In all, there were 11,188 Catholics over a large area of 200 miles from north to south and 50 to 70 miles from east to west, covering the two districts of Purnea and the Santal Parganas.[209]

2.3.6. The Mission Stations – Reaching Out to Mongalpara, Torai

The rise in missionary zeal was heightened because there was desire from the priests to reach out to more people and open up unknown territories to bring other cultures to the Santals. Yet another element of this increased mission activity was the desire to make more Christians. The message of Vatican II is very clear though these missionaries had already preached before the Vatican II:

> Divinely sent to the nations of the world to be unto them "a universal sacrament of salvation," the Church, driven by the inner necessity of her own catholicity, and obeying the mandate of her Founder (cf. Mark 16:16), strives ever to proclaim the Gospel to all men. The Apostles themselves, on whom the Church was founded, following in the footsteps of Christ, "preached the word of truth and begot churches." It is the duty of their successors to make this task endure "so that the word of God may run and be glorified (2 Thess. 3:1) and the kingdom of God be proclaimed and established throughout the world.[210]

This missionary zeal heightened the expansion of more mission stations and the increase of priests. Thus, unknown territories opened up and brought other cultures to the attention of the newly formed mission stations. The missionaries felt the need to reach out to more people and more places so that there would be more Santal Christians in the Catholic Church.

There were about 2,000 converts by March 1931 in Kasturi. Since Kasturi was too small a place to permanently settle down Fr. Benjamin Cauchi moved a few miles away to Mongolpara. His settlement in this area had advantages and disadvantages. What was favourable to him was that he could visit the different

209 De Steenhault, Yves SJ, History of the Jesuits in West Bengal Part I, 192.

210 AG, 1.

village chapels in the vicinity and he was surrounded by 50 Christian families. He was not well received at first, but gradually the number of the converts increased. The government was quite indifferent to the activities of Fr. Cauchi. The Protestants were determined to put an end to his activities because many Protestants were joining the Catholics. "On December 7th they held a meeting and decided:

1. To write books and pamphlets against the Catholics.
2. To write to the authorities against the fathers and forbid them to stay among the Santals.
3. To follow the missionaries and their catechists wherever they go.

Such a hostile atmosphere did not frustrate the mission of Fr. Cauchi; he built another school next to his residence and accommodated 50 boarders of whom 25 were orphans."[211]

Missionary Zeal for More Conversions

An experience is narrated by Fr. Cauchi in Mongalpara. The headman of Mongalpara, Mr. Misir Murmu, and Mr. Pandit Murmu were very close friends. They wanted to change their religion and attended the Methodist Mission close by but refused to be baptized because it did not meet their expectations. Therefore, they began a religion of their own, which consisted of administering medicine to the sick. Once a tribal girl (non-Christian) was dying in the village and at first the local healers were called to heal her but they failed and finally they called Misir Murmu and Pandit Murmu. They poured water on the head of the girl and invoked the name of God. They were probably doing what they had learnt from the Methodists. The girl was almost instantaneously cured. They later narrated their experience to their friends and they all laughed saying that in spite of their efforts they had not found the true religion. The people directed the two men to Kasturi village saying, "they would find two Sahibs (term used - to mean the foreigners) dressed in white, wearing big beards and above all....with no wives and children."[212]

The story did not end there. They invited the fathers to their village. Fr. Grech Combo kept his word and visited the village. But when he reached there, he did not find them as they had gone to town. Fr. Grech Combo was not disappointed because he found two families who were willing to be baptized. The two friends were disappointed when they came back and so they invited the fathers once again. Fr. Grech Combo and Fr. Cauchi paid them another visit and this time celebrated mass there. The headman and his friend were very helpful to the priests. They even built a hut with three rooms for the fathers. Their influence

211 De Steenhault, Yves S.J., History of the Jesuits in West Bengal Part I, 124.

212 Scicluna, John SJ, Can You face a Challenge? 28.

on the people made many more villagers become Catholics. Thus most of the families from that village and the neighbouring village as well were baptized.[213]

Fathers Joseph Cordaro and John Grech-Cumbo joined Fr Benjamin Cauchi in the year 1932. Fr. Cauchi then moved to Dumka, the district headquarters of Santal Parganas, about 60 miles away from Mongolpara. He tried to get a plot of land there with the intention of settling the headquarters of Santal Mission there. When he visited Dumka he was invited by the headman of Sibinigor village and he could stay there as his guest as he desired to remain there. He accepted the invitation thinking that the founding of another station would be the centre of activity within the Dumka sub-division. Fr. Joseph d'Espieres, a Belgian Jesuit, came to assist Fr. Cauchi here. But as Sibinigor was not a central place the activities did not last long there. Therefore, Fr. Cauchi moved to Guhiajori, about six miles away from Dumka. He started with a hut on borrowed land. Later some land was bought to build the church and the bungalow with the consent of the people. Archbishop Perier wanted these structures to be immediately built.[214]

By then the Sisters of Capitanio came from Majlispur to help the fathers at Mongolpara and Guhiajori. For the first time in their life the people saw such strangely dressed people in white habits and wearing peculiar headgear. The women from the villages benefited a lot from the visits of the sisters. They taught catechism to women and children. The sisters would soon be living in the village in the midst of the people.[215]

The Sisters' work was effective among the women. A small incident is narrated in an Italian magazine named, *Ai Nostri Amici*. An old lady came once to one of the Sisters to confess her sins because she was afraid to go to the priest. She knew that if she did not confess her sins she would go to hell. What is important is not the fact that she came to confess her sins to a nun, but the fact that the woman could easily approach the nun. The catechism and the understanding of the Sacrament that she learned may be aspects in question. However, the incident is a clear indication of the successful work of nuns among women. In the Indian context, women are needed to work among women especially in villages. The sisters were like mothers to the children in the villages. They would even baptise them if they were in danger of death. If they refused to be baptised, the sister would ask the children to wash their hands and face.[216] The sisters used such dubious methods to get families to Christianity as they thought that Christianity was the only religion that confirmed salvation. The remarkable aspect of their mission is their enthusiasm and courage to travel far and wide almost always on foot, even in monsoon season.

---

213 Scicluna, John SJ, Can You face a Challenge? Madras: St. Joseph's Technical School, 1961, 29.

214 Scicluna, John SJ, Can You face a Challenge? 31.

215 Scicluna, John SJ, Can You face a Challenge? 32.

216 Cordaro, Guiseppe, SJ, Ai Nostri Amici (Diario 1938), Palermo: Rettoria Casaprofessa, 1938, 127.

At Mongalpara the missionaries were taught a lesson about Damin-i-koh land regulations. Fr. Cordarao after handing over charge to Fr. Grech Combo went further away to the Rajmahal hills. On 11 October 1932, the headman of Mongalpara, Misir Murmu, died of snake bite. His death changed the situation radically. His son was a minor and so he could not become the headman. His uncle took over as headman and the situation was no longer under control. The fathers had trusted Misir Murmu and had gone ahead with the building activities with the hope of establishing a mission station. On 14 December summons were sent to the headman, Pandit Murmu to appear in the Magistrate court at Pakur on 11 January 1933. He was charged with having transferred his land to non-Santals. The fathers had thought that the villagers, whom they had helped with medicine and other things, would support them. But they turned against them in court. The headman escaped by evading the case by siding with the people and the fathers were summoned. They could not provide sufficient evidence to prove that they possessed the land. The case was adjourned to 25 July 1933, and the verdict was passed to the effect that they had unlawfully occupied the land. Thus, the fathers lost the case and the buildings had to be demolished. On 13 October1933, the father's residence was demolished. After two days, the church was demolished after a Eucharistic celebration. Even the school was not spared.[217]

In these trying circumstances, the Archbishop wrote to his sorrowing missionaries and consoled them saying that it was a big cross and they had to be resigned to the will of God. He felt deep concern about the future of the mission. He now advised the fathers to look for land elsewhere, from where they could visit the Santal villages. A government official at Pakur also offered a solution. He advised the missionaries to go to Calcutta and stay in some comfortable palace. The fathers thanked him for his valuable suggestion and replied that there were enough trees in Santal Parganas to shelter them. They were in serious doubt whether they had failed in their mission and had to give up the hopes of founding a mission in Santal Parganas. They realised that God had not abandoned his tiny mission. The days of trial began to pass and the radiance of God's grace was to penetrate into the very heart of the land.[218]

Fr. Grech Combo had the good sense to accept that he had been taught a lesson and he did not lose courage. He decided to shift his place from the Damin-i-koh. Pakur was the sub-divisional town on the East India Railway. He succeeded in finding a place (Torai) and buying a house near Pakur. Gradually Torai developed into a large station with a church and a school. Torai was a place with plenty of Muslims. Although their conversion was not easily possible, they

---

217 De Steenhault, Yves SJ, History of the Jesuits in West Bengal Part I, 125.

218 Scicluna, John SJ, Can You face a Challenge? 33.

were not hostile. In fact, a Muslim family offered him a house to stay during the rainy season when his house was flooded with water.[219]

Torai was an ideal place even for travelling to other places because of the facility of the railway station. From here, he went further north as prospects of conversion were excellent. He found that there was a railway station at the foot of three hillocks called Tinpahar (the name is suggestive of three hills). He found a good house which he took in lease and settled down there. A few families of converts also settled there, building their own huts. Everything was alright till 1 May 1935. On 2 May 1935, a sudden fire broke out and all the huts of the Santals were gutted. The father's house was not much affected because it was mainly of bricks and stones. He said that it was providential because the house on a hillock was not ideal as a mission station. He managed to acquire a better place not very far from the railway station. A lawyer helped him to do the transactions with regard to getting the land.[220] Eventually Tinpahar became one of the largest mission stations of the Santal Mission. There was a bungalow, a church and a school. However, a major problem in this stony area was, water. Water dried up in summer season and they had to dig new wells again and again.

Fr. Grech Combo was an adventurer and a wanderer. He wanted to explore the possibility of venturing into other areas. He travelled to another place called Sahibganj, a railway township, on the banks of the river Ganges. There were some Anglo-Indian families living there and he had to say mass for them. He bought some land from the government and without much delay he began building a church there. It was also the meeting place of the Santals who worked in the railway colony or in nearby stations. Eventually Sahibganj became the site for an English medium school.[221]

The New Centres: Dumka, Dudhani, Guhiajori

From Guhiajori preparations were made for a new parish to be set up at Dudhani. Meanwhile Fr. Cauchi was in Sibnagar where he had settled down temporarily. He had entrusted Mongalpara to Fr. Grech Combo. Then he was looking for a place to house the headquarters of the Mission. He succeeded in buying a plot of land at Dudhani, only a mile away from the district town, Dumka. There were no local converts there and so he requested the Sisters of Capitanio to see the possibility of working there. Fr. Cauchi accompanied the sisters to Dudhani and then proceeded to Guhiajori where he had succeeded in buying land and had begun to build a bungalow. Dudhani was an ideal place for the children who had been evacuated from Mongalpara after the house was demolished. Here they

219 Guiseppe, Cordaro SJ, Ai Nostri Amici (Diario 1938), Palermo: Rettoria Casaprofessa, 1938, 132.

220 De Steenhault, Yves SJ, History of the Jesuits in West Bengal Part I, 125.

221 De Steenhault, Yves SJ, History of the Jesuits in West Bengal Part I, 126.

separated the boys and girls. The boys were accommodated in Guhiajori and the girls in Dudhani with the sisters.[222]

On 31 March 1935, the church and the convent at Dudhani were blessed by Archbishop Ferdinand Perier. The missionaries of Santal Parganas, Frs. Anthony Debono and a Jesuit priest of the Patna Mission and eight sisters (Sisters of Capitanio) were present on the occasion. By August 1935, eight girls joined the boarding school, but within a week, the young girls ran away. The girls could not cope with the rules and regulations. The freedom that they enjoyed at home made them leave the boarding school. This happened in 1935. (The situation has improved today, but still there are many cases of such happenings, children running away from the boarding school). The sisters were not discouraged by this first experience of such an incident. By April 1937, the sisters were running a Hindi medium high school for girls. Here the girls learned to read and write. The sisters also opened a training centre to prepare girls for marriage. The problem was that the house was not big enough to accommodate all the girls who wanted to come there for the programme.[223]

Fr. Cauchi continued his work and now he was helped by two Belgian Jesuits, Frs. d'Espieres of Calcutta Province and George Andries of Ranchi Province in Guhiajori. The building work went on fast as Fr. d'Espieres was a self-made building engineer. By September 1934, both school and church were blessed by Archbishop Perier. Fr. d'Espieres went ahead with buildings, and by early 1936, the bungalow for the fathers was ready. After a few years, he was transferred to St. Joseph's school in Darjeeling. He died at the age of 91 in January 1986. Fr. Andries was in-charge of the hostel in Guhiajori. There were 135 Catholic boys who came from nearly 100 villages of the sub-divisions of Dumka, Rajmahal and Pakur. The school was only up to class VI and the major problem was to get well-trained teachers.[224]

2.4. The Second World War and After: The Effect on the Mission

Although, India was far from the war affecting Europe the effect of it was very much experienced in India. The fathers were not free to go around. Some of them were kept under custody as they were of Italian origin. Missionaries stopped coming to India and communication with Europe was reduced to the minimum. This affected the work in the mission stations because the necessary funds needed for the work could not be obtained. Adding to these problems, the sisters were not allowed to go to visit villages. Not only was there a shortage of missionaries but the few available ones were appointed as Railway Chaplains for the British people because they wanted to have regular masses and probably confessions. Really

222 De Steenhault, Yves SJ, History of the Jesuits in West Bengal Part I, 126.

223 De Steenhault, Yves SJ, History of the Jesuits in West Bengal Part I, 126.

224 De Steenhault, Yves SJ, History of the Jesuits in West Bengal Part I, 127.

surprising indeed! Thus, the new process of evangelization which began not long ago had to undergo the lull and the developmental work had to be curtailed.[225]

2.4.1. The New Situation in Mission Stations

In the parishes, however, the new religion, the Santals accepted or converted to, thrived. The Santals found meaning in practising the new religion, Christianity. In several centres, the people wanted the priest to go to their villages so that they could have the liturgy properly conducted. Even the schools at Majlispur, Guhiajori, Tinpahar, Torai and Dudhani were well attended.[226]

In Torai there was a plan to start a convent. The fathers had begun an upper primary school in 1936 and that was housed in a building bought from a Mohammedan. At that time, the fathers could make no better arrangement than converting that building into a convent, after necessary modifications. By the year 1952, the Fatima convent of the Daughters of St. Anne started a school and named it Maria Goretti. This was the first convent of Daughters of St. Anne in the Santal Mission. A second convent was to be at Tinpahar and the building was ready by the beginning of 1954. The sisters started a boarding school for girls there.[227]

Until 1938, there was no resident priest in Sahibganj. From Tinpahar the fathers were visiting the railway colony at Sahibganj. In 1955, a property on the banks of the Ganges was bought for starting a school for Catholics and non-Catholics. Fr. Anthony Sammut, SJ, who was residing in a house near the church now moved to the new bungalow and began making preparations for the school. In a year's time, Sahibganj was to become the Mission's headquarters. By now, 30 years after the inception there were nine parishes and three sub-stations with 20,596 Catholics.[228]

Everybody expected peace to dawn. When it was announced that the war was over it was definitely good news for all. Many Santal families wanted to be converted to Christianity. But they wished to wait for the head of the family to return from war. Many Santal men had gone as soldiers to different parts of the country and even the world. Once again, there was hope of more missionaries and funds coming to India for the missionary work. Thus further development of the mission could be continued.[229]

The church was becoming more organized among the Santals, and gradually it began to get more human and material resources. Thus they were even specializing in it, namely, undertaking missionary work. Initially a normalized church structure was established in the mission area, often starting with special

225 Scicluna, John SJ, Can You face a Challenge? 37.

226 Scicluna, John SJ, Can You face a Challenge? 38.

227 Scicluna, John SJ, Can You face a Challenge? 46.

228 Scicluna, John SJ, Can You face a Challenge? 46.

229 Scicluna, John SJ, Can You face a Challenge? 37.

jurisdictions, and later more churches were built and areas bifurcated for better administration. Over the years, as indigenous churches among the Santals matured the people became the driving force in missions because many people began to play active roles in the process of evangelization. The situation has not always remained the same. There were times when Santals did not turn to Christianity and in fact, they turned against the missionary activity. The missionaries needed to find out ways and means of evangelizing and educating Santals.[230]

Fr. Benjamin Cauchi's observations of 1946 are quoted by Yves de Steenhault:

> Conversions today are not so numerous as they were at the beginning but the number of Christians is always on the increase. A chief cause of the slow expansion is the small number of missionaries. At times we wonder how the people remain Christians when they are visited only once or twice a year. By June 1947 the number of Catholics had risen to 15,914. It is not much higher than the natural increase of births over deaths, taking however into account the almost complete lack of medical facilities available to Santals and other villagers, and the near-famine conditions that prevailed for several months every year not mentioning the fatal year 1943, the year of the Bengal famine.[231]

After the war, education in the Santal Mission was given a new impetus. Until now, there were no high schools in the Mission. In January 1946 in Guhiajori they started class VIII, the first section of high school. Thus, Guhiajori became the first high school of the Santal Mission. Every year one section was increased, till they reached matriculation. The first batch of students who appeared for the examination was very successful. The following year St. Joseph's High School was officially recognised by the Bihar State Education Board. The first Santal Jesuit, Anthony Murmu was an ex-student of this school.[232]

2.4.2. Administrative Changes: Formation of Dioceses

A major event that needs to be mentioned is the separation of the Maltese island from the Jesuit Province of Sicily. Malta was erected into a Vice-Province on 29 June 1947. In those days Maltese Province had 95 members. The next nine years were years of great importance because the Maltese vice-Province was able to send 23 missionaries to India. The first vice-Provincial of Malta, Fr. Joseph Delia SJ, paid a visit to his missionaries in India in 1948. He was cordially and affectionately welcomed by the villagers, whichever villages he visited. Many people were baptised during his visit. He said that he had a very rich and meaningful experience in the Santal Mission.[233]

230 De Steenhault, Yves SJ, History of the Jesuits in West Bengal Part I, 192.

231 De Steenhault, Yves SJ, History of the Jesuits in West Bengal Part I, 192-93.

232 Scicluna, John SJ, Can You face a Challenge? 38.

233 Scicluna, John SJ, Can You face a Challenge? 40.

The missionary work in Santal Parganas and Purnea districts was in progress and it meant that decisions had to be taken on the spot. The problem was that the Jesuit Superior was in Calcutta and so there would be delay in the work. Therefore, on 1 July 1949, he appointed Fr. Portelli SJ, the parish priest of Tinpahar, the District Superior of the Santal Mission. Together with this appointment came another one from the Archbishop appointing him Father Vicar Forane of the Santal parishes. The development of the Santal Mission owes much to Fr. Cauchi who had been the Vicar Forane. He played a very important role in building up the mission in the early years.[234]

Formation of a New Diocese: Dumka

As early as 1921, even before the Jesuits officially landed in Santal Parganas, Fr. General Wlodimir Ledochowski of the Society of Jesus and Fr. Ferdinand Perier, the then Superior Regular of the Bengal Mission discussed the possible transfer of Santal Parganas and Purnea districts to a new diocese separate from the Calcutta archdiocese. The matter was left untouched for some time. In 1954 another General of the Society of Jesus, John B. Janssens, and Superior Regular, Fr. John Henrichs dealt with the topic again. In 1955 two 'ternae' (list of three names of possible candidates) were submitted to the Holy See for the appointment of the first bishop for the Santal Parganas and Purnea. But no decision was taken. In 1960, the Archbishop of Calcutta, Ferdinand Perier, resigned and was succeeded by his coadjutor Archbishop Vivian Dyer on 14 November 1960. In February 1961, the Apostolic Pro-Nuncio, Archbishop James Robert Knox, together with Archbishop Vivian Dyer visited Santal Parganas. Once again, a new list of Candidates for the new bishopric (diocese) was sent to Rome. The sudden death of Archbishop Dyer in 1962 delayed the establishment of the proposed new diocese.[235]

The long awaited news was broadcast on 3rd September 1962. The Vatican announced that on 8 August Pope John XXIII had established the new diocese of Dumka, and appointed Fr. Leo Tigga SJ of Ranchi Jesuit Province as the first Bishop. Because of the imminent inauguration of the Vatican Council on 11th October 1962, the Episcopal ordination of Mgr. Leo Tigga, together with that of Mgr. Eric Benjamin of Darjeeling took place at St. John's Co-Cathedral in Valletta, Malta on 7 October 1962. Archbishop Michael Gonzi of Malta was the ordaining prelate who was assisted by Archbishop Pius Kerketta of Ranchi and Bishop Stanislaus Tigga of Raigarh-Ambikapur diocese in Chattisgarh State. The retired Archbishop Ferdinand Perier was present with other bishops on the occasion.[236]

---

234 Scicluna, John SJ, Can You face a Challenge? 44.

235 Steenhault, Yves SJ, History of the Jesuits in West Bengal Part II, Ranchi: Catholic Press, 2003, 178.

236 Steenhault, Yves S.J., History of the Jesuits in West Bengal Part II, 178-79.

Establishment of Santal (Jesuit) Region

The developments in Santal Parganas required a different sort of administration because it was no longer possible to manage the activities from Calcutta. On 1July 1949, Fr. Joseph Portelli was appointed District Superior of the newly formed Santal Parganas Region. In 1956, the Jesuit General, John Janssens, planned the reorganization of all the Jesuit administrative units in India. He appointed Fr. Douglas Gordon, Provincial of Madurai Province to find out the views of the Jesuit Fathers with regard to administration. At that time, there were only 16 priests, 3 brothers and only 1 Indian scholastic. In Malta, there were 22 scholastics and 3 brothers who had applied to join the Santal Mission. They remained legally members of the Maltese vice-Province until they pronounced their final vows. Because of these reasons, the Santal Mission could not be made into a province. It was made into a Region which would have its own Major Superior appointed by Father General. To some extent, the Region remained dependent on Calcutta vice-Province. Fr. Portelli was appointed as the first Regional Superior.[237]

The second Regional Superior was Fr. Anthony Savona who had just completed his term of office as vice-Provincial in Malta. He assumed office on 4 February 1961. Until the year 1965, the office of the Superior was in Xavier house, Sahibganj. Then it was transferred to Ignatius Residence also at Sahibganj. This office remained until 1982 when it was transferred to Dumka. On 8 March 1967, Fr. Lawrence Caruana, SJ took over as the third Regional Superior. On 31 July 1972, (on the Feast of Ignatius of Loyola) Fr. Alfred Agius, SJ became the fourth Superior. He was then appointed Vice-Provincial of Maltese Province. Fr. Agius was succeeded by Fr. John Scicluna in Santal Region in 1978, on 30 March. The sixth Regional Superior was Fr. Emmanuel Stellini, SJ who took over on 3 November 1982.[238]

By this time, Santal Region had made substantial progress in different apostolates, namely, pastoral, educational, social, communication, etc. There were enough Jesuits to manage the different apostolates. It was felt that there was no need to depend on another Jesuit Province, Calcutta. Therefore, it was thought that it could be an independent administrative unit of the Society of Jesus. Keeping this in mind the Provincial Congregation of Calcutta in 1974 sent a postulate to the Superior General requesting to convert Santal Region into a vice-Province and Calcutta a Province. Calcutta became a Province in 1976. But the Santal Region remained a Region till 1989.[239]

237 Steenhault, Yves S.J., History of the Jesuits in West Bengal Part II, 177.

238 Steenhault, Yves SJ, History of the Jesuits in West Bengal Part II, 177.

239 Steenhault, Yves SJ, History of the Jesuits in West Bengal Part II, 178.

Formation of the New Diocese: Raiganj

Dumka diocese had two thirds of its territory in Bihar and the rest in West Bengal. The two states have two different languages, although Santals in both the states speak Santali. The laws regarding land and education differed in both the states. Besides that, the Episcopal See was located in the south-western part of the Diocese. Communication was not easy because of the river Ganges in between the two districts. After much consultation, the Holy See was petitioned to divide the diocese of Dumka. The two districts of Malda and West Dinajpur (both in West Bengal State) could form another diocese. On 8 July 1978, the Vatican announced the establishment of Raiganj Diocese by dismembering the two districts in West Bengal from Dumka diocese. Bishop Leo Tigga of Dumka was transferred to the newly created See of Raiganj. Fr. Telesphore Toppo, a diocesan priest of Ranchi archdiocese, was appointed as the second bishop of Dumka. His Episcopal ordination took place at Dumka on 7 October 1978.[240]

Dumka diocese had this time only 31,404 Catholics out of a total of 50,225. The parishes of Majlispur and Islampur which were part of Bihar state also became part of the new diocese of Raiganj. When Dumka diocese was established, there was no bishop's house or cathedral. After the first session of the Vatican Council when Bishop Leo Tigga returned to India, he stayed as a guest at St. Xavier's School, Sahibganj and later in St. Ignatius Hostel. The Bishop could stay in the Bishop's house in Dumka only in 1974. Here he laid the foundation for a new church and it was completed in the year 1976. The Apostolic Pro-Nuncio, Archbishop John Gordon blessed the completed Church on 3 November 1976 and it was officially declared the cathedral of the diocese.[241]

Jesuit Collaboration with the Dioceses

The Jesuits have always collaborated with the diocese. The Jesuit Regional Superior was always a consulter of the diocese together with some other Jesuits. Fr. Anthony Savona, SJ was the treasurer of the diocese from its establishment till his death; that was 27 years of service. He also served as the secretary to the bishop. On several occasions, in the absence of the bishop, he was appointed as the diocesan administrator. The first Vicar General of Bishop Leo Tigga was Fr. Paul Aquilina, SJ and later Fr. Aloysius Camilleri, SJ who was also the vicar General of Bishop Telesphore Toppo in Dumka. Fr. John Scicluna, SJ served as the chancellor and secretary to the Bishop in Dumka.[242]

The new changes in the dioceses affected the Jesuit Mission. Initially the involvement of the Jesuits in the new Diocese of Raiganj was limited because this area was a restricted area for the non-Indians. They required special permission

240 Steenhault, Yves SJ, History of the Jesuits in West Bengal Part II, 180.

241 Steenhault, Yves SJ, History of the Jesuits in West Bengal Part II, 180.

242 Steenhault, Yves SJ, History of the Jesuits in West Bengal Part II, 183.

to reside in this area. The Indian Jesuits were still in training. When Dumka Diocese was established in 1962, there were no diocesan priests in the Santal Mission. There were some seminarians in training. Until 1962, all the parish priests in Santal Parganas and Purnea were Jesuits. Gradually as the diocesan clergy increased, the process of handing over the parishes to the diocesan clergy began. Several parishes were taken over by the diocesan priests and a few parishes continued to remain in the hands of the Jesuits.[243]

Many mission stations were opened in the dioceses. The parish of Dudhani was very extensive. In 1966, Fr. John Baptist Panepinto SJ bought a property with a bungalow at Asanbani, about 50 kilometres away from Dumka. The first resident priest in Asanbani was Fr. Joseph Zerafa, SJ from 1968. In 1975, Fr. Zerafa started a hostel for the tribal boys to attend the local school in the village. Until now, there was no church building there. As the number of Catholics increased, the need for a parish church was realized. In 1985, Fr. Scicluna, SJ blessed the foundation stone of the church. Frs. Joseph Zerafa and Julian Cachia managed to collect the funds for the same.[244]

The Silver Jubilee of the Mission

"By a happy coincidence in the Holy Year 1950, the Santal Mission and its Mother House, Majlispur celebrated their silver Jubilee."[245] It was definitely a happy occasion and everyone had reason to be grateful to God for the graces and blessings showered upon the Mission and the people. The celebration took place at Majlispur on 10 and 11 May and before the celebrations began, a retreat was preached to the people by Fr. Grech Combo. On 10 May a solemn High Mass was celebrated by the dean and superior of the Mission, Rev. Fr. Portelli, SJ, with Fr. Debono, the pioneer and founder of Majlispur. The following day a solemn Requiem Mass was sung for the fathers and sisters who had died in the past twenty-five years and for the many benefactors who have gone for their eternal reward.[246]

In his letter of October 10th, 1950, Very Rev. Fr. John Janssens, the Superior General of the Society of Jesus greeted and congratulated the missionaries of the Santal Mission in connection with the Silver Jubilee of the Mission.

In 1953, on July 27 the new vice-Provincial, Fr Savona, SJ, was appointed in Malta. Four months after taking office, he visited the Santal Mission. He organised a meeting of all the fathers working in the mission to discuss the problems and needs of the Province. They all unanimously agreed that they needed more missionaries. Nevertheless, the work already done was remarkable in such a short time. When he reached Malta, he requested the Vice-Province for volunteers for

243 Steenhault, Yves SJ, History of the Jesuits in West Bengal Part II, 181.

244 Steenhault, Yves SJ, History of the Jesuits in West Bengal Part II, 181.

245 Scicluna, John SJ, Can You face a Challenge? 44.

246 Scicluna, John SJ, Can You face a Challenge? 44.

the Santal Mission. The response was more than expected. But all could not be sent as there would be hardly anyone left in the Vice-Province. Therefore, he chose only ten of them who came in three separate groups. Just then, Fr. Anthony Savona did not think that he would be going to India. In fact, he was going to take over a great responsibility. He was appointed Regional Superior of the Santal Mission in 1960. He was aware of the needs and problems of the Mission and for nearly 15 years he was the Mission's procurator in Malta and so he was a suitable candidate to be the Superior.[247]

New Phase of the Mission and Missionaries

My own analysis of the situation is reasonably positive because of the hard work of the missionaries in trying situations. However today I would not appreciate the method and means they used to convert people to Christianity. There is no doubt in saying that after the silver jubilee celebrations there was a feeling that the Santal Mission had made substantial progress among the Santals. But, it was no time to sit back and relax. There was an element of satisfaction at all that was happening in different centres. The genuine work for God and people requires constant struggle and new ventures. There was still much more to be attained in terms of missionary work in the Vineyard. The new phase of the mission had to begin by the starting of new centres and new activities and different methods of evangelising. I mean to say that evangelisation is not merely converting people to Christianity. This dimension of evangelisation is also dealt with in the later part of my reflection.

Majlispur under Fr. Bernard Bugeja

Fr. Bernard Bugeja was parish priest and Theophil Roussos (a Greek Jesuit) was his assistant. Fr. Roussos was on a visit to Majlispur and his observation is so quoted:

The mission centre is in the midst of paddy fields. A group of Bengali catechumens at Kakulbari are unable to make up their minds about taking the final step....Islampur is a big settlement, almost exclusively Muslim. Fine plot of ground belonging to the Mission, a large bamboo hut for the Fathers, another one for the nuns. An ideal spot for a future mission station. Besides Santals, a large number of Bengali Harijans are interested.[248]

In one letter Fr. Calleja Gera, a Regent in Majlispur narrates a small incident about a quarrel between Fr. Bernard Bugeja and another Hindu, manager of Raja P.C. Lal's estate, about a plot of land. Fr. Bugeja paid him a visit and managed it so well that both struck up a friendship which stood our Jesuit in good stead in the years to come. He also wrote that Fr. Bugeja was an excellent missionary, quiet but strong and deeply spiritual. His district was very vast and so could not

247 Scicluna, John SJ, Can You face a Challenge? 41.

248 Steenhault, Yves SJ, History of the Jesuits in West Bengal Part I, 193.

be easily visited. It was thus necessary to start a new mission station. But there were no priests available to stay in the new centre.[249]

It is to be remarked that Islampur was basically an off-shoot of Majlispur. The fathers who were in Majlispur had regularly visited the place, Islampur. It was a big settlement almost exclusively Muslim. In 1938, there was a fine plot of ground belonging to the Mission. There was only a bamboo hut for the fathers. The sisters too had a similar hut. The possibility of acquiring land for school, playground and convent was not very difficult there. The few Christians who were present then were all Bengali Harijans (low caste). As always, the beginnings in Islampur were hard and humble. Fr. Laferla had to wait until 1952 to shift to a small building consisting of one big room and two small ones. In the same year, he was appointed parish priest. The area was about 2500 sq. miles. Here 75% of the population were Muslims, 5% Santals and the rest Hindus. There were only 700 Catholics. In 1953, Fr. Francis Wirth was appointed to help Fr. Laferla. By now, there was already a hostel to accommodate the boys to facilitate their education.[250]

Fr. Bugeja received financial support also from the governor. When the governor was passing by car from one district to another he stopped at Majlispur as it was on the way. The schoolchildren put up an arch to welcome the governor. The governor stopped for 10 minutes and inspected the children and asked them questions about the school and the mission. Then he drove off. Fr. Bugeja was there for the official reception. The governor was full of admiration for the work of the fathers and sisters in the school and parish. He promised to give a good share of the money from the governor's fund to the mission. Adding to this he also received help from a friendly businessman to repair ´the two mile road` to the mission. He even wanted to come for the Christmas mass and the drama but was prevented by probably other Hindus. But to make up he sent two silver medals for the best actors of the play and Rs. 50/- for the feast. This was something unexpected from a Hindu.[251]

Fr. Bugeja had his share of problems and difficulties too. He narrates a moving account of a woman unjustly accused of witchcraft by the local witch doctor and saved by a Catholic Santal. He is so quoted:

> The witch doctor invariably picks on one of the old women of the village and from that moment the poor creature's life becomes unbearable. She is dragged out of the house, severely turned out of the village and often put to death. In one place there was to be a meeting of the village to decide whether a certain woman was a witch. The decision of that meeting was that the woman was a witch, and had

249 Steenhault, Yves SJ, History of the Jesuits in West Bengal Part I, 194.

250 Steenhault, Yves SJ, History of the Jesuits in West Bengal Part II, 59.

251 Our Field (Calcutta Jesuit Mission Newsletter) Jan - Feb 1945, 9.

> to be dealt with accordingly. Then a Catholic stood up and said, "we have come to the conclusion that this woman is a witch, but according to me, it is not she, but her husband who should be punished (this man was at the meeting). He must have known it before; why did he marry her and bring her into the village? If he knew it after marriage, why did he keep her in the house?" Needless to say, the woman was saved.[252]

Dudhani under Fr. Benjamin Cauchi

I refer back here, before the Second World War to highlight the progress that had taken place in Dudhani. By November 1937, the construction of a church at Dudhani began and by Christmas, the roof was ready. On 9 January, the wife of the Governor of Bihar, H. E. Lady Hallett, visited the school in Dudhani. The headmistress of the school even requested her to stay a little longer so as to meet the children as well. She appreciated the children and the sisters for their warm and cordial reception. Such contacts and visits by political leaders were beneficial for the school. It had to be noted that the Bambina Sisters (Sisters of Charity) were soon ready to begin a hostel with 90 girls. The number of girls in the hostel increased every year.[253]

Fr. Cauchi wrote in 1939, "What interest can your distinguished readers have to hear that my little church at Dudhani accommodated over 600 people last Christmas? On an ordinary Sunday the congregation, schoolchildren included, is about 200 people and the church is fairly full; one can imagine how it was on Christmas-day."[254]

One of his worries in this place was with regard to the burial of the dead. At first he began to bury them in his own compound because all his attempts to get a burial ground failed. Soon he realized that such a thing was not wise and could not continue. The need for the burial ground was further increased because on and off the hostel children died and had to be buried. The district hospital was only a mile away from the parish. When a catholic patient died, he/she had to be buried. Adding to such worries, he had to tackle other problems. Once a Catholic patient died in the hospital. Fr. Cauchi sent a message to a village close by asking to be allowed to bury the body there. The non-Christian village did not allow him to bury the body there. The event took place on the eve of Christmas. He then sent a message to the government officer asking permission to bury the body at a particular plot. Since he did not receive any message from the officer, he asked another village and he was allowed to bury the body. The kind officer had in fact come personally to meet Fr. Cauchi but as he was not available and so he

252 Steenhault, Yves SJ, History of the Jesuits in West Bengal Part I, 194.

253 Steenhault, Yves SJ, History of the Jesuits in West Bengal Part I, 194.

254 Our Field (Calcutta Jesuit Mission Newsletter) March, 1939, 44.

left the message with a villager granting him permission to bury the body. But the villager did not care to communicate the message to the priest. Twelve days later, he received a written message from the officer in favour of the burial.[255]

Guhiajori: An Important Centre of the Mission

Guhiajori was the first full-fledged high school for boys in the Santal Mission. It was also pastorally very good in terms of developments. Fr. Joseph Portelli narrates a pastorally important event while he was on a mission tour. In one village, a non-Christian boy of 8 years was betrothed to a non-Christian girl. The parents were also non-Christians. Two years later the parents and children became Christians. So the parents of the boy claimed back the money (bride price) from the girl's parents. The others refused to pay the money back and thus a quarrel started. The uncle of the boy, still a non-Christian, together with the non-Christians of the village sided with the girl's parents and encouraged them not to return the money. This led to a village meeting and the headman of the village decided that the two Christian families should be cast out from the village, and that nobody should mix with them and if anyone did not abide by the decision, they would be fined.[256]

In the meeting, they abused the Christians and even threatened to poison the catechist and hang his corpse on the tree. After three weeks, the catechist asked Fr. Portelli to arrange for a meeting with the *pargana* (headman of several villages). The *pargana* a good-natured "pagan" obliged for the meeting and he informed the headman and his colleagues to attend the meeting. There were 200 people in the meeting. After much shouting and discussion, the *pargana* succeeded in getting the non-Christians to desist from molesting the Christians. The *pargana* told them if they did not oblige by the decision, the matter would be reported to the head-quarters. (It is to be understood that usually (used to be) the tribal people make their own decisions in the village and only when it is beyond their limit it goes to the government authority). The Christians were definitely jubilant at the decision made by the *pargana*.[257]

Hatimara: A Renovated Centre

Calcutta Archdiocese had a plot of land at Hatimara village which is about 80 kilometres away from Dumka. There was a high percentage of Santals in this village. Adding to that in a nearby village, Chandrapura, there was also a small chapel constructed by Fr. Joseph Cordaro, SJ. Fr. Joseph Borg, SJ, the parish priest of Cilimpur was looking after the basic needs of this place. He was also trying to make a real parish there. In 1977, he built a mud-wall hut at Hatimara and made it a sub-station of Cilimpur. In 1978, Bishop Leo Tigga gave the place to the

255 Our Field (Calcutta Jesuit Mission Newsletter), 44.

256 Our Field (Calcutta Jesuit Mission Newsletter), 168.

257 Our Field (Calcutta Jesuit Mission Newsletter), 169.

Jesuits to develop. In 1980, it was established as quasi-parish and Fr. Cachia, SJ became the first resident priest there. In 1981, he built a chapel and later the same year he started St. Stanislaus School and Hostel.[258] Now there are a big church, a school, and hostels for both boys and girls, a Carmelite Convent of the Sisters, and a medical centre.

Torai: Memories Renewed

Torai was the mission station built on the fringes of the Damin-i-Koh next to the ruins of the bygone Mongolpara, where from the beginning things were in better condition. In 1939, Fr. Joseph Cordaro was already busy with building the bungalow and next to it the church. It was a pity that he had to leave the place and go to a camp as he was a Sicilian. However, he did not reach the camp. He was detained in Patna in the school run by the American Fathers, pending examination of his case. He was released since he had been in India for 16 years without returning to Italy during the Fascist regime. After his release, he was transferred to Majlispur where he suffered a stroke in 1945. He was taken to Calcutta for better treatment. He did not respond to the treatment given to him and so he breathed his last on 1 April 1946. He was one of the first to come to India from the Sicilian Province. He was only 51 years old and had spent 22 years in India. He was remembered for his activities in Torai. Other than the church he built in Torai, he also built a number of chapels. That was a sign that the number of Catholics had increased during his tenure.[259]

Stories of Concern

Fr. John Grech Combo narrates his adventures in this region. An adventure of a more spiritual nature is quoted by Yves de Steenhault:

> A sick call. In one of the villages that I visited during my last tour, I found a man about thirty, in the last stages of consumption. He was all alone, for his wife, seeing him in that condition and probably not mindful of the promises she had made at the altar, "for better or for worse", "in health or in sickness", had thought it better to run away – a very common occurrence among the Santals. He asked me to give him the Last Sacraments. I was very edified indeed, for it is generally the last thing they think of, if they ever think of it! He was well disposed and very piously inclined. I told him that after mass I would do the needful. And so I did. I brought him the Viaticum; I anointed him, and gave him the Apostolic Blessing. He received all this with great fervour and in full senses. I remained with him talking for some time, about heaven and all the happiness he would get there.

258 Steenhault, Yves SJ, History of the Jesuits in West Bengal Part II, 187.

259 Steenhault, Yves SJ, History of the Jesuits in West Bengal Part I, 198.

> He seemed to be convinced and also very happy, when all of a sudden he sat up in bed and asked me for MONEY. This request ruined all my consolation.[260]

The work in this region was not at all easy. First of all it was difficult to get land. The land which were usually in possession of the mission, often belonged to the Christian Santals. Sometimes the Christians gave land for the purpose of building chapels because they had ulterior motives. They would wait until the church or chapel was built and once ready, they would gradually use it for their purpose, even to the extent of using it as a stable. Adding to these problems there were other problems related to the sacrament of marriage. A marriage could be easily dissolved by bribing the headman of the village before the village meeting took place. Prenuptial instructions, sermons and lectures had often no effect. They do not consider the exchange of consent very important. The "good news" however was, that in June 1947 there were 4202 Catholics and 50 Catechumens.[261]

Tinpahr under Frs. Grech and Portelli

Fr. John Grech Combo was initiated to the mission work by Fr. Joseph Portelli in Tinpahar. Tinpahar is part of the Rajmahal hill range which demarcate the boundary of the Damin-i-koh. Here all the arable land is occupied by the Santals. On these hills live two primitive tribes, namely, Mal Paharia and Sauria Paharia who live usually on the hills. The efforts to convert them were met with little success.[262]

The most serious problem in Tinpahar is water as mentioned earlier. It is a rocky area and so to dig a well one has to explode rocks. The fathers have always tried to find places to dig wells. Very often, they find water in these wells but the tragic side of the story is that the water does not last for several months. They have to keep trying in other places.[263] Fr. Joseph Portelli's narration of the incident is so quoted:

What bluffs every Priest here is the hard granite that covers our property: dig a few feet and you find this stumbling block. Though we have surface water in 3 wells during the rains, from January to the monsoon we have to get our supply of water with a bullock cart from the neighbours' wells, mostly Hindus. Our Christians were confronted with strong objections against their faith. 'How is it' said a Hindu friend, 'that your Padre prays so much, yet has not succeeded in finding water in his well? Is it because the God of the Christians is not as strong

260 Steenhault, Yves SJ, History of the Jesuits in West Bengal Part I, 56.

261 Steenhault, Yves SJ, History of the Jesuits in West Bengal Part I, 199.

262 Steenhault, Yves SJ, History of the Jesuits in West Bengal Part I, 200.

263 Steenhault, Yves SJ, History of the Jesuits in West Bengal Part I, 200.

as our own gods?' After this challenge to the true faith, all of a sudden and for no reason water has begun to ooze from the bottom of our big well.[264]

Fr. Grech Kombo managed to get land in Tinpahar to build the church and bungalow. On 8 December 1939, the church was blessed. The Catholic community was grateful to Archbishop Perier who provided the fund for the building. The fathers kept themselves very busy by running the school and touring villages saying mass for the Catholics. They had to be also taking care of the parish at Tinpahar. It was reported that for Christmas, 1945, there were 600 Catholics for the midnight mass. In the year 1947, Tinpahr had more Catholics than the other Mission Stations of the Santal Mission with 4625 and 72 catechumens.[265]

However, by 1953, the number of Catholics dwindled to 4591. Being a centre of communication, the focus was on education. In 1949, there were 179 boys in the school, all Catholic Santals. In 1954, Class VIII was opened. At this juncture they tried to get the recognition from the government, but no reply came.[266]

Some Reminiscences

One of the most difficult experiences of living in mission stations, parishes, is one of loneliness. In some of these mission stations, the fathers had to spend several years alone. Even when there were two priests, often one priest went touring the villages. After coming back from the tour if nobody was there, the priest had to sit alone on the veranda, alone with his thoughts and worries and alone to bear the burden of overwhelming work and ever-accumulating complications. Only in such situations, one realized the need of a companion and the value of one was never appreciated when we had one. At times the missionary found himself unable to fulfil the most urgent and most elementary duties of a priest; for example when there was a sick call he was unable to administer the sacrament because of distance, lack of transport, or urgent unavoidable commitment in the parish. Such situations when they recurred, could lead the person to despondency.[267]

New Mission Stations of the Seventies

As the number of priests increased, the need also was felt to start new centres, new parishes and mission stations. Ongoing support came from other Jesuits, priests and lay people through participation in the missionary activity and a supportive environment helps to start more mission stations. The healthy church initiative seeks to multiply healthy programmes through multiplying healthy Disciples of Christ. The missionaries should develop a balanced, biblical model of ministry that can transform lives and empower people to walk on their feet. Support

264 Steenhault, Yves SJ, History of the Jesuits in West Bengal Part II, 57.

265 Steenhault, Yves SJ, History of the Jesuits in West Bengal Part I, 200.

266 Steenhault, Yves SJ, History of the Jesuits in West Bengal Part II, 56.

267 Our Field (Calcutta Jesuit Mission Newsletter) June, 1939, 173-74.

from other older mission stations was also provided for new ministries in the new mission stations. Great care was taken to nurture new churches because the initial support of the people can gradually dwindle and they may even turn away from the initial enthusiasm. However, in order to begin new mission stations the missionary needs to have faith and hope in the work of God. I briefly describe some of the new mission stations which were started to reach out to more people. Some of these centres are not described in any books and therefore I had to rely on my own personal experiences. I have visited many of these places, and have discussed with various people (priests and lay people) the history and development of these places.

Daharlangi: This village lies between Dumka and Sahibganj, by the side of the road. When Fr. Joseph Gauci Sacco, SJ was the parish priest in Torai, he bought the land here and later a few rooms were built. In 1979, this place was inaugurated and a school started. Later in 1983 Fr. Chacko Puthuparambil, SJ used this building temporarily for the purpose of his apostolate among the Paharias. Fathers were appointed to reside here to carry on with the mission. But they discontinued due to constant sickness.[268]

Boropahari: Boropahari parish was part of Cilimpur. Fr. Joseph Borg was responsible for this centre. He saw great hopes in this area and accordingly he began the apostolic activities here. One need not say that there were many mission stations and activities in other villages. Boropahari later became a flourishing parish. At present, there are a parish, a school, a convent, hostels for boys and girls. All these managed by the Salesian Fathers and Sisters.

Madhupur and Jamtara: The church here existed from 1908. It was built for the Anglo-Indian community. The parish was established in 1946. When Fr. Cauchi was parish priest of Madhupur he envisaged a new mission station, Jamtara. He bought a property with a house near the railway station. Three Jesuit Fathers, Anthony Scicluna, Calleja Gera and Henry Schembri were the resident priests. But in 1971 the Mission Station was closed. Later the mission was reopened in 1980 when the SCN (Sisters of Charity of Nazareth) sisters arrived. But, the priest stayed in Madhupur and regularly came to Jamtara.[269]

Mariampahar: This mission station was originally a part of Tinpahar parish but it was not where the church is today. It was about 2 kilometres away. In 1968 the Bishop of Dumka, Leo Tigga entrusted the mission station to the Jesuits. In 1975, the mission station was established as a parish. In the adjoining village, Sitapahar,[270] there was a hillock and it was bought by Fr. Borg. Later a school was built below the hillock and on top of the hillock the church was built and the

268 Steenhault, Yves SJ, History of the Jesuits in West Bengal Part II, 183. (Daharlangi: This region is infested with Malaria and many people die of the same).

269 Steenhault, Yves SJ, History of the Jesuits in West Bengal Part II, Ranchi: Catholic Press, 2003, 189.

270 (Sitapahar: Sita is the wife of Hindu God Ram and Pahar means hill or hillock).

name of the place was changed from Sitapahar to Mariampahar. At present, there are a parish, a school, a convent of the Sisters of the Holy Cross, a hospital and a training centre for women.[271]

Jiapani: Jiapani is a village 40 kilometres away from Guhiajori. Fr. Bernard Bugeja visited this village regularly when he was parish priest at Guhiajori. In 1957, he acquired some land here and built a hut to be used as a chapel and a small room for the priest to stay. In 1972, it was a sub-station of Guhiajori and on Sundays, they had mass. In December of the same year, Fr. Anthony Mallia, SJ became the first resident priest there. He bought more land to develop this centre. Later Fr. Mathew Thadathikuzhy, SJ took over the place. Gradually the place began to take shape. Now there are a church, a middle school, a convent and a small clinic. Hostels for boys and girls are necessary in most of the mission stations and they are here too.[272]

2.4.3. Formation Centres: Schools

We know that education is central to development and a key to attaining at least certain goals in life. It is one of the most powerful instruments for reducing poverty and inequality and lays a foundation for sustained economic growth. It empowers people and strengthens nations. It is a powerful "equalizer", opening doors to all to lift themselves out of poverty. It is said that even the thrust of the World Bank is to help countries integrate education into national economic strategies and develop holistic education systems responsive to national socio economic needs. The World Bank is committed to help countries achieve education for all and build dynamic knowledge societies.

The World Bank has supported education in developing countries since 1963 during which period it has transferred more than US $39 billion in loans and credits for education. The Bank's strategic thrust is to help countries integrate education into national economic strategies and policies and develop holistic and balanced education systems which are responsive to the socio-economic needs of countries. The World Bank is a major supporter of Education for all, an international effort to provide every boy and girl in the developing world with a full, good-quality, free and compulsory primary school education.[273]

Adding to the above declaration the Constitution of India declares: "The State shall endeavour to provide, within a period of ten years from the commencement of this Constitution, for free and compulsory education for

271 Steenhault, Yves SJ, History of the Jesuits in West Bengal Part II, Ranchi: Catholic Press, 2003, 190.

272 Steenhault, Yves SJ, History of the Jesuits in West Bengal Part II, Ranchi: Catholic Press, 2003, p. 188.

273 Education and the World Bank, available from: http://web.worldbank.org/Wbsite/External/Topics/Exteducation/0,,contentMDK:20606691~menuPK:1463878~pagePK:148956~piPK:216618~theSitePK:282386,00.html, accessed on 13.05.2008.

all children until they complete the age of fourteen years."[274] Education is very much needed in the context of the Santals. Unless they are educated many of the existential problems will remain as part and parcel of their life. Educating themselves to stand on their feet can give the Santals a better standard of living.

St. Joseph's School (Guhiajori)

The Santals were slow in Education. In 1944, the result of the middle school examination showed very poor results. The school rolls recorded 120 boarders and 19 day-scholars. Fr. Cauchi had a different opinion altogether. He was of the opinion that education spoils the Santals. His reasons were in a way valid; because instead of uplifting them, education turns Santals into *dikus* (strangers and oppressors like Hindus and Muslims according to the perspective of Santals). The eternal problem all over the world was the same. Instead of becoming an agent of progress in the village, they went to town and became bourgeois city dwellers.[275]

In spite of differing views about the school and the type of education offered to the children, the interest in running the school at Guhiajori was very firm. In July 1948, there were 230 boys on the rolls. The school was developed as the first Santal High School of the mission. In 1949 class X was opened. In 1950, the school was recognised by the Patna board of secondary education up to class VII. In the following year with the official recognition of Class XI, St. Joseph's Guhiajori became a full-fledged high school. The strength of the school by then was 400. All the students who appeared for the Examination, to everyone's surprise, passed.[276]

The high school in Guhiajori had its beginning in Torai by Fr. Grech Cumbo, SJ and then shifted to Guhiajori. As soon as Fr. John Milanes, SJ was appointed parish priest, he acquired a plot of land. He had the foresight to realize that as the number of the pupils increased the high school section of the school had to be shifted to another location. In 1965, when Fr. Aloysius Camilleri, SJ was headmaster, the construction of the high school block had begun. In July 1968, during the headmastership of Fr. Alfred Agius, SJ another storey was added to the school building to serve as a hostel. In February 1969, the construction of the science block was started. Only in 1970, they managed to get electricity supply to Guhiajori school.[277]

In 1978 the headmaster, Fr. Anthony Scerri, SJ was transferred from Guhiajori to Tinpahar high school and thus ended the line of Jesuit Headmasters from Fr. Salvatore Nobili, to Fr. Anthony La Greca, to Fr. Aloysius Camilleri, to

274 Constitution of India, Article 45, available from: http://lawmin.nic.in/coi.htm, accessed on 13.05.2008.

275 Steenhault, Yves SJ, History of the Jesuits in West Bengal Part I, 197.

276 Steenhault, Yves SJ, History of the Jesuits in West Bengal Part II, 58.

277 Steenhault, Yves SJ, History of the Jesuits in West Bengal Part II, 186.

Fr. Alfred Agius and to Fr. Anthony Scerri. The administration of the school then passed into the hands of the diocesan clergy.[278]

St. Joseph's School: Rajibpur: Defeat and Success

Rajibpur was/is part of West Bengal State. It belonged originally to the Malda Prefecture until 1962. The Malda Prefecture started a school, St. Joseph's School, in the early fifties. It was recognised by the West Bengal government as a high school and a layman was appointed headmaster of the school. The fathers were not very much engaged in the work here and discipline at the school was very bad. In 1966, Fr. Anthony Scerri, SJ was appointed hostel superintendent to improve the situation at the high school. In January 1973, the Jesuits took up the administration of Rajibpur parish and to solve the school discipline problems three Jesuit Fathers were appointed, namely, Salvatore Nobile, Anthony Gatt and Emidio Saliba. The school had to pass through serious crises of indiscipline and mismanagement leading to many painful and unpleasant situations.[279]

According to the West Bengal government, the representation of the founding society was always a minority in the Christian schools. This was a plus point for the prevailing administration to do what they wanted and the Jesuits who tried to create discipline in the school has less possibility to administer. To remedy the situation the Christian schools of West Bengal formed an association and applied to the West Bengal government for special Rules for the composition of the managing committee of Christian schools. The special Rules were granted and the Church's representation became a majority in the Managing Committee which was also to include a teachers' representative and two guardians. When the bishop asked the teachers to elect their representative they filed a case in the high court at Calcutta in December 1974, claiming that the school had been established by them.[280]

Fr. Scicluna, SJ was assigned to follow this case in the High Court. He managed to contact the right advocates and started studying the case thoroughly collecting all possible documentary evidence in support of the case. This was a long process and the work of Fr. Scicluna was not in vain. The High Court decided in favour of the fathers. The teachers asked for a compromise. They would recognise the ownership of the school by the Church and requested that the staff members not be victimised. The Justice of the High Court in 1976 accepted the compromise petition and dismissed the teachers' appeal.[281]

278 Steenhault, Yves SJ, History of the Jesuits in West Bengal Part II, 186.

279 Steenhault, Yves SJ, History of the Jesuits in West Bengal Part II, 193.

280 Steenhault, Yves SJ, History of the Jesuits in West Bengal Part II, 194.

281 Steenhault, Yves SJ, History of the Jesuits in West Bengal Part II, 194.

St. John Berchmans' High School: Tinpahar

The middle school in Tinpahar existed from July 1954 and in 1962, it was recognised by the state government. Gradually the need was felt to upgrade it to a high school. The middle school building built during the time of Fr. Portelli was inadequate as the number of pupils had increased. In 1973 when Fr. Salvatore Nobile was the parish priest and headmaster, he started the construction of the High School wing. Fr. Anthony Scerri was the assistant headmaster from 1961 to 1962 and then again from 1979 to 1985. Fr. Anthony La Greca was Headmaster from 1964. The high school was built in 1973 under the direction of Fr. Lawrence Caruana, SJ[282]

From the beginning of the school, there were hostel boys though there was no separate hostel building. There was a makeshift arrangement to accommodate the boys. When classes were over, the classrooms were used as study halls for the hostel boys. At night, they slept in the same places by rearranging the classrooms. In 1970, the construction of the hostel began; a part of the hostel was used for the residence of the fathers. In 1981, the hostel was extended and in 1982, a spacious chapel was built.

St. Xavier's School: Sahibganj

The Jesuits bought a property in 1954 with three bungalows on it. When the Santal Region was established one of the bungalows became the residence of the Regional Superior. It was known as Xavier House. In 1957, the new English medium school was begun in the same house. There were just seven students. Scholastic Roland Ghirlando, SJ was the first principal of the school. The construction of the school building began in 1959. In 1960, they named the school, St Xavier's. In 1968, the school was affiliated to the Board of the Indian School Examination. The school building was made bigger by building more rooms and a science block. Already in 1966, the construction of the Hostel wing was begun and by 1968, it was ready for accommodation. The first batch of students appeared for the ICSE (Indian Certificate of Secondary Education) examination in 1969 and all of them passed. There was also the need for a new residence for the Jesuits and so the residence with an attached chapel was started in 1968 and completed in 1970.[283]

Fr. Francis Wirth, SJ was appointed as the vice-rector of the School in 1962 and Fr. Salvino Azzopardi, SJ was the first rector of the school in 1968. During the time of Fr. Emmanuel Stellini, rector and principal in 1972, the new block for the Primary building started under the supervision of Bro. Joseph Bonello. In 1980 when Fr. Anthony Gatt was rector and principal the construction of the new science block with a large basement began. Later the Jubilee auditorium was built. In 1982, the Jubilee celebrations were inaugurated by Mother Teresa of Calcutta.

---

282 Steenhault, Yves SJ, History of the Jesuits in West Bengal Part II, 197.

283 Steenhault, Yves SJ, History of the Jesuits in West Bengal Part II, 195.

She addressed the large audience of parents and children who warmly welcomed her and appreciated her presence in their midst.[284]

The number of children in the school has been on the increase ever since. There are about 3,000 children studying in the school at present. There are ICSE and ISC (+2) (Indian School Certificate) in the school programme. Today the school is one of the famous schools in the country and the ex-students are all over the world, many of them well placed in life. Of this group, some of them are very grateful to the school and the Jesuits; there are also some ex-students against the school; some others are neutral and still others help people who are less fortunate in life. Attached to this English medium school there is a Hindi medium school now in order to facilitate the children coming from other Hindi medium schools.

About a kilometre away from St. Xavier's School the Jesuits bought a property in 1959. The following year it was used for the boys attending school at St. Xavier's. It was named St. Ignatius' Hostel. Later the boys were shifted to St. Xavier's school premises and the building was used as a hostel for tribal (mainly Santal) students who were attending Sahibganj College. Later the students were shifted to the hostel run by the college. In 1970, St Ignatius' Hostel was made into a hostel for the tribal boys who wanted to study in St Xavier's School. Fr. Laferla was the hostel superintendent. He was succeeded by Fr. Steno De Raffaele, SJ who remained there for several years until he was appointed Principal of St Xavier's School in 1986.[285] Fr. Varghese Palli, SJ was his successor until 1999 and then Fr. Nirmal Raj took charge as principal of the school.

St. Xavier's School: Raiganj

In the diocese of Raiganj in West Bengal the Jesuits did not have great impact as there were not many Jesuits or many institutions. One of the means of having influence in the district is by having a good school. The Bishop of Raiganj, Alphonse D'Souza requested the Jesuits to start an English medium School. So the Province decided to start an English medium school in Raiganj diocese. In 1999, the school was begun up to class V. The first principal was Fr. Varghese Palli, an experienced Principal who had served as Principal in St Xavier's School, Sahibganj for nearly 10 years. Every year a section was added to the school. Today the school has more than 1,500 children. There is also a hostel for the tribal children, not only Santals but also Oraons, Kharias and Mundas.

2.4.4. Formation Centres for Priests and Sisters

In secular usage, religious education is the teaching of a particular religion and its varied aspects, its beliefs, doctrines, rituals, customs, rites and personal roles. In a secular culture, religious education implies a type of education which is largely separate from academic and which (generally) regards religious belief as a

284 Steenhault, Yves SJ, History of the Jesuits in West Bengal Part II, 195.

285 Steenhault, Yves SJ, History of the Jesuits in West Bengal Part II, 195.

fundamental tenet and operating modality, as well as a prerequisite condition for priests and nuns. They have their own particular centres of formation where only those people who belong to the same group stay together. The candidates who want to become priests or nuns had to undergo special training separate from the other people. To some extent, they are cut off from the ordinary life situations. The history of the church has been so, and it is kept up.

Vinay Bhawan

In August 1975 Robertson Manor (a residence which had belonged to an Anglo-Indian couple, who donated it to the Jesuits) was acquired at Sahibganj with a view to becoming the candidates' house. However, in 1975 the candidate house started in Purnea. Until then the candidate house was in Guhiajori for a few years. Until 1982, the candidate house for the Jesuit candidates as well as for the diocesan seminarians was in Purnea. Then it was transferred to Vinay Bhawan, Sahibganj. The director of the candidates was Fr. Henry Schembri, SJ. Since then the candidates undergo one year training here and stay here and attend the near-by college, for the next two years. After this training if they are fit and willing to join the Society of Jesus they are sent to the novitiate.

Jesuit Novitiate

In 1970, Fr. Panepinto, SJ bought a piece of land in Dumka, a few metres away from the Bishop's house, to build the residence of the regional superior. More land was bought again in 1975 and 1977. In 1976, Fr. General of the Society of Jesus, Pedro Arrupe, gave permission to the Santal Jesuit Region to have its own novitiate. A plan for the novitiate building was made by Fr. Anthony Formosa, SJ and assisted by Bros. Bernard Kisku, SJ and Anthony Lakra, SJ. The construction work started without much delay. On 29 June 1977, the Novitiate was canonically established. It was named "Jisu Jaher" (which in Santali means *Sacred Grove of Jesus*). Fr. Cecil Azzopardi, SJ was the first novice master. On the same day, ten Novices started their novitiate. The programme of Juniorate also began there under the guidance of Fr. Emmanuel Stellini, SJ. The regional superior's curia was shifted to JisuJaher in 1983 and a few years later the Provincialate was constructed in the same compound under the supervision of Fr. L. Caruana, SJ.[286] Due to scarcity of novices and the need for combined formation (novices from different provinces to come together), the novitiate, JisuJaher, was closed down in 2017.

Poor Clare's Monastery

The Jesuits played a very important role in bringing the contemplative group of sisters. Fr. Savona, SJ was entrusted with the responsibility of getting the sisters to the diocese because the suggestion for a contemplative congregation of sisters came from him. He first requested the Carmel sisters but they could not accept his

286 Steenhault, Yves SJ, History of the Jesuits in West Bengal Part II, 184.

request. Later when he visited the Poor Clare's Monastery in Kerala he requested them and they obliged to come to Dumka. In 1977, they started the construction of the monastery and already in 1978, the nuns were in the monastery and a few candidates joined the monastery in a short time.[287]

2.4.5. Formation Centres for Catechists

Catechists are very important co-workers of the parish priest. Often the mission stations belonging to a parish are far away from the parish, and it is not easy to reach the mission stations (villages) due to lack of transport. In such situations, catechists are the only refuge to conduct the Sunday Services. It is to be noted that many people in the villages are illiterate, and so it is very difficult to find a person who can read and write a little. One has to be satisfied with someone who can be of some help. The positive aspect is that they can communicate in their own language to their own people. They can do this quite effectively. Still they need to be trained in catechetical, religious instruction. It was usually done on Sundays after mass. Catechists from different centres gather together in the parish and they are given instructions. Keeping this in mind several parish priests realized that this training was not enough. They need a systematic, longer and deeper formation. The bishops of other Santali speaking dioceses (Bhagalpur in Bihar state and Calcutta) also requested the Santal Jesuits to open a school for catechists.

The diocese of Dumka had a small plot of land in Torai. This plot of land was transferred to the Society of Jesus for the proposed catechists training centre (CTC). Fr. Scicluna, SJ managed to get the required amount of money from Missio for the construction. Construction work started under the supervision of Fr. Caruana, SJ. On 15 September 1976, Bishop Leo Tigga blessed the Centre and inaugurated the first course for the full-time catechists from Dumka and other neighbouring dioceses. Fr. Paul Aquilina, SJ was the first Director of the CTC. The catechetical course is divided in three parts and each part lasts for three months. Courses are also held for other catechists (men and women) who are not full timers. The CTC also serves as a pastoral centre for seminars and retreats. Every year a month-long Santali language course used to be conducted for priests, nuns and seminarians.

2.4.6. Social Service Centres

Social justice is a concept that some use to describe the movement towards a socially just world. In this context, social justice is based on the concepts of human rights and equality. The Constitution of India is committed to the cause of the marginalized in Indian society: "The State shall promote with special care the educational and economic interests of the weaker sections of the people, and,

287 Steenhault, Yves SJ, History of the Jesuits in West Bengal Part II, 184.

in particular, of the scheduled castes and the scheduled tribes, and shall protect them from social injustice and all forms of exploitation."[288]

The Society of Jesus has made a preferential option for the poor and the marginalized of society. In the Decree 4 on Our Mission Today: The Service of Faith and the Promotion of Justice of the GC (General Congregation) 32, it is explicated, "Our faith in Christ Jesus and our mission to proclaim the Gospel demand of us a commitment to promote justice and to enter into solidarity with the voiceless and the powerless. This commitment will move us seriously to verse ourselves in the complex problems which they face in their lives, then to identify and assume our own responsibilities to society."[289]

Social Development Centre

Bishop Telesphore Toppo intended to have a coordinating centre for all the diocesan apostolates and activities. In Islampur (West Bengal) Fr. Laferla, SJ was the Director of Caritas and the C.R.S. (Catholic Relief Services). When the diocese was divided in 1978, the activities remained within Raiganj diocese. In 1979 Fr. Aloysius Camilleri, SJ was appointed diocesan director of Caritas and C.R.S. in Dumka diocese. He soon began the plans for a construction of this centre. In June 1980, Fr. Anthony La Greca, S.J. was appointed director of the new centre which was blessed on 8 September 1981.[290]

Sademarsal

Sademrasal was another venture by two fathers, Joseph Gauci Sacco, SJ and Anthony Micallef, SJ. Both were interested in mass media. They prepared slides with commentaries in Santali and prepared religious filmstrips for the Santals. With the encouragement and support of Bishop Telesphore Toppo they prepared a plan for a mass media centre at Dumka. The centre was meant to help the Santali speaking dioceses and was blessed on 8th October 1980. The centre prepared charts for catechetical, educational and medical instructions. Many Santali music cassettes were produced. Fr. George Muscat wrote several radio-plays which were recorded in the centre.[291]

The Missionaries of Charity

The presence of the Missionaries of Charity or Mother Teresa Sisters as they are called is easily felt by people. They have been in the diocese since the 1970s. They first came to Kundli, a village about 90 kilometres north of Dumka, where Fr. Albert Said, SJ had begun a leprosy rehabilitation centre. This centre was later

288 Constitution of India, Article 46.

289 Decree 4 of the 32nd General Congregation of the Society of Jesus, No: 42, Rome: 2.12.1974 – 7.03.1975.

290 Steenhault, Yves SJ, History of the Jesuits in West Bengal Part II, 184.

291 Steenhault, Yves SJ, History of the Jesuits in West Bengal Part II, 185.

taken up by the sisters. Later they also started a convent in Dumka. The sisters have a large centre for old and sick people and go to the villages to visit the poor and supply medicine. Many people, both Indian and foreign, flock to them all year round, some as benefactors and others as beneficiaries.

Social Apostolate

Social apostolate was/is part and parcel of the Jesuit charism. The social aspect was always an integral part of their ministry. As soon as a mission station was started, the opening of a school was a priority and together with that, social work was inevitable. In the earlier stages, there was what was called "Food for Work" projects mainly to help the people. The fathers in parishes and mission stations helped people through these projects. This approach was not sufficient to help people stand on their feet. In 1968, Fr. Anthony Savona, SJ then diocesan treasurer launched a savings scheme for the benefit of the parishioners and for those working in diocesan and religious institutions. The scheme has helped many people to save money from the little that they have. From 1962, Fr. Laferla, SJ was the diocesan director of Caritas India and C.R.S. His efforts were substantially helpful to the refugees who fled from East Pakistan (Bangladesh) to India in 1971 (Indo-Pak war of 1970-71). Many of these people were in the border districts of Malda and West Dinajpur which formed part of the diocese. Fr. Laferla was appointed by the Indian government as the coordinator of the relief and medical services in these two districts. His sense of dedication and admirable organization earned him lot of praise from government authorities and relief organizations. Some Jesuits began to feel that this way of helping was not enough to tackle the unjust and oppressive situation prevailing in Santal Parganas.

Kodma: Social Apostolate among the Santals

Fr. Anthony Murmu was the first Santal Jesuit of the Santal Mission. In July 1969, a false case was filed against Anthony Murmu and a number of other Santals from Banjhi, 15 kilometres away from Sahibganj, for attempted murder of a police officer. Several months were needed to get bail for the accused and they had to go up to the High Court in Patna, capital town of Bihar. When the case was finally heard, the charge was not proved and thus it was dismissed. After this incident, Fr. Anthony Murmu wanted to stand as a political candidate in the general election in the national parliament. He needed to receive an indult of exclaustration by the Holy See. Later he was dispensed from his priestly obligations. He was elected and became an M.P. (Member of Parliament). His term of office was over and later he lost the elections. He continued to live in Banjhi (a Santal village in Jharkhand) and fight for the rights of the Santals.

Banjhi was a scene of trouble. There had been problems and tensions between the Santals and the other local people, mainly Hindus and some Muslims. Anthony Murmu was the tribal leader and spokesperson of the Santals. There had been previous grievances against the Hindus and Muslims and the Santals had informed the police about the prevailing difficulties and problems (land grabbing, extorting too much interest on the loans, etc). The police had assured the Santals that they would punish the culprits for their earlier crimes and safeguard the lives of the Santals. But, what happened was just the opposite. The police too worked against the Santals and joined the Hindus and Muslims. Anthony Murmu organised the Santals and they demanded justice from the administration. A delegation went to meet the police on the 19 April 1985. On that day, Anthony Murmu and 15 other Santals were killed in the police firing in Banjhi. After the incident, the Santals in Banjhi and the surrounding areas lived in fear of the local Hindus and Muslims.

It was during this period that the Jesuits assembled together to discuss the prevailing situation in Banjhi because the fathers used to visit this place to celebrate mass occasionally. During the meeting, it was unanimously felt that the Jesuits should show solidarity with the people in their dire need. They needed assistance during the judicial inquiry by the Bihar Government. The Jesuit Regional Superior appointed Frs. Thomas Kavalakat, SJ and Michael Raj, SJ to Banjhi village for this uncharted work. They stayed with the people for nearly a year, surveying, studying their difficulties and problems and learning from the situation. Then they realized the need to stay in some place permanently. So they shifted their abode to Kodma, about 5 kilometres away from Banjhi, in the midst of Santals. They constructed a small house like that of the Santals. Since then the Jesuits in Kodma are engaged in conscientizing (motivating and organizing people to flight for their rights) the people as well as in implementing economic and agricultural programmes which have helped the people a lot. The apostolate here is very challenging and risky because of the conflicting situation. The Hindu and Muslim *mahajans* and *zamindars* are against the work done for the Santals. I have also worked there for a year (1987-88) and so I can confidently speak of the prevailing situation. Today the situation of the people has considerably improved.

Satia: Social Apostolate among the Paharias

In 1983, Fr. Chacko Puthuparambil, SJ was commissioned to start a new apostolate among another tribe of Santal Parganas, called Paharias (already mentioned above). This tribe had always lived on hills without having much contact with the rest of people. They survived by collecting fruits and vegetables and hunting animals. But, as the forest and minerals began to dwindle by the encroachment of greedy business people, the Paharias could no longer manage with what they could find on the hills. Illiteracy, poverty and oppression are the "hallmark" of these people. Economically they are worse than the Santals. Many of the Santals own some land (little as it is) but the Paharias own almost no land. Many of them cultivate beans on hilltops which they do not own. Forests are owned by the government and often many Paharias lose their cultivation rights when the regime is not very friendly or are instigated by non-tribal businesspersons against the Paharias.

It is these people that Fr. Chacko ventured to evangelize. It meant that he had to learn their language which was completely different from the other languages that he had already learned. It was no easy task approaching these people; they did not know whether he was their friend or foe like any other non-tribal. He spoke the language of the oppressors and looked like them. So, it was not easy for the people to understand what he really was and what he was up to. Gradually they knew that he was no oppressor or enemy, but still they kept him away from their circle. Once they understood his motive, they accepted him and he could easily walk into their villages though there were no Christians among them.

A Paharia village is quite different from a Santal village with regard to the house construction and facilities. They are simpler and often smaller with fewer facilities. For Fr. Chacko it was a challenge of his commitment to Christ, to remain or to go away from there. He stayed on to experience the struggle and pain, joys and celebrations of their life. It was no easy task. He was often sick due to lack of regular and nourishing food, and also because the place was prone to sicknesses like malaria, jaundice and typhoid. Infant mortality in these villages was very high, as medical facilities were limited. In fact, I was also a victim of malaria when I stayed here.

Gradually he started visiting people in different villages. He realized that hardly any children went to school and the parents were unaware of the benefits of school or education. He decided to stay on in a village; the village was Satia. Soon a school was opened and a hostel for the children to stay. Without a hostel, it was unthinkable to expect the children to come to school. Gradually a herbal medical centre was opened to meet the immediate medical needs of the people.

Another area of concern was to channel the government projects meant for the Paharias to reach the people properly. The people were not aware of many of the projects allotted to them. This meant that he was taking up a challenging and often risky mission because the government authorities had been utilising the full benefits of the projects for themselves without ever reaching out to the people. There were difficulties and problems but gradually the people were able to receive a substantial amount of help from these projects. Today a number of activities go on here: school, hostel, night school, medical centre and social training centre.

2.4.7. Press and Publications

The importance and necessity of Catholic literature was found by the Jesuits especially in a new mission context. However illiterate they were they could still appreciate stories and news when someone read for them. Many of the fathers realized the need to write and convey the message to people who needed to understand the new religion they accepted. Fr. Portelli wrote a number of booklets (in Santali) of catechism, prayers, hymnal, short lives of saints and the gospels.

He was also the founder editor of the Santali Monthly, *"Marsaltabon"* (which means Our Light) from 1946 until 1956. For the next 34 years, Fr. Panepinto, SJ was the editor of this little booklet which the people greatly appreciated. He also published a number of plays for boys and girls as supplements to "*Marsaltabon.*" Adding to these he also translated the Sunday and Feast Day Lectionary into Santali, published first as supplements to *Marsaltabon* and later in book form. He also translated the Missal into Santali with the help of Mr. George Soren (an educated Santal teacher) and Fr. Paul Aquilina, SJ. His great works are the translation and publication of the New Testament and of the deuterocanonical books as well as the Lectionary in three volumes.[292]

It was felt at this time that a printing press would be of great help in order to publish more materials in Santali. In 1979, the Santal Region started a printing press, *Loyola Chapasal* at Tinpahar. In 1981, the Press was transferred to Sahibganj and named it Vinay Press. Br. Benjamin Sarapurti, SJ was trained in printing work and took over as the director of the press in 1981. From June 1982, the monthly, *Marsaltabon* was published from there. At present, the press has an advanced method of printing faster and better compared to what had been in 1979. Br Benjamin has undergone training to manage these machines and he manages the work efficiently and continues to be the director of the press. Unfortunately, the press had to be closed down in 2014.

2.4.8. Alterantive Health Care Clinic, Kalidanga

Alternative Health Care Clinic is a project (Healing Ministry) of the Dumka-Raiganj Jesuit Province. Fr. (Dr.) M. J. Peter, SJ as the director and Christopher Dungdung as the Administrator, the clinic is run today in Kalidanga, Rampurhat, West Bengal. It has gone through tremendous changes and growth during the last several years. The healing ministry that began as a very simple and private home project has become a renowned and popular nation-wide project.

It was in the year 1992 that the idea about Magnetic treatment emerged in the mind of Fr. Peter. By then he was a priest for 6 years and had tried many innovative ways of working with the people and particularly with the Santal youth in the villages. It was during his stay in Cilimpur, a remote parish of Dumka diocese, that he got this inspiration. As though a bolt from the blue it struck him when he visited a mission station. He saw a few magnets there on the table and he asked the Father in charge what they were. He said that they were magnets that heal. Fr. Peter's friend, who accompanied him, had a little headache and he asked the father in-charge whether the magnets would be useful to get rid of the headache. He said that they would be very beneficial. The magnets were placed on the forehead and after a few minutes, the headache was healed. Peter got the details about the magnets and the way of treating diseases. In a few weeks' time, he bought a few magnets and started experimenting them on the people in the

292 Cf. Steenhault, Yves SJ, History of the Jesuits in West Bengal Part II, 192.

house. The venture that he began with a few magnets and small machines, now has become a great ministry of the Jesuit province. Today the ministry has become very successful and the number of people who come for treatment continue to increase and has spread to more people and places. Thus, more magnets and equipment were required. As the need arose, more electronic and magnetic instruments were bought.

As Peter by nature is a very friendly and outgoing person, many people came to know about the treatment in no time. It was then that he realized that he could not treat people without proper medical training. He immediately launched on a hard and big project of learning and studying treatments systematically. It took him a few years to complete the studies and he was so successful that to his surprise he realized that his competence was not less than many doctors in the town in terms of diagnosis and knowledge of anatomy. From 1992 to 2000 were years of rigorous study and learning. By then he had completed the studies in Homeopathy, Alternative medicines, Magnetic Therapy, Physio-therapy and many more things useful to be an effective doctor. No one can doubt his efficiency in diagnosis and friendly way of dealing with patients. His diagnosis is so accurate that many other experienced doctors are wonder struck.

As time passed, the place was developed with a hospital and other requirements meant to accommodate patients. By the end of 1999, it was realized that the clinic had to be shifted as more facilities were required and more people had to be accommodated. A place close to the road would be easily accessible for patients. The earlier place (cilimpur, Birbhum Dist.) was very remote and no proper conveyance was available. Thus, in the year 2000 Frs. C. M. John, SJ and M. J. Peter shifted to the new place, Kalidanga, Rampurhat, W. Bengal.

Many patients come here as a last resort because they found no relief in other hospitals and medical centres. Many of them had realized that their money were merely wasted. Another impressive thing about the clinic is that majority of the people who come for treatment are mainly very poor Muslims, Hindus and Christians, of whom many are tribals and dalits. Since the charge is very low, they can easily afford to pay. They know in any other hospital they have to pay exorbitant amount of money and they end up with negative results. In spite of the low charge, some of them are still given concession, as they cannot afford even that amount.

At present, other than Peter, there is a Jesuit priest (Administrator), there are 2 well-trained doctors, a physiotherapist and 16 nurses. The dedicated team of doctors and nurses convey the message of hope and healing to the patients in the clinic. The atmosphere in the clinic is so pleasant that the patients feel comfortable and at home. According to many people who have received treatment here, this clinic is considered the best place for effective treatment in the locality and even the state and neighbouring states.

2.4.9. Establishment of Dumka-Raiganj Jesuit Province

In 1956, the Calcutta mission was established as the independent Vice-Province of Calcutta, including the dependent Regions of Darjeeling and Santal; and in 1976, the Vice-Province was raised to the status of a Province, retaining the two Regions.

During the period from 1956, the Santal Region has notably grown in numbers and apostolic works. The Maltese Province has given continual assistance and generous support in the building of the Region. The Region has its own house for candidates and novitiate; the range of its apostolic works now extends to educational institutions and student hostels, to pastoral apostolate through parishes and a specialized centre for catechetical and pastoral training, to the social apostolate and the apostolate of communication media. Considering all these factors the Society of Jesus decided to make Santal Region into a Province of the Society of Jesus. When the new Province was established in 1989, the new Provincial, Fr. Angelus Kujur, SJ, was appointed.

2.4.10. Formation of Purnea Diocese

Pope John XXIII, by the Apostolic Bull, "Exultet Sancta Mater Ecclesia", established the diocese of Dumka on August 8, 1962. Thirty-six years later hence the diocese of Purnea is born from Dumka through a declaration of Pope John Paul II on August 11, 1998 and the first Bishop was Vincent Barwa from Ranchi Diocese. As already mentioned in the beginning of this chapter Fr. Knockaert, SJ took charge in Purnea and worked in the region until 1921 except for a gap of three years. He pioneered the work among the Santals of Purnea district. His work led to the opening of Majlispur (now in Raiganj diocese) which today is considered to be the cradle of Jesuit Santal work, and was the launching pad for work among the Santals of Santal Parganas. The Jesuits continued their work in Purneauntil 1978 to May 1981, and Rev. Michael Minj, a diocesan priest was the parish priest of Purnea.[293]

On December 8, 1989, the foundation stone for a big and spacious church was blessed and laid adjacent to the old church. The church was solemnly blessed and dedicated on March 8, 1992 by Bishop Stephen Tiru, and now it is the cathedral of Purnea diocese. According to the decree of Pope John Paul II the diocese of Purnea consists of the northern portion of the diocese of Dumka, beyond the river Ganges, viz. the four civil districts of Purnea, Katihar, Kishanganj and Araria of Bihar state, covering an area of 15,733 sq. kilometres. The majority of the Catholic population consists of Santals, Oraons and Mundas.[294]

On 3 May1981, the Salesian Fathersbegan to administer the parish in Purnea. Soon the Purnea mission witnessed rapid growth and development. Church work

293 Purnea Diocese, available from: http://www.cbcisite.com/Purnea.htm, accessed on 13.05.2008.

294 Purnea Diocese, available from: http://www.cbcisite.com/Purnea.htm.

was given priority and new parishes and stations were opened, most of them with their own chapels. Besides these, hostels for boys and girls, schools, parish houses, community centres and other works in the service of the poor sprung up one after another. In this period of history, covering a span of 15 years, Fr. Jim (James) Gimenez, SDB, played a gigantic role in the development and progress of the Purnea deanery. Katihar, which had been an important part of Purnea, where a church had been in existence from 1940, became a quasi-parish in 1980 and a parish on April 26, 1987. Katihar too underwent rapid development and expansion under the care of the Salesians of Don Bosco, and it has given birth to two more parishes; Gopalpur in 1994 and Baghela in 1997.[295]

Kishanganj station was established with a resident priest-in-charge in June 1983, and it became a parish in 1994. In 1991 Thakurganj was opened as a station under Kishanganj, and then subsequently made it to a parish in 1995, and is being administered by the T.O.R. (Third Order Regular) fathers. Raniganj, 47 kilometres northwest of Purnea had become a station in 1986. It was bifurcated from Purnea to be made an independent parish in 1994. Satmi, 60 kilometres West of Purnea too was a place regularly visited by priests from Purnea. A chapel had been built there in 1954. It too became a full-fledged parish in 1994. Banmankhi is another fast-developed mission-station under Purnea with two resident priests.[296]

From September 2004 until January 2007, there was no bishop in Purnea. In 2007, Fr. Angelus Kujur of Dumka-Raiganj Jesuit Province was appointed Bishop of Purnea.

2.5. The Statistics of the Dioceses

Bishops of Dumka Diocese

Adam Grossi, P.M.E. (Pretres de Missions Etrangeres, or Fathers of the Foreign Mission Society) (Prefect: 28 March 1952 to 1962).
Leo Tigga, SJ (8 August 1962 – 8 June 1978).
Telesphore Placidus Toppo (8 June 1978 – 8 Nov 1984).
Stephen Tiru (18 Apr 1986 – 1 Apr 1995).
Julius Marandi (14 June 1997 - ....).
Total population according to the census in 2004: 4,059,716.
Catholics: 141,051.
Diocesan Priests: 50.
Religious Congregations (Men): 7.
Religious Congregations (Women): 31.
Total number of Parishes: 44.[297]

295 Purnea Diocese, available from: http://www.cbcisite.com/Purnea.htm.

296 Purnea Diocese, available from: http://www.cbcisite.com/Purnea.htm.

297 The Catholic Bishops' Conference of India, Catholic Directory of India 2013, Bangalore: Claretian Publications, 2013, 695.

Bishops of Raiganj Diocese

Leo Tigga, SJ (8 Jun 1978 – 29 Jan 1986).
Alphonsus F. D'Souza, SJ (26 Jan 1987 –30 April 2016).
Fulgence Aloysius Tigga (8 June 2018 - ....).
Total Population: 7,814,142.
Catholics: 95,664.
Diocesan Priests: 102.
Religious Congregations (Men): 3.
Religious Congregations (Women): 13.
Female Religious: 183.
Secular Institute: 1.
Total number of Parishes: 33.[298]

Bishops of Purnea Diocese

Vincent Barwa (27 June 1998 - 29 Sep 2004).
Angelus Kujur SJ (20 Jan 2007 - ...).
Total Population: 8,349,215.
Catholics: 16,201.
Diocesan Priests: 44.
Religious Congregations (Men): 4.
Religious Congregations (Women): 9.
Secular Institute.: 1.
Total number of Parishes: 16.[299]

Conclusion

The question was raised as to why there was no real mass conversion of the Santals as it happened among the Oraon Tribe in Chotanagpur. The probable analysis was that Santals are five times more numerous than the Oraons. The Oraons were concentrated in well-defined areas. In all these areas, they were persecuted at the hands of the landlords and the semi-independent Rajas (Kings). To these people the missionary was the liberator from oppression. Christianity meant for them a rise in human dignity, an end of slavery, and the salvation of their souls. The Santals on the other hand were perpetual migrants, spread over large areas, scattered among other communities, from Orissa, Jharkhand, Bengal up to Assam and even Bangladesh. The only district where they are real owners of the land is Santal Parganas. The intervention of the British regime kept the missionaries away from being liberators except in rare cases.[300]

298 The Catholic Bishops' Conference of India, Catholic Directory of India 2013, 1685.

299 The Catholic Bishops' Conference of India, Catholic Directory of India 2013, 1661.

300 Steenhault, Yves SJ, History of the Jesuits in West Bengal Part I, 201.

Santals outside Damin-i-koh usually possess no land. Besides that, they are scattered on wide areas in small groups. Because of these reasons, conversion also was difficult. However, Christianity was more impressive to the Santals than other religions. Muslims and Hindus were not successful in converting them. Moreover, the Santals were always prejudiced against the Hindus as their long history reveals. They (Hindus) were considered to be dikus (strangers) and did not want to integrate into their culture. Because of these reasons, Christianity was more impressive and they found the schools run by the fathers useful for their education. Therefore, they helped the people in situations of injustice and conflicts. The fathers stood by the people in their difficulties and helped them.[301] It is also argued that the lower castes or tribes have converted to Christianity only because the missionaries took up their case of social justice in terms of being exploited, particularly in land matters. It is also argued that if there were any material inducements used then the number of converts would have been much higher than that is seen in the country. Is it wise saying that the achievement of bringing about social justice was accidental?

Many tribal people (the Santals too) feel obliged to Christian missionaries for having given to them the 'true religion' and having saved them from the fear of punishment and hell. They no more need to fear the indigenous spirits and deities and their worship and propitiation. In fact many people were often afraid of their gods and spirits; on many occasions it was because they were told about the impending punishment and dire consequences that would befall them, they obliged to propitiate these spirits. The Christian God is seen as more powerful than all other gods. The other gods are mere manifestations of the devil and they are considered evil and pagan. God the Father, Jesus Christ the Son and the Holy Spirit have replaced all the other tribal spirits and the Supreme Being of the tribal religion. There was also a change from the oral tradition to literary, religious tradition; they received written scriptures and learned catechism and learned prayers and socio-religious conduct and behaviour.[302]

Tribal religion was mainly a concern of adult and aged people almost excluding women and children. With the Christian religion, they had an active role to play, of course within the limits of certain periphery. All Christians are expected to undergo certain religious training in order to receive the sacraments. The Christian sacraments replaced initiation and purification practices of the Santals. These aspects of religion were unknown to the non-Christian Santals. There are organisations for women, children and for the whole parish to see to the better functioning and needs of the community. The sacred groves and places were substituted with churches, chapels, grottos and statues of saints. Most of the tribal feasts and festivals were discarded and Christian feasts and festivals like

---

301 Steenhault, Yves SJ, History of the Jesuits in West Bengal Part II, 60.

302 Cf. Sahay, K. N., *Dynamics and Dimensions of Tribal Societies: Regional and Indian Perspectives*, New Delhi: Commonwealth Publishers, 1998, 310-11.

Christmas, Easter and other feasts of saints took their place. The new Christians did not have to contribute much for these celebrations while earlier they had to give on and off for the tribal celebrations.

On the other side, some of them feel that they are cut off from the rest of the tribe who are not Christians. They feel uncomfortable taking part in tribal feasts and festivals. Thus, they feel alienated from the tribe. Sometimes there are difficult situations to face and tackle. The non-Christians come to the Christian Santals in the same village for the preparation of feasts, both for financial help as well as manual work. They (Christians) are hesitant to help in such situations because they feel that by cooperating in such activities they will not be true Christians. This can lead to conflicts and even ostracism from the village. It is a very delicate and challenging situation for us to deal with. One way of tackling the situation is by telling the Christians that they are Christians and they should keep away from the devilish and barbarous activities of the non-Christians. Probably that had happened earlier because of the type of theology the missionaries had learned. They were full of enthusiasm and zeal to evangelize, to baptize, so that the people would not go to hell, as they believed. They found no salvation outside the church.

We should know that some of the information given above should be taken with caution as some of these writers hold Hindu fundamentalist views and ideologies. They also try to spread hatred and anti-Christian feelings. However, we need to ponder over some of these thoughts and ideas and see for ourselves how meaningfully we can work as Christians. We need to appreciate the good intention and enthusiasm the missionaries had, to be "authentic" missionaries of Christ in those days. Many of the missionaries lived before the Second Vatican Council and so the theology of the time was different from what we may understand today. We should understand the situation today in a different perspective. We need to interpret and inculturate to the situation meaningfully and read the signs of the times to be relevant to people. We need to know the need of the hour. The earlier missionaries did not think of inculturation of the gospel. Unless we are ready to understand the situation in the right perspective and inculturate ourselves to each situation of the people there will be incredible amount of problems. Our task is to understand the context of the local Church so that inculturation becomes relevant for the Santals in their context.

"To know the truth of history is to realize its ultimate myth and its inevitable ambiguity." Roy P. Basler.

3

Inculturation as a Revolutionary Theme for the Santals

"The split between the gospel and the culture is the drama of our time",
(Pope Paul VI)

3.1. Introduction

We human beings live in a time of great insecurity where humanity is faced with many grave threats and challenges; from climate change to political instability, de-culturation of cultures or even their extinction (as is happening in the Indian tribal culture), from species extinction to poverty, financial crisis and warfare. Fear has eaten its way into the human psyche. The rise of fear is more intense today than ever before in history. From this perspective, we human beings are in great crisis. Although, this crisis can mean danger, change and transformation are also possible. Thus, we human beings are at a crossroad; our future depends on how we choose and deal with the situations in which we are.

How and what do we choose? The primary focus at this time in our history in the context of the Santals is the building up of a truly local church in their midst. Why is this so in India at the present time? We need to ask also, how is such a church built up? The idea of "becoming a local church" in most cases does not mean starting from nothing. It means that the gospel is meeting a living group of people in every moment of history. Inculturation becomes inevitable if a local church has to be created. We need to know what inculturation is. To know what inculturation is we need to know what culture is.

3.2. Culture: Its Meaning

Culture (from the Latin cultura stems from colere, meaning "to cultivate,") generally refers to patterns of human activity and the symbolic structures that give such activities significance and importance. Different definitions of "culture" reflect different theoretical bases for understanding, or criteria for evaluating, human activity.[303] One of the important, largely appreciated, definitions is the one by Sir Edward Tylor, "that complex whole which includes knowledge, belief, art, morals, law, custom and any other capabilities and habits acquired by man as a member of society."[304] Culture is manifested in music, literature, painting and sculpture, theatre and film. Although, some people identify culture in terms of consumption and consumer goods (as in high culture, low culture, folk culture or popular culture), anthropologists understand "culture" to refer not only to consumption of goods but to the general processes which produce such goods and give them meaning, and to the social relationships and practices in which such objects and processes become embedded. For them, culture thus includes technology, art, science, as well as moral systems.[305]

Anthropologists use the concept of culture in a very wide and comprehensive sense. According to them culture is not confined to elitist or folkloristic niceties or to achievements related to humanistic learning; everything is culture which is not nature. Culture cannot be identified with literary education or with industrial development. Economically poor or illiterate people may be well advanced culturally or spiritually. Culture is comprehensive of all activities of men and women. We can say that culture is the complex of patterned activities characteristic of a specific group of people.[306]

Culture may be also understood in a holistic sense, as a set of meanings and values that shape human consciousness, which are expressed in the thought-patterns, artistry, language and aspirations of a given group or nation. Culture is a reality in a constant process, formed by generations of ancestors, transmitted as traditions, customs, that are changing under the impact of various influences in time and space. Even inside the very compact culture of one nation or one ethnic group there are many sub-cultures that are conditioned by different life situations and the smaller groups which constitute and shape the larger entity.[307] Some features of culture would clarify this perspective.

3.2.1. Culture as Dynamic Reality

A generation ago the question: "Is there progress?" would have been regarded by many as unabashed heresy and stupidity, because of the technological, scientific progress and radical changes. However, the shock-treatment experience of two

303 Culture: available from: http://en.wikipedia.org/wiki/Culture, accessed on 04.11.2008.

304 Shorter, Aylward, Toward a Theology of Inculturation, London: Geoffrey Chapman, 1988, 4.

305 Culture: available from: http://en.wikipedia.org/wiki/Culture, accessed on 04.11.2008.

306 Chiromba, Frederick E, Evangelization and Inculturation, Gweru (Zimbabwe): Mambo Press, 1989, 6-7.

307 Inculturation: available from: http://eapi.admu.edu.ph/eapr94/nemet.htm, accessed on 04.11.2008.

world wars, the insidious spread of totalitarianism, the revival of slavery in the form of forced labour, and the horrifying power of the propaganda lies, now leave serious doubts. The god of *progress* has been worshipped alike by crass materialists, visionary intellectuals, and incurably optimistic devotees. Most societies look back to a Golden age, which may reflect the nostalgia of older people for a time when they enjoyed somewhat greater prestige or may be the dream fulfilment of an ethnocentric pride. In view of serious maladjustments in modern life, dire threats to personal liberty, and hideous fear of atomic destruction, are we justified in seeing any substantial progress or change in human culture?[308]

No group of people, whether primitive or civilized, has a completely static culture, for everything is subject to and in the process of change. This is true of our own culture even though we may not recognize it because we are flowing imperceptibly with the tide. Our own lives are constantly changed by streamlined automobiles. But more important than these mechanical features of life are the factors of millions of people flocking to our impersonal cities, the rising juvenile delinquency, the breakdown of home life, and the general replacement of religion and purpose of life. The tempo of change may vary, but whether slow or fast, life never remains the same for succeeding generations.[309]

Though culture is universal, it has its local and unique manifestations. It is dynamic and at the same time stable. There is continuous change in certain aspects like eating and dressing habits but marriage and burial of dead do not change so easily. Culture is the learned portion of human behaviour.[310] We learn and borrow from one another for a better and meaningful life.

"Even the simplest of cultures are in debt to others for important contributions to their life. Composite cultures, such as the European, are monumental agglomerations, resulting largely from the process of borrowing. The language is Germanic, but more than half of the vocabulary has been borrowed from non-Germanic sources. The Christian religion had its origin in Jewish culture, and the Bible was written in Hebrew, Aramaic, and Greek. The philosophy came originally from Greece."[311] Thus, nothing has remained static as pre-planned. Depending on the need and context, adjustments had to be made to suit the people's need.

3.2.2. Highbrow Culture vs. Lowbrow Culture

There is in the human milieu a 'highbrow culture' relating to classical music, opera, serious theatre, literature, poetry, art. It belongs to the so-called educated

308 Nida, Eugene A., Customs, Culture and Christianity, London: The Tyndale Press, 1963, 247-48.

309 Nida, Eugene A., Customs, Culture and Christianity, 224.

310 Cf. Chiromba, Frederick E, Evangelization and Inculturation, Gweru (Zimbabwe: Mambo Press, 1989, 7.

311 Nida, Eugene A., Customs, Culture and Christianity, London: The Tyndale Press, 1963, 234.

class and possesses a superior taste. The Church had held this classical view of culture. It was the opposite of barbarism. It was a matter of acquiring and assimilating thc tastes and skills, the ideals and virtues of the liberal arts. It claimed itself to be universal and its philosophy was the perennial philosophy. The classical assumption was that there was just one culture. That culture is not attained by the simple faithful, the natives and the barbarians. It depended on the study of ancient Greek and Latin and learning scholastic philosophy and theology.[312]

Until recently, culture was identified with and defined in terms of this classical view: painting, music, dance, poetry, drama, etc., and the ability to produce them or to appreciate them. This bourgeois approach viewed culture as an éliteprivilege, a leisure-time activity separate from the labour which sustains life. This bourgeoisie culture was entertainment and fashionable commodity which was highly appreciated by one class of people. Karl Marx criticised this view and use of culture as dehumanised and fetishist. He tried to restore the ancient holistic tradition of culture by re-integrating it into the totality of human activity. His analysis disclosed a web of interdependence between production relations and the other social and cultural expressions. According to Karl Marx, the impact is mutual. Culture does not begin after the serious business of economics has been taken care of. The two proceed together, affecting each other. Socio-economic activity is an integral part of the cultural process.[313]

Since the Church held on to the classicist, normative view of culture the Church's missionary activity was inhibited. Probably it distorted the Church's own understanding of itself. Christians failed to recognise cultural changes and developments and thus the interpretation of the Christian message through history was affected. The consequence was to come; for the new generation the situation of the Church is traumatic. It means that the whole of Church history and the history of theology must be rewritten so that there is human growth.[314]

3.2.3. Culture and Human Growth

Culture is a metaphor deriving from cultivating the soil. Actively it refers to the process of developing an existing potential; passively it denotes the resultant product, state or condition. This second objective meaning is the more modern. Culture is what human beings grow or create. It is the result of human intervention, and is distinguished from nature which is given, and grows and

312 Shorter, Aylward, Toward a Theology of Inculturation, London: Geoffrey Chapman, 1988, 19.

313 Rayan, Samuel SJ, Local Churches, available from: http://www.sedos.org/english/rayan1.htm, accessed on 10.01.2009.

314 Shorter, Aylward, Toward a Theology of Inculturation, London: Geoffrey Chapman, 1988, 20.

develops independently of our minds, wills and hands. The skin is nature, the shirt is culture.[315]

There is also a spiritual element in culture. Every culture embraces a multitude of values: material and utilitarian values, (like housing, clothing, food, health): intellectual and artistic ones (poetry, painting, philosophy): moral values (respect for life, love of truth, sense of freedom, concern for justice): and religious values (faith in the Absolute, relation to the Holy, its expressions in rites, liturgies, icons, temples). There are also various skills and refinements of mind, heart and hands connected with each and all of the above. Cultures entail spirituality also in the sense that they are people's responses to the reality of human needs, possibilities, historical situations and events as well as to their implications and promises. As these evolve and unfold, new openness and responses are called for from the human side. And that means spirituality too keeps growing and putting forth new buds and blossoms.[316]

Human beings learn or acquire culture as members of society. Culture comprises the learned aspects as opposed to the inherited aspects of human thinking and human behaviour. It is what human beings share culturally, their customs, values and distinctive way of living that constitutes them as a recognisably distinct human group or society. Human societies not only possess culture, but are distinguished by it from other human societies. Since human beings interact with one another, culture is not only about behaviour but also about ideas. Culture is a transmitted pattern of meanings embodied in symbols, a pattern capable of development and change, and it belongs to the concept of humanness itself. Thus, if religion is a human phenomenon or human activity it must affect and be affected by culture.[317]

3.2.4. Culture as Resistance to Oppression

Culture has also another meaning: resistance to oppression. But no theory of oppression can make sense unless it is cast in native (local) terms or categories, i.e., in terms and categories used by the victims of our times. The victims see that concepts such as development, growth, history, science and technology have become new 'reasons of the state' and mystifications for new forms of violence and injustice. Therefore, there should be resistance to modern oppression. The victims are also sceptical and wary of the modern nation-state, of modern science and technology and of the large forces of history. Unfortunately, in most Asian and African societies, the state has become the major instrument of corruption and violence towards its own people. Modern science has become the basic model of domination and the ultimate justification for all institutionalised violence.

---

315 Cf. Rayan, Samuel SJ, Local Churches.

316 Rayan, Samuel SJ, Local Churches.

317 Cf. Shorter, Aylward, Toward a Theology of Inculturation, London: Geoffrey Chapman, 1988, 4-5.

Attention has been drawn to the fact that the Third World societies usually maintain within their borders exactly the same violent, exploitative, ethnocidal systems which they confront in the larger world. Unfortunately, this is a sad reality of the world.[318]

Culture is for the formation of a just society as everyone is a participant for the growth of the state. In this context what was said in the Encyclical, *Sublimus Dei* was significant because he was convinced that human beings anywhere in the world are created in the image and likeness of God and all are called to resist destruction and receive the Faith:

> The enemy of the human race, who opposes all good deeds in order to bring men to destruction, beholding and envying this, invented a means never before heard of, by which he might hinder the preaching of God's word of Salvation to the people: he inspired his satellites who, to please him, have not hesitated to publish abroad that the Indians of the West and the South, and other people of whom we have recent knowledge should be treated as dumb brutes created for our service, pretending that they are incapable of receiving the Catholic Faith (SD).

Human beings, though unworthy, exercise on earth the power of our Lord and seek with all their might to bring those sheep of His flock that are outside, into the fold committed to the charge. It was a question those days whether these people living in the forests were really human beings.[319] The Indians (of the Americas) are truly human beings and that they are not only capable of understanding the Catholic Faith but, according to information, they desire exceedingly to receive it. Later the Church tried to remedy the harm she had done (SD).

What Fr. Felix Wilfred says is also very relevant in this context, "The process on inculturation will be affected by the various cultural streams among the people living in a particular area, region or nation. The Church should not allow itself to be dominated by the culture of the socially, economically and politically dominant group or groups, but should be sensitive to the culture and tradition of the weaker sections of the people."[320] Thus, the resistance to oppression is a very important function of culture.

---

318 Rayan, Samuel SJ, Local Churches.

319 It was thought that Indians did not have souls because they were "animals" in human form. Therefore, it was believed they could be hunted down like animals. It was only in 1537 CE that Pope Paul III (1468-1549; pope 1534-49) declared that the Indians were human. Having established their humanity, it was decided that they must be inducted into Christianity. As the Indians were unwilling, this was accomplished by force. Though the change in their status from animal to human might appear to be an improvement, in reality, little changed in their plight (available from: http://freetruth.50webs.org/A4a.htm, accessed on 08.01.2009).

320 Wilfred, Felix, Sunset in the East? Madras: SIGA, 1991, 172.

3.2.5. Culture and Historicity

In *Gaudium et spes* we find that culture as something very vital for humanity and very much related to nature because culture is historically situated.

Man comes to a true and full humanity only through culture that is through the cultivation of the goods and values of nature. Wherever human life is involved, therefore, nature and culture are quite intimately connected one with the other. The word "culture" in its general sense indicates everything whereby man develops and perfects his many bodily and spiritual qualities; he strives by his knowledge and his labour, to bring the world itself under his control. He renders social life more human both in the family and the civic community, through improvement of customs and institutions. Throughout the course of time he expresses, communicates and conserves in his works, great spiritual experiences and desires, that they might be of advantage to the progress of many, even of the whole human family (GS 53).

According to GS, the human culture has necessarily a historical and social aspect and the word "culture" also often assumes a sociological and ethnological sense. Thus, we may speak of a plurality of cultures. Different styles of life and multiple scales of values arise from the diverse manner of using things, of labouring, of expressing oneself, of practising religion, of forming customs, of establishing laws and juridical institutions, of cultivating the sciences, the arts and beauty. It is also in this way that there is formed the definite, historical milieu which enfolds people of every nation and age and from which they draw the values which permit him to promote civilization (GS 53).

We need to consider that all are called to fraternally unite in one human family and so we are asked some questions so that we human beings may realise our mission.

What is to be done to prevent from disturbing the life of communities, from destroying the wisdom received from ancestors, or from placing in danger the character proper to each people? How is the dynamism and expansion of a new culture to be fostered without losing a living fidelity to the heritage of tradition? What can be done to make all men partakers of cultural values in the world, when the human culture of those who are more competent is constantly becoming more refined and more complex? Finally how is the autonomy which culture claims for itself to be recognized as legitimate without generating a notion of humanism which is merely terrestrial, and even contrary to religion itself? In the midst of these conflicting requirements, human culture must evolve today in such a way that it can both develop the whole human person and aid man in those duties to whose fulfilment all are called, especially Christians fraternally united in one human family (GS 56).

It is true that the Church has contributed much to the development of culture. But experience shows that, for circumstantial reasons, it is sometimes difficult to harmonize culture with Christian teaching. Though such difficulties do not necessarily harm the life of faith, they can stimulate the mind to a deeper and more accurate understanding of the faith. The recent studies and findings of science, history and philosophy raise new questions which affect life and which demand new theological investigations. Theologians are invited to seek continually for more suitable ways of communicating doctrine to the people of their times; for the deposit of faith or the truths are one thing and the manner in which they are enunciated, in the same meaning and understanding, is another. In pastoral care, sufficient use must be made not only of theological principles, but also of the findings of the secular sciences, especially of psychology and sociology, so that the faithful may be brought to a more adequate and mature life of faith (cf. GS 62).

3.2.6. Culture and Modernity

The classical definition of culture was in vogue by the late 18th century. This period may be referred to as modernity, with the Enlightenment's belief in universal reason, equality, individual freedom, and limitless progress achieved through technology. Before this period even Christian missions, both Catholic and Protestant, were imbued with the classical understanding of culture; indeed, the Church's work of evangelization was intimately tied with the White Man's *mission civilisatrice,* which consisted in the Westernization of the non-Christian parts of the globe, chiefly through education, health care, social welfare, and technology. The modern concept of culture is represented by the anthropological concept of culture that emerged as a theoretical construct after the 1920s, especially on the American scene. This concept was used to account for differences in customs and practices of a particular human society. They are explained in terms of cultures rather than in terms of God's will, racial or generational variations, or environmental factors, or differences in origin. Furthermore, in this understanding of culture, no evaluative judgment is made as to whether a particular culture represents a less noble or less developed stage of human evolution. In other words, no culture is inherently superior or inferior to another.[321]

3.2.7. Culture and the Task of Scholars

It is the task of qualified philosophers and theologians to study the dominant scientific and technological culture and competently to identify challenges to the proclamation of the Gospel. They should also find positive points of contact. Thus, philosophical and theological formation will need to be revised, since dialogue and inculturation depend on a theology which is perfectly in tune with the deposit of faith. Science and faith play a vital role. Therefore, pastoral approach to culture also calls for Catholic scientists who will offer their due contribution to the life of the Church by sharing their reflections on the encounter between

321 Phan, Peter C., Evangelisation in a Culture of Pluralism: Challenges and Opportunities, available from: http://dlibrary.acu.edu.au/research/theology/ejournal/aejt_9/phan.htm, accessed on 11.01.2009.

science and faith. The lack of people who are both qualified in theology and competent in science makes for a patchy presence of the Church at the heart of a culture produced by scientific research and its technical applications. Yet we are living in a period which is particularly favourable to the dialogue between science and faith.[322]

The above-mentioned information about culture makes us know that culture is what brings us together as human beings, as social creatures. We can work together to achieve what is not possible individually. We interact in accordance with the natural laws of social behaviour, respecting each other's individual rights and respecting one another's property. This description should lead us to understand inculturation.

3.3. Inculturation: Meaning and Background

"The origin of the term, inculturation, goes back to Melville Jean Herskovits' coining of the sociological term 'enculturation', a general notion referring to the gradual process by which a social reality (idea, institution or person) situates itself within a given cultural environment. This was subsequently transformed in missiological circles into 'inculturation', a theological notion describing the way in which the Christian message inserts itself into a given culture. In October 1974, during a synod on evangelisation in Rome, the Bishops of Africa and Madagascar declared obsolete the theology of adaptation in the process of evangelisation, and recommended the development of a theology of incarnation. In the wake of further missiological study, the Magisterium recognised the theological significance of the similarity between the idea of 'inculturation' and the mystery of incarnation.[323] In the Encyclical *Slavorum Apostoli* it is said: "Inculturation is the incarnation of the Gospel in native cultures and also the introduction of these cultures into the life of the Church."[324]

In fact, it was Fr. Pedro Arrupe (former Superior General of the Society of Jesus, (1907-1991) who introduced the term ′inculturation` into the Catholic Church. According to him, inculturation is "the incarnation of Christian life and of the Christian message in a particular cultural context, in such a way that this experience not only finds expression through elements proper to the culture in question (this alone would be no more than a superficial adaptation) but becomes

322 Cf. Poupard, Paul (Cardinal), Towards a Pastoral Approach to Culture, Vatican City, 23 May 1999, no. 12.

323 Amaladoss, Michael SJ, Beyond Inculturation, available from: http://www.google.com/search?q=beyond+inculturation, accessed on 04.11.2008

324 *Slavorum Apostoli* (Encyclical Epistle), Given in Rome, at Saint Peter's, by John Paul II on 2 June, the Solemnity of the Most Holy Trinity, 1985.

a principle that animates, directs and unifies the culture, transforming it and remaking it so as to bring about a new creation."[325]

3.3.1. Purpose of Inculturation

It is known to almost everyone that to a great extent the early missionaries had no knowledge of the culture of the people they were evangelising and the significance and meaning of their ritual actions and the missionaries did not in any way want to know about such cultures which were unchristian. Consequently, they considered most of these rituals as devilish and incompatible with the gospel message and the Christian rituals. As a result, Christians were forced to part completely with their native way of worship of their sacrifices and celebrations of feasts and festivals. The newly converted people were threatened with sanctions from the Church and the 'fires of hell', and they were not allowed to include anything traditional in their religious and cultural practices. In many places, the situation remains almost the same even today. It is this situation that demands inculturation. More than ever before, we are conscious of the existence of the world's many religions. There are not only the major religions of Judaism, Islam, Hinduism, and Buddhism, but also a host of smaller yet enduring religions and religious movements of tribal peoples. It is necessary to give them their rightful place in their own contexts.

Wine has to be imported into the Philippines for the celebration of the Eucharist. What better symbol can we have? How can the important symbol of baptism express cleansing and inclusion when, in the Masai culture of Africa, pouring water over a woman`s head is a ritual cursing her to barrenness? Christianity's insistence on monogamy and condemnation of polygamy ignores an important structure for women's security in African societies where women outnumber men and kinship patterns and obligations differ significantly from those of Europe.[326]

When communication began to take place with America, Asia and Africa the procedure that followed was not proper. Since missionary expansion mainly started from Europe and the missionary enterprises coincided with the expansion through navigation, trade, colonization and conquest, it happened that the cultures of these countries were imposed on the colonial people. Knowingly or unknowingly, the missionaries transmitted along with the gospel the cultures of the countries from which they came. The new Christians accepted the faith along with the western cultural expressions. Gradually they came to be known as "Christian culture."[327] What was practised during the time of Jesus and later the Apostles was kept aside.

325 Arrupe, Pedro SJ, Letter to the Whole Society on Inculturation, 1978, in *Toward of Theology of Inculturation* Shorter, Aylward, London: Geoffrey Chapman, 1988, 11.

326 Bevans, Stephen B., Models of Contextual Theology, New York: Orbis Books, 1994, 5.

327 Amalorpavadass, Duraiswami Simon, Gospel and Culture, Bangalore: National Biblical Catechetical and Liturgical Centre, 1978, 29.

Inculturation implies and should bring about not one single universal Christian culture, but many particular Christian cultures. It is no longer one Christian culture but many. It means that the indigenous culture of every country and region must be permeated by the spirit of Jesus Christ, purified, enriched and fulfilled by the gospel values. There could be as many Christian cultures as there are cultures in the world. Our fidelity is to the Word of God and not to the culture of the missionary who announced the word. Fidelity to the Word of God may also depend on keeping the tradition of the time of Jesus and the Apostles.[328]

Inculturation is Already in Tradition

Indigenisation is very much related to a very ancient and venerable tradition that can be tracked back to Jesus Christ, the Word incarnate. When the Word was made flesh, he identified himself fully with the Jewish people, spoke their language (Aramaic), followed their customs and traditions and was involved in the Jewish society. The early celebration of the Eucharist has been patterned on the synagogue prayer service and the Paschal meal. There was also at the same time the danger of Christianity identifying with one Judaic culture as the first Christian community was formed of Jews. Paul was the champion of freedom and universality. It was during the council in Jerusalem (Acts 15) the triumph for the values of universality and freedom were affirmed and so an affirmation of indigenisation. When the Gospel penetrated into the Greco-Roman societies, the languages of Greek and later Latin and socio-cultural signs were integrated into the liturgy. Theology was thus elaborated on the Greco-Roman modes of thought. The same changes took place when the Gospel was preached to Syria, Egypt and Europe. In all these situations, the spirit of the Gospel permeated the cultures of the place, transformed them profoundly and enriched them. Because of this inculturation, the Gospel became a living reality; the Church became more catholic and was adorned with an ever richer variety.[329]

To Deal with the Cruel Human Reality

The Latin American bishops clarify the purpose for inculturation as they saw the cruel reality of the people and they issued the statement in 1979 at Puebla.

The situation of pervasive extreme poverty takes on very concrete faces in real life. In these faces, we ought to recognise the suffering features of Christ the Lord, who questions and challenges us. The faces of young children, struck down by poverty before they are born, their chance for self-development blocked by irreparable mental and physical deficiencies.

328 Cf. Amalorpavadass, Duraiswami Simon, Gospel and Culture, Bangalore: National Biblical Catechetical and Liturgical Centre, 1978, 30.

329 Amalorpavadass, Duraiswami Simon, Gospel and Culture, Bangalore: National Biblical Catechetical and Liturgical Centre, 1978, 28-29.

- The faces of young people, who are disoriented because they cannot find their place in society.
- The faces of labourers who frequently are ill-paid and who have difficulty in organising themselves and defending their rights;
- The faces of the underemployed and the unemployed, who are dismissed because of the harsh exigencies of economic crises.
- The faces of old people who are frequently marginalised in a progress-oriented society that totally disregards people not engaged in Production.[330]

To deal with this situation of cruelty, pain and poverty a proper understanding of inculturation is needed so that people can experience the good effects of inculturation. "If we wish Gospel values to penetrate a given cultural context, we must recognise that evangelisation, as an expansion of Christ's incarnation, must be offered as a liberating gift. It is imperative to exclude from our minds any proselytising afterthought."[331]

To Play the Prophetic Role

Throughout history, the message of Christ has presented itself as a challenge and a task to its hearers and believers. Theologians have often spoken of its prophetic dimension. Jesus himself fulfilled this prophetic role throughout his life and up to his death on the cross. Jesus set us an example that he himself lived out. The inculturation of the Gospel message, therefore, should bring about a more vivid consciousness of God's presence in every cultural and religious context.[332]

The Kingdom of God which is operating in the world, far from putting aside the mission of the Church in Asia, challenges the Church to find a new role for itself and for its efforts of inculturation in Asia. The Church in this new situation is called to be at the service of the Kingdom, towards realizing the Father's Kingdom and its values together with the whole of humankind. This work consists of building up a new human community. The process of inculturation is no longer a question of a search for external adaptation to Asian reality and way of living, but a question of an existential nature: being and living in Asia and with Asians, becoming involved in all the aspects of life, collaborating with all the forces which are working actively to build up the Kingdom. It is a call to a radical change in our life situation. An inculturated local church in the service of the Kingdom

330 Eagleson, John & Scharper Philip (ed), in *Puebla and Beyond*, Maryknoll, N.Y: Orbis Books, 1979, 128-29, quoted in Schineller, Peter, SJ, A Handbook on Inculturation, New York: Paulist Press, 1990, 96.

331 Amaladoss, Michael SJ, Beyond Inculturation, available from: http://www.google.com/search?q=michael+amaladoss%2C+beyond+inculturation, accessed on 10.01.2009.

332 Cf. Amaladoss, Michael SJ, Beyond Inculturation.

is finally the sacrament of the same Kingdom. This is a prophetic role which everyone is called to take up.[333]

3.4. Inculturation and its Biblical Basis

The Gospel and therefore evangelisation are certainly not identical with culture, and they are independent in regard to all cultures. Nevertheless, the Kingdom which the Gospel proclaims is lived by men who are profoundly linked to a culture, the Gospel and evangelisation are necessarily incompatible with them; rather they are capable of permeating them all without becoming subject to any of them. The split between the Gospel and culture is without a doubt the drama of our time, just as it was of other times. Therefore every effort must be made to ensure a full evangelization of culture, or more correctly of cultures. They have to be regenerated by an encounter with the Gospel. But this encounter will not take place if the Gospel is not proclaimed (EN, 20).

It is a known fact that in the first century after Christ, the apostles, particularly Peter, James, and Paul recognized the difficulty of transplanting the Gospel message beyond its culture of origin. The experience and efforts by these apostles in Acts 10-11, Acts 15, and theologized by Paul in Galatians 1-3, demonstrate how they resolved such problems. Though they were very strongly based in the Law of Moses and Abrahamic covenantal act of circumcision, in order to follow the new faith the sanctions were given to follow Christ without being circumcised. In the critical section in Acts, Luke depicts "Gentiles" becoming Christians without having to embrace aspects particular to and deemed important to some Christians of Jewish ethnicity. The conflict of table fellowship between Jews and Gentiles and the issue of Gentile circumcision are again at the centre of the conflict (Acts 2:11-13, and allusion to circumcision in 2:12, 3:3). For Paul, the Gentile Christians have gained access to the family of God by faith in Christ and are in need of no further requirement (2:15-21).[334]

The Christian Gospel is not limited by any one cultural expression and, as such, is trans-cultural. The Lukan narrative of the first-century apostles, and the manner in which they understood the nature of the Gospel, demonstrates an early recognition of the trans-cultural aspect of this perspective. The experiences of different places serve as a constant reminder of the deep cultural desire to make Christianity "at home" within its society and illustrate the trans-cultural ideas.[335]

---

333 Inculturation FABC, available from: http://eapi.admu.edu.ph/eapr94/nemet.htm, accessed on 06.01.2009.

334 Pruitt, Richard A, The Inculturation of the Christian Gospel, available from: http://edt.missouri.edu/Fall2007/Thesis/PruittR-121207-T9136/research.pdf, accessed on 11.12.2008.

335 Cf. Pruitt, Richard A, The Inculturation of the Christian Gospel, available from: http://edt.missouri.edu/Fall2007/Thesis/PruittR-121207-T9136/research.pdf, accessed on 11.12.2008.

3.4.1. Inculturation in the Old Testament

The Old Testament was able to form the Israelites into the people of God because it incorporated their worldview, their histories, their wisdom, their culture, their aspirations and their total identity. The Bible therefore remains the first and powerful source and principle of any inculturation.[336] The process of inculturation was a process which developed in many ways. The people of Israel throughout their history preserved the idea that they were the chosen people of God. The Old Testament, comprising the life and culture of the people of Israel, is also the history of salvation. They took from neighbouring peoples certain forms of worship, but its faith in the God of Abraham, Isaac and Jacob was firm. However, there were modifications, and often changes in the form, as it incorporated these elements into the religious practice in order to celebrate the memory of God's wonderful deeds in history. The adjustments and adaptations were for a better purpose, to honour their only God.[337]

3.4.2. Jesus and the Incarnation

On coming to the earth the Son of God, "born of a woman, born under the law" (Gal. 4:4), associated himself with social and cultural conditions of the people of the alliance, with whom he lived and prayed. In becoming a man, he became a member of a people, a country and an epoch and in a certain way, he thereby united himself to the whole human race. For we are all one in Christ and the common nature of our humanity takes life in him. Christ, who wanted to share our human condition (cf. Heb. 2:14), died for all in order to gather into unity the scattered children of God (cf. Jn. 11:52). By his death, he wanted to break down the wall of separation between humankind, to make Israel and the nations, one people. By the power of his resurrection he drew all people to himself and created out of them a single new man (cf. Eph. 2: 14-16; Jn. 12:32). In him a new world has been born (cf. 2 Cor. 5:16-17), and everyone can become a new creature. In him, darkness has given place to light, promise became reality and all the religious aspirations of humanity found their fulfilment. By the offering that he made of his body, once for all (cf. Heb. 10: 10), Christ Jesus brought about the fullness of worship in spirit and in truth in the renewal which he wished for his disciples.[338]

Incarnation and Inculturation

The incarnation of the Word determines the nature of the Church; and the Church expresses and functions in indigenisation. Therefore, indigenisation is

336 Waliggo, John Mary, Making a Church that is truly African, in Inculturation: Its Meaning and Emergency, Africa: St. Paul's Publications, 1986, 20.

337 Cf. Inculturation and the Roman Liturgy, available from: http://www.adoremus.org/doc_inculturation, accessed on 14.01.2009.

338 Cf. Inculturation and the Roman Liturgy, available from: http://www.adoremus.org/doc_inculturation, accessed on 14.01.2009.

a logical consequence of the nature of the Church and the Incarnation of the Word. The choice then is not between indigenisation and non-indigenisation but between being an authentic Church of Christ and not being a Church at all. In virtue of the principle of incarnation, the Church expresses herself, in her being and action, through an incarnational procedure, and this procedure is called indigenisation or inculturation.[339]

The Word of God though invisible became visible by being incarnated. The humanity of Christ is the enfleshment of God's self-gift (Jn. 1:12). Likewise, the spirit of Jesus, dead and risen, is invisible but becomes embodied and is manifest in the visible community of Christ's disciples. This community is nothing else but a group of people imbued with the spirit, transformed by him and led by him. Just as Jesus was endowed with the power of God and manifested his power in words and deeds and in sign of wonders, so the power of the Gospel needs visible expression and concretisation in the context. The values of the Gospel and the Kingdom or the reality of the new era and new creation are to be translated and communicated to others. When this is actualised then it is called integration of the Church in a socio-cultural religious milieu, incarnation of the Church in a place, time and people. The living Gospel lived by the Church in a living culture with all the transformations and realities it entails is what is called inculturation.[340]

Jesus Christ, the model of incarnation and inculturation, had to speak differently to different people. He spoke differently to his apostles, the scribes and Pharisees, the Samaritan woman and Peter. He was sensitive to the generosity of the widow at the temple and to the need for affection on the part of the children who sought his blessing. His entire life and ministry remain the central paradigm for revealing and inculturating Gospel values of the Kingdom into particular contexts.[341]

The narration about Jesus is multifaceted, and the communities to whom the good news was preached were also diverse. There were Jewish Christians, some were Gentiles; some were struggling under persecution while some others were flourishing and expanding. The Jews retained many of the Jewish ways of praying, the Jewish law of circumcision and some of the dietary laws. Each of the Evangelists provides both a model for inculturation and also a message to be inculturated. Each of them presents this good news in its own particular creative and inspired way.[342]

The attitude towards inculturation is conditioned by one's understanding of creation and relationship with the world. Though the world is affected by sin

339 Amalorpavadass, Duraiswami Simon, Gospel and Culture, Bangalore: National Biblical Catechetical and Liturgical Centre, 1978, 18-19.

340 Amalorpavadass, Duraiswami Simon, Gospel and Culture, Bangalore: National Biblical Catechetical and Liturgical Centre, 1978, 19-20.

341 Schineller, Peter, SJ, A Handbook on Inculturation, New York: Paulist Press, 1990, 7.

342 Schineller, Peter, SJ, A Handbook on Inculturation, New York: Paulist Press, 1990, 8-9.

and bears its imprint in all realities, the first creation through Christ's work of reconciliation and redemption has become good again. That is the reason why the Word has been present in the whole of creation and through human history revealing Himself in various ways to various people. The seeds of the Word (AG) are found in all religions and temporal realities.[343]

Can we ask, "Could inculturation be described as the incarnation of the Christian faith, that is, as the 'process by which the Church becomes inserted into a culture?" Christian faith does not exist except in concrete cultural forms. I think it is very difficult to conceive of a Christian experience that is culturally pure, uncontaminated by any culture. We understand that incarnation is Word becoming flesh and it became flesh in the Hebrew context. So, the Word of God was addressed in history in a specific context. Jesus became real to the world.[344]

3.4.3. Revolutionary Message of Paul and the Early Church

Paul although a Hebrew of Hebrews (cf. Phil 3:5) has a universal perspective (generally speaking Judaism was not mission-oriented during the first centuries). Given the reluctance of Judaism to seek conversions actively, it is incredible to think that Paul should make a massive campaign to take his deviant form of Judaism to the Gentile world. Paul himself does not explain why he shifted from a Particularist to a Universalist. He was moved to deviate from Judaism to Gentile mission. Probably he realised that only by evangelising the pagans could Judaism itself become revived and complete (A divine demonstration of mercy to the Gentiles will enable the Jews to see the meaning of God's wrath, Rom 9:14-29; If the Gentiles are included it will make Jews jealous and therefore more open, Rom 11:11-16).[345]

The speech of Paul at Athens (Acts 17) is a good example of this dimension of openness and inculturation. He speaks of the good news of Jesus Christ, present and risen, to the Greek philosophies and religion of the day. Paul's missionary activity to the Gentiles was an especially difficult test case in inculturation for the early Christian community. His situation is of great significance to deal with inculturation and pastoral problems of today.[346] During this period, the Church entered a new epoch or era, which has important implications for the meaning of inculturation. At the council of Jerusalem, the decision was made to allow

343 Cf. Amalorpavadass, Duraiswami Simon, Gospel and Culture, Bangalore: National Biblical Catechetical and Liturgical Centre, 1978, 17-18.

344 Soares-Prabhu George S.J., Biblical Themes for a Contextual Theology by., Pune: Jnana-Deepa Vidyapeeth Theology series, 1999, 92.

345 Cf. Snyder, Graydon F., Inculturation of the Jesus Tradition, Pennsylvania: Trinity Press International, 1999, 25-26.

346 Schineller, Peter, SJ, A Handbook on Inculturation, New York: Paulist Press, 1990, 8.

Gentiles, non-Jews, to become Christians through baptism without imposing on them the Jewish law of circumcision.[347]

What is remarkable about primitive Christianity is that it had a revolutionary nature, not in terms of war but in ideology. Jew and Roman, Greek and Barbarian, free and slave, rich and poor, woman and man, accepted one another as brothers and sisters. It was indeed a sociological impossibility but the small Christian community caused the wonder.[348]

The challenge which faced the first Christians, whether they came from the chosen people or from a pagan background, was to reconcile the renunciations demanded by faith in Christ with fidelity to the culture and traditions of the people to which they belonged. And so it will be for Christians of all times, as the words of St. Paul affirm: "We proclaim Christ crucified, scandal for the Jews, foolishness for the pagans" (1 Cor. 1:23).[349]

The Christians who came from paganism had to renounce idols, myths, superstitions (cf. Acts 19:18-19; 1 Cor. 10:14-22; 2:20-22; 1 Jn. 5:21) when they adhered to Christ. But whatever their ethnic or cultural origin, Christians had to recognise the promise, the prophecy and the history of their salvation in the history of Israel. They had to accept as the word of God the books of the Old Testament as well as those of the New. They welcomed the sacramental signs, which could only be understood fully in the context of Holy Scripture and the life of the Church.[350]

Inculturation was a new term expressing an old reality in the history of the Christian Church, i.e., the insertion of Christianity into different cultures and the establishment of new kinds of Christian communities. The church borrowed elements from Roman civilisation such as the hierarchically structured imperial system, the legal system, and the territorial division in provinces and dioceses. Through creative assimilation, the church gave new meaning to the Jewish Passover and Christmas celebrations replaced the Roman winter festival. Later, theological concepts were reformulated in Aristotle's philosophical categories.[351]

The history of the Church is one of the strongest arguments in support of inculturation. The rules of communications require that the speaker adapt himself/herself to the audience and in order that his/her message be understood, it has to be clothed in the thought pattern of the hearers. This process has been taking place

347 Schineller, Peter, SJ, A Handbook on Inculturation, New York: Paulist Press, 1990, 29.

348 Bosch, David J., Transforming Mission, New York: Orbis Books, 1996, 48.

349 Inculturation: Varietates Legitimae 19, 20, available from: http://www.adoremus.org/doc_inculturation, accessed on 06.01.2009.

350 Cf. Inculturation: Varietates Legitimae 19, 20, available from: http://www.adoremus.org/doc_inculturation, accessed on 06.01.2009.

351 Gibbs, Philip SVD, Pearls in the Deep: Inculturation and Ecclesia in Oceania, in Australian EJournal of Theology, ISSUE 3 - ISSN 1448 – 632, August 2004, available from: http://dlibrary.acu.edu.au/research/theology/ejournal/aejt_3/Gibbs.htm, accessed on 02.11.2008.

in Christianity right from the beginning. When the centre of Christianity moved from Jerusalem to the Gentile world in the second half of the first century, the Christian message and organisation had to be adapted to the existing milieu. The passage of the Church from three centuries of severe persecutions to Constantine's era of peace, witnessed an adjustment of the message and Church order to the circumstances of the times. Whatever genuine movement that has taken place in the Church has been a result of an honest attempt to inculturate Christianity to the times and cultures of contemporary peoples.[352]

3.5. Inculturation and the Church Documents

Although the term "inculturation" may be of recent origin within Christian theology and language, the reality it signifies has been present in various degrees in the Church since its foundation. There has been a noticeable development in our understanding of the inculturation movement and this is evident from the terminology used. Adaptation is the term used for a long time to signify the same idea. After that, the term indigenisation was used. It referred to the same process but underlined the necessity of promoting indigenous church ministers in every locality. Soon after the second Vatican Council, the term incarnation of the Christian message came into general use. Christianity has no alternative but to do the same in every culture and time in order to continue the salvation brought by Christ. This terminology has never been superseded. Inculturation came to express that same reality while underlying the importance of cultures as the instrument and the means for realising the incarnation process of the Christian religion. Inculturation means the honest and serious attempt to make Christ and his message of salvation evermore understood by peoples of every culture, locality and time. It means the reformation of Christian life and doctrine into the very thought-patterns of each people.[353] It is the ongoing way of engaging in Christian life and mission. This engagement takes place within families, schools, seminaries and parishes, whether in the United States or in Africa. That is the reason why the Church began to think about it seriously in order to be more effective in evangelising.

The church council exists to create a strategic plan for a local congregation. Therefore, its primary work is one of leadership rather than management. This is an important distinction to make. Leadership is the visionary, which assesses critically where the congregation is at the present moment, where God is calling it to be in the future, and what resources will be required to move from the current reality into the desired reality. Management is the essential work that must be accomplished on a daily basis to make the congregation effective. The three

352 Waliggo, John Mary, Making a Church that is truly African, in Inculturation: Its Meaning and Emergency, Africa: St. Paul's Publications, 1986, 14.

353 Cf. Waliggo, John Mary, Making a Church that is truly African, in Inculturation: Its Meaning and Emergency, Africa: St. Paul's Publications, 1986, 12.

councils played important roles to shape up the running of the church. In fact, the Council of Trent lasted 18 years and its objective was the definitive determination of the doctrines of the Church in answer to the heresies of the Protestants; a further object was the execution of a thorough reform of the inner life of the Church by removing the numerous abuses that had developed in it.[354]

Three centuries after the Council of Trent (1545), the First Vatican Council (1869 – 1870) took place. It expressed more withdrawal and retrenchment on the part of the Church. The Church was more afraid of new liberal attitudes and modern ideas and the influence of the enlightenment led the Catholic Church toward centralisation and further standardisation. The papacy received new power and emphasis at the expense of the local churches under their bishops. The council reaffirmed the Catholic emphasis upon faith and reason, but it was very wary of contemporary intellectual movements and issued condemnations rather than calls for dialogue.[355]

3.5.1. Vatican II

According to Karl Rahner, a new era of the world church in Christian history, began with Vatican II. The setting for the discussion of these changes was St. Peter's, Rome. There were more than two thousand council fathers assembled. Many of these bishops came from Africa, Asia and Latin America. The universality and catholicity of the Roman church became visible with the presence and representation of so many cultures and traditions. The council itself was an exercise in inculturation as the church tried to open its windows to the modern world, with its joys and sorrows, hopes and anxieties. The Sacred Liturgy called for the revision of the liturgy in accordance with the particular situations and cultures. The vernacular could be used instead of the so-called universal Latin language. This was definitely a very radical change.[356] In fact, Vatican II, far from teaching a new doctrine and instead of initiating a new tradition re-affirmed the age-old Christian principle of incarnation. In so doing, it re-launched the process of incarnation which had been impeded during the last several centuries.[357]

> The seed which is the word of God, watered by divine dew, sprouts from the good ground and draws from thence its moisture, which it transforms and assimilates into itself, and finally bears much fruit. In harmony with the economy of the Incarnation, the young churches, rooted in Christ and built up on the foundation of the Apostles, take

354 Church Councils, Catholic Encyclopaedia, available from: http://www.newadvent.org/cathen/15030c.htm, accessed on 16.01.2009.

355 Schineller, Peter, SJ, A Handbook on Inculturation, 37-38.

356 Schineller, Peter, SJ, A Handbook on Inculturation, 39-40.

357 Cf. Amalorpavadass, Duraiswami Simon, Gospel and Culture, Bangalore: National Biblical Catechetical and Liturgical Centre, 1978, 31.

> to themselves in a wonderful exchange all the riches of the nations which were given to Christ as an inheritance (cf. Ps. 2:8). They borrow from the customs and traditions of their people, from their wisdom and their learning, from their arts and disciplines, all those things which can contribute to the glory of their Creator, or enhance the grace of their Saviour, or dispose Christian life the way it should be (AG, 22).

The people who have not yet received the Gospel are also related in various ways to the people of God. We need to remember the people to whom the testament and the promises were given and from whom Christ was born according to the flesh. Because of their fathers these people remain most dear to God, for God does not repent of the gifts He makes nor of the calls He issues. That does not mean that the others are excluded from the plan of God. In the first place, amongst these there are the Mohamedans, who, professing to hold the faith of Abraham, along with us adore the one and merciful God, who on the last day will judge humankind. God is not far from those who seek in images the unknown God, for it is He who gives to all people life and breath. He wants all people to be saved. Others who through no fault of their own do not know the Gospel of Christ or His Church can also attain salvation provided they sincerely seek God and do His will according to the dictates of conscience. Nor does Divine Providence deny the helps necessary for salvation to those who, without blame on their part, have not yet arrived at an explicit knowledge of God and with His grace strive to live a good life. The Church looks upon the good or truth that is found among them as a preparation for the Gospel. She knows that it is given by Him who enlightens all people so that they may finally have life. But often people are deceived by the Evil One, and have become vain in their reasoning and have exchanged the truth of God for a lie, serving the creature rather than the Creator. There are also some people who, living and dying in this world without God. In order to promote the glory of God and procure the salvation of all and mindful of the command of the Lord, all of us are expected to preach the Gospel to every creature (LG, 16).

Jesus told the apostles, "Go, therefore, make disciples of all nations, baptizing them in the name of the Father and of the Son and of the Holy Spirit, teaching them to observe all things whatsoever I have commanded you. And behold I am with you all days even to the consummation of the world" (Mt. 21:18-20). Jesus was actually doing the will of His Father. The Church has received this solemn mandate of Christ to proclaim the saving truth from the apostles and must carry it out to the very ends of the earth (cf. Acts 1:8). That is why St. Paul would say, "Woe to me, if I do not preach the Gospel", (I Cor. 9:16) and continues unceasingly to send heralds of the Gospel until such time as the infant churches are fully established and can themselves continue the work of evangelising. For the Church is compelled by the Holy Spirit to do her part that God's plan may be fully realized, whereby He has constituted Christ as the source of salvation for the whole world. By the proclamation of the Gospel, she prepares her hearers to receive and profess the faith. Through her work, whatever good is in the minds and hearts of people, whatever good lies latent in the religious practices and cultures of diverse peoples, is not only saved from destruction but is also cleansed, raised up and perfected unto the glory of God, the confusion of the devil and the happiness of humanity. All Christians are obliged to spread the faith. Thus are fulfilled the words of God, spoken through His prophet: "From the rising of the sun until the going down thereof my name is great among the gentiles, and in every place a clean oblation is sacrificed and offered up in my name" (Mal. 1, 11). In this way the Church both prays and labours in order that the entire world may become the People of God, the Body of the Lord and the Temple of the Holy Spirit, and that in Christ, the Head of all, all honour and glory may be rendered to the Creator and Father of the Universe (LG, 16-17).

3.5.2. Evangelii Praecone

Pope Pius XII was aware of the missionaries toiling all over the world that the word of the Lord may run its course triumphantly. Therefore, he said, that the Catholic missionary movement both in Christian and in pagan lands had gained such force and momentum and was of such proportions as perhaps had been never witnessed before in the annals of Catholic mission. Another end had to be achieved; and he wanted that all should understand that fully. The Church from the beginning down to the present time has always followed that wise practice. No one should by introducing the Gospel into any new land, destroy or extinguish whatever the people possess that is naturally good, just or beautiful. For the Church, when she calls people to a higher culture and a better way of life, under the inspiration of the Christian religion, does not act like one who recklessly cuts down and uproots a thriving forest. No, she grafts a good scion upon the wild stock that it may bear a crop of more delicious fruit (EP, 56). It only suggests and in fact demands that we are called to propagate the Gospel to the people in their cultural milieu without interfering with their culture.

3.5.3. Pacem in Terris

Pope John XXIII was aware of the prevailing situation in several of the European colonies and so he wanted to establish universal peace in truth, justice, charity and liberty. Peace on Earth can only be established by the diligent observance of the divinely established order. Indeed, the best interests of justice are served by those public authorities who do all they can to improve the human conditions of the members of these minority groups, especially in what concerns their language, culture, ancient traditions, and their economic activity and enterprise (PT, 96). Once again, our task is to establish order on this earth by preserving their tradition and culture.

3.5.4. Evangelii Nuntiandi

The people, who sincerely accept the Good News, gather in Jesus' name in order to seek together the kingdom. They want to build up the Kingdom of God and live it. They make up a community that is ready to evangelise. The command to the Twelve to go out and proclaim the Good News is also valid for all Christians today in the world, though the method of reaching out to people might be in different ways. It is precisely for this reason that Peter calls Christians "a people set apart to sing the praises of God" (1 Pt 2:9) those marvellous things that each one was able to hear in his own language (cf. Acts 2:11). Moreover, the Good News of the Kingdom which is coming and which has begun is meant for all people of all times. Those who have received the Good News and who have been gathered by it into the community of salvation can and must communicate and spread the message to the world (EN, 13).

If one reads the New Testament and the origins of the Church, one may follow her history step by step, one can understand how she lived and acted in the mission of Jesus. The Church herself is sent by Jesus to evangelise and so in turn the Church herself sends out evangelisers. She puts on their lips the saving Word, she explains to them the message of which she herself is the depositary, she gives them the mandate which she herself has received and she sends them out to preach. To preach not their own selves or their personal ideas, but a Gospel of which neither she nor they are the absolute masters and owners, but a Gospel of which they are the ministers, in order to pass it on with complete fidelity (EN, 15). In other words, it is a mission given by God.

The document (EN) expresses the idea of evangelizing very succinctly, "All this could be expressed in the following words: what matters is to evangelise man's culture and cultures (not in a purely decorative way, as it were, by applying a thin veneer, but in a vital way, in depth and right to their very roots), in the wide and rich sense which these terms have in Gaudium et spes, always taking the person as one's starting-point and always coming back to the relationships of people among themselves and with God" (EN, 20).

It is asserted that evangelisation can lose much of its force and effectiveness if it does not take into consideration the actual people to whom it is addressed. It is supposed to use their language, their signs and symbols. It should answer the questions they ask, and should have an impact on their concrete life. But on the other hand, evangelisation risks losing its power and disappear altogether if one empties or adulterates its content under the pretext of translating it; if, in other words, one sacrifices this reality and destroys the unity without which there is no universality, out of a wish to adapt a universal reality to a local situation. Now, only a Church which preserves the awareness of her universality and shows that she is in fact universal is capable of having a message which can be heard by all, regardless of regional frontiers. Legitimate attention to individual Churches cannot fail to enrich the Church. Such attention is indispensable and urgent. It responds to the very deep aspirations of peoples and human communities to find their own identity ever more clearly (EN, 63). None of us Christians can yearn for anything more ardently than to serve the people of the modern world with mounting generosity and success. If we do this then we are fulfilling the mission of God.

3.5.5. Slavorum Apostoli

John Paul II travelled further and visited more countries than any other pope, it is said. His worldwide pastoral journeys confronted him with the cultural pluralism and problems and he had to find reasonable answers to emerging situations. In many circumstances, he had to deal with the issue of faith and culture. During his visit to Africa in 1980, John Paul II spoke to the bishops of Zaire on the topic of inculturation of the Gospel, the Africanisation of the Church. The Pope told the bishops that it was up to them to promote and harmonise the advance in the field of inculturation, after mature reflection and in union with the universal church and with the Holy See. Inculturation for the people as a whole cannot be, but the fruit of gradual maturity in faith.[358]

The encyclical *Slavorum Apostoli* was to commemorate the evangelisation of Cyril and Methodius who were presented as the apostles of Slavic people. "They realized that an essential condition of the success of their missionary activity was to transpose correctly Biblical notions and Greek theological concepts into a very different context of thought and historical experience. It was a question of a new method of catechesis" (SA, 11). These two great men were determined persons who assimilated and identified themselves with the needs and aspirations of the Slav people. These saints are in fact great examples of inculturation.

It is not only the evangelical content of the doctrine proclaimed by Saints Cyril and Methodius that merits particular emphasis. Also very expressive and instructive for the Church today is the catechetic and pastoral method that they applied in their apostolic activity among the peoples who had not yet heard the Sacred Mysteries celebrated in their native language, nor heard the word of God proclaimed in a way that completely fitted their own mentality and respected the actual conditions of their own life. The Church or People of God takes nothing away from the temporal welfare of any people by establishing that kingdom. Rather does she foster and take to herself, insofar as they are good, the abilities, resources, and customs of each people. Taking them to herself she purifies, strengthens, and ennobles them. This characteristic of universality which adorns the People of God is a gift from the Lord himself. In virtue of this catholicity each individual part of the Church contributes through its special gifts to the good of the other parts and of the whole Church. Thus through the common sharing of gifts and through the

358 Cf. Shorter, Aylward, Toward a Theology of Inculturation, London: Geoffrey Chapman, 1988, 222-26.

common effort to attain fullness in unity, the whole and each of its parts receive increase (SA, 16).

As early as the ninth century, they already thought of the universal Church and each context to be respected for its own particularity. Ever since the ninth century in Christian Europe, a new organization was emerging. Saints Cyril and Methodius held out a message clearly of great relevance for our own age, which precisely because of the many complex problems of a religious, cultural, civil and international nature is seeking a vital unity in the real communion of its various elements. The two evangelisers were known for their love for the communion of the universal Church both in the East and in the West, and, within the universal Church, love for the particular Church that was coming into being in the Slav nations. The present generation can learn from them how Christians and people of our time can live together in communion (cf. SA, 26).

3.5.6. Redemptoris Missio

The Encyclical *Redemptoris Missio* published in 1990, dealing with Evangelisation, deals also with inculturation. It takes Saint Paul as the model for inculturation. "In the name of the whole Church, I sense an urgent duty to repeat this cry of St. Paul" (RM, 1).

The speeches in Lystra and Athens (cf. Acts 14:15-17; 17:22-31) are acknowledged as models for the evangelization of the Gentiles. In these speeches, Paul enters into "dialogue" with the cultural and religious values of different peoples. To the Lycaonians, who practiced a cosmic religion, he speaks of religious experiences related to the cosmos. With the Greeks he discusses philosophy and quotes their own poets (cf. Acts 17:18, 26-28). The God whom Paul wishes to reveal is already present in their lives; indeed, this God has created them and mysteriously guides nations and history. But if they are to recognize the true God, they must abandon the false gods which they themselves have made and open themselves to the One whom God has sent to remedy their ignorance and satisfy the longings of their hearts. These are speeches which offer an example of the inculturation of the Gospel (RM, 25).

In the context of the encyclical, it is understood that salvation is for all and not only for the Christians. Such a perspective is very much needed in the context of India.

> The universality of salvation means that it is granted not only to those who explicitly believe in Christ and have entered the Church. Since salvation is offered to all, it must be made concretely available to all. Since Christ died for everyone, and since the ultimate calling of each of us comes from God and is therefore a universal one, we are obliged to hold that the Holy Spirit offers everyone the possibility of sharing in this Paschal Mystery in a manner known to God (RM, 10).

When the Church carries out missionary activity among the nations, she encounters different cultures and becomes involved in the process of inculturation. The need for such involvement has marked the Church's pilgrimage throughout her history, but today it is particularly urgent. The process of the Church's insertion into peoples' cultures is a lengthy one. It is not a matter of purely external adaptation, for inculturation means the intimate transformation of authentic cultural values through their integration in Christianity and the insertion of Christianity in the various human cultures. It is important that the missionaries need to immerse themselves in the milieu of those to whom they are sent. They must learn the language of the place in which they work, become familiar with the most important expressions of the local culture, and discover its values through direct experience. Without this experience, it will be difficult to bring to people the knowledge of the mystery of God in a fruitful way. Therefore, the missionaries should be well equipped to communicate effectively, adopting a manner of living which is a sign of gospel witness and of solidarity with the people. Only in such a context can the missionaries develop ecclesial communities, inspired by the Gospel and gradually they will be able to express their Christian experience in original ways and forms that are consonant with their own cultural traditions, provided that those traditions are in harmony with the objective requirements of the faith itself. In effect, inculturation must involve the whole people of God, and not just a few experts, since the people reflect the authentic *sensus fidei (*A supernatural appreciation of the faith shown by the universal consent in matters of faith and morals manifested by the whole body of the faithful under the guidance of the Magisterium) which must never be lost sight of. Inculturation needs to be guided and encouraged, but not forced. If forced, it gives rise to negative reactions among Christians. It must be an expression of the community's life, one which must mature within the community itself. The safeguarding of traditional values is the work of a mature faith (RM, 52-54).

Those Primarily Responsible for Missionary Activity

Just as the risen Lord gave the universal missionary mandate to the College of the Apostles with Peter as its head, so this same responsibility now rests primarily with the College of Bishops, headed by the successor of Peter. So, also today all are called to new evangelization and the universal mission.

> I have travelled all over the world in order 'to proclaim the Gospel,' to 'strengthen the brothers' in the faith, to console the Church, to meet people. They are journeys of faith; they are likewise opportunities for travelling catechesis, for evangelical proclamation in spreading the Gospel and the apostolic Magisterium to the full extent of the world. My brother bishops are directly responsible, together with me, for the evangelization of the world, both as members of the College of Bishops and as pastors of the particular churches. In this regard the

Council states: “The charge of announcing the Gospel throughout the world belongs to the body of shepherds, to all of whom in common Christ gave the command." It also stated that the bishops "have been consecrated not only for a particular diocese but for the salvation of the entire world." This collegial responsibility has certain practical consequences. Thus, "the Synod of Bishops should, among the concerns of general importance, pay special attention to missionary activity, the greatest and holiest duty of the Church. The same responsibility is reflected to varying degrees in Episcopal Conferences and their organisms at a continental level, which must make their own contribution to the missionary task” (RM, 63).

3.5.7. Orientale Lumen

“The light of the East has illumined the universal Church, from the moment when "a rising sun" appeared above us (Lk 1:78): Jesus Christ, our Lord, whom all Christians invoke as the Redeemer of man and the hope of the world” (OL, 1). Pope John Paul intended the encyclical to deal with the context of East; he desired to restore unity with all the Christians of the East. It is to be taken for granted that East and West have used different methods and approaches in understanding and confessing divine elements. Sometimes one tradition has come nearer to a full appreciation of some aspects of a mystery of revelation than the other, or has expressed them better. In such cases, these various theological formulations are often to be considered complementary rather than conflicting (OL, 5).

By giving great value to the Christian East and their culture, the Word of God is praised in different languages. In other words, inculturation is a necessary requirement to evangelise meaningfully. Revelation is proclaimed satisfactorily and becomes fully understandable when Christ speaks the tongues of the various peoples, and they can read scripture and sing the liturgy in their own language with their own expressions, as though repeating the marvels of Pentecost. At a time when it is increasingly recognized that the right of every people to express themselves according to their own heritage of culture and thought is fundamental, the experience of the individual Churches of the East is offered to us as an authoritative example of successful inculturation (OL, 7).

3.5.8. Ecclesia in Asia

Ecclesia in Asia emphasises the dimension of culture as a very vital aspect of evangelisation. Culture is the vital space within which the human person comes face to face with the Gospel. Just as culture is the result of the life and activity of a human group, so the persons belonging to that group are shaped to a large extent by the culture in which they live. As persons and societies change or transform, the culture changes or transforms with them. It becomes clear now why evangelisation and inculturation are naturally and intimately related to each other. The Gospel and evangelisation are certainly not identical with culture; they are independent of it. Yet the Kingdom of God comes to people who are profoundly linked to a culture, and the building of the Kingdom cannot avoid borrowing elements from human cultures. In the process of encountering the world's different cultures, the Church not only transmits her truths and values and renews cultures from within, but she also takes from the various cultures the positive elements already found in them. The obligatory path for evangelisers is to present the Christian faith and make it part of a people's cultural heritage. The Church, through inculturation becomes a more intelligible sign of what she is, and a more effective instrument of mission. This engagement with cultures has always been part of the Church's pilgrimage through history. But it has a special urgency today in the multi-ethnic, multi-religious and multi-cultural situation of Asia, where Christianity is still too often seen as foreign (EA, 21).

An important aspect of inculturation according to *Ecclesia in Asia* is the *formation of evangelisers.* The future of the Church and evangelisation depends on them.

> In the past, formation often followed the style, methods and programmes imported from the West, and while appreciating the service rendered by that mode of formation, the Synod Fathers recognized as a positive development the efforts made in recent times to adapt the formation of evangelizers to the cultural contexts of Asia. As well as a solid grounding in biblical and patristic studies, seminarians should acquire a detailed and firm grasp of the Church's theological and philosophical patrimony. The Synod also expressed concern for the formation of men and women in the consecrated life, making it clear that the spirituality and lifestyle of consecrated persons needs to be sensitive to the religious and cultural heritage of the people among whom they live and whom they serve, always presupposing the necessary discernment of what conforms to the Gospel and what does not (EA, 22).

All these need to lead communion and solidarity among the particular Churches themselves in the context of Asia. Attention has to be given to local needs, but communion requires that the particular Churches remain open to one another and collaborate with one another, so that in their diversity they may preserve and clearly manifest the bond of communion with the universal Church. Communion calls for mutual understanding and a coordinated approach to mission, without prejudice to the autonomy and rights of the Churches according to their respective theological, liturgical and spiritual traditions. History however shows how divisions have often wounded the communion of the Churches in Asia. Down the centuries, relations between particular Churches of different ecclesiastical jurisdictions, liturgical traditions and missionary styles have sometimes been tense and difficult. The Bishops present at the Synod acknowledged that even today within and among the particular Churches in Asia there are sometimes unfortunate divisions, often connected with ritual, linguistic, ethnic and caste differences. Wherever communion is weakened, the Church's witness and missionary work suffer. There are many centres of theology, spirituality and pastoral activity across Asia which foster communion and practical cooperation. It must be the concern of all to see these promising initiatives develop further for the good of both the Church and society in Asia (EA, 26).

This analysis shows that as early as the Old Testament times there was need to practise inculturation. The Israelites had to find meaningful ways to express their love and devotion to their God and so they had to borrow methods and means from others. No culture may be complete in itself as we human beings depend on others for our life and as we can learn from others. In our context today, our reflections and analysis should conclude in Jesus as the supreme example of inculturation through his incarnation. Though he was equal to God, he emptied himself to be born as a man in an ordinary human situation (cf. Phil 2:5-8).

3.6. Methods of Inculturation

All theology, ministry and inculturation are at the service of human needs. But, there are positive and negative elements in every situation. The positive elements are stepping stones for pastoral action. In this context, the first task of the agent of inculturation is to become acquainted with the situation and know the reality as well as values present and absent. The myths, dreams, idols and worldview of the people involved must be carefully listened to and studied. This analysis cannot be done by the agent of inculturation alone but the people in the situation should also be involved. It should be understood that no analysis is ever complete since every situation is changing and cultures are evolving.[359]

Once the situation is well understood, Christian values are brought to bear on that situation. A pastoral strategy is formed that accords with God's word and truth, especially as focused in the life and message of Jesus Christ. This is done by examining the ways in which God has revealed himself in human history; through scripture, tradition, and contemporary embodiments and manifestations. The minister of inculturation should have critical understanding of, and working familiarity with the scripture. Other than the scripture the past and present of the Christian community also functions as part of the Christian message. The Christian message has to be read and interpreted from one's own particular tradition and in light of the tradition of interpretation by the church through its magisterium as well as its theologians and biblical scholars. As we are also prophetic people, God speaks to us as He had spoken through the prophets. In

359 Cf. Schineller, Peter SJ., A Handbook on Inculturation, New York, Paulist Press, 1990, 63-65.

other words, in order to know exactly what the Christian message is, there should be much study, dialogue and prayer.[360]

The minister or agent of inculturation should be aware of his/her own strengths and weakness, biases and prejudices. When the agent of inculturation is an outsider to the culture, there is a need for team work and collaboration. Through the help of the community, we can achieve solutions that are helpful and lasting.[361] The role of the agent is very specific according to Peter Schineller:

The agent of inculturation becomes a trusted authority and resource for those in the cultural situation. The ministry of inculturation means serving, putting the needs of the situation before one's own agenda. The agent of inculturation enters the situation with respect and humility, knowing that he or she treads on holy ground and at the invitation of those concerned. He or she comes with the conviction that God is already present in the situation. The task of the facilitator is to let the power and love of God more deeply illuminate and guide that context or culture.[362]

Once these elements interact together dynamically then the truth emerges. It emerges when the values and goals of these elements mutually confirm, challenge, and corroborate each other. They actually will resonate when the truth emerges. The result will be directed towards peace, though the process itself is not always so peaceful because as it is prophetic there is a possibility of being critical. Only in such a context, Gospel may be inculturated.[363]

3.6.1. Dialogical Process of Inculturation

In the inculturation of the life and message of the Gospel in Asia, there have been hesitations and mistakes in the past, but we are more than ever convinced that dialogue with our fellow Asians whose commitment is to other faiths is increasingly important. We also urge on all a deep respect for the culture and traditions of our peoples, and express the hope that the catholicity of the Church, the root of our diversity in the oneness of faith, may serve to help Asians remain truly Asian, and yet become fully part of the modem world and the one family of mankind.[364]

A dialogical process of inculturation happens in communities where people live their common-life-situations in the midst of the Asian reality. The reality of Asia is complex; nevertheless, it operates as one in every moment of history. If there is any attempt to specify, divide and analyse the three different elements of the Asian reality as separate entities, it is inspired and justified more by an effort to

360 Schineller, Peter SJ., A Handbook on Inculturation, 66-67.

361 Schineller, Peter SJ., A Handbook on Inculturation, 68.

362 Schineller, Peter SJ., A Handbook on Inculturation, 69.

363 Schineller, Peter SJ., A Handbook on Inculturation, 70-72.

364 Jonathan Yun-Ka Tan, Towards Asian Liturgical Inculturation, FABC Paper No. 89, available from: http://www.ucanews.com/html/fabc-papers/fabc-89.htm, accessed on 05.11.2008.

clarify the different elements than to affirm their separate existence in the real-life situations. It shows the reality of Asia is very authentic and Asian in its deepest nature. That is why inculturation should take the Asian reality holistically. But the holistic approach has another meaning as well: it is not only a characteristic of the Asian reality; it is a characteristic of the mentality of Asians. Thus, human being is always part of the totality of the universe: of the cosmos and of the earth, involved in all the aspects of life, in its full complexity.[365]

It is the updating of the language which the church uses for evangelisation, in keeping with the language which the Spirit speaks in other religions and secular ideologies that shape the lives of the people. It amounts to speaking in such way that everyone understands the message in his or her native tongue. It is also a powerful Word of protest against the rule of Mammon that all religions repudiate.[366]

How can a dialogical process lead towards inculturation? What happens with the values and meaning embodied in the Gospel and in cultures/religions involved in a dialogical process? The process of inculturation starts at the grassroots level, in a constant dialogue of life with religions, cultures, and the poor. It should be analysed with the help of experts through the theological, ethnological, anthropological sciences, to find out the compatibility of the process. It should also correspond with the living Tradition of the Church.[367]

Dialogue may take place in an encounter between individuals or groups where communication between the different sides of the encounter plays an essential role. Thus, dialogue and a dialogical process may be understood as a communication problem between two or more individuals or communities. Dialogue as communication can be realized on different levels: it can be a simple argumentative discourse, a presentation of two different points of views which can then lead to a second level: a deeper encounter of ideas, meanings and the different realities of the partners in the dialogue. On the third level, dialogue is an interaction of partners who force themselves to enter into the world of meanings and symbols of the other. They try to find common symbols and meanings which can be understood in both partners' world of symbols, leading thus to a possibility of interaction, exchange and mutual enrichment. A meaningful inculturation takes place on the third level of dialogue, perceived as an understanding of the two different systems of values and meanings involved in the process of inculturation, finding common symbols which can then serve as the basis for a new creation.[368]

---

365 Cf. Inculturation FABC, available from: http://eapi.admu.edu.ph/eapr94/nemet.htm, accessed on 06.01.2009.

366 Pieris, Aloysius SJ, Inculturation as a Missionary/Evangelical Presence in a Religiously Plural Society, available from: http://eapi.admu.edu.ph/eapr95/pieris.htm, accessed on 08.01.2009.

367 Inculturation FABC.

368 Inculturation FABC.

Inculturation is the ongoing dialogue between faith and culture or cultures. The insertion of the faith into a culture is an extremely important moment in the process. Christian faith cannot exist except in a cultural form because Christian faith or Christian life is a cultural phenomenon. This distinct way of life can operate only culturally. It is essentially a dialogue between faith and culture; faith in cultural form. Human culture is thus enlivened by the Gospel from within.[369]

With regard to the theological foundations of dialogue and the dialogical process of inculturation, the documents of the FABC see them in the inner-trinitarian dialogical life reality of the Father, Son and the Holy Spirit which leads to mutual enrichment of the divine Persons. In this way, the final result will not lead to a dubious syncretism but to integration, profound and organic in character, of all that is best in our traditional ways into the treasury of our Christian heritage.[370]

3.6.2. Dealing with Life Situations of Asia

Inculturation in Asia has to start from the actual Asian reality. And this reality is characterized by different elements which can be defined according to the First General Assembly of FABC as "the living traditions, the cultures, the religions, all the life-realities of the people in whose midst it (the local church) has sunk its roots deeply and whose history and life it (the local church) gladly makes its own."[371]

Inculturation is the process of dealing with the dimensions of living religio-cultural and socio-economic contexts (religious pluralism, widespread poverty, cultural diversity and unjust and oppressive structures). It is a process of integration of Christian faith with local culture, cultures. There is an ongoing process of reciprocal and critical interaction. Because culture is dynamic there is a never ending process.[372]

This process of inculturation also presupposes certain human attitudes, practiced in an atmosphere of freedom and mutual respect, knowledge of both the Gospel with its implications and of the local cultures, religions and life-situations. This is the reason why the real agents of inculturation should be the members of local origin, who know of the local cultural and the religious backgrounds necessary to find common meanings and values in them which are later used in the process of inculturation.[373]

A very important factor that characterises and decisively influences the local churches and their inculturation efforts on this continent: poverty and the

369 Shorter, Aylward, Toward of Theology of Inculturation, London: Geoffrey Chapman, 1988, 12.

370 Cf. Inculturation FABC.

371 Inculturation FABC.

372 Dorr, Donal, Mission in Today's World, New York: Orbis Books, 2002, 94.

373 Inculturation FABC.

phenomenon of the poor. Half of the population of this enormous continent live in poverty. In 1970, the Asian Bishops' Meeting in Manila took up the problem of poverty and since then the poor have been occupying a very important position in the documents of FABC. Generally, poverty stems from two main reasons in Asia: it can be voluntary (as it is practiced and highly appreciated in great religions like Hinduism, Buddhism and Christianity) and it can be structural: the people are poor in this sense: they are 'deprived' deliberately. Because of this two-fold understanding of poverty, local churches should make different answers to the challenges posed by poverty. The critical approaches to cultures and religions cannot be limited only to a scientific analysis of the situation. Structural poverty, often the result of greed and injustice should be fought with all the means of the Church. On the other hand, the local churches should enter into a dialogue of life with the poor, in order to listen to the aspirations and needs of these groups, to be able to proclaim the Gospel to them according to their expectations. In such life-contacts and experiences, the poor can teach the Church humility, solidarity, and detachment from material wealth. If a local church really wants to become inculturated, truly indigenous, it has to become a church not only for the poor but of the poor, with the poor and among the poor.[374]

3.6.3. Considering Great Religious Traditions of Asia

The great religious traditions of Asia have a privileged place in the process of inculturation. The understanding of the role of great religions and how the Church is supposed to relate to them has been in constant development in the various documents. There are two starting points: firstly, the great religions are expressions of God's salvific will, as well as human being's free response to God's invitation. This idea is constant in all documents of FABC. Secondly, in all the religions the presence of the seeds of the Word is acknowledged while stressing the task of the Church to recognize these seeds and bring them into the Church in order to enrich the local churches, and through the local churches the universal Church. This implies that, because of the presence of the Holy Spirit in these religions, they are an authentic way of life leading their followers towards God, and in interaction and dialogue with them; Christians can discover new expressions and insights into their own faith. There is mutual giving and taking.[375]

Explicitly, this perception leads to a receptive pluralism: that is to say, the many ways of responding to the prompting of the Holy Spirit must be continually in conversation with one another. Here, there is a shifting of the accent from collecting the seeds of the Word in religions and inserting them into the local church, to constructive collaboration and dialogue that can lead to the recognition of the deepest values and aspirations of Asian people, the clarification of meanings and symbols, and the ability to work hand-in-hand in realizing the common

374 Cf. Inculturation FABC.

375 Inculturation FABC.

destiny of all the nations and people on the continent. This perception leads slowly to a realization that all the religions are complementary in the historically and culturally conditioned ways in which people in a pilgrim state have experienced and expressed their relation to and the significance to life of the Absolute.[376]

The principal criterion in this interaction and collaboration is orthopraxis, the authenticity of the participants to serve all the members of the community in achieving a better, more human society and fullness of life. Inculturation in such understanding does not mean extracting selected elements from different religions, whether purely philosophical notions or religious values, and the subsequent incorporation of these elements into Christianity; but it is a dialogical process of collaboration and critical interaction for the realization of the fullness of life in Asia.[377]

3.6.4. Dynamic Equivalence in Inculturation

Three other methods suggested by Anscar J. Chupungco may be of help to understand inculturation better. Correct method is the key to correct inculturation. They are: the method of dynamic equivalence, the method of creative assimilation, and the method of organic progression. Dynamic equivalence starts with what exists in Christian liturgy and how culture can further develop its process, which is the composite of the rite. Dynamic equivalence may be described in terms of translation. In other words, it re-expresses the liturgical process in the living language, rites, and symbols of a local community. It consists of replacing elements of the liturgical process with something that has an equal meaning or value in the culture of the people, and hence can suitably transmit the message intended by the process. The opposite of dynamic equivalence is 'stationary or static.' It is called static because it remains on the level of form or shape or external appearance. It does not take into consideration the cultural patterns, history, and life experience of the local community. The temptation to settle easily with formal correspondence is strong among Roman Catholics whose liturgical formularies are in most instances translated from the Latin. Dynamic equivalence is an extremely difficult method of translation. On the other hand, static method tends to be no more than a literal, word-for-word or phrase-by-phrase, translation to the point of ignoring the linguistic characteristics of the audience.[378]

Some examples of static translations are cited here; but they are no more than mere transliterations. Examples are the words "mystery" for *mysterion* and "sacrament" for *sacramentum*. Such transliterations, though they are doctrinally safe, do not enrich the people's understanding of what the liturgy is talking about.

---

376 Inculturation FABC.

377 Inculturation FABC.

378 Chupungco, Anscar J, O.S.B, Liturgical Inculturation: Sacramentals, Religiosity, and Catechesis, Minnesota: The Liturgical Press, 1992, 38.

Consider such common words as "baptism", "Eucharist", "Amen", "Alleluia", and a myriad of other traditional words we use in our worship services. The people are surely familiar with these words, but familiarity with foreign words does not mean that they have become embedded in the cultural consciousness of the people.[379]

3.6.5. Creative Assimilation in Inculturation

In the time of writers like Tertullian, Hippolytus, and Ambrose, the age of patristic creativity, inculturation was often done through integration of pertinent rites, symbols, and linguistic expressions, religious or otherwise, into the liturgy. Examples are anointing at baptism, the giving of the cup of milk and honey, and the foot washing of neophytes. Greeks and Romans had commonly practised these rites during the first four centuries. Some of them belonged to household rites, others to religious acts like what are known as mystery rites. By the method of creative assimilation, they became part of Christian worship. They elaborated the core of the liturgical rite; they developed the shape of the liturgy. For example, the rite of baptism developed from the simple apostolic rite of washing in water with the word to a full-blown liturgical celebration.[380]

3.6.6. Organic Progression in Inculturation

Organic progression connotes the work of supplementing and completing the shape of the liturgy established by the Constitution on the Liturgy and by the Holy See after the council. This method involves 'filling in the gaps,' as it were, that have been left in the treatment of liturgy since Vatican II. While offering principles that serve the universal Church and preserve the unity of the Roman rite, the Council could not possibly have envisioned all the possible expressions and situations that would bear on the inculturation of liturgy. The new liturgical forms, which were not envisaged by the *Constitution on the Liturgy* or the typical editions, should have been there all along. They would surely have been included in the liturgical rite had it been drawn up today. This method is progressive because of the new shape it gives to the liturgy. It is organic because its result complies with the basic intention of the liturgical documents and also with the nature and tradition of the liturgy.[381]

3.6.7. Models of Inculturation

The historical fact that helps us to understand the necessity and importance of inculturation is found in the numerous official documents and instructions of Propaganda Fide (Department (Congregation) of the Holy See) since its establishment in 1622 and the constitutions and regulations for missionaries from their founders. In these documents, it is clearly mentioned that the church

379 Chupungco, Anscar O.S.B, 38.

380 Cf. Chupungco, Anscar O.S.B, 44-45.

381 Chupungco, Anscar O.S.B, 47-48.

in its missionary endeavour has constantly tried to insist on those principles of adaptation which alone could assure Christianity's success in those countries outside Europe. Propaganda Fide insisted on the need for evangelisers to respect the cultures of the peoples evangelised, so that they might accept Christianity and be able to regard it as their own. Missionaries were told by their founders to take time to study the languages and cultures of the people they were evangelising and to avoid as much as possible turning their converts into Asian or African-Europeans, but rather make them Asian and African Christians. In fact, the missionaries were advised to forget their own cultures and categories of thought so that they could adjust themselves better to the situation.[382]

Evangelisation of the American Indians

The revocation of the 15th century papal bull, *Inter Caetera,*[383] definitely announced before the world community that the Vatican no longer supported the principle of subjugation that it promulgated five and a half centuries ago. The Roman Catholic Church would be demonstrating its seriousness about respecting the rights and dignity of all peoples. The revocation of Inter Caetera was an extremely important spiritual and symbolic gesture of peace and healing in creating a culture of peace on earth. It is a fact that the European colonists were very cruel to the natives and considered them like animals. However, missionary activity has been a proven source of evangelical inculturation. The evangelisation of the American Indian in the sixteenth century, for example, represents an exemplary parable of the process of inculturating the Gospel. The missionaries rejected the model of Germanic[384] evangelisation and hoped to imitate the style of true Apostles: to refrain from using weapons, to respect the laws of the peoples, to defend the rights of the native inhabitants, to study and adapt to their psychology, to become familiar with their religious beliefs. However, the Spanish colonizers were violent and dishonest: a painful thorn of counter-witness. Nonetheless, the fact remains that evangelisation triumphed over immense problems.[385]

---

382 Waliggo, John Mary, Making a Church that is truly African, in Inculturation: Its Meaning and Emergency, Africa: St. Paul's Publications, 1986, 15.

383 Inter Caetera was a papal bull issued by Pope Alexander VI on 4 May 1493, which granted to Spain (the Crowns of Castle and Aragon) all lands to the "west and south" of a pole-to-pole line 100 leagues west and south of any of the islands of the Azores or the Cape Verde Islands.

384 The culture of central and northern Europe was tribal in nature. When a tribal chief or key elder embraced Christianity, mass conversions within that tribe often followed. The cultural disintegration came about, some anthropologists would say, because of the impact the "higher" culture had on the "lower" one, available from: http://home.snu.edu/~HCULBERT/400.htm, accessed on 19.01.2009.

385 Inculturation: available from http://www.ewtn.com/library/Montfort/Handbook/Incult.htm, accessed on 07.01.2009.

The Model of Matteo Ricci for China

As early as in the 16th century the Italian Jesuit missionary Fr. Matteo Ricci was fully convinced that to make any impact on a sophisticated culture, he had not only to learn the language but also to adapt himself to the way of life of the people. He realised that if Christianity were to enter deeply into the life of China, it had to find points of contact with Confucianism. He was one of the few missionaries allowed to enter the Chinese society. It was something unheard of in those days because the Chinese people were not welcoming to foreign cultures. He transcended his status as a foreigner by mastering the Chinese language and the Confucian literary classics. The imperial court and the educated class recognized him as a distinguished scholar. He wore the appropriate attire for a Chinese scholar, silk dresses and published works on such topics as astronomy, science and philosophy. He was particularly admired for his map-making skills as well as for being an accomplished teacher of mnemonic techniques, that is, ways of memorizing things. Through his knowledge of mathematics and science, Ricci managed to gain entry into the intellectual circles of China even up to the emperor himself.[386]

Ricci did not initially concern himself with making many converts. As a Confucian scholar he was convinced that the ethical precepts of Confucianism were reconcilable with Christian morality. He attempted reconciling the Gospel with Confucianism which played an important role in Chinese culture. He was highly regarded by the Chinese. At his death, at age 58, hundreds paid their respects. The emperor decreed that he be buried in a special tomb, an unheard of honour for a foreigner and even rare for any Chinese. Ricci's entire project was however rejected by the Vatican I and many, even within the Church, considered the activities and views of Ricci as derogatory to the Church Teachings. As there were not many converts to Christianity in China Ricci was considered a total failure by the Church.[387]

The Model of Roberto de Nobili for India

In the 17th century, the Italian Jesuit missionary Roberto de Nobili (1577-1656) understood that if he wanted to convert Hindus to Christianity he had to change his western ways of life. He observed that the *sadhus* (Hindu religious mendicant) and Brahmins were highly respected in the society. He also noticed that generally the Portuguese foreigners, *parangis,* as they were known, were poorly regarded; and were looked down. The local elite found the Europeans' leather shoes, alcohol consumption and carnivorous diet rather offensive. That was compounded by the foreigners' disdain for the indigenous religion and culture. They were therefore kept

---

386 Cf. Inculturation, Enculturation, the soft method, available from: http://ssubbanna.sulekha.com/blog/post/2008/05/inculturation, accessed on 07.12.2008.

387 Cf. Inculturation, Enculturation, the soft method.

on the outer fringe of the respectable society. De Nobili reckoned that converting only the illiterate and the lower classes of Indian society brought no credit to Christ. It seemed to him that if Christianity was to be a credible religion in India, it was imperative to convert educated upper class and Brahmin scholars. That would help him serve his mission better. Having that in view, he tried entering in to the core of the orthodox Hindu society. He distanced himself from the image the people had about the uncouth Portuguese. He presented himself asa *kshatriya,* (warrior caste, one of the castes of the Hindu society a *Raja-sanyasi,* kingly, Hindu religious mendicant from the country of Rome). People of Madurai (a district in Tamil Nadu, India) did take notice of him but could not appreciate the strange amalgam of a foreigner, a *kshatriya* and a *sanyasi* spreading the message of an alien god. He remained at best an object of curiosity and was not taken seriously.[388] The Hindu society had taken for granted that all foreigners were Christians and the Hindus were deeply rooted in their religion. The Brahmins were/are the priestly class and they had to keep the Hindu religion. There was no easy way to convert them.

De Nobili was of the opinion that the adoption of brahmanical customs was the only way in which Christian faith could be presented to the people in India. He insisted that his method was in accordance with the practices of the early Church; whatever was not directly contrary to the Gospel could be employed in its service.[389]

Opposition to Inculturation, and Uniformity of Culture

In the early 17thcentury, the inquisition and those who advocated a narrow view of the missions objected to the inculturation methods of Matteo Ricci in China and Roberto de Nobili in India. From the Council of Trent onwards Catholic renewal stressed the necessity of uniformity. Thus, inculturation was not within the framework of uniformity of the Church. The achievements of these missionaries were lost to Catholicism because by then the Church became a Latinised Church. The Latin rite became the rule for all evangelised by the Latin Church. Uniformity was aimed at discouraging future dissensions and divisions within the Church. Christian doctrine was clearly defined and *anathemas* (formal ecclesiastical ban, curse, or excommunication) attached to each of them.[390]

The hierarchical Church had the fear of losing her identity. Any kind of adaptation and indigenisation of Christianity in a particular culture, and if it assimilated even the values, good elements and inspiring practices of another

388 Inculturation...Enculturation ...the soft method, available from: http://ssubbanna.sulekha.com/blog/post/2008/05/inculturation, accessed on 07.12.2008.

389 Inculturation...Enculturation ...the soft method, available from: http://ssubbanna.sulekha.com/blog/post/2008/05/inculturation, accessed on 07.12.2008.

390 Waliggo, John Mary, Making a Church that is truly African, in Inculturation: Its Meaning and Emergency, Africa: St. Paul's Publications, 1986, 16-17.

religion, would lead to losing the distinctive character of the Church. The missionaries were advised to preach a 'pure' and 'simple' Gospel divested of any sociological garb and cultural expressions. In other words, one was to preach the Gospel with a socio-cultural expression of Western Europe dating back to the middle ages. In order to save the purity of Gospel, to preserve the identity of Christianity, to safeguard doctrinal orthodoxy, and to avoid the dangers of syncretism, superstition and doctrinal compromise, the missionaries had to avoid indigenisation. In the process, a western cultural form of Christianity was imposed.[391] Therefore, western form of Christianity was the Christian culture.

3.7. Goal of Inculturation

We need to have a definite goal as to why we need inculturation in our context. The theologian's task consists in re-thinking and re-expressing the original Christian message in the given cultural milieu. In fact, it is the task of every Christian. The task is that of confronting the Christian faith and local culture. In this process there is interpenetration of both; integration of faith and culture and from it, is born a new theological expression that is local and Christian.

3.7.1. Inculturation as Unifying Factor

The attitude for inculturation should be that of Jesus. He did not cling to his equality with God but humbled himself and became a slave and accepted death and death on a cross (Phil 2:5-6). Fr Pedro Arrupe says, "Inculturation may be looked at from many view points and seen at different levels, which must be distinguished but cannot be separated. Yet amid the multiple formulations of the problem which we have to reckon with the fundamental and constantly valid principle is that inculturation is the insertion of Christian life and the Christian message in a particular context in such a way that the experience not only finds expression through elements proper to the culture in question but become a principle that animates, directs and unifies the culture, transforming and making it so as to bring about a new creation."[392]

3.7.2. Inculturation as Participation in the Paschal Mystery

Inculturation is based on the mystery of the Church which is analogically modelled upon the mystery of incarnation. This incarnation is a not a simple incarnation but a redemptive one. Inculturation recognises the presence of evil in the world, the reality of sin and its implications in all realities of the world and human life. "For our sake God made the sinless into sin, so that in him we might become the goodness of God" (2 Cor. 5:21). He took upon Himself

391 Amalorpavadass, Duraiswami Simon, Gospel and Culture, Bangalore: National Biblical Catechetical and Liturgical Centre, 1978, 12.

392 Arrupe, Pedro S.J., "Letter on Inculturation" in Aixila, Jerome (Ed), Jesuit Formation and Inculturation in India Today, Delhi: 1978, 181-82.

the whole of humanity and redeemed them through his death and resurrection. Hence, the Church is a community of those who have died and risen with Christ by being identified with his body. The Church has to live the paschal mystery in her life and mission as an on-going reality. Any authentic inculturation will reject false doctrines, superstitions, all forms of sin and evil. Nothing can be integrated into theology, liturgy and spirituality unless they have values in them and unless they can survive a prophetic critique and unless they acquire a Christian meaning through a Christian interpretation.[393]

Inculturation is a process by which the church joins the paschal journey of the poor and acquires the faith, the hope and the love by which the simple folk of all faiths anticipate, in small daily glimpses, the glory that awaits them on the threshold of failure and frustration. A church that is part of the struggle, a struggle which requires the church's withdrawal from or rejection by the power structures of a country, is truly inculturated.[394]

3.7.3. The Kingdom of God More than the Church

We believe that Christ is the total, ultimate and definite revelation of God, and even though this Christ is present in the Church, we should not identify Christ with the Church. He is not imprisoned in the Church. Self-sufficiency can be attributed only to God and to Christ but not to the Church. Like every other sign it is less than the reality; the Kingdom is present in the Church, but the Church and the Kingdom are not identical. The Church is in continuous pilgrimage and tends towards fullness and total consummation. The Church has to be open to an ever-widening fellowship and dynamism towards universality. That means also that the Church can and should borrow from other religions, their customs, traditions, their wisdom their art and science which can contribute to the glory of God. Though this may be difficult for many Catholics due to their earlier training by which they were made to think that the other religions are erroneous, idolatrous and superstitious. Thus, inculturation realises the Church's universality, fullness and unity.[395] Inculturation is complete when we are able to experience the Kingdom of God within us. That is by being among the poor and thus by being with Jesus and about the work of Jesus. To incarnationally live this life is to be announcing the Kingdom of God.

393 Amalorpavadass, Duraiswami Simon, Gospel and Culture, Bangalore: National Biblical Catechetical and Liturgical Centre, 1978, 36-37.

394 Pieris, Aloysius SJ, Inculturation as a Missionary/Evangelical Presence in a Religiously Plural Society, available from: http://eapi.admu.edu.ph/eapr95/pieris.htm, accessed on 08.01.2009.

395 Amalorpavadass, Duraiswami Simon, Gospel and Culture, Bangalore: National Biblical Catechetical and Liturgical Centre, 1978, 38-40.

Conclusion

Universality can be realised through particularities and localisations, unity through variety, and pluriformity, and authenticity through freedom and originality. Even though God is universal and eternal, transcending time and space, the encounters between God and human beings have been particular and specific. He revealed himself to particular persons and groups in a particular place and time, within a specific socio-cultural milieu. So also, inculturation supposes particular cultural expressions in all domains. Universality and unity are to be found at the core of realities: God, Spirit, the Gospel and faith; it is concerned with every aspect of the Church's life and with every sector of its activity. It implies creativity, originality, dynamism, community responsibility and relevance. Therefore, inculturation challenges our whole life and our whole surrounding.[396]

The Spirit of God is no religion's monopoly but present in every human heart. Similarly, the saints, to whatever religious traditions they belong, Sri Ramakrishna Paramahamsa (a famous mystic of nineteenth century India), Mahatma Gandhi, Mother Teresa and Jesus Christ now free of time space limitations of earthly existence, are present to every human being. What God has already accomplished through the death and resurrection of Jesus Christ is for all human beings. Therefore, evangelization is mostly inter-religious dialogue, inquiring from other religious followers how God has spoken to them in history and is present to them in their traditions.[397]

Inculturation must be a constant of all theology and ministry, whether in the rain forests or Sahara Desert of Africa, or amid the skyscrapers and slums of New York or Rio. In Latin America they have set the gospel and the Christian tradition over against their contemporary political, religious, and social situation. Their reflection has moved them to confirm the good in the culture and the church. In this way both culture and church can approach more closely the vision of the kingdom.[398] "Each tradition is understandable only within its proper background, and any pretension to universality is itself particular. This affirmation is the core of contextual theology."[399] A good understanding of inculturation can lead us to a meaningful contextual theology, which is a necessary element for the Santals.

"If you want to make a thing real, make it local." G. K. Chesterton.

396 Amalorpavadass, Duraiswami Simon, Gospel and Culture, Bangalore: National Biblical Catechetical and Liturgical Centre, 1978, 43-54.

397 Chethimattam, John B(Ed), Inculturating Our Theological Thinking, in Jeevadhara Vol. XXX No. 179, Sep. 2000, 436.

398 Schineller, Peter, SJ, A Handbook on Inculturation, 97.

399 Padinjarekuttu, Isaac, "George Soares-Prabhu S.J. and the Quest for a Contextual Theology" in Soares-Prabhu George S.J., Biblical Themes for a Contextual Theology by., Pune: Jnana-Deepa Vidyapeeth Theology series, 1999, xx.

4

Contextual Theology
A New Way for the Santals

The challenge of the living God and man's response to it today cannot be judged by the yardstick of petrified formulae derived from earlier ages. Rather it should be the other way round. The value of tradition must be assessed in the light of God's contemporary word.[400]

4.1. Introduction

There is an Indian story: "Once a parachutist found himself caught up in a storm and he was swept off several kilometres away from his scheduled location. He landed somewhere on the top of a tree, and was only too happy that his life was saved. He saw someone passing by, called out to him and asked, "Sir, could you tell me where I am?" Back came the answer, "You are on the top of a tree!" At this, the parachutist asked, "Are you a theologian?" The other man was wonder struck. He asked the parachutist, "Yes, I am, but how do you know that?" The parachutist replied, "Oh that is easy, because what you said is correct, but useless!"[401]

We live in a time in which the entire human situation must be explored, a time in which our perspective must move from the particular to the universal because universalism is abstract; particularity is concrete. This move implies a serious encounter with ethnic theological programmes everywhere. The context of belief, life and action must now be given priority. Different contexts demand different theologies. It is imperative to have a theology from the perspective of

400 Sebastian Kappen, available from: http://en.wikipedia.org/wiki/Sebastian_Kappen, accessed on 26.02.08.

401 Wilfred, Felix, On the Banks of Ganges (Doing Contextual Theology), Delhi: ISPCK, 2002, ix.

the specific history, needs, and vision of a particular group insofar as such a voice has been repressed and absent. Insofar as it makes an essential contribution to the universality of Christian theology, it can become truly universal only through the concrete incorporation of the various particularities, not through the external imposition of a particular theology.

Theology can become absurd and futile when it fails to focus itself in a particular place. We may say that in the traditional understanding theology would be a theology "on top of the tree", on the clouds, away from the reality of the people. Every theology ought to be contextual within its specific location. Time and space are very fundamental categories that define our concrete human existence. Equally important is the question of space and context. The location of theology is very important.[402] The location in which I want to concentrate is not general India which is very vast; I focus on a very particular region related to the Santal tribe.

Christianity in India is considered as a 'foreign religion' even after many centuries of its existence in India. In the past few decades, especially inspired by the renewal of theology at Vatican II, there has been a theological quest to 'incarnate' the Church in India. There is an ever-growing, ever-strengthening plea to make the church 'fully Indian and authentically Christian.' The multi-religious, multi-cultural and multi-caste context of Indian society and the Indian Church call for an ever-renewed ecclesiological reflection so that the Church in India can be the salt of the earth in India, a true witness of Jesus and his Gospel. There is talk about 'A New Way of Being Church.'[403] In spite of the many good things that are prevalent and done for them there are still many problems and difficulties which we need to challenge. We know that the early understanding of theology was quite different from what it is today or it has to be different. We have to interpret theology differently so that the tribal people benefit. Let the theologian not remain on the treetopinstead, he/she should try to understand the reality of the tribal people.

Tribal theology is a contextual theology. Like liberation theology, it is theology from "below" "underside of history." It seeks to reflect on the faith experience of the tribal people and aims to liberate people from their inferiority complex, from oppressions and discriminations. To achieve this, it attempts to rediscover the liberative motifs in the tribal culture and reinterpret the Bible and Christian traditions. Hence, the focus and goal of tribal theology is liberation. It embraces social, economic, cultural, political and ecological dimensions. In the process of working at their own liberation, the tribal people pursue the liberation

402 Cf. Wilfred, Felix, On the Banks of Ganges (Doing Contextual Theology), Ix.

403 Fox, Thomas C, Pentecost in Asia: A New Way of Being Church, New York: Orbis Books, 2002.

of both the oppressors and the oppressed. Therefore, it is a theology that includes liberation of the whole humanity and of God's creation.[404]

4.2. Theology: Definition

Traditionally theology was understood as "faith seeking understanding." Two important elements in this understanding were "wisdom" and "rational knowledge." Theological reflection – that is, the understanding of faith – arises spontaneously and inevitably in the believer, in all those who have accepted the gift of the Word of God. Theology is intrinsic to a life of faith seeking to be authentic and complete and is, therefore, essential to the common consideration of this faith in the ecclesial community. There is present in *all believers* – and more so in every Christian community – a rough outline of a theology.[405]

The function of theology as critical reflection on praxis has its roots in the first centuries of the church. It was deeply rooted in the life and culture of the people. In fact, the Augustinian theology is based on a true analysis of the signs of the times. Faith is understood as an act of trust, a going out of one's self, a commitment to God and neighbour, a relationship with others. Faith is the total human response to God who saves through love. It is a commitment to God and neighbour, a relationship with others. Theology becomes critical reflection on humankind, on basic human principles. It is to reflect upon the presence and action of the Christian in the world. It implies openness to the world, gathering the questions it poses, being attentive to historical transformations. Reflection in the light of faith must constantly accompany pastoral action of the Church. It fulfils a prophetic function as it interprets historical events with the intention of revealing and proclaiming their profound meaning.[406]

4.2.1. Classical Task of Theology

Two functions of theology were considered classical: theology as wisdom and theology as rational knowledge. In the early centuries of the Church, theology was closely linked to the spiritual life. It was essentially a meditation on the Bible, geared toward spiritual growth. This theology was above all monastic and therefore characterized by a spiritual life removed from worldly concerns. It offered a model for every Christian wanting to attain spiritual perfection.[407]

The traditional discursive orientation of classicist theological methodologies which are invariably metaphysical in orientation, have traditionally focused upon wisdom *(sapientia)* or rational knowledge *(scientia),* and are often detached from the daily living experiences of its target audience. "This theology used Platonic and Neoplatonic categories. In these philosophies it found a metaphysics which

404 Parapullil, Anthony, SJ, "Tribal Theology", Sevartham Vol. 2, 1977, 28.

405 Gutierrez, Gustavo, A Theology of Liberation, Maryknoll: Orbis Books, 1993, 3.

406 Gutierrez, Gustavo, A Theology of Liberation, 10-11.

407 Gutierrez, Gustavo, A Theology of Liberation, 4.

stressed the existence of a higher world and the transcendence of an Absolute from which everything came and to which everything returned. The present life was regarded as essentially contingent and was not valued sufficiently."[408]

Theology as rational knowledge may be associated mainly with saints Albert the Great and Thomas Aquinas. Thomas Aquinas' view was based on Aristotelian categories and he said that theology was not only a science but also wisdom flowing from the charity which unites a person to God. According to him, theology was an intellectual discipline, born of the meeting of faith and reason. In this sense, theology may be regarded not as a science but as rational knowledge. The function of theology as rational knowledge is permanent because of the meeting between faith and reason. Reason has in today's context more manifestations than philosophical ones. The understanding of faith too is following new paths today, namely, the social, psychological and biological sciences. The social sciences are very important in today's context.[409]

4.2.2. Theology: Away from the Context

Although, Christianity was born in Asia and reached Europe only later, the present day Churches of Asia have their source in the missionary zeal of the European and North American churches. Their labours gave birth to Christian communities in Asia. But, oftentimes in many countries the missionaries went hand in hand with colonizers, both traders and soldiers. For example in India, the foreign missionaries had to be chaplains of the soldiers and officers who were oppressing Indians. Hence, they could not but be partially tainted by the designs of the searchers for gold, spices, land, slaves and colonies. They were zealous for souls, but they tended to think that the commercial and military expansion of western peoples was a providential opportunity for the salvation of souls and the spread of the evangelical message. All that mattered was baptising the ′infidels and pagans` and not what happened to their material or cultural well-being.[410]

Missiologists were aware of the need to contextualize theology in every culture. In practice, their success has been limited because of the identification of Christian theology with the Western philosophical worldview. Merged with this view was the imperialist view of the Western world as the highest form of thinking. Then it was understood that the rest of the world should be taught to think in the same way in order to truly comprehend the reality. It was understood that the Bible represents the revelation of God contextualized in the Hebrew and

408 Gutierrez, Gustavo, A Theology of Liberation, 4.

409 Gutierrez, Gustavo, A Theology of Liberation, 4-5.

410 Balasundaram, Franklyn J, Contemporary Asian Christian Theology, Bangalore: ISPCK, 1998, 5.

Hellenized Hebrew cultures. But this perspective was confined to one culture and it took many years to accept other cultures as important.[411]

The missionaries thought of spreading Christianity in terms of transporting the institutions of their Euro-American churches with the framework of imperial destination. In the process, the new Christians were segregated from their fellow human beings, alienated from the traditional religions, cultural heritage and their community way of life. The liturgy was imported wholesale from the "mother churches." The ecclesiastical structures and theology too were imported. Western theology was overly concerned with content. Dogmatic theology defines divine doctrine, unalterable whether one theologizes in Rio, Rome, Rwanda or in a tribal village in India.[412]

> In the early phases of Western expansion, the churches were allies in the colonisation process. They spread under the aegis of colonial powers: they benefited from the expansion of empire. In return, they rendered a special service to western imperialism by legitimising it and accustoming their new adherents to accept compensatory expectations of an eternal reward for terrestrial misfortunes including colonial expansion. The gospel was thus used as an agency for a softening of national resistance to the plunder by the foreigners and a domestication of the minds and cultures of the dominated converts.[413]

God of Mammon and Universalism

The great Western expansion was characterized by the unquestioned syncretistic mixture of the gods of Mammon and the Christian God of eternal life. Since the Constantinian inversion, the syncretism had been developing in Western Christianity. The Empire and the Kingdom were fused into one coherent though contradictory cosmo-vision. In this strange synthesis, there was a curious mixture and interdependency of God and gold, material wealth and salvation, earthly property and heaven, charity and cruelty, love and violence, enslavement and emancipation, military power and spiritual power, church and state.[414]

Theology as developed in Europe and America is limited in its approach. A "universal" arising from the experience of a small sample is a myth. Christian theologians so unaware of the thought and belief of peoples elsewhere in the world make only false claims to universalism. There is no completely universal perspective, since all human thought and belief are limited by structural bounds.

411 Gill, Kenneth D., Toward a Contextualized Theology for the Third World, Frankfurt: Peter Lang, 1994, 241.

412 Balasundaram, Franklyn J, Contemporary Asian Christian Theology, 6.

413 Balasundaram, Franklyn J, Contemporary Asian Christian Theology, 6.

414 Boff, Leonardo and Elizondo, Virgil (Eds), Any Room for Christ in Asia? Maryknoll: Orbis Books, viii.

However, there can be openness to the universal. When it is objected that we are dealing with a universal revelation, we must raise the issue of finite human understanding, through which God's self-disclosure is communicated. The eventual locus of divine revelation is our personal, social, cultural, and ethnic existence.[415]

European theology lacks self-criticism in its accomplishments and to the historical anachronism because it still thinks what was useful once upon a time should be always useful. Such an outlook implies that theology is profoundly ahistorical. Such a theology was not conscious that it was theologizing from the vantage point of the geopolitical centre of the world. It failed to see that the world is not identical with the centre and cannot be understood from the standpoint of the centre.[416]

Clash of Civilization and Colonisation

It is ironic that Christianity, with its roots in the Middle East, has come to be considered by most contemporary Asians as a foreign religion, a product of Western colonial expansion (there are some exceptions – the Orthodox churches and the Syro-Malabar Church. But unfortunately, the Syro-Malabar Church has become more Roman than the Roman Church). In recent decades, the growth of anti-Western feeling throughout Asia has meant that Christianity had to dispose of its Western baggage and leadership, and to develop forms more palatable to an Asian population. Since Christianity is directly associated with the West, the same suspicion and mistrust is extended to the local Christian communities. Thus, it is a common experience to see a church bombed or Christians attacked in an Asian country, as a reaction to foreign policies of the Western countries. The local church stands right in the middle of a clash of civilizations. We have to undergo this is the experience today in Jharkhand state.

The theology of the Christian churches during the colonial period suited the colonization process and further supported the colonization. The sense of military and commercial superiority of the European people was underpinned with the view that Christianity was superior to other religions which had to be replaced by the "truth." The western theology could plunder the Asian continent with its people and civilization. Thus, the Church in Asia during the colonial and post-colonial period served as a handmaid of the imperial powers and thus could not be in any way prophetic and in fact misused its prophetic office and was not faithful to its calling. The reasons why the Church today is often persecuted in non-Western societies are of course complex. The principal reason is "alienation," of which there are two main levels: spiritual and cultural. There is nothing we can do about spiritual alienation since it comes with the distinctiveness of the Cross. However, most of the problem of cultural alienation is correctable because

415 Balasundaram, Franklyn J, Contemporary Asian Christian Theology, 7.

416 Sobrino, Jon, The Church and the Poor, London: SCM Press, 1985, 36.

it comes from unwise missiological methodologies of foreign evangelists and from the way the newly found local church forms her sub-cultural identity.[417]

Christian theologians may generally be numbered among the colonizers of the peoples of the Third World. Many have been "God's colonizers" not by intention but by default; the results have been the same. As a theologian, Albert Schweitzer went beyond most of his peers in his involvement in Africa. Paradoxically, it is the manifestation of this European mind, set in an African context, which dramatizes that his philosophy of civilization is pro-Western. Aristotelian logic and Platonic dualism do not exhaust the thought-structures of the human race. It is arrogant for persons who have been exposed only to these categories of thought and their derivatives to speak *ex cathedra* (from the chair, the Chair of Peter) for all Christians. Non-Western religions were often dismissed as heathen; the highest compliment was to accept such a religion as a preparation for the gospel. Western missionaries were not aware that the very gospel which they sought to transplant was blighted by the "Constantinian captivity" of the church. In their pharisaic approach, they did not observe anything of worth in other religions or in the cultures that sustained them.[418]

Misrepresentation of Jesus

According to Fr. Tissa Balasurya O.M.I. (Oblates of Mary Immaculate), Jesus is one of the most represented and misunderstood person in Asia. Jesus was presented to Asia in modern times in the manner he was thought of in modern Western Europe and later North America. This understanding of Jesus suited the Christian religious institutions which had become the handmaid of the Roman Emperors and later on medieval feudal lords and rulers, including the Papal States. The Christians regarded the western Expansion as a God given opportunity for missionary activity. In the process they neglected liberation from social exploitation. Thus, Jesus was seen as the one who had to redeem the human race from the consequences of the original sin of Adam. His life and death were seen as an act of obedience to the will of God rather than as a logical working out of his own personal options made in the context of the society of his time. His love for the underprivileged and marginalised of society and the consequential liberative process were almost bypassed.[419] I think such an understanding neglected the gospel narratives. In the gospel we see the life and death of Jesus within the social and political context of his time and place.

Jesus was seen from an individualistic point of view and one had to attain one's salvation by doing good to others. The highest form of doing good was realized in converting people to Christianity. The mission of Christ was in relation to the Church and the Church became the unique means of salvation.

417 Cf. Balasundaram, Franklyn J, Contemporary Asian Christian Theology, 6.

418 Balasundaram, Franklyn J, Contemporary Asian Christian Theology 6-7.

419 Cf. Balasundaram, Franklyn J, Contemporary Asian Christian Theology, 20.

Christ was said to reside within the Church. The understanding of Jesus became as the sweet Jesus, meek and humble, obedient unto death like a lamb. Thus, Jesus was presented as a conformist, domesticated and apolitical person. Jesus was considered as an enemy of modernity, democracy, socialism, the struggle of the proletariat for social justice. Human beings were supposed to accept all problems and difficulties as the will of God and they would get their eternal reward in the next world. These people had no option other than accept the reality of life as it was because if they protested against the injustice done to them they would be denying the salvation promised to them. Was Jesus such a passive, anti-social, anti-human, conformist as he has been made out to be, during so many centuries?[420]

4.3. Need for Contextual Theology

Contextual theology is not another/separate subject at all. It is a way of doing theology that begins with the experience of a community. It is a way of discerning God's presence in a people and in a concrete situation. Contextual theology is not one particular theology or method but it is theology by its very nature. It is an ongoing and transforming process for teacher, student, church, society. It is a radical critique of theological suppositions and existing models. It is a challenge to the institution and to our way of being church in our own context.[421]

Contextual theologies are different interpretations of life, which are distinguished through a common view of the method of theology. Contextual theologies have grown up on the continents of the globe since the demand for the contextualization was formulated in 1973. Christians in different regions have developed the concept formation of the word context in relation to the notion theology according to their own geographical situation.[422] Traditional theology is a response to western demands, and people's (contextual/tribal) theology is a response to dehumanization and colonialism. Traditional theology rejects local belief and culture while people's theology respects local culture.

"The Latin American liberation theology may be considered a contextual theology without hesitation because the base communities and the theologians shape it in an indissoluble integration with a political situation of conflict and thereby independently make use of sociological theories."[423]

Theology today must take into consideration context for various reasons. The factors involved in this are external and internal factors. External factors consist in historical events, intellectual currents, cultural shifts and political

---

420 Balasundaram, Franklyn J, Contemporary Asian Christian Theology, 20-21.

421 Yun-Ka Tan, Jonathan, Theologizing at the Service of Life: The Contextual Theological Methodology of FABC, FABC Papers No. 108, accessed on 08.03.2008, available from: http://www.ucanews.com/ html/fabc-papers/fabc-0.htm.

422 Bergmann, Sigurd, *God in Context: A Survey on Contextual Theology*, Burlington: Ashgate Publishing Company, 2003, 32.

423 Bergmann, Sigurd, *God in Context: A Survey on Contextual Theology*, 32.

forces. The external factor is related to the general dissatisfaction all over the world with classical approaches to theology. Many theologians have abandoned philosophy as a basis for theology. These external factors bring to light some internal factors which are essential factors for doing theology in context. This factor is the incarnational nature of Christianity. God became human so that God could grasp the human nature and communicate with humanity meaningfully.[424] Therefore, contextual theology is a necessary aspect to express our nearness to God and humanity.

4.3.1. Historical Development of Contextual Theologies

As far back as the Book of Exodus, The Book of Prophets (especially Amos), the Old Testament, and the Book of Beatitudes, the Christian message has been reflected and interpreted as a means of liberation of the poor. In Latin America, the first call for the Church to address policy issues came at the turn of the 15th century, when Pope Alexander VI granted control of the Latin American church to the kings of Spain and Portugal in exchange for political support of papal political endeavours in Europe. Then in 1537, Pope Paul III declared the American natives "truly human." In early industrial Europe, the Church also took position in 1891 with Pope Leo XIII's encyclical letter *Rerum Novarum* (New Things) which dealt with the conditions of the European working class.[425]

The history of the theological developments of the Christian Church documents is an ongoing tension. On the one hand there is need to keep the teachings of Jesus and the apostles intact and passing them on to the next generation of believers. On the other hand, there is the obligation of preaching the Gospel to every creature. The tension arises because of making the Gospel relevant to particular worldviews and cultures. This tension existed from the very beginning of the primitive Church too as the Gospel was brought to the Gentiles. Christian leaders in the more dominant cultures attempted to impose their concepts on the Church. The situation was complicated because the Gospel was spread to different groups and nationalities in the world.[426]

In Latin America

> Latin American Liberation theology was born at the crossroads of a changing Catholic Church and the revolutionary political-economic ferment of the late 1960s and early 1970s. In the first case, the second Vatican Council (1962-65) opened the door for a fundamental

424 Bevans, Stephen B., Models of Contextual Theology, New York: Orbis Books, 1994, 5-6.

425 Cf. Jean-Pierre Cloutier, Theologies: Liberation Vs Submission, accessed on 08.04.2008, available from: http://www.cyberie.qc.ca/jpc/haiti/theology.html.

426 Gill, Kenneth D., Toward a Contextualized Theology for the Third World, Frankfurt: Peter Lang, 1994, 241.

rethinking of the relation between Christian faith and the world by asserting the value of secular historical as part of God's work.[427]

The modern wave of liberation theology, however, dates back to the sixties and originates in Latin America where it is intertwined with direct political action. Significantly, Latin America was the cradle of colonial Christianity but the anti-imperialist guerrilla phenomenon burgeoning at the time forced individuals or groups, including members of the clergy, into radical involvement. A current emerged from this radicalism, revolution theology, the vibrant symbol of which was a Colombian priest Camilo Torres, killed in 1966 as he was fighting at the side of rebel groups. But the movement gained momentum after the Vatican Council II, which was held in late 1965 under Pope Paul VI. Emphasis in the debates had been put on the Church being the people of God, and on the Bible being the corner stone of Christian doctrine. This was somewhat of a change in doctrinal attitude because the Church had been based on a rigid hierarchy having the Pope at the summit of the pyramid, and second, it revalorized the presence of God in historical terms. Before the Council, a saying existed in the Roman Catholic Church that exemplified Rome's undisputed authority: *Roma locuta, causa finita* (Rome has spoken, the case is settled). But after Vatican II, some sectors of the Church felt empowered with more autonomy that they had previously experienced. At the time, then-Bishop Karol Wojtyla from Poland had championed the reforms. After his election to the Holy See, his first trip was to Puebla, Mexico, to address the first conference of Latin American bishops in almost 20 years. He was later to halt liberalization, after his election as Pope John Paul II.[428]

In the late 60s, a new social and intellectual movement appeared on the Latin American continent. The movement is rooted in the Christian faith and Scriptures and seeks its ideological superstructure based on the religious reflection in close association with the Church organization. It is typical not only for Latin America but for the entire Third World, the social situation of oppression. Members of the religious orders are committed to the vow of poverty and do not own property individually, nevertheless they enjoy a standard of living and security that separates them from the daily agony of the poor. The question then arose for some of them: What is the ideal of poverty in a situation where most people are suffering dehumanizing poverty and what should the Church and Christians do about it? Liberation theology thus emerged as a result of a systematic, disciplined reflection on Christian faith and its implications. The theologians who formulated liberation theology usually do not teach in universities and seminaries; they are a small group of Catholic or Protestant clergy and have direct contact with the grassroots groups as advisors to priests, nuns or pastors. Since they spend at least

427 Petrella, Ivan, The Future of Liberation Theology, London: SCM Press, 2006, 1.

428 Jean-Pierre Cloutier, Theologies: Liberation Vs Submission.

some time working directly with the poor themselves, the questions they deal with arise out of their direct contact with the poor.[429]

In Asia

> As Asians, our mode of thinking is unitive rather than analytic, experiential rather than representational, existentialist rather than essentialist. The dichotomies western thought has thrown up — matter and spirit, faith and reason, nature and grace, temporal and eternal, human and divine, and the like — are foreign to us. For us thinking is communing, not conquering; is being present to what presents itself, not re-presenting it through concepts; is being one with the oneness of all, not exploding the one into the manifold. Our ancient seers would have questioned even the 'and' in the customary formulation, God and man, if taken in the additive, disjunctive sense; so finely attuned were they to the underlying oneness of the many. These cultural specificities are ignored by the church when she compels us, Asians, to think as do people in the West. What is this but cultural imperialism and colonisation of the mind?[430]

The quest for harmony in the task of theologizing in the Asian milieu is rooted in the FABC's firm belief that there is an Asian approach to reality, a world-view, wherein the whole is the sum-total of the web of relationships and interaction of the various parts with each other in a word, *harmony,* a word which resonates with all Asian cultures. Within the many Asian worldviews, harmony is perceived as "the spiritual pursuit of the totality of reality in its infinite diversity and radical unity" which "evolves by respecting the otherness of the other and by acknowledging its significance in relation to the totality." Harmony is also predicated upon the commonly-held view that since "the ultimate ground of being is unity-in-plurality, the divergent forms of reality [in the Asian milieu] are perceived in the convergent rhythm that harmonizes them."[431]

An important factor that helped the development of Indian theology is the experience of the 1960s and the 1970s. It was the time of the emergence of the so-called grassroots action-groups. The most important feature about these groups was that it consisted of people hailing from upper and middle class backgrounds. They were moved by the prevailing situation of injustice and oppression. Many of them renounced their bright prospective careers and chose to be in solidarity with the marginalized, and struggle for their liberation. These groups were spread all over India and took up issues of the people depending on their contexts. All

429 M. Hillar and H. R. Leuchtag, eds, Liberation Theology, Published in Humanism and Social Issues. Anthology of Essays, Houston: American Humanist Association, 1993, 35.

430 Sebastian Kappen, available from: http://en.wikipedia.org/wiki/Sebastian_Kappen.

431 Cf. Jonathan, Yun-Ka Tan, Theologizing at the Service of Life.

the groups imparted non-formal education to the people and lead them to the awareness of their bondage and exploitation. Since they were disillusioned by the unfulfilled promises of the political parties, they did not join any political parties. They wanted to work as volunteers for the marginalized people of the country.[432] These elements have also helped theology to be contextualised.

4.4. Basic Principles of Liberation Theology

Facing enormous problems in society, some theologians realized that the traditional theology concerned with religious dogmas and abstract religious concepts had no relevance in the present human society. It became an abstract speculation removed from the original spirit of the Gospel message and out of touch with real life. On the social level, it served the rich. They realized that if one really cared for and believed in the Christian ideals one had to answer the question: how to be a Christian in a concrete historical situation? The basic concerns in Latin America shifted thus from "whether one can believe what Christianity affirms to what relevance Christianity has in the struggle for a more just world." Out of such considerations was born "liberation theology" outlined for the first time by Peruvian theologian Gustavo Gutierrez O. P. (Dominican priest) a few weeks before the Medellín conference in 1968. Gutierrez defined theology as a "critical reflection on praxis in the light of the word of God." Liberation theology has two basic principles: first, it recognizes a need for liberation from any kind of oppression - political, economic, social, sexual, racial, and religious; second, it asserts that the theology must grow out of the basic Christian communities and should not be imposed from above, that is, from the infallible source book or from the *magisterium* of an infallible Church.[433]

4.4.1. Critical Reflection on Praxis

The basic principle of liberation theology is that it is a critical reflection on praxis in the light of faith. Leonardo and Clodovis Boff succinctly formulated: "Faith helps the Christian endorse and support those historical movements that have a greater affinity with the ideals of the gospel. Today, for example, we perceive that the Christian ideal is closer to socialism than to capitalism. It is not a matter of creating a Christian socialism. It is a matter of being able to say that the socialist system, when actually carried out in reality, enables Christians better to live the humanitarian and divine ideals of their faith."[434] Church has the duty to act as agent of liberation. It must attempt to articulate its words, its catechesis, its liturgy, its community action, and its interventions with established authority, in the direction of liberation.[435]

432 Wilfred, Felix, On the Banks of Ganges (Doing Contextual Theology), 85.

433 Petrella, Ivan, The Future of Liberation Theology, 1.

434 M. Hillar and H. R. Leuchtag, eds, Liberation Theology, 38.

435 M. Hillar and H. R. Leuchtag, eds, Liberation Theology, 39.

Liberation theology's foundational texts, those of its inception and expansion, were written from a particular worldview of critical reflection. They share the following presuppositions: (a) a sharp dichotomy between revolution and reformist political action, the first seen as necessary while the second is deemed as ineffectual or as an ideological smokescreen that supports the status quo; (b) the poor were seen as the primary, and at times exclusive, agents of social change; (c) a sharp dichotomy between socialism and capitalism, socialism as the social system that could remedy the injustice of the latter; (d) priority was given to politics in the narrow sense of struggle over state power, with little attention to issues of gender, ecology, race and popular culture.[436]

The term orthopraxis was coined by the liberation theologians as a counterpoint to insistence on orthodoxy, meaning correct belief. Liberation theologians argue that what is most fundamental is correct action - that is, effort leading to human liberation. Most liberation theologians say the accent on orthopraxis is a matter of balance. They wanted to remedy a centuries-long Christian inclination to overemphasize belief at the expense of action.[437] Gustavo Gutierrez said that the intention was not to deny the meaning of orthodoxy understood as proclamation of and reflection on statements considered to be true. Rather it was only to keep away from an obsolete tradition. It is also to recognize the work and importance of concrete behaviour, of deeds, of action, of praxis in the Christian life.[438]

Liberation theology is and will continue to be needed by the church and by the world as long as poverty and oppression exist. But what it means to believe in and work for a new society of justice is being expanded significantly in Latin America today. The revolutionary fervour of the 1980s has not abolished the gruelling poverty that some now call an economic holocaust for the poor in Nicaragua, Honduras, El Salvador, Guatemala and, more recently, Costa Rica. So this new generation of Latin American theologians is "rereading the Bible," searching for words to describe what Christians have traditionally called the "new creation", a transformation that ultimately alters the political and economic spheres, though it does not begin there.[439]

4.4.2. Social Analysis and Hope of the Poor

Liberation theology places a premium on social analysis. To remedy injustice, they believe, one must first understand the social mechanisms that produce it. To do this, many liberation theologians were drawn to Marxism. Critics found this alarming, insisting that one cannot distinguish between Marxist "science"

436 Petrella, Ivan, The Future of Liberation Theology, 1.

437 Cf. Gutierrez, Gustavo, A Theology of Liberation, xxxiv.

438 Gutierrez, Gustavo, A Theology of Liberation, 8.

439 Smith, Alex, Latin American Christians Reshape Liberation Theology, available from: http://www.villagelife.org/church/archives/pres_latinamerican.html, accessed on 10.04.2008.

and its ideological underpinnings, atheism, materialism and totalitarianism.[440] Liberationists see a hidden violence in social arrangements that create hunger and poverty. Thus, when critics accused theologians of advocating revolutionary violence (which most did not), they often responded: "But the church has always tolerated violence." They meant that by endorsing the status quo, church leaders were acquiescing in a system that did violence to millions of people (crusades, inquisition, counter-reformation, colonialism, etc.). Liberation theologians also argued that there is a social dimension that is more than the sum of individual acts. Examples frequently cited include neo-colonialism and the feudal nature of the relationship between the Latin American oligarchy and the peasants. By extension, the redemption from sin won by Christ must be more than the redemption of individual souls. It must redeem, transform the social realities of human life.[441]

In Latin America, the suffering of the people plays the active role in the process of understanding. Moreover, this suffering provides the authentic analogy for understanding God: the recognition that the present history of the world is the ongoing history of the suffering of God. At the crowning moments of divine revelation, there has always been suffering: the cry of the oppressed in Egypt (Exodus 3:7-8); the cry of Jesus on the cross (Mark 15:34); the birth pangs experienced by the whole of creation as it awaits liberation (Romans 8: 18-23). Thus, Latin American theology gives a privileged place to the cries of the oppressed.[442]

In Latin America, liberation theology has focused spontaneously on the historical Jesus for guidance and orientation. Since it arose out of the concrete experience and praxis of faith within a lived commitment to liberation, it soon realized that the universality of Christ amid those circumstances could only be grasped from the standpoint from the concrete Christ of history.[443] Therefore, they interpret Christian faith out of the suffering, struggle, and hope of the poor. It critiques society and ideologies sustaining it; pretends not to lay down specific rules for how to struggle for justice, but stresses that a responsible commitment with class conflict is an expression of love for one's neighbour. Through solidarity with the poor theologians of liberation advocate the transcendence from class division to a new type of society. It critiques the activity of the Church from the angle of the poor.[444]

The main theme, liberation, is considered at three levels of meaning which are interconnected. At the social and political level, liberation is an expression of aspirations of the oppressed classes and peoples. This liberation emphasizes

440 Gutierrez, Gustavo, A Theology of Liberation, 60.

441 Gutierrez, Gustavo, A Theology of Liberation, 103.

442 Sobrino, Jon, The Church and the Poor, 28.

443 Sobrino, Jon, Christology at the Crossroads, New York: Orbis Books, 1985, 10.

444 M. Hillar and H. R. Leuchtag, eds, Liberation Theology, 38.

the conflict in the economic, social and political process between the oppressed and the oppressors. At the human level, liberation is conceived as a historical process in which people consciously develop their own destiny through the social changes. At the religious, salvific level, liberation means liberation from sin, the ultimate source of all deviation from fraternity, of all injustice and oppression. It brings human beings back into communion with God and fellow human beings, which is radical, total liberation. For the first time sin was formulated in social terms as a concrete social act and not in traditional way as an abstract, and even an allegoric personification in the person of Satan, or at best, a personal act. For the first time the religious, salvific plan was explicitly linked to the human experience in a society. The perception of social reality is that it condemns the capitalistic system as the source of evils. The theological reading of social reality in the light of faith is based on the Bible.[445]

Latest figures published in the Encyclopaedia Britannica Book of the Year indicate that there are 1.06 billion Christians in the world. The West Indies, Central and South America have more than 400 million believers in the Bible, and although Liberation Theology has gained no stronghold in the Northern Hemisphere, except in Poland, it has developed into a major force within these people south of the U.S. border. It is also growing in influence in Africa. By the year 2000, half of Christianity was in the Third World countries, in countries where the majority are poor and for which Liberation Theology has more to offer than the traditional Theology of Submission. Submission to a state, to a highly hierarchal Church, leads the people to a fate of poverty and hunger.[446]

4.5. Asian Contextual Theology

From the various official documents of the FABC, one sees the development of a new way of doing theology with Asian resources in multi-religious, multi-ethnic, multi-lingual and pluri-cultural Asia, which may be described as the *contextualisation of* the salvific message of the Christian Gospel in the diverse and pluralistic Asian *Sitz-im-Leben.* Implicit in the FABC's contextual theological methodology is the acknowledgment and acceptance of a fundamental ontological, soteriological and existential relationship between the salvific message of the Christian Gospel and the Asian peoples with their rich religious and cultural traditions, as well as their daily socioeconomic challenges. As a new way ofdoing theology in the Asian milieu, the contextual theological methodology ofthe FABC seeks to theologize with Asian resources in response to the many pressing challenges which arise out of the concrete specificity of the diverse and pluralistic Asian life experiences.[447]

445 Cf. M. Hillar and H. R. Leuchtag, eds, Liberation Theology, 39.

446 Smith, Alex, Latin American Christians Reshape Liberation Theology.

447 Jonathan, Yun-Ka Tan, Theologizing at the Service of Life.

4.5.1. Indian Theologies

A major concern in the context of India is for the oppressed and subjugated people – the tribal people, Dalits, women and so on to recover their authentic selves. Liberation from poverty and economic exploitation is only one dimension of their life. It does not define the whole reality of the people. The alienation of their true selves and the loss of their dignity and identity has been the worst thing that has happened to them. The historical subjugation of women in India, even based on religious tradition, is something the Latin American theology cannot define, experience or offer to solve. However, the concern for liberation and the need to begin as a methodological starting point could be shared with liberation theology.[448] In the Indian context, we need to have more than one type of theology; Dalit theology and tribal theology take prime place.

Dalit theology is drawing attention today because it springs up from the experience of one of the most oppressed groups in the world today. The Dalits constitute 16.48% or about one fifth of India's population. They are the poorest of the poor among the 48% of Indian population living below the poverty line. The Dalits are marginalized in the villages and abandoned in the cities. The majority of the Christians, two thirds of all Indian Christians, are from the Dalits. The roots of Dalit theology lie in the experience of this most discriminated people. Being a Dalit is an experience different from that of slaves in the ancient world or serfs in the feudal society.[449] I am unable to describe the experience of the Dalits. I have only heard heart-rending stories of Dalits and have talked with them but I have never lived in their midst. I can only imagine how terrible it would be to undergo such inhuman treatment. A theology emerging from this group definitely should have some meaning for life.

The Dalits undergo oppression and discrimination in every sphere of their life. Their powerlessness lies in the political, economic and cultural fields. All these religiously legitimized and any vivid description of their misery, poverty and oppression will not actually reflect their real experiences. They are excluded from social contacts because they are considered as untouchables and they must live on the outskirts of the village because they cause impurity to the higher castes.[450] "In his work on Social Contract, Jean Jacques Rousseau made this famous statement: *'Man is born free, but he is in chains everywhere.'* Had he known about the Dalits, he would have refused to state, "man is born free." For here, is a portion of humanity, who is born not free but bonded, as stigmatised and designated by

448 Wilfred, Felix, On the Banks of Ganges, 100.

449 Cf. Wilfred, Felix, On the Banks of Ganges, 113.

450 Narrain, Siddharth, Justice for Dalits still a Dream, in *The Hindu* (Indian Newspaper) Thursday, May 11, 2006.

birth as untouchables. They carry the consequences of their birth, for which they have no responsibility.[451]

Tribal people are the most exploited and divided people in the world, perhaps as pitiable as the Dalits. Theirs is a history of defeat, suffering and oppression. Throughout generations, they suffered discrimination, genocide, exploitation and alienation. They lost their self-esteem because of conquest and slavery. In addition, in recent years, globalisation makes the situation worse; it causes further marginalisation to their continuity as people. Indigenous people suffer from suppression. Dominant societies do not listen to their cries and do not acknowledge their human rights and dignity making them resort to armed struggle. The dominant government, instead of recognizing the movements as a struggle for justice, attempts to silence the movements by hostility. Soldiers killed innocent people, raped their women and burned their villages to ashes.[452] One may think that these atrocities are not happening today but such human right violations have been going on endlessly.

Tribal theology came out of the experiences of various forms of injustice and exploitation. Their theology is an attempt to express Christian faith in socio-cultural, traditional and liturgical thought patterns of people. Tribal theology can be considered as resistance theology. It is a resistance to the destruction of the dignity of life, dances, songs and tribal people's spirituality. It emerges as a response to different forms of barbaric atrocities, human rights violations, ethnic conflicts, poverty, injustice, ecological destructions, and all that negate their identity as tribal people.

4.6. Basic Principles of Asian Contextual Theology

The task of Asian theologians is more complex than that of the theologians from Latin America. The Latin American theologians can communicate in the common idiom. The situation is not the same in Asia. Asians are not able to consult each other's theologies except in a non-Asian idiom, thus neutralizing the most promising feature in our methodology. We Asians professionally theologize in English; it is the language in which most of us think, act, read and even pray. The many languages of the continent remain a barrier to really discover the true Asian theology.[453] However, we need to understand the context and make efforts to personalise the reality of the people with whom we live and share our life with them. Without such an effort, no Asian contextual theology is possible.

451 Wilfred, Felix, On the Banks of Ganges, 136.

452 Ahmed, Syed Khalique, Rape of the Tribal, in *Indian Express* (Indian Newspaper) Monday, December 14, 1998.

453 Cf. Pieris, Aloysius SJ, An Asian Theology of Liberation, Edinburgh: T&T Clark, 1988, 71.

4.6.1. Third Worldness (Asian Character)

> Any discussion about Asian theology has to move between two poles: the *Third Worldness* of our continent and its peculiarly *Asian* character. More realistically and precisely, the common denominator linking Asia with the rest of the Third World is its overwhelming poverty. The specific character defining Asia within the other poor countries is its multifaceted religiousness. These two inseparable realities constitute in their interpretation what might be designated as the *Asian Context*, the matrix of any theology truly Asian.[454]

The quest for harmony in the task of theologizing in the Asian milieu can also be understood as the FABC's theological contribution to the "the cause of unity of the peoples of Asia marked by such a diversity of beliefs, cultures and socio-political structures. In the rich diversity of ancient Asian cultures and faiths is a vision of unity in diversity, a communion of life among diverse peoples. Ours is a vision of holistic life, life that is achieved and entrusted to every person and every community of persons, regardless of gender, creed or culture, class or colour. At the heart of our vision of life is the Asian reverential sense of mystery and of the sacred, a spirituality that regards life as sacred and discovers the Transcendent and its gifts even in mundane affairs, in tragedy or victory, in brokenness or wholeness. This deep interiority draws people to experience *harmony* and inner peace and infuses ethics into all of creation. Briefly, despite religious, ethnic, linguistic and cultural diversity, one can perceive a unity of values and perceptions which is epitomized in the spirit of harmony. Harmony, in the created universe, within the human family, and internalized in the individual person, has for centuries been an ideal to which peoples of the region have striven.[455]

Believers of all faiths have an urgent responsibility to open themselves once again to the voice of nature and its mystery, to return to their primordial attachment to and respect for nature, to grow in a creation-centred spirituality. Believers in any place are called to come together in silence and love before creation, to accept the God-given order and harmony of nature, to counteract the forces of exploitation and ruin. Harmony with nature brings harmony of hearts and harmony in human relationships.[456]

4.6.2. Dialogue with Asian Cultures

The rationale for local churches engaging in a dialogue with cultures has been explained by the FABC Office of Theological Concerns as follows: Each culture not only provides us with a new approach to the human, but also opens up new

454 Pieris, Aloysius SJ, An Asian Theology of Liberation, 69.

455 Jonathan, Yun-Ka Tan, Theologizing at the Service of Life.

456 Jonathan, Yun-Ka Tan, Theologizing at the Service of Life.

avenues for the understanding of the Gospel and its riches. When the Gospel encounters the tradition, experience and culture of a people, the undiscovered virtuosities will surface; riches and meanings yet hidden will emerge into the light. That is why it is so important to reinterpret the Gospel through the cultural resources of every people; this reinterpretation enriches the Christian tradition. This dialogical encounter facilitates the incarnation of the Good News in the various cultures creating new ways of life, action, worship and reflection, to help the growth of the local Churches and to realize the catholicity and fullness of the mystery of Christ.[457]

The importance of engaging in a dialogue with the Asian religions was first recognized by the 1970 Asian Bishops' Meeting:

> We pledge ourselves to an open, sincere, and continuing dialogue with our brothers of other great religions of Asia that we may learn from one another how to enrich ourselves spiritually and how to work more effectively together on our common task of total human development.It has been suggested that interreligious dialogue is not merely an activity of Asian Christians, but rather it enters into the very definition of what it is to be a Christian in Asia. To be Christian is not an abstraction, but a contextual reality.[458]

4.6.3. Interreligious Dialogue and Popular Religiosity

Interreligious dialogue has to be the nature of the Church, a community in pilgrimage journeying with peoples of other faiths towards the Kingdom that is to come. In particular, religious dialogue is not just a substitute for or a mere preliminary to the proclamation of Christ. It should be the ideal form of evangelisation, where in humility and mutual support we seek together with our brothers and sisters that fullness of Christ which is God's plan for the whole of creation, in its entirety and its great and wonderful diversity.[459] The First FABC Plenary Assembly explained that the local churches have to participate in a "dialogue of life" with the poor, which involves a genuine experience and understanding of the poverty, deprivation and oppression of many of the Asian peoples. Here, the term "poor" is understood in a dialectical sense: Poor, not in human values, qualities, nor in human potential. But poor, in that they are deprived of access to material goods and resources which they need in order to create a truly human life for themselves.[460]

The First FABC Plenary Assembly has emphasized that it is only through dialogue that the Asian local churches are able to give due reverence and honour

457 Cf. Jonathan, Yun-Ka Tan, Theologizing at the Service of Life.

458 Jonathan, Yun-Ka Tan, Theologizing at the Service of Life.

459 Jonathan, Yun-Ka Tan, Theologizing at the Service of Life.

460 Jonathan, Yun-Ka Tan, Theologizing at the Service of Life.

to these Asian religions and acknowledge that God has drawn these religions to Godself. In giving a privileged place to the religious traditions of the Asian peoples, the First FABC Plenary Assembly pointed out that they accept the great religious traditions as significant and positive elements in the economy of God's design of salvation. These traditions have to be recognized and respected because they contain profound spiritual and ethical meanings and values. Over many centuries, they have been the treasuries of the religious experience of the ancestors, from which the contemporaries do not cease to draw-light and strength. They have been (and continue to be) the authentic expression of the noblest longings of their hearts, and the home of their contemplation and prayer. They have helped to give shape to the histories and cultures of the nations.[461]

Popular religiosity of the people is another aspect that has to be taken into consideration when one develops a truly contextual theology. This needs to include and be in balance with the elements of scripture and tradition. Therefore, the word contextualization might be considered the best way of describing the process that has been called inculturation, indigenization or incarnation of the gospel.[462]

4.6.4. Critical Introspective Contemplation

Critical introspective contemplation begins with an acknowledgment that Asia is a continent of ancient and diverse cultures, religions, histories and traditions, a region like Joseph's coat of many colours. It also recognizes that the great religious traditions of Asia are: significant and positive elements in the economy of God's design and salvation. Critical introspective contemplation seeks to present a holistic vision of life in Asia which integrates the liberative action of dialectical social analysis within the wider religiousness and spirituality of the Asian peoples, because this mosaic of rich and deeply profound religious sentiments play a very significant role in shaping the life experiences of the Asian peoples. This holistic perspective of critical introspective contemplation reveals the fact that the contextual theological methodology of the FABC is more than just a preferential option for the poor and marginalized; it is also a preferential option for Asian cultures, spirituality and religiosity, in recognition of the fact that the Asian milieu is defined by both its varying degrees of economic poverty as well as its multifaceted religiousness. It seeks to draw upon the spirit of compassion and interiority, asceticism and renunciation, as well as intuition and mysticism of the religiosity of the Asian peoples to undergird the pursuit of integral human liberation.[463]

461 Cf. Jonathan, Yun-Ka Tan, Theologizing at the Service of Life.

462 Bevans, Stephen B., Models of Contextual Theology, New York: Orbis Books, 1994, 21.

463 Yun-Ka Tan, Jonathan, Theologizing at the Service of Life.

4.6.5. Dialectical Social Analysis

The stage of *dialectical social analysis,* seeks to identify and analyse the structural causes of, as well as focus attention on the impact of socioeconomic, political and cultural forces on the suffering and marginalization of the Asian peoples. This analysis is carried out through reading the "signs of the times" and confronting "the dark realities in the heart of Asia", a continent which is perceived in dialectical terms as "an arena of conflict and division, the world's exploited market place, the continent of suffering humanity," while at the same time, a "cradle of culture, birthplace of great religions, a continent awakening to new and gigantic responsibilities." It also aims to overcome the destructive forces in the life experiences of the Asian peoples and free them from structures which have created new forms of bondage, so as to foster human dignity, freedom and a more fully human life, as well as to create a more genuine communion among the multi-religious, multi-ethnic, multi-lingual and pluri-cultural Asian communities. Therefore, it is not surprising that dialectical social analysis is a ubiquitous aspect of the FABC's contextual theological methodology.[464]

Effect of Capitalism

It is necessary to have a social analysis of the country in order to theologize properly. What prevails in India is a form of dependent capitalism characterized by vast concentration of the means of production (agricultural and industrial) in a few hands. Capitalism in India has created wide disparities in income and opportunity. Only ten per cent of the population live in relative affluence, forty-seven percent are doomed to live below subsistence level. Adding to this on the political front, the affluent classes, the landlords, the rich capitalist peasants and the medium bourgeoisie are able to use democratic institutions to their own purposes. They manipulate elections, create powerful lobbies in the assemblies and the parliament, corrupt the bureaucracy and control local self-government bodies.[465]

The challenge for the Indians is very clear. They need to restructure the economy in such a manner that production for profit is replaced by production for social needs; to give power back to the people so that they mould their own lives; to create a counterculture consonant with the dignity of the human being and with the positive values of tradition. The task of liberation theology in India is an attempt to solve this contradiction.[466]

---

464 Cf. Yun-Ka Tan, Jonathan, Theologizing at the Service of Life.

465 Kappen, Sebastian, S.J., Jesus and Culture, Delhi: ISPCK, 2002, 114-15.

466 Kappen, Sebastian, S.J., Jesus and Culture, 115-16.

Cultural Crisis

The cultural crisis has affected the country at a deeper level. There is a real conflict between tradition and bourgeois modernity transplanted from outside. On one side is the traditional caste culture coupled with an obsolete religiosity; on the other side is the bourgeois modernity patronized by sections of the westernized urban elite. It is this monstrous un-culture that holds sway over the vast majority of the Indian people. It is here white money has its counterpart in black money, genuine goods in adulterated ones, true ownership in false ownership, bourgeois democracy in mafia politics, the written law in the unwritten law of might and manipulation, genuine religion in the worship of spurious god-men and god-women.[467]

Understanding Indian society is a very difficult task as it is bound up with the mythos.

It is through vibrant narrations, myths, epics and stories extant in the everyday life of the people that the real nature of the present society in uncovered and understood. Such a reading of the society appeals not only to the intellect, but to the whole being. The awareness of the social reality created through the rereading of the present with reference to the living myths and stories among a people has greater energizing force in terms of transformative praxis.[468]

In fact, a rational analysis of society in the context of India does not encourage the people to work out their liberation from oppressive conditions.

Situation of Poverty and Double Marginalisation

The term poverty designates in the first place material poverty, that is, the lack of economic goods necessary for a human life worthy of the name. This is something degrading and is rejected by the conscience of contemporary people. But, poverty has been thought of and experienced by Christians as part of the condition of marginalized people and is seen with certain fatalism. The poor are seen as an object of our mercy. Economic realities prevent the poor from finding true happiness in this life, so religion tells them that their situation is alright because they will find true happiness in the next life. They are diverted from the path of revolution by administering to them promises of an eternal heaven and paradise where those who bear injustice in this world will live forever in comfort and pleasure. But today social classes and nations are becoming aware of their poverty and when they see its root causes, they rebel against it.[469]

There is a double marginalization of the Christian Gospel and the Asian local churches. The FABC identified some socioeconomic and cultural-political challenges facing the Asian *Sitz-im-Lebe:* poverty and the inequitable

467 Cf. Kappen, Sebastian, S.J., Jesus and Culture, 115.

468 Wilfred, Felix, On the Banks of Ganges, 102.

469 Gutierrez, Gustavo, A Theology of Liberation, 163.

distribution of wealth; economic dependency; unjust trade and aid conditions; unfair economic policies which discriminate against labour; landlessness and the destruction of the rural economy and small family farms; unemployment and underemployment; poor working conditions and inadequate wages. Moreover, there are also dehumanizing plight of slum dwellers, landless peasants and migrant workers; unjust exploitation of workers; child labour; marginalization of indigenous people; unjust exploitation and discrimination of women; exploitative tourism (including sex-tourism); the plight of refugees; unrestrained exploitation of natural resources; pollution, environmental and ecological damage; as well as social and cultural dislocation.[470] These factors of Asian reality affect the people to their core.

Dimension of Social Justice and Freedom

There is need for a genuine commitment and effort to bring about social justice in the Asian societies. In so doing, the FABC affirmed the Statement of the 1971 Special Synod of Bishops on Justice in the World and pointed out that "evangelization and the pro-motion of true human development and liberation, are not only not opposed, but make up today the integral preaching of the Gospel, especially in Asia" (FABC I, art. 23). Hence, the poor are seen as ultimately the privileged community and agents of salvation. Life is seen with integrity and dignity, a life of compassion for the multitudes, especially for the poor and the needy. It is a life of solidarity with every form of life and sensitive care for all the earth. It is thus a life that unites us Asians among ourselves and with the whole of creation into one community of life. The ecological question or the harmony and balance of the natural environment in relation to the life of human are fundamental. The destiny of humankind is inextricably bound up with the way they cultivate the earth and share its resources. Harmony and peace call for respect for the earth. She is the mother of whose dust we are made and to whose womb we shall all return. The usurpation of the fruit of the earth by some and deprivation of others of the same, results in the rupture of harmony among peoples.[471]

Although the liberationists are staunch champions of justice, they recognise that forgiveness is an integral part of the life of faith. The struggle for the liberation of the oppressed majorities of the world is not simply a struggle for justice. Authentic liberation is only possible if mercy and forgiveness are an integral part of that struggle. God is merciful and forgiving. Our human experience shows that actual achievement of justice is meagre and fragile, though human life would be ignoble and impossible if we did not keep trying to achieve it; and justice alone is not enough to maintain peace.[472]

---

470 Cf. Yun-Ka Tan, Jonathan, Theologizing at the Service of Life.

471 Yun-Ka Tan, Jonathan, Theologizing at the Service of Life.

472 Bell, Daniel M., Liberation Theology after the end of History, London: Routledge, 2003, 154.

The capitalist form of production as it functions in today's world in the dependent countries creates a form of human existence characterized by artificiality, selfishness, the inhuman and dehumanizing pursuit of success measured in terms of prestige and money, and the resignation of responsibility for the world and for one's neighbour. The solution is to know that class struggle is a fact and abandon the theology of conciliation so that we love the oppressed, defending and liberating the people and accusing and combating the oppressor. Love demands that there is a need to fight for the liberation of those who live under a condition of objective sin.[473]

According to Aloysius Pieris, a major problem that confronts Asian theology is the association of people with mammon in terms of acquisitiveness and greed. This is on the increase through massive development programmes with which Asian churches consolidates themselves into western oases (big private educational, technological or agricultural establishments run with foreign aid) thus forcing a non-Christian majority to depend on a Christian minority for material progress. This use of Mammon, imposingly and manipulatively present in Asia, is a continuation in a new way, of the Missiology of conquest and power characteristic of the colonial era. When people revolt against such establishments, the churches speak of themselves as being persecuted. But in reality they are being trampled upon, like salt without flavour (Matt. 5:13).[474]

Marxists are of the opinion that it is religion that will die so that the poor may have life. I think it may not be true of the Asian context. For the majority of the peoples in Asia there is no existence without religion.

> Theoretically at least, Marxism is more consistently anti-mammon than purely antipoverty, in contrast with capitalist technocracy. In fact, no religious persecution under a Marxist regime can be compared to the subtle undermining of religious values that capitalist technocracy generates in our cultures. Marxism may purify institutional religion of its unholy alliances with the creators of poverty; capitalism pollutes religion by betraying it to Mammon.[475]

Because Asian theology focuses on liberation, it must also be a servant theology - one arising out of a commitment to serve the poor and the oppressed. No theology is seen to be neutral; each must take sides in the struggle for freedom. As expressed in a national group report prepared by the Philippine delegation to the conference, the basic question here is: "*for whom* are we theologizing?" In order to serve the poor in their liberation struggle, it is necessary for theology to have included in its methodology the critical component of social analysis.

473 Siggmund, Paul E., Oxford: Liberation Theology at the Crossroads: Democracy or Revolution? Oxford: Oxford University Press, 1990, 54.

474 Cf. Pieris, Aloysius SJ, An Asian Theology of Liberation, 74.

475 Pieris, Aloysius SJ, An Asian Theology of Liberation, 76.

How can theology serve the poor if its spokespersons do not understand the reasons for poverty? It is not enough for theology to proclaim freedom; it must also participate in the struggle for freedom. Yet the liberation of the poor is real only when the poor themselves participate in their own struggle for relief from poverty and oppression. This participation occurs authentically when the concept used to analyse the situation of the oppressed is derived from their own history and culture. Hence, Asian theology cannot ignore the culture of its people as it is expressed in the living faiths of the area. The trust of the people and the belief that they can theologize and are the real theologians is central to the idea of theologizing.[476] Thus, Asian theology is the way of sensing and doing things as revealed in the Asian people's struggle for spiritual and social emancipation. This theology is expressed in the idioms and languages of the cultures such struggles have created. Therefore, in that sense theology is not mere 'God Talk' as defined in classical theology.

4.6.6. Commitment and Solidarity with the Poor

One of the main elements of contextual theological methodology is *commitment and service to life* which goes beyond a mere personal, existential, ontological or metaphysical quest for a systematic way of theologizing. This commitment and service to life arises out of a holistic view of life together with a traditional sense of reverence which sees God's Spirit as active in the diverse and pluralistic Asian milieu. In this regard, one notes that the final statement of the 1994 FABC International Theological Colloquium began simply with the following statement: "Life. Vibrant life pulsating in the fecundity of Asia." Such a statement aptly describes the panorama of religious and cultural diversity in Asia, which comprises a rich and colourful mosaic of many of the world's ancient religious, philosophical and socio-cultural traditions.[477] As the Sixth FABC Plenary Assembly points out: "We Asians are searching not simply for the meaning of life but for life itself. We are striving and struggling for life because it is a task and a challenge. But life is a gift too, a mystery, because our efforts to achieve it are far too short of the ultimate value of life. We speak of life as a *becoming* - a growing into, a journeying to life and to the source of life. Ours is a vision of *holistic life.* We envision a life *with integrity and dignity, a life of compassion* for the multitudes, especially for the poor and needy. It is a life of *solidarity* with every form of life and of *sensitive care* for the earth."[478]

Thus, one sees clearly that this commitment and service to life reveals the communal character of the FABC's contextual theological methodology, viz., theologizing is rooted in the local community's experiences of life, rather than in

476 Cone, James M., Asian Theology Today: Searching for Definitions, taken from *Christian Century,* New York: Orbis Books, May 23, 1979, 589.

477 Yun-Ka Tan, Jonathan, Theologizing at the Service of Life.

478 Yun-Ka Tan, Jonathan, Theologizing at the Service of Life.

the intellectual arena of the academy. Theology is not something which is being carried out *for* the benefit of the community, or even *about* the community, but rather, *together with* the community and in solidarity with their life experiences. What is more important is that we are with the people rather than what we do for them. In particular, such a call for a personal commitment to and active solidarity with the life experiences of the Asian peoples entails more than mere sympathy, empathy or occasional encounters of theologians, bishops and other pastoral leaders with the daily lives of the Asian peoples, especially the poor and marginalized. Rather, it calls for their personal commitment, deep immersion and experiential participation in the lives of these peoples, not as outsiders who drop by to visit, but as insiders who are bound in solidarity with them.[479]

Christian poverty has meaning only as a commitment of solidarity with the poor, with those who suffer misery and injustice. It is a struggle to protest against the evil of poverty and struggle against it. This poverty is lived not for its own sake but rather as an authentic imitation of Christ. It takes on the sinful human condition to liberate humankind from sin and all its consequences. The classical example of this may be found in Acts of the Apostles, "None of the members was ever in want as all those owned land or houses would sell them and bring the money from the sale of them to present it to the apostles; it was distributed to any who might be in need" (Acts 4:34). Only authentic solidarity with the poor and a real protest against the poverty of our time can provide reflection on the witness of poverty. This witness is a much-needed sign of authenticity of the mission.[480]

Poverty and the Bible

Commitment and solidarity with the poor has its basis in the Bible. In the Bible poverty is a scandalous condition inimical to human dignity and therefore contrary to the will of God. There are several terms used in the Old Testament in order to refer to the poor. For example: *ebyon* (one who desires), the beggar, *dal* (the weak one), *ani* (the bent over one), *anaw* (humble before God). In the New Testament, the Greek term *ptokos* is used to speak of the poor person (the one who does not have what is necessary to subsist or the wretched one driven into begging). All these terms, indigent, weak, bent over, wretched, express a degrading human condition.[481]

It is very explicit that poverty is not caused by fate but by the injustice of the oppressors. The text from Job expresses this perspective: "The wicked move boundary marks away, they carry off flock and shepherd. They drive away the orphan's donkey, as security they seize the widow's ox" (Job 24:2-3). The prophet condemns the deeds of the wicked: "I have made my decree and will not relent because they have sold the upright for silver and the poor for a pair of sandals,

479 Yun-Ka Tan, Jonathan, Theologizing at the Service of Life.

480 Gutierrez, Gustavo, A Theology of Liberation, 173.

481 Gutierrez, Gustavo, A Theology of Liberation, 165.

because they have crushed the heads of the weak into the dust and thrust the oppressed to one side" (Amos 2:6-7). According to Prophet Isaiah, some people are poor because they are victims of others: "Woe to those who enact unjust decrees, who compose oppressive legislation to deny justice to the weak and to cheat the humblest of my people of fair judgement to make widows their prey and to rob the orphan" (Isa. 10:1-2). The prophets condemn every kind of abuse, every form of keeping the poor in poverty.[482]

Poverty contradicts the very meaning of the Mosaic religion. Moses led the people out of slavery, exploitation, and alienation of Egypt so that they could inhabit a land where they could live with human dignity. God is the one who saves the people from servitude and will not allow them to be subjected to it again. Exploitation in any form goes against the mandate of Genesis. Humankind is created in the image and likeness of God and is destined to dominate the earth. Human being is also the sacrament of God. Therefore, to oppress the poor is to offend God; to know God is to work for justice. We meet God in our encounter with other people; what is done for others is done for God. Poverty is an expression of a sin and a negation of love.[483]

There is another dimension to the poverty we have already mentioned, that is spiritual poverty. It finds its expression in the Beatitudes of the New Testament. The version in Matthew expresses the idea of spiritual poverty, "Blessed are the poor in spirit" (5:1). It is being totally at the disposition of the Lord. This poverty has no direct relationship to wealth. In this situation, we should have no other sustenance than the will of God. In Luke the term used is, "Blessed are you who are poor: the kingdom of God is yours" (Lk 6:26). It does not mean that the poor should accept their poverty because later this injustice will be compensated for in the Kingdom of God. It could mean that the time has come to eliminate the exploitation and poverty that prevent the poor from being fully human. They are blessed because the coming of the Kingdom will put an end to their poverty by creating a world of fellowship.[484]

4.6.7. God Encounter

The starting point of theology according to Fr. Sebastian Kappen S.J. is God-encounter. How does this encounter take place? It cannot be at the level of religious symbols. No symbol is capable of expressing the richness of the original experience, which is ineffable and unfathomable. The danger with regard to forms and symbols is that they will subsequently lead to institutionalization and thus alienate. That is the reason why this encounter has to be beyond religion. The primary focus of theological reflection should be our meeting with God in the contemporary historical situation. It is the reality of practical life, individual

482 Gutierrez, Gustavo, A Theology of Liberation, 166-67.

483 Gutierrez, Gustavo, A Theology of Liberation, 168.

484 Cf. Gutierrez, Gustavo, A Theology of Liberation, 169-71.

and social. This is the world of praxis, meaning the historical process whereby we transform ourselves in transforming our environment of things, persons and structures; structures of economic, social, political and cultural elements.[485]

"To encounter God is to become both a wielder of the sword and a herald of peace. Through the one who has encountered God, the divine No to misery, injustice and exploitation and the divine Yes to whatever furthers the fullness of human beings reverberate in history and radiate to the ends of the earth."[486] The response of the person mediates the presence of God in the world. To have encountered and responded to God in this manner is a pre-condition for any valid theological reflection. A genuine theological reflection will respond to the challenge of God embedded in history. This encounter should direct itself to the divine challenge and the human response.[487]

Christian Doctrine and Experience

"For a theology to be authentically Christian, it must not only enunciate sound Christian doctrine, or reflect on an authentic Christian experience, but it must be done in a specifically Christian way. The Christian way will be the biblical way. For the Bible as the written record of the founding experience of the Christian community, is the ultimate norm of all Christian theology."[488] The Second Vatican Council affirms this, "Sacred theology rests on the written word of God, together with sacred tradition, as its primary and perpetual foundation. By scrutinizing in the light of faith all truth stored up in the mystery of Christ, theology is most powerfully strengthened and constantly rejuvenated by that word" (DV, 24).

The Christian analysis of society is based on the foundational Christian experience which is a sharing in the "Abba Experience" of Jesus himself. This theology is based on human experience and problems in a social context. It must include all aspects of life such as politics, economy, and socio-culture, which are directed to the deeper internalization of the Gospel in such reality. It is expected that the Church will live not for itself but for the Reign of God, for its neighbours of other religious traditions and for the whole world. All are the concerns of God. It is therefore not primarily a matter of trying to reconcile individual people but a matter of trying to change unjust structures so that people will not be pitted against one another as oppressor and oppressed. This is possible only if the language of theology is authentic and contextualized.[489]

---

485 Cf. Kappen, Sebastian, SJ, Jesus and Culture, 80-82.

486 Kappen, Sebastian, SJ, Jesus and Culture, 82.

487 Kappen, Sebastian, SJ, Jesus and Culture, 83.

488 Soares-Prabhu, George SJ, "Theology of Liberation: An Indian Biblical Perspective", in: Francis X. D'Sa (Ed), *Collected Writings of George Soares-Prabhu S.J. Vol. 4,* Pune: Jnana Deepa Vidyapeeth Theology Series, 2001, 14.

489 Cf. Soares-Prabhu, George SJ, 20-21.

Theology is not an attempt to flee from the concrete world of praxis to the world of sterile abstractions. It is a process of immersion in reality, in the reality of God's challenge enfleshed in history. Theological reflection must take place in a spirit of communion with all that is and compassion for all who belong to the human family. Our encounter with God has also a cosmic dimension because our being with others and the material world are extensions of humanity. The historical dimension of God-encounter must be focused. In this context, to respond to God is to proclaim the challenge one has accepted of working for total human freedom.[490]

The process of liberation in order to maintain the purely Christian character implies the acceptance in its praxis of the Paschal experience. The Catholic Church because of its unbroken link with Jesus Christ is a special institutional articulation of Christianity with the clearest interpretation of the mystery of God and human. Yet it is a sinful and pilgrim organization far from the Father's house.[491]

Conformity to the Bible

The content of Christian theology must conform to the Bible. A genuinely Christian theology must be biblical not only in what it teaches but in how it is done. In other words, our theology and theologizing should be biblical. To understand this we need to go to the Bible. Yahweh is understood as the god who freed his people from bondage in Egypt in order to make them his people. "I am Yahweh and I will bring you out from under the burden of the Egyptians, and I will deliver you from their bondage, and I will redeem you with an outstretched arm and I will take you for my people" (Ex 6:6-7). Therefore, Yahweh has brought them out of the bondage of the Egyptians and led them to a good land so that they might build there a community in which there would be no poor among them. This experience of the freedom of God leads Israel to the vision of an alternative society. The Exodus is the fundamental experience for the Jewish people. Every year the community of Israel gathers to celebrate and relive the Exodus. They are to remember that their God frees them from oppression and injustice. If they are to be faithful to God, they must free the oppressed and do justice toward others. In the legal tradition of the Old Testament, we find the theme of concern for the oppressed and poor of society, "The resident aliens, the orphans, and the widows in your towns, may come and eat their fill so that the Lord your God may bless you in all the work that you undertake" (Deut 14:28-29).[492]

Liberation in the Bible is a religious experience of the poor, for what liberates is the redeeming love of God, and the final fruit of liberation is the saving knowledge of God. Biblical liberation is more than class struggle. It is the God-encounter of the poor, the poor by choice (the renouncers) and the poor by

490 Kappen, Sebastian, SJ, Jesus and Culture, 87.

491 Sigmund, Paul E., Liberation Theology at the Crossroads: Democracy or Revolution, 81.

492 Cf. Soares-Prabhu, George S.J., 15-16.

circumstances (the *anawim* of Yahweh). Liberation is seen as a joint venture of God and the poor people covenanted into an indivisible Saving Reality. Human efforts and divine initiatives merge into one liberating enterprise.[493]

Concern for the oppressed and the poor was at the core of the Israelites' calling. This concern was rooted not only in the covenant, but more so, in the very nature of God. God is the defender of the oppressed, the One who liberates the captives, the One who feeds hungry people, "The Lord executes justice for the oppressed; gives food to the hungry. The Lord sets the prisoners free; the Lord opens the eyes of the blind" (Psalm 146:7-8).

God of Justice and the Prophets

To know God is to do justice to the poor. The Old Testament explicates this message in relation to God and neighbour. "You must not exploit a poor and needy wage-earner, be he one of your brothers or a foreigner resident in your community. You must pay him his wages each day, not allowing the sun to set before you do, since he being poor, needs them badly, otherwise he may appeal to Yahweh against you, and you would incur guilt" (Deut. 24:14-15). When justice does not exist, God is not known; God is absent. If justice is done, if the alien, the orphan and the widow are not oppressed, "Then I will let you stay in this place, in the country I gave for ever to your ancestors of old" (Jer. 7:7). In the Biblical understanding to love Yahweh is to establish just relationships among persons, it is to recognize the rights of the poor.[494]

Throughout Israel's history, the prophets reminded Israel to remain faithful to the covenant. Their primary mission was to lead the people back to the path of righteousness and justice. The prophets were sent not only to speak God's word, but also to speak on behalf of those who had no voice. God complained through the prophets that the people had forgotten who it was that gave them their land and provisions. They, who once were hungry and oppressed, refused to feed the hungry and themselves became the oppressors. The people of Israel spoke folly and left the craving of the hungry unsatisfied (Isaiah 32:6). The prophets of the Old Testament protested against a system that was not appealing to the Mosaic Law. This situation could be seen like this: "Solomon effectively reversed the movement of the Mosaic revolution by countering Israel's economics of equality (Ex 16:18) with an economics of affluence founded on the concentration of wealth (1 Kings 4:20-23); by subverting its politics of justice (Lev 23:35-42) with a politics of oppression which restored forced labour (1 Kings 5:13-18); and by replacing its religion of the absolute freedom of God with a "state religion" in which Yahweh, confined to a temple, was domesticated as the legitimizing patron of his imperial system. The pre-Exodus situation of Egypt was neatly restored!"[495]

493 Cf. Pieris, Aloysius S.J., An Asian Theology of Liberation, 123-24.

494 Cf. Gutierrez, Gustavo, A Theology of Liberation, 110-11.

495 Soares-Prabhu, George SJ, 18.

The prophets condemn idolatry. The people (Israelites) are expected not to forsake Yahweh for other Gods (Jer 2:20-28; Ezek 6:1-7). They are not supposed to make Yahweh into an idol to legitimize their money power and human power. The prophets also criticised social injustice. They could not tolerate the situation of exploitation and oppression that result from the legitimizing idolatry (Amos 2:6-9; Is 3:13-15; Jer 5:20-29). Social protest and critique of religion go closely in the preaching of the prophets. The prophets based their criticism on the vision of Exodus and it involves a radical change in the prophets' consciousness and perception. Amos' justification was simple. God had called him and so he must speak. Amos and the other prophets of his time knew that God called his people to live in justice and peace. The other surrounding peoples also lived unjustly and woe would come upon them. But the people of Israel and Judah had been blessed and chosen by God and so should live accordingly.[496]

Amos was one of the strongest in calling the people back to the way of justice. Israel was at the height of her economic and political power when God sent the poor shepherd Amos to call the people of Israel to repentance. These people had often transgressed against the covenant. One transgression was that they trampled on the poor man and extorted levies on his wheat (cf. Amos 5:11a). The injustice that the rich engaged in completely negated the value of their worship, "I hate, I despise your festivals, and I take no delight in your solemn assemblies. Even though you offer me your burnt offerings and grain offerings, I will not accept them; and the offerings of well-being of your fatted animals I will not look upon. Take away from me the noise of your songs; I will not listen to the melody of your harps. But let justice roll down like waters, and righteousness like an ever-flowing stream" (Amos 5:21-24). When there is no justice, life is barren and worship of God is a sham.[497]

The task of prophesying is not merely to proclaim the new age of freedom but to actualize it in the world here and now. Then theology becomes world transforming praxis. But, theology can become power only if it is appropriated by the oppressed masses in whose interest it is to change the world. This theology has to express the mute longings of the downtrodden and the unwanted of the earth.[498]

A desire for justice and peace; for a more equitable distribution of the world's resources; a longing for a more compassionate society - these are themes common to many people of good will, of many faiths and none. Indeed, they are part of what it really means to be a human being.

The parable of the Final Judgement (Mat. 25:31-46) may be considered as a very meaningful passage regarding the love of neighbour. According to Gustavo Gutierrez, it summarizes the essence of the gospel message. Some believe that

---

496 Soares-Prabhu, George SJ, 18.

497 Cf.Soares-Prabhu, George SJ, 18-19.

498 Kappen, Sebastian, SJ, Jesus and Culture, 87.

this is a judgement of all people – Christians and non-Christians – according to their love of neighbour, particularly of the needy. It is very clear from the passage, "anything you did not do for one of these, you did not do for me" (25:45). To abstain from serving is to refuse to love; to fail to act for another is as culpable as expressly refusing to do it. Charity exists only in concrete actions (feeding the hungry, giving drink to the thirsty), etc. The parable of the Good Samaritan conveys the same message (Luke 10:29-37). St. James says, "Faith without deeds is useless" (James 2:14). Therefore, to sin is to refuse to love, to reject communion and fellowship, to reject even the very meaning of human existence.[499]

4.7. Basic Principles of Indian Theology

In a broad sense, the roots of Indian liberation theology go back to the Indian experience of anti-colonial and anti-imperialist struggles. The backbone of liberation in India was the experience of the struggles of the marginalized people. More particularly, I should point out the many battles waged by the tribal people, menial workers, agricultural labourers, fishermen and others in the effort to free themselves from the oppression to which they were subjected. The energies released in anti-colonial struggles were kept alive even after independence.[500]

4.7.1. Religious in Dynamism (Inter-religious Character)

> There is a striking difference between the liberation theology as formulated in Latin America and the Indian experience. In India, the project of liberation is not confined to the context of Christians reading and re-interpreting Christian sources and traditions. In India, liberation cannot but be an *inter-religious* project. In the pluralistic Indian society, the poor cut across the various religious affiliations. Therefore any liberative endeavour should be attuned in its very dynamics to this *inter-religious* character.[501]

India is known not only for its inter-religious character but also for its religiosity. Many of the major religions of the world are found in India: Hinduism, Buddhism, Jainism, Sikhism, Zoroastrianism, Islam and Christianity. These religions have also contributed to the negative reality of India, though there is a tradition of religious tolerance from the time of Asoka and Akbar. The causes of such conflicts are various and complex. There are economic reasons as well as religious reasons. Many of the people are very religious to the extent of fundamentalists and they want their religion to be prominent. On the other hand, different groups feel threatened because of the minority – majority balance. This

499 Cf. Gutierrez, Gustavo, A Theology of Liberation, 112-13.

500 Wilfred, Felix, On the Banks of Ganges, 84.

501 Wilfred, Felix, On the Banks of Ganges, 95.

is an important factor that one has to be aware of when one theologizes in the Indian context.[502]

If we believe that Jesus continues to be with all humanity through his Spirit, how could we discount the ever-new encounters of people with him and his teachings? It is important to note that the encounter with Jesus and his message have effected deep transformations in people for whom what is most important is not a conceptual definition of the reality of Jesus, but the vivid narration of their deeper experiences. The Christian community should learn to appreciate and value not only the experiences and encounters of its neighbours with Jesus Christ, but should also realize the widespread influence of these encounters on the larger society. Many Indians know Sri Ramakrishna Paramahamsa who was an almost illiterate man but a great mystic. No one, perhaps, has influenced the contemporary religious life of India as this illiterate mystic. He narrated his own mystical experience of Jesus, so much so that when the Ramakrishna Mission was founded on Christmas day, it is said that the monks took the oath to be "Christs." Who can deny the influence of the teachings of Jesus on Ram Mohan Roy, the influence of the self-sacrifice of Jesus and his Sermon on the Mount on Gandhi? Popular religiosity assumes great importance in the context of India. All Indians are aware of the fact that India is pulled apart by ethnic, linguistic and communal strife. There is a need for unity, harmony and concord based on justice. Though religions cause conflicts, riots and violence it is also a force of cohesion.[503]

4.7.2. Liberative in Praxis

The poor, the oppressed and the marginalized Indians are the active subjects of the process of liberation. Their experiences and struggles give rise to a genuine theology of liberation. The praxis of liberation is by the suffering masses and those in solidarity with them, most of whom do not share the same faith as Christians. The various religious traditions are composed of many strands and streams characterized by historical, geographical, cultural and ethnic differences. It is in these traditions that the heart and soul of the poor and the oppressed come alive in myriad forms.[504]

4.7.3. Inculturation and Role of Active Groups

Inculturation is an issue of central importance in Indian local churches. This is based on the belief and historical understanding that Jesus was born in a Jewish culture and tradition. It could be found in the way he lived, thought and taught. Only if we know the context of Jesus' time and culture can we understand

502 Arulsamy, Santiago, Liberation Theology in Asia, taken from: Indian Theological Studies, 22 (3), September 1985, 271.

503 Wilfred, Felix, Sunset in the East, Madras: Siga, 1991, 199.

504 Wilfred, Felix, On the Banks of Ganges, 97.

Jesus well. Though Jesus was reinterpreted after his resurrection, his historical background and culture cannot be discarded.[505]

For the Second Vatican Council, the history of evangelization has been and continues to be a process of cultural adaptation. The council noted that the Church profits from the treasures buried within the diversity of human culture and that from the beginning of her history, the Church has learned to express the message of Christ with the help of the ideas and terminology of various peoples, and has tried to clarify it with the wisdom of philosophers, too. Her purpose has been to adapt the gospel to the grasp of all as well as to the needs of the learned, insofar as such was appropriate. For thus the ability to express Christ's message in its own way is developed in each nation, and at the same time there is fostered a living exchange between the Church and the diverse cultures of people. To promote such exchange, especially in our days, the Church requires the special help of those who live in the world, are versed in different institutions and specialties, and grasp their innermost significance in the eyes of both believers and unbelievers (GS, 44).

One way of being inculturated and responding to the situation in India is by joining the voluntary groups which are active in India. The process of liberation is active in India in spite of the oppressive forces all over the country. The self-assertion of the people has found heavy-handed reprisal on the part of the upper castes and classes. There is a need to challenge such a situation. Some of these groups or NGOs (Non-Governmental Organizations) were to help the Dalits, tribal people, peasants, people living in slums, tribal women working in urban areas, and to foster communal harmony in situations of communalism. Another group that cannot be neglected is the movement of ecology. Some of these activists renounced their religions because of the religious fundamentalism which destroyed and distorted the country. As a theology student I have also worked with some these activists during my theological studies in Delhi. It was a profound experience, coming to know the activists and their deep commitment to the poor and the exploited. It was a time of plenty of work, to do my theology and then be part of the organizations. I found theology, celebration of the Eucharist, and prayer profoundly meaningful. I realized that I was doing a theology emerging from the life and situation of the people.

Adding to these voluntary agencies and groups there are also other groups working in the Indian sub-continent; some of these groups have taken revolutionary steps, to the extent of using arms and ammunition. One such group that emerged because of the prevailing situation is the naxalite which sprung up in West Bengal and Andhra Pradesh. Their main target was rich landlords and wealthy, corrupt politicians. The members of the naxalite group consisted of young men from middle class families and most of them unemployed. Many corrupt politicians were kidnapped and killed and so were many landlords. An

505 Wilfred, Felix, Sunset in the East, 185.

offshoot of this naxalite group existed also in Kerala in the early 1970s with the same goal. After a few years, the naxalite group was "almost" annihilated because of lack of mass support, and the use of violent means was not appealing to the people. There were however individuals and small groups functioning in remote areas of the country.

The Sampradayikta Virodhi Andholan (Anti-communalism Movement) is a group of concerned individuals formed in November 1984 specifically to engage in an all-around struggle against communalism. Communalism must be understood, first and foremost, not in the Hindu, Muslim, and Sikh variants and manifestations, but in general as an ideological and political method. It is rooted both in the power-hungry delusions and fantasies of certain obscurantist intelligentsia, and in their common hatred for democracy and secular values.[506] I have worked with this group between 1989 and 1992. It is a group of dedicated people from different religions and even atheists who are committed to the cause of communal harmony and the welfare of the poor people in slums. From my own experience of working with this group shows that these groups can also help us form a theology that is contextual.

4.8. Basic Principles of Santal Theology

> Can one speak meaningfully of a tribal theology? Can there be a theology special to a particular Church? Is not Catholic theology universal? Will not a tribal theology narrow down our perspectives and lead us into a ghetto? Can we have a tribal theology, even if we wish to have one? Theology presupposes a philosophy as its handmaid. How do we pass from the myths, symbols and rituals of the tribals to a theology? What is the link between tribal Christian experience and theologising? These doubts would raise a deeper question. What is theology today? Will not his pluralism lead to fragmentation of the Church and wreck its unity? I do not expect to be able to allay all these fears.[507]

These are some of the questions raised by Fr. Michael Amaladoss SJ. Though he is not a tribal himself, according to me the questions are very relevant and we need to find answers to these questions if we want to make sense to doing theology in the tribal context.

The starting point and context of a tribal/Santal theology should be our faith experience. The question here is: whose experience? It is primarily the experience of the group that is theologising. It is not an easy task to bear the experience of

506 Cf. On a Struggle against communalism, available from: http://www.questia.com/, accessed on 06.03.2008.

507 Amaladoss, Michael S.J., "Theologising in a Tribal Context: Some Methodological Observations", 3.

the tribal community. Through sympathy and participation, they should make the experience of the people their own. It is not enough to be mere spectators of the difficulties and problems, tensions and sufferings, joys and achievements, hope and aspirations of the people. Tribal people say that non-tribal people will not easily understand them. That is why there should be a concerted effort from the part of those who theologize to participate in the life of the people as much as possible. Tribal people themselves at times may participate in the process of theologising.[508]

Human encounter with God does not take place in a vacuum, instead we meet the living God with minds and hearts shaped by ideas, values, beliefs, attitudes, myths and symbols handed down to us from past generations. These factors determine the way we are attuned to the mystery of human existence and also to God.[509]

4.8.1. The Context: Physical and Spiritual

The general context may be classified under three main headings: geographical, socio-cultural and political. All these elements are necessary requirements for the theologising. For a structural analysis of society, one needs to know these factors and how they are operative in a particular society. What is understood by the term geographical is in relation to its physical confines. It is a territory located in the north of India.

To know the context properly, the reality of the tribal people, we need to analyse the experience. The analysis should be comprehensive enough to deal not only with the socio economic and political situation but also with the psychological, cultural and the religious factors. This is an important part of doing theology because we need to know the whole reality of the people. The people have their own particular perspectives on certain things in their life and a non-tribal will understand it in a different way. We may take an example; the community's experience of suffering when someone in the family is sick. The sickness may be caused because of malnutrition which is due to lack of food. This scarcity is caused because of oppressive socio-political structures. But due to the prevailing situation, the people think in terms of evil spirits and punishment. Such a situation should be dealt with properly.[510]

The experience of the Christian tribal people today is a very different one. To a great extent they have lost their 'tribalness.' The tribal world-view, values and structures have inevitably blended with the Christian world-view. The tribal people today are part of a democratic polity in which, in different places, namely,

508 Amaladoss, Michael S.J., "Theologising in a Tribal Context: Some Methodological Observations", Sevartham Vol. 4, 1984, 6.

509 Kappen, Sebastian, S.J., Jesus and Culture, 88.

510 Amaladoss, Michael S.J., "Theologising in a Tribal Context: Some Methodological Observations", 7-8.

schools, offices of government, etc, they have to relate to non-tribal people, not as intruders and oppressors but as fellow citizens. Such an experience gives them a new dimension to their search for self-identity, freedom, justice and fellowship. Adding to these, tribal people are forced to come to the so called main stream of the country, industrialization, urbanization - meaning, this leads to the denial of their own culture and values.

4.8.2. Tribal Worldview

Tribal people have many myths, stories and events which contain aspects of liberation. The creation myth itself is an experience of chaos and final liberation. Initially there was only water and no earth. The earth was later formed by the Supreme Being with the help of other creatures. The human beings were created and multiplied and filled the earth. The aspect of sin and punishment and restoration are also found in the Santal myth. Further explanation reveals that the Santals had to flee from their own land and after wandering for some years, they reached the place where they are now (mainly Jharkhand).[511]

Tribal Understanding of God and Spirits

All the major tribes have the idea of a Supreme Being/God. The Supreme Being is called by different names in different tribes. The Santals call Him Sing Bonga or Marang Buru. He is the creator God and beyond all human beings and realities of the earth. He is all good and pure. He may also inflict pain and suffering on human beings when they turn away from the path of God. In other words, when people sin He may punish them. He is omnipotent, author, ruler and controller of all minor spirits. Sacrifices are offered to Him to give thanks and to be liberated from suffering. He himself does not act. He appoints his agents, spirits, to do the task of blessing or harming people. People receive punishment or reward according to the measure they have pleased or displeased the Supreme Being.[512]

Tribal people believe that there are several minor spirits which can do good or harm to the people. The good spirits are benevolent to them and protect them. On certain occasions, they have to be given sacrifices and the priest prays for the protection of the people and village. Adding to these, the malevolent spirits have to be propitiated so that they do not cause harm to the people. The concept of an intermediary between God and human being is very much prevalent among the tribal people. That is why animals (fowls, goats) are sacrificed on feast days so that the spirits intercede for human beings. The Supreme Being cannot be accessed directly as He is the Master and Creator of the Universe though he is depicted in an anthropomorphic way. That is the reason why there are intermediaries. It

511 Kujur, Jacob, S.J., Liberative Aspects in Tribal Theology, in Sevartham Vol. 22, 1997, 110.

512 Parapullil, Anthony, S.J., "Tribal Theology", 30.

is believed that the sacrificial victim intercedes for their forgiveness for their sins and well-being.[513]

The tribal people attribute the creation of the world to the Supreme Being. This God is personal and even commits mistakes in creation and he corrects the mistakes later. The other creatures help Him in the process of creation. There is a significant place for human beings in the whole of creation. God created other things for the benefit of human beings. Thus, human beings remained as the crown of creation. As in the Bible, the tribal people too have the idea of sin and punishment. When human beings turned away from God, they were punished. Tribal understanding of sin is that it is not only an offence against God/Supreme Being but also against society/community. They had to repent and turn to God and to community to attain belongingness.[514]

The tribal people have not only the idea of sin and punishment but also the idea of salvation which is inevitable for their life. Life after death is considered important. The memory of the ancestors is always cherished in their day-to-day life. Almost all tribal people remember their ancestors everyday of their life, while they eat and drink. Every time they eat and drink a few grains of rice and a few drops of rice beer are offered to the ancestors. Their happiness in the next world is proportional to the moral conduct here on earth. They attain communion with the ancestors and so they need the ancestors as intermediaries like the saints of Christianity.[515]

Understanding of Land

Tribal people want to be associated with nature and that is the reason why they are real tribal people or adivasi people, meaning:

> Original, indigenous people, earth born and nature-evolved people. As imitators of nature, the Tribals are verbally non-expressive people. They are not only silent listeners, doers and sufferers like nature, but are also incapable of expressing their feelings and sentiments verbally. In fact, they have no words for expressing their feelings and sentiments. For example, they have no words for expressing love, gratitude, anger, sadness and joy. All such feelings and sentiments they express through various symbolic actions.[516]

For the tribal people land is the greatest asset. It is the core of tribal life and their spirituality which gives them distinct religious and cultural identity. Land binds all indigenous people as one body with the Supreme Being and ancestors.

513 Parapullil, Anthony, S.J., "Tribal Theology", 33.

514 Parapullil, Anthony, S.J., "Tribal Theology", 33.

515 Parapullil, Anthony, S.J., "Tribal Theology", 45.

516 Kullu, Paulus, S.J., Theology in Tribal Religio-Cultural Context, in Sevartham Vol. 28, 2003, 67.

The greatest culture of the aborigines is agriculture and it will continue to be so decades to come. Crops, cattle and children are their most prized blessings. Land is the source of every life everything that exists on the face of the earth has its origin in soil. The Supreme Being taught human beings how to till the ground and cultivate for their livelihood.[517]

For tribal people land is not only a factor of production but also a source of spirituality. Land is sacred to them. It is a gift given to the ancestors by God. That is the reason why land belongs to the community and not to the individual. The community is not only the living members but also the ancestors and future generations. The present generation has the sacred duty to maintain the sanctity of the land, and hand it over to the coming generation as an ancestral heritage. Land is thus the foundation of tribal religion and belief system. There are several feasts and festivals related to the land. Tribal people have to fulfil some sacred duties, such as giving food and drinks to the ancestors. The food and drink are the produce of the land. From these elements, a liberative tribal theology should evolve in order that the tribal people overcome every form of injustice, and unite them to God and their ancestors.[518]

4.8.3. Tribal Community and Identity Crisis

Tribal community spirit is the feeling of great equality, solidarity and togetherness. The tribal community is considered sacred. This sacred component is acquired during rites of passages, through the changing of situations in life. Part of this sacredness is achieved through the transient humility learned in these phases; this allows people to reach a higher position. They share common experiences, usually through a rite of passage. This brings everyone onto an equal level, even if one is higher in position. But, this spirit is now in crisis because of forces that are beyond the tribal perspective.

All human beings have certain basic quests in life especially when they are faced with negativities of life, namely, suffering and death. They ask themselves: Where do I come from? Where am I going? What happens to me after death? Why am I in this world? The answers to these questions cannot be found unless we go the scriptures of our religions. These answers set before us a goal, rooted in the past but progressively realizable in the present. The rituals are symbolic mediations of this on-going realization that is taking place in daily living.[519]

The tribal Church today, which is conditioned by the historical realities of tribal society, is undergoing an identity crisis caused by challenging factors from within and without. Internal and external factors are affecting the very existence and faith life of the people. There is a mutual relationship between the Church

517 Tirkey, Amrit, S.J., Tribal Land: A Theological Reflection, in Sevartham Vol. 30, 2005, 25.

518 Kujur, Jacob, S.J., Liberative Aspects in Tribal Theology, in Sevartham Vol. 22, 1997, 113-14.

519 Amaladoss, Michael S.J., "Theologising in a Tribal Context: Some Methodological Observations", 3.

and the world; and so the tribal church and tribal society are interacting on one another. Hence, there is a need for a close analysis and deep reflection on the existing realities. In this context, we need to know, how the tribal church can become a leaven in the society and an effective visible reality of establishing the Kingdom of God in the tribal society.[520]

Theologising in the tribal context is characterised by immense diversity. It means to do theology in the midst of contradictions and conflicts with unprecedented challenges at all levels. To understand what Indian theology and particularly tribal theology means, one has to transport oneself psychologically and spiritually into another world, which is quite unfamiliar terrain for many people. It is by entering into their life, their tradition, culture, history, religion and dynamics of contemporary society, that we could make some sense of what it means to do theology in the tribal context. This is a concrete engagement which contains challenges and risks because there are serious threats and conflicts and death dealing powers of darkness. This is no intellectual discussion but relating to the realm of praxis. That is why theology cannot be an end in itself but has to be pursued and cultivated in service of something much greater; it is for life in its various forms and expressions, with its manifold demands and challenges. This is something that can take place in the concrete, in a particular context, in a particular history.[521]

4.8.4. Faith Commitment

The symbolic mediations of the on-going process are connected with our faith commitment. As Christians, we understand the commitment that we have towards the Creator God and Jesus Christ who suffered, died and rose from death. Christians are called to participate in this mission of the Kingdom of God and partakers in the life of Christ. This new life in Christ is not simply promised for a future after death. That would be alienating. It demands however the building up of a new humanity of justice, freedom and fellowship here and now. Christian faith is a commitment to this creative process. It is an involvement in life in the present, in history. Thus, faith and life enter into a dialectic; a conflicting and challenging situation of life goes on here. Life is incarnating faith in the here and now of history; faith is challenging life to become what it ought to be.[522]

In the dialectical process of life and faith, culture has an important function. Culture is the world of language and symbols, of socio-political and economic structures through which a particular group of people humanize nature and promote and regulate life in community. It reflects the socio-historic experience

---

520 Kujur, Raphael, "Tribal Church in Chotanagpur: Identity and Mission", Sevartham Vol. 23, 1998, 43.

521 Wilfred, Felix, On the Banks of Ganges (Doing Contextual Theology), 5.

522 Amaladoss, Michael SJ, "Theologising in a Tribal Context: Some Methodological Observations", 4.

of a people. In order to be effective faith must find embodiment in a culture. This embodiment is called religion. It is in this context of dialectic between faith and life that we need to understand the nature and function of theology. Theological reflection is to find meaning in life here and now. The faith that theology interprets is not a thing of the past but it is a living faith of the here and now of history and an element of the consciousness of the community. It is a memory: it evokes a past through scripture and tradition; but it has to be made alive in contemporary experience, finding a new meaningfulness, offering a challenge and indicating a new direction. It is a contemporary search, localised in the here and now of history, situated by life-experience.[523]

The life of faith planted in the people of a particular culture, interacts with that culture: its history, philosophy, its religious experiences, and concretisation and institutionalization of these experiences into religious institutions. From such interaction and inner dialogue emerges the flowering of the faith in that culture in the form of an indigenous theology, indigenous liturgy, indigenous Church institutions and structures. It is exactly as Christ was presented within a particular culture so that the particular people could experience His presence in their midst sensibly and immanently. It is Christ's confrontation of a particular people in their own culture that converts and transforms them.[524]

4.8.5. Enriching Elements in Tribal Religion

In such a context the development of a Tribal Christian Theology is inevitable. The tribal religions could be encountered by Christian faith because they are open to light, truth and goodness. What Pope Paul VI said about non-Christian religions is applicable also to the tribal religions: "These religions venerate God by sincere acts of piety, a piety which like their convictions, forms the foundations of their moral and social life."[525] What Vatican II says is quite significant here:

> The Church rejects nothing which is true and holy in these religions. She looks with sincere respect upon those ways of conduct and life, those rules and teachings which, though differing in many particulars from what she holds and sets forth, nevertheless often reflect a ray of that Truth which enlightens all men. We cannot truly pray to God the Father of all if we treat any people in other than brotherly fashion, for all men are created in God's image (NA, 2).

These truth and goodness are found in unique expressions in these religions. These expressions need to grow up ever more for the further progress of the religious pilgrimage. So, a tribal Christian theology develops through expressions,

523 Amaladoss, Michael SJ, "Theologising in a Tribal Context: Some Methodological Observations", 5.

524 Parapullil, Anthony, SJ, "Tribal Theology", 27.

525 Parapullil, Anthony, SJ, "Tribal Theology", 28.

namely, their philosophy, anthropology, forms of worship and symbolism. The task for us is to make Christ present in the midst of the tribal people and allow Him to confront them in their own cultural expressions of truth and goodness. Such a confrontation will lead to a Christian theology, liturgy and local Church institutions and way of life. But, we should realize that it is not an easy task or process. It will be the result of an inner growth of Christian life lived in the tribal culture. So, we need to find out the truth and goodness inherent in these religions.[526] If we are able to do this there is a possibility of forming a tribal theology that is liberative.

4.9. Critical Function of Theology: Against Power and Idolatry

In order to theologize meaningfully we need to renounce three aspects, namely, money, power and the anti-God. All the evils of an economy based on private property, competition, and exploitation are expressed in the money form. Because it creates divisions in society into employers and workers, consumers and producers, it alienates people from other people. People use God as a means to legitimize their own class interests and exploit the poor. The rich can buy the favour of God by making donations to religious institutions or by having religious services held for their spiritual benefit. The rich believer develops a religious attitude to money and a monetary attitude to God. We need to understand then that the God who is exchanged for money is not the living God but a product of the human brain. In order to develop a theology that is faithful to the living God, theologians have to opt out of the institutional Church or at any rate dissociate themselves from its practice. They have to make a historic option in favour of the poor and the oppressed; they have to declass themselves.[527]

Power can be used as a weapon to suppress and manipulate others. Those who exercise power for such purposes fail to encounter the living God. Religious authority is vested with secular power, and secular power with religious authority. God thus becomes *kingified*, and kings deified. In either case human beings are reduced to slaves. In medieval times there were magistrates who enjoyed Episcopal powers, and bishops vested with magistrate's power. Today the structure of power in the Church is very much feudal, characterized by dependence and patronage. In India domination is enhanced by the inflow of foreign money. The emergence of a theology of the living God will be possible only when theologians have the courage to renounce all power and, like Jesus, identify themselves with the powerless and the downtrodden of today.[528]

When people use God to legitimize their own interests of exploitation and domination then gives birth to the Anti-God. Other factors like cult may be involved too. Cult is authentic when it is part of a person's response to the

526 Parapullil, Anthony, SJ, "Tribal Theology", 29.

527 Kappen, Sebastian, SJ, Jesus and Culture, 90.

528 Kappen, Sebastian, SJ, Jesus and Culture, 91.

demand of God as revealed in history. This can lead to creative, liberating praxis. It becomes inauthentic, alienated and alienating, when it is detached from the dialectic of divine challenge and human response. False cult leads to making a God whom people can manipulate and dispose of as they please. This God is neutral to the rich and the poor and dispenses favours to the exploiter and the exploited. The Anti-God breeds and is bred by dogma. Dogma de-historicizes and fixes God into eternal and immutable concepts.[529] This is something we should reject constantly in order to see and experience the real God of the Bible.

4.10. Credibility and Authenticity of Contextual (Santal) Theology

All theology is culturally conditioned and contextual but some contexts are wrong (when we do not read the signs of the times properly). The context has to be addressed consciously. Context is both global and local; one has to be aware of the political and economic elements in a given culture. Context decides the meaning of language. The experience of a community is that of a community suffering, rejoicing, weeping, dancing, and hoping. Contextual Theology does not begin in a mind filled with information but in a compassionate heart ready to listen. To do contextual theology is to take a faithful stance; it involves risk.[530]

The credibility and authenticity of contextual theology could be judged within the matrix of a creative tension between the *vertical* and the *horizontal* dimensions of theologizing, whereby tradition and experience encounter each other in a mutual dialogical relationship which in turn generates the fruits of exciting, new possibilities of theologizing. The *vertical* dimension of contextual theology refers to its *internal* coherence with the deeply profound and rich heritage of 2000 years of diverse and pluralistic ways of doing theologies within the Catholic theological tradition which is handed down from one generation to another. Its *horizontal* dimension refers to its *external* coherence with a local community's experiences and actions which are being carried out in specific *local* multireligious, multi-ethnic, multi-lingual and pluri-cultural contexts. To the extent that the contextual theology is authentic and credible, it should be able to define, articulate and uphold in a holistic manner the *hyphenated* character of all Asian local churches: all Asian local churches are/should be authentically Christian yet truly Asian in every sense of the word.[531]

Conclusion

> Whether they are called *bidonvilles* in Haiti, *favellas* in Rio de Janeiro, *barriadas* in Lima, *tambos* in Bolivia, *ranchitos* in Caracas or *ciudadesperdidas* in Mexico, a slum is a slum, overcrowded, dirty, with

529 Cf. Kappen, Sebastian, SJ, Jesus and Culture, 92-93.

530 Cf. Yun-Ka Tan, Jonathan, Theologizing at the Service of Life.

531 Yun-Ka Tan, Jonathan, Theologizing at the Service of Life.

> no water or sanitary conditions, no health services, housing millions of jobless, lost cities where even hope is hard to come by. Theologian Elizondo explains: Liberation Theology came out of the context of poverty because most of the people in Latin America are poor. The Church asked the question, 'what does it mean to be a Christian here and now?'[532]

Deane William Ferm says that they who live in the West should not, of course, adopt Asian theology wholesale; that would be the begging approach. The Asians' imagery speaks to their situations; the West couldn't do much with water-buffaloes and sticky-rice. But that does not mean that they have nothing to learn from them (Asians). Indeed, they should forswear forever the imperialistic "ugly monster" of the one-way teacher approach which has so deeply infected the Western attitude towards the Third World. They should formulate a "rice-roots" approach for the poverty and oppression within their own context (megatrend theology? computer theology? multinational theology?); they should develop their own sensitivity, their own concern for the "sinned against", their own sensitivity to the mystery of the others. Perhaps in this way they can become full-fledged participants in an ongoing worldwide struggle for a full humanity – an effort which will not only mean good news for the "underside of humanity" but will lead to their (Western) own liberation as well. And that, after all, is what Christianity is all about.[533]

> The primary locus of theology, therefore, cannot be the closed community of Christians but the open community of all those who hunger and thirst for justice and freedom. And if the theology that emerges out of dialogue with the Lord of history bursts the old wineskins of tradition, none need shed a tear over it except the makers of old wineskins![534]

The theological task here would be to make the tribal people a progressive community without cutting them off from their tribal roots. The tribal people should know the strength and weakness of their culture. Only then can they remove the weaknesses like the lack of work-culture, easy-going life, addiction to alcoholic drinks, lack of high aims and determination to achieve them at all costs. They need to work on these areas of their life to improve their situation and only then they can stand on equal footing with others.

Emphasis on liberation, service, social analysis and culture leads to a focus on the Bible and Jesus Christ. To be sure, the presence in Asia of various faith groups

---

532 Cloutier, Jean-Pierre, Theologies: Liberation Vs Submission.

533 Ferm, Deane William, Outlining Rice-Roots Theology, in *Christian Century* January 25, 1984, 78.

534 Sebastian Kappen, accessed on 26.02.08.

means that the biblical Christ does not dominate the emerging shape of Asian theology as might be the case in other Third World theologies. However, it would be incorrect to suggest that Christ has been excluded. On the contrary, he occupies a central place in Asian Christianity, even among the Santals of Jharkhand; the emerging theologies are simply reinterpreting the pastoral approach suitable for the people today. We believe that Christ frees us that we may free others because we experience God's revelation is in all nature, all history, and among all peoples. It is our task to observe where God is at work and to join in the liberation of the oppressed, poor and marginalised. Each must discover God in Christ at work where he or she is and move from that centre, being guided by the Spirit, toward making life more human and more liveable. It is thus that we are set free as human beings both from the slavery of sin and the sin of slavery. It is thus that we participate in liberation in order to uproot the systems of bondage; there may be no slaves or masters, but a co-humanity in Christ Jesus our Lord, in the church as an extension of the incarnation and consequently among all people. Such an experience of God interpreted in contextual theology can lead us to a meaningful pastoral approach for the Santals. We need to understand their needs and possible approaches to the situation today. Only then can we be effective catalysts for the holistic liberation of the Santals.

"Mission is to be passionate for God's Reign." Diego Irarrázaval

5

New Pastoral Vision in the Context of the Santals

"Do not wait for leaders; do it alone, person to person." Mother Teresa

5.1. Introduction

"I have never been able to comprehend how Christianity, which is essentially a message of liberation, managed to allow the rise of the capitalistic system and then came to safeguard it. This fact is all the more lamentable and incomprehensible because injustice, oppression, and manipulation are the most striking and obvious features of that system."[535] These features have ruled Christianity and we find today a pallid Christianity living the life of a vegetable. The revolutionary and creative import of its message of love seems to have been lost. The Christian faith seems to have been stripped of its subversive content, namely, its commitment to the creation of an ever more humane world and its opposition to every type of dehumanisation. Christianity then associated revolutionary nature with atheists because Christianity had become radically debased. In such a situation if we believe that God revealed himself in an act of socio-political liberation, we are invited to participate in fashioning a real communion by establishing the Kingdom of God here on earth.[536]

Christianity in India appears as a foreign religion to people. Expressions like, "fullness of revelation", and the "only way", are subjective faith expressions.[537] Today we need to choose a new way of proceeding. Do we have to choose the

535 Perez-Esclarin, Antonio, Atheism and Liberation, London: SCM Press, 1980, 1.

536 Cf. Perez-Esclarin, Antonio, Atheism and Liberation, 1-2.

537 Chethimattam, John B(Ed), Jeevadhara Vol. XXX No. 179 Inculturating Our Theological Thinking, Sep. 2000, 419.

old culture and say no to the new one or do we choose the other way? Should we critically see the reality of the world and people? People have the freedom to choose and act accordingly. If we choose the vision for a new humanity it is a cause for celebration because many people are trying to follow it already. It is hoped that this attempt to work for a new humanity will provide sustainable solutions to humanity's greatest threats. Because we know that our mission is supposed to be oriented to connect people, who, through personal and social transformation, aim to build a just, peaceful, and sustainable world, reflecting the unity of all humanity in the world and in a special way in the context of the Santals. In order to achieve this goal, we need to start from below, from the local church where we should know the mission and vision of Jesus.

We believe that Jesus came to earth for us. What is most important about Jesus' mission is that it directly affects our life. Jesus came to restore our relationship to God the Father. If we choose to receive Jesus' body and blood as a sacrifice for our sins, and are willing to give Him our life, then we receive His life. Jesus' name describes His mission and purpose of coming to earth. And Jesus went about all Galilee, teaching in their synagogues, preaching the gospel of the kingdom, and healing all kinds of sickness and all kinds of diseases among the people. Then His fame went throughout all Syria; and they brought to Him all sick people who were afflicted with various diseases and torments, and those who were demon-possessed, epileptics, and paralytics; and He healed them (Matt 4:23-24). Jesus explained His mission to the twelve apostles. "For even the Son of Man did not come to be served, but to serve, and to give his life as a ransom for many" (Mk 10:45). If anyone had a right to be served, it was Jesus. He is God, King of Kings, and Lord of Lords. Millions of angels serve Him night and day. However, when Jesus came to earth, He came to serve others and give his life as a ransom for sinners. If we believe in this vision of Jesus, we need to follow him in his path.

5.2. Need for A New Vision of Mission

The primary focus at this time in our history in the context of the Santals is the building up of a new pastoral vision for the mission so as to have a true local church. This is based on the understanding of the people (Santals) and their situation. In the first chapter of my dissertation I have elaborated their situation, their world view. Two striking aspects of their life are their link to nature and communitarian approach. These aspects should be affirmed in our understanding of the tribal people. The other important thing in their life experience is the experience of their untold misery and oppression at the hands of local leaders and government leaders. It is incredible to think that such oppression can exist under the sun. I have seen the tears of the oppressed and they had no one to comfort them. The oppressors had power and wealth, but they used their power and wealth only to oppress and hoard up more wealth for themselves. In the second chapter I have explained the history and growth of the church. All their (missionaries') good intentions and missionary activities had a substantial effect on the people but that was not all. They thought that the priority of the church was focused on its own existence and rituals. They forgot that such a church is only in its infancy. In the process many of the tribal people lost their cultural values and tradition. When the church tries to bottle up the Spirit within herself, she acts contrary to her nature. It is the nature of the church ever to be enlarging her borders, and it is the nature of the Spirit to transmit his life to ever-widening circles. An authentic church is one that lives for others. Today we need to rethink and find ways and means of remedying the situation by finding new modes of dealing with the people. It is here that we should think about how the building up of such a church is possible as the primary task in the Santal context, also in India at the present time. The idea of "becoming a local church" in most cases does not mean starting from nothing. Becoming a local church means that the Gospel is meeting a living group of people in every moment of history.

One of the primary steps in dealing with the situation of the Santals is by inculturating ourselves in the context of the Santals. The third chapter clarifies the method and approach of inculturation in the context of the tribal people. If we have the context (their world view and life experiences) we can understand their situation better in order to live our life in their midst meaningfully. To live meaningfully in their midst, we need to inculturate ourselves to their reality. With these elements we should be able to theologise and formulate a theology that is suitable to the context of the Santals. In this theology Christian faith is interpreted from the perspective of the suffering, struggle, and hope of the poor; there is a critique of society and the ideologies sustaining it. There is also a critique of the activity of the church and of Christians from the angle of the poor. This is what I have described in the fourth chapter. From this analysis we may be able to find some remedies and possible ways to deal with the Santal life and situation. However, I might say as well that all our possible remedies and solutions may not always be right as people themselves are the real planners and decision makers. We can only help them find solutions. First of all, we need to make our options clear.

5.2.1. Option for the Poor as our Motivation

In order to achieve the goal Jesus had to abolish Roman imperialism and bring in the Kingdom of God through a religio-political movement. There is no evidence that after Jesus left Jordan he ever baptised or sent anyone to John the Baptist to be baptised. Instead he went to seek out, help and serve the lost sheep of the house of Israel. He went to live and share his life with the poor, the little ones, the marginalised of society. These people lived in a dark and fearful world in which they were threatened from all sides by hostile spirits and equally hostile people. Jesus wanted to fill these people with the Spirit of God.[538] The situation of the Santals is similar. Therefore, the Jesuits of Dumka-Raiganj Province made

538 Nolan, Albert, Jesus Before Christianity, New York: Orbis Books, 1978, 49.

a preferential option for the poor and marginalised of society. The basis for this option is based on the General Congregations (ultimate governing body in the Society of Jesus) of 32, 34 and 35. In all these General Congregations (GC) they emphasised the dimension of mission in favour of promoting justice in which faith is an integral part.

General Congregations of the Society of Jesus and Our Mission Today

The need was felt from different parts of the world by the Jesuits to know the guidelines for the mission today. The 32nd General Congregation of the Society of Jesus held in Rome very firmly asserted:

The mission of the Society of Jesus today is the service of faith, of which the promotion of justice is an absolute requirement. For reconciliation with God demands the reconciliation of people with one another.In one form or another, this has always been the mission of the Society; but it gains new meaning and urgency in the light of the needs and aspirations of the men and women of our time, and it is in that light that we examine it anew. We are confronted today, in fact, by a whole series of new challenges.[539]

The Society of Jesus was aware of the new challenge to our apostolic mission in a world increasingly interdependent but, at the same time, divided by injustice: injustice not only personal but institutionalized - built into economic, social, and political structures that dominate the life of nations and the international community. This unjust situation needs our response; a response that will be unavailing unless it is total, corporate, rooted in faith and experience, and multiform. It is total because we are expected to give our all, persons, communities, institutions, ministries and resources. It is corporate because all are expected to use their talents and functions in collaboration with others to give life to the whole body. It is rooted in faith and experience because we need to respond to new situations. It is multiform because the situations are different in different parts of the world. We need to be adjustable and flexible to situations within the steady aim of the service of faith and promotion of justice.[540]

This mission we are called to share is the mission of the Church itself, to make known to men and women the love of God our Father, a love whose promise is eternal life. The mission originates in God the Father who appointed Jesus to carry on His mission. Thus, Jesus was sent by the Father "not to be served but to serve, and to give His life as a ransom for many" (Matt. 20:28). The mission of Christ, in turn, gives rise to the mission shared by all Christians as members of the Church sent to bring all men and women the Good News of their salvation and that "they may have life and have it to the full" (Jn 10.10; Matt. 9.36). It is this understanding of Jesus' mission that moved St. Ignatius and his first companions

539 GC 32, Decree 4, Our Mission Today: The Service of Faith and the Promotion of Justice, December 2nd, 1974 - March 7th, 1975, Nos. 48,49.

540 GC 32, Our Mission Today, 52-56.

to a searching consideration of the world of their own time in order to discover its needs. As they contemplated, they turned their eyes to where God's gaze was fixed, and saw for themselves the men and women of their time, one after another, "with such great diversity in dress and in manners of acting. Some are white, some black; some at peace, and some at war; some weeping, some laughing; some well, some sick; some people coming into the world, some dying, etc" (Spiritual Exercises,[541] 102, 106, Contemplation on the Incarnation). That was how they learned to respond to the call of Christ and to work for the establishment of His Kingdom.[542]

If we analyse the reason why the Society of Jesus was founded, we know that it was chiefly for the purpose of striving especially for the defence and propagation of the faith, and for the progress of souls in Christian life and doctrine, by means of public preaching, lectures, and any other ministrations whatsoever of the word of God. They were also expected to help by means of the Spiritual Exercises, the education of children and unlettered persons in Christianity, and the spiritual consolation of Christ's faithful through hearing confessions and administering the other sacraments. Another important mission was in reconciling the estranged, in assisting and serving those who are found in prisons and hospitals, and indeed in performing any other works of charity, according to what will seem expedient for the glory of God and the common good. This primordial statement remains for us a normative one. Therefore, our Jesuit communities have to help each of us overcome the reluctance, fear and apathy which block us from truly comprehending the social, economic, and political problems which exist in our region or country, as well as on the international scene. Only by understanding these problems well, will we be able to preach the Gospel better and to work better with others in our own particular way to promote justice.[543]

The 34th General Congregation again emphasised the commitment to the poor and renewed our commitment to the promotion of justice as an integral part of our mission.

> The promotion of justice requires, before all else, our own continuing personal conversion — finding Jesus Christ in the brokenness of our world, living in solidarity with the poor and outcast, so that we can take up their cause under the standard of the Cross. Our sensitivity for such a mission will be most affected by frequent direct contact with these friends of the Lord, from whom we can often learn about faith. Some insertion into the world of the poor should therefore be part of

541 The Spiritual Exercises of St. Ignatius of Loyola are a month-long programme of meditations, prayers, considerations, and contemplative practices that help Catholic faith become more fully alive in the everyday life of contemporary people. They are set out in a brief manual or handbook.

542 Cf. GC 32, Our Mission Today, 62, 63.

543 Cf. GC 32, Our Mission Today, 66, 92.

> the life of every Jesuit. And our communities should be located among ordinary people wherever possible.[544]

In order to achieve this aim in each of our different apostolates, we must create communities of solidarity in seeking justice. We have to work together with our colleagues, so that every Jesuit ministry can and should promote justice. Only then can we have direct service and accompaniment of the poor, develop awareness of the demands of justice joined to the social responsibility to achieve it and participate in social mobilization for the creation of a more just social order.[545]

Realising the great need of the time the recent General Congregation 35 (held in January to March 2009 in Rome) highlighted and termed it *Challenges to our Mission Today: Sent to the Frontiers*, showing the dire need of our mission today.

> Our commitment to establish right relationships invites us to see the world from the perspective of the poor and the marginalised, learning from them acting with and for them. In this context the Holy Father reminds that the preferential option for the poor is implicit in the Christological faith in a God who became for us became poor, to enrich us with his poverty (2 Cor 8:9). He invites us with a prophetic call to renew our mission among the poor and for the poor.[546]

In fact, this decree was derived from the understanding of Jesuit Identity which is an inseparable part of the Mission of the Society. The Mission document takes into consideration our concrete experience of good and evil which affect human beings in their everyday life. This document was therefore considered the people's decree. The identity of the society should have this charism to be at the service of people. Jesuits are thus called to be sent to the frontiers to serve in faith, promote justice and dialogue with cultures and religions. This prophetic call may lead us to confrontations with the powers that be. At times we may even have to pay a price for our call. It is like making an option like Jesus made. Just as Ignatius sent the Jesuits to the mission regions, today we are called to serve the marginalised, the poor and unwanted of society. We have to create reconciliation in a world torn apart by violence, strife and injustice. We need to create new relationships to celebrate the justice God. To achieve this, we need to be deeply rooted in the love of God, need to be united with one another and obedient to being sent to any situation. If we are ready for this, we can build right relationships

---

544 GC 34, Decree 3, Our Mission and Justice, January 5th – March 22nd, 1995, No. 66.

545 GC 34, Decree 3, Our Mission and Justice, 68.

546 GC 35, Decree 3, Challenges to Our Mission Today: Sent to the Frontiers, January 7th – 6th March 2008, No. 27.

at three levels, namely, with God, one another and creation. This message is very vivid in the Spiritual Exercises (SpEx) of St. Ignatius.[547]

The Spiritual Exercises of St. Ignatius and Our Option

The Spiritual Exercises of St. Ignatius are very clear about the type of options and choices in the life of Jesuits. Ignatius suggests ways to make our option very clear. At first, we consider the call of the temporal king to his subjects. If we understand what is meant by the call of the temporal king, how much more worthy of consideration is it to see Christ our Lord, King eternal, and before Him all the entire world, which and each one in particular He calls, and says: "It is My will to conquer all the world and all enemies and so to enter into the glory of My Father; therefore, whoever would like to come with Me is to labour with Me, that following Me in the pain, he may also follow Me in the glory." Those who want to be more devoted and signalise themselves in all service of their King Eternal and universal Lord, not only will offer their persons to the labour, but even, acting against their own sensuality and against their carnal and worldly love, will make offerings of greater value and greater importance.[548]

In the meditation on *Two Standards* once again Ignatius recommends that we choose the standard of Christ and follow him rather than following Lucifer and his team. If we choose Christ it would mean we consider the discourse which Christ our Lord makes to all His servants and friends whom He sends on this expedition, recommending them to want to help all - bringing them first to the highest spiritual poverty, and if His Divine Majesty would be served and would want to choose them, no less to actual poverty. Adding to this there could be scorn and contempt; because from these two things humility follows. There are three steps that follow: the first, poverty against riches; the second, contempt against worldly honour; the third, humility against pride. And from these three steps let them induce to all the other virtues.[549]

This idea is further highlighted by Ignatius in another meditation on Three Classes/Pairs of Men. The first two classes are committed to some extent but for a radical commitment the third option is recommended. The third want to rid themselves of the attachment, but want so to rid themselves of it that they have even no liking for it, to keep the thing acquired or not to keep it. They only want to want it or not want it according to how God our Lord will put in their will and as will appear to them better for the service and praise of His Divine Majesty. They want to be totally at the service of the Lord and accept or reject as the Lord wants them to do. This is done in perfect humility. Ignatius therefore speaks of

547 Cf. Kujur, Marianus, SJ, Sent to the Frontiers – Decree on Mission, in Jivan: News and Views of Jesuits in India, August 2008, 4-6.

548 Cf. Mulla, Elder, SJ, (Translator), Spiritual Exercises of St. Ignatius, Second Week, Nos. 95, 97.

549 Mulla, Elder, SJ, (Translator), Spiritual Exercises of St. Ignatius, Second Week, No. 146.

three types of humility to show the intensity of our commitment to the Lord. The first manner of humility is necessary for eternal salvation. The second is more perfect humility than the first; namely, if I find myself at such a stage that I do not want, and feel no inclination to have, riches rather than poverty, to want honour rather than dishonour, to desire a long rather than a short life, the service of God our Lord and the salvation of my soul being equal; I would not deliberate about committing even a venial sin. The third is most perfect humility; namely, when, including the first and second, and the praise and glory of the Divine Majesty being equal, in order to imitate and be more actually like Christ our Lord, I want and choose poverty with Christ, poverty rather than riches, opprobrium with Christ replete with it rather than honours; and desire to be rated as worthless and a fool for Christ, who was first held as such, rather than wise or prudent in this world.[550] It is this radical option that orients us towards Christ's mission and the Kingdom of God.

5.2.2. Option for the Poor Vital for the Kingdom of God

Jesus' mission was to present eternal life and knowledge of the only true God. This mission is unique in that up until this point, knowledge of the only true God was not known. The identity of God is only revealed to us through Jesus Christ who is the Son of God, who came to die for our sins. In that sense, Jesus is saying that we can have true knowledge of God only when we realize that Jesus Christ died for us. Jesus had to reveal this to humanity. Therefore, Jesus' mission has its basis on the experience of Jesus with His Father. Jesus addresses the awesome God of Israel as Abba. He experiences His God as gracious, loving and compassionate. What is interesting to note is that Jesus' personality is described in terms of His mission. It occupies his whole being and life. Therefore, Jesus had to confront the structured forms of sins embodied in every group within his own people and in humanity as a whole. Being sent into the world meant he had to confront the structures of sinfulness that enslave human beings. At times it is a sad reality that human beings enjoy the bondage because it affords them refuge and security. Authentic freedom and personal responsibility are not desired by people in general. So, Jesus wants to go beyond the framework of such views and practice of people and bring to life the more authentic human.[551]

To bring about the authentic human Jesus made the Kingdom of God as the central motif. This symbol made him articulate his mission to Israel. The idea of the Kingdom of God was long in the minds of people. It had a special significance in the life of Israel. It was related to their saving relationship between Yahweh and His people. This God was recognised as the one who ruled all peoples. Israel looked to the future vindication of its hopes by God's might alone. God would come to establish His rule. The people were convinced that God had ultimate

550 Cf. Mulla, Elder, SJ, (Translator), SpEx of St. Ignatius, Second Week, 155, 166-68.

551 Comblin, Jose`, The Meaning of Mission, New York: Orbis Books, 1978, 31.

authority over the life of His people and was intent on rescuing His people. We shall experience God as the absolute Lord of all at the appointed time, the kairos(the appointed time in the purpose of God).[552]

For us Christians, therefore, the story of Jesus does not end with the cross. God raised Jesus up, through whom (we believe) creation has once and for all been redeemed. His claims are vindicated by the resurrection from the dead. The emergence of life from death guarantees the ultimate triumph of God's act of creation. The Resurrection validates Jesus' proclamation that the Reign of God has come. God's salvation does not come by coercive power but through the revelation of God's love. The Reign of God which Jesus brings is, according to the New Testament, both present and future, already and not yet. So, it is a process which has begun but not yet ended. The awareness of God's love has entered into the world through Jesus, and is at work among us transforming hearts and structures, and so liberating people from Mammon (greed) and Satan (structured evil). The process of liberation is taking us towards the "new heaven and new earth."[553]

The mission of Jesus must permeate our land through the community of his disciples, the Church. It is not a displacement of other religions but it is a call to be the servant of the Kingdom. Christians and followers of other religions too should defend the values of life together and in respect for every person. All are called to show God's mercy and compassion, working to make the entire human race God's family on earth.[554] Mission is always integral as the New Testament understands it. It includes healing as well (Matt 4:23; 9:35) and it strives for the growth of the whole of creation, the total and integral liberation of human and cosmic history into the fullness of the eschatological Kingdom (Matt 10:7).

The radical dimension of this Kingdom is that, the so-called outcasts, sinners and prostitutes are included. This is so because Jesus is a man of the people, a person of the labouring class. He knows the struggle of the people, their sorrow and their heart's yearning for liberation, though society keeps them out. The wretched life of the poor is contrary to God's purposes and Jesus has come to put an end to their misery.[555] In this process we have a role to play because God's reign is a gift and a task. The fulfilment of the creation is not without human effort. We are not passive receptors of God's reign but active collaborators in its growth. Christian mission therefore must not forget the primacy of God's reign and so the ultimate primacy of God. Like all Christian life, Christian mission is

---

552 Senior, Donald and Stuhlmueller, Carroll, Biblical Foundations for Mission, London: SCM Press Ltd, 1983, 144.

553 Soares-Prabhu, George S.J., Expanding the Horizon of Christian Mission, 13.

554 Kavunkal, Jacob, SVD, The "Abba" Experience of Jesus: Model and Motive for Mission in Asia, Indore: Satprachar Press, 1995, 176.

555 Bosch, David J, Transforming Mission, New York: Orbis Books, 1993, 28.

theocentric, not Christocentric, much less ecclesiocentric. It is always God and God's reign that is the goal; therefore, our option is very clear, for the poor.[556]

The preferential option for the poor is definitely following Jesus and as such a Christological question as Professor Franz Weber (Theology Faculty, University Innsbruck) considers. Any Christian is called to make this option for the poor because he or she has opted for Christ. The option for the poor is not just a spiritual motivation but it is very much related to the biblical-theological, socio-ethical, systematic-theological, practice-theological as well as philosophical motivation which we need to express in different situations.[557] In other words it has to be a comprehensive reality, concerning all our life because God has become human.

God did not become just any human being but He became a poor human being. This is a clear indication of His bias in favour of the poor and the powerless, evident beyond any doubt in God's historical incarnation – in Jesus of Nazareth, which was considered an insignificant and God forsaken place from whence no good could come. But God's choice to belong to Nazareth was deliberate. This deliberate choice is very evident in Jesus' dealings. He had to even suffer for it unto death. That is the reason why we need to make a deliberate choice in our life.[558] This choice is very clear when Jesus says, "I am not asking you to take them out of the world, but I ask you to protect them from the evil one. They do not belong to the world, just as I do not belong to the world. Sanctify them in the truth; your word is truth. As you have sent me into the world, so I have sent them into the world. And for their sakes I sanctify myself, so that they also may be sanctified in truth" (Jn 17:15-19).

We human beings understand that all women and men are endowed with a rational soul and are created in God's image; they have the same nature and origin and, being redeemed by Christ, they enjoy the same divine calling and destiny; there is a basic equality between all and it must be accorded ever greater recognition. Therefore, there should not be room for inhuman inequalities and injustice in the world. To experience this inhuman situation Jesus was sent to experience the reality of the world (GS, 29). So we are also sent on this mission.

"Just as our being, all our actions must bear a clear stamp of an unmistakable bias in favour of the poor and the powerless and Christ's message leaves us in no doubt about this bias we all need to have. Whether we are involved in parish ministry or preaching or education, or formation or health services or as writers, or whatever, this bias in favour of the poor should become an integral part of

556 Soares-Prabhu, George S.J., Expanding the Horizon of Christian Mission, 13.

557 Cf. Franz Weber, Option für die Armen, Innsbruck, 1198, 23-25.

558 Kocherry, Thomas, My Vision of Mission in India: From a personal mission to a global vision, in The Church in Mission, Malipurathu, Thomas and L. Stanislaus (eds), Gujarat: Gujarat Sahitya Prakash, 2002, 111.

our life and evangelisation ministry."[559] The preferential option for the poor is not an option to exclude the rich from God's salvation plan. It is an attitude and action to follow Jesus who has proclaimed the reign of God. The proclamation is an invitation for everybody to become brothers and sisters for all; where there is no gap between the poor and the rich, where there are neither the exploiters nor the exploited, neither the oppressors nor the oppressed; and where all people 'eat together.' The rich joyfully and happily find God's own solidarity in their solidarity with the poor.

We become human and Christian only when we allow ourselves to be challenged and are converted every day by the poor and by different religious traditions. The poor and the various religious and secular traditions and ideologies challenge us with the kairos. We have to learn not only the art of being tolerant but also to appreciate positively, cherish and to promote the wealth of goodness and holiness that is found in other scriptures and religious traditions. The marginalised people of our society, the tribal people, the Dalits and the landless labourers are agents of conversion for us. It is in these situations that we find God.[560]

If we join these people in their world, we can form a Church inculturated into the world of the poor who are struggling for survival in the socio-economic, political-cultural sphere of life. Our ministries and services should be carried out from the perspective of these people - the poor; the economically poor and oppressed (mainly dalits and tribals). Since we have many religions in India we need to work closely with other people's movements and make our commitment more effective.[561]

5.3. Prophetic Role of the Church among the Santals

In the Old Testament God reveals himself to us as the liberator of the oppressed and the defender of the poor (Ex 23:1-3; Deut 16:18-20; Prov 20:8; Isa 59:14-15; Jer 22:1-4; Amos 5:7).He demands faith in him from people and justice towards one's neighbour. It is only in the observance of the duties of justice that God is truly recognized as the liberator of the oppressed.[562] Though God was so depicted the Israelites had made Yahweh the legitimating deity of the monarch. Worse still Solomon conscripts forced labourers throughout Israel (1 King 5:15). Nothing could be more poignant than this. God had made them a contrast community by liberating them from bonded labour in Egypt. Now the king of Israel has bought back bonded labour into Israel. Thus, the Exodus has been reversed.

It is precisely at this moment in the biblical story that the great writing prophets appear. Amos, the first of them taught in the Northern Kingdom round about 780 B.C.E. The prophets form a protest movement which calls back Israel

559 Kocherry, Thomas, My Vision of Mission in India, 114.

560 Kocherry, Thomas, My Vision of Mission in India, 113.

561 Cf. Kocherry, Thomas, My Vision of Mission in India, 115-16.

562 Catholic Social Teaching, Justice in the world, No. 30.

to the original vocation. The preaching of the prophets emphasises two basic themes; the denunciation of idolatry and a passionate condemnation of social injustice. The two themes are related. To worship Yahweh implies that we do justice to people. Biblical prophetism thus becomes Yahweh's continuing call to Israel to fulfil its destiny as a contrast community.[563]

God the Father is presented in the Scripture as the harvest master and vineyard owner (Cf. Mt 20:1-16; 21:33-43). Mission, therefore, originates with the Father; mission is God's project. The Father determines its parameters. Jesus declares openly that he has been sent by his loving Father; precisely, the phrase "the Father who sent me" occurs 46 times in the Gospel of John. And, a salvific thrust is evident in the missioning of Jesus by his Father. Vatican II expresses Jesus' mission as a reconciling presence: "to establish peace or communion between sinful human beings and Himself. Jesus Christ was sent into the world as a real Mediator between God and men" (AG 3). In Paul's theology, mediation and reconciliation are vital elements of the *mysterion* (Cf. 2 Cor 5:19; Col 1:13; Rom 5:1). Jesus' continuing "Abba-experience" enabling him to faithfully accomplish his mission has several dimensions: his coming or proceeding from the Father, his remaining with the Father (Cf. Jn 10:38; 16:32), and his eventual return to the Father (Cf. Jn 16:5; 7:33; 13:36). This means that Jesus fulfils his mission in light of a particular consciousness: continual intimacy with his Father. Luke tells us that before making such a decisive move in his ministry as the choice of the twelve, Jesus "went out to the mountains to pray, spending the night in communion with God" (Lk 6:12). Mission in the Jesus mode has its source, continuation, and fulfilment in the "Abba-experience." This dimension in Jesus' pattern of living mission provides evangelizers an inviting model for their own mission consciousness.[564]

Jesus clearly and unequivocally understood his mission in terms of the authentic Old Testament tradition. The missionary nature of Jesus' ministry is revealed in the foundational characteristic of his kingdom ministry. "It launches an all-out attack on evil in all its manifestations. God's reign arrives wherever Jesus overcomes the power of evil. Then as it does now, evil took many forms: pain, sickness, death, demon-possession, personal sin and immorality, the loveless self-righteousness of those who claim to know God, the maintaining of special class privileges, the brokenness of human relationships. Jesus is however, saying: if human distress takes many forms, the power of God does likewise."[565]

If we rely on Jesus then the role of the Church is as the prophetic critic of society. It is unfortunately neglected today; instead, the chief emphasis is on the healing ministry of the church, on Christianity as the antidote for anxiety, on the gospel's promise of peace of mind. This is not the role of the prophetic Church.

563 Soares-Prabhu, George S.J., Expanding the Horizon of Christian Mission, 9.

564 FABC Document, No. 61, Mission Today, James H. Kroeger, "Aware we are Sent", 4.

565 Bosch, David J, Transforming Mission, 32-33.

Our mission demands that we should courageously denounce injustice, with charity, prudence and firmness, in sincere dialogue with all sections of society concerned. There is no turning back or running away from this task. Our faith demands that the Church is obliged to live and administer its own goods in such a way that the Gospel is proclaimed to the poor. It implies that the Church is not expected to be among the rich and the powerful of this world. Then credibility of the Church is diminished.[566]

Such an understanding of mission is appropriate for the Christian community today. George Soares-Prabhu says that Missiology, like theology, is historically and culturally conditioned. There is no uniform, unchanging, universal understanding of mission valid always and everywhere. It is part of the finitude and historicity of Christian existence that our understanding of mission should vary in place and grow in time. The Indian Church must therefore develop its own understanding of mission which should correspond with our life and activity so that we find ways and means to help them in their day to day life.[567]

5.3.1. Pastoral Planning for the Santals

Jesus has done his work and gone. What remains is that we have to continue his mission. We tell people who Jesus was, how he lived, healed and reconciled people and empowered the poor. The fundamental task now placed before us is that of accepting the Lord's invitation to His people to journey together to bring about a new society where justice, peace and love reign. In order to work effectively we should be rooted in the Source of our being, the Father, whose love was made known to us in Jesus Christ and to live as He lived. This demands conversion and renewal in our life by authentically fulfilling the mission entrusted to us. Some of the prerequisites to be authentic are suggested by the Dumka Synod Document (held in the diocese of Dumka in 2000): First of all, we have to be a *praying community*. Praying together and participating in the Eucharist are to discover ever anew the wonders of God's love, to grow in knowledge of Jesus and deepen our relationship with Him. Only through this communion with the Lord can we become worthy witnesses to the values of Christ. Once we are a praying community then we can also become a compassionate community. This community becomes aware of the condition of the oppressed and marginalised brothers and sisters of our society. Through this solidarity we become a servant church.[568]

We need to express our solidarity not in words but in deeds. In a place like Jharkhand we need to ask ourselves, should we not be masters of our own home,

566 Cf. Catholic Social Teaching, Justice in the world, 47, 57.

567 Soares-Prabhu, George S.J., Expanding the Horizon of Christian Mission, in Jnana-Deepa Vidyapeeth, Theology Series Vol - I, Pune: 1999, p. 3.

568 Synod Document, Diocese of Dumka, Ranchi: Catholic Press, 2000, 2.

of our own country? It is unthinkable that as we stand before the rich natural resources, our hands should be tied, while the makers of the factories, industries and so on want to sign up our workforce for their own use and benefit. They take our riches away with them, extracted and transformed by our home workforce. When the situation is so, how can our natural resources and minerals contribute to our economic liberation? But we do not give up hope. With our experience in community building we can provide community building support to small groups and organisations which are working for people's rights. On their own it may be difficult to obtain inputs and information.

We need to implement developmental programmes in tribal villages (irrespective of religion, Christian or non-Christian) through local community participation. We must meet their basic requirements of housing, drinking water, education, health services, etc., by linking up with either government departments like Tribal Welfare, Forest Department or similar organisations. Unfortunately, these departments are unfriendly and unhelpful to the tribal people. Therefore, we need to support them in these situations. We have to encourage communities to build up local sustainable institutions to prevent the constant exploitation that keep occurring, forest protection committees, health and education committees and farmers' associations. These are essential groups which need to function properly.

General Development

In the biblical world the distinction between the religious and the socio-political reality are not compartmentalised. The religious realm overflows into the socio-political. The king is also the priest. The people are both an ethnic and a religious group. The prophet is a social reformer. A religious movement, like the one started by Jesus, will have great political consequences. That is why Jesus was crucified under Pontius Pilate (Cf. Mk 15:26). His religious proclamation included a vision of society. For Jesus the Kingdom of God would stand for the New Israel, that is, for the eschatological realisation of the community which he inaugurated when he appointed twelve of his followers to represent the twelve tribes of the covenant people (Cf. Mk 3:13f; Mt 19:28). In this theme of the Kingdom of God we shall discover his vision of the new society. In this Kingdom of God, the outcasts, the poor and the marginalised are included.[569]

If we want to follow the model of Jesus in our commitment, we need to also take part in political activities. It does not mean party politics, as we know very well that all parties have their own vested interests. Our involvement in politics has to be on a different footing or a different paradigm which will be holistic in nature. This can be seen from the perspective of our involvement in

569 Cf. Soares-Prabhu, George, SJ, *Theology of Liberation: An Indian Biblical Perspective*, in Collected Writings of George M. Soares-Prabhu, SJ, Vol 4, D'Sa, Francis X., SJ (Ed), Pune: Jnana-Deepa Vidyapeeth Theology Series, 2001, 223-25.

the protection of the weak and poor against imperial and despotic rule. This can be termed as prophetic politics or messianic politics. "With justice he will judge the poor and defend the humble in the land of equity. Like a rod his verdict will strike the ruthless and with his sword he will slay the wicked. He will wear the belt of justice and truth will be his girdle" (Isa 11:4-5). Thus, we have to design our participation in politics. In a country like India where the democratic system prevails, we can be of great support. Though the democratic system and the Christian understanding of human being have similarities we live with contradictions in our political life. Here we have to work towards quickening the process which will help in establishing a social democracy and will pave the way to establishing a just society.[570]

Efforts must also be made to implement patterns of development that provide the basic essentials for all, food, housing, health services and education. Our goal is greater economic and political democracy that is genuine participation of the people in decision making in daily work and civic affairs. An area to be specially considered is agricultural development as Santals are generally dependent on land. Land utilisation, crop production, irrigation, animal husbandry and dairying are part of this development. Community plantations, social forestry are useful elements for the tribal people. Many herbs and medicinal plants are found in the forest. They could use them effectively (as most of the herbal medicines are without side effects) as they had used them once upon a time.

As the basis of all economic activity, land can either serve as an essential asset for the Santal community to achieve economic growth and social equity, or it could be used as a tool in the hands of a few to hijack a country's economic independence and subvert its social processes. Our goal is to avoid what the British colonizers did two centuries ago. During colonialism, India's traditional land ownership and land use patterns were changed to ease acquisition of land at low prices by British entrepreneurs for mines, plantations etc. The introduction of the institution of private property de-legitimized community ownership systems of tribal societies. Moreover, we are today at a juncture where land, mostly for the urban, educated elite, who also happen to be the powerful decision-makers, has become more a matter for housing, investment and building infra-structure. In the bargain, the existence of land as a basis of livelihood – for subsistence, survival, social justice and human dignity has largely been lost. Finding effective means to relieve poverty is a defining mission for development economics. Our attempt today is to favour the Santals that they are able to make use of their land properly. We need to change the deteriorating plight of the Santals today. In fact, there used to be occasional efforts by the government to consider the problems of the tribal people. The national objective of abolishing poverty envisaged simultaneous

570 Cf. Massey, James, Socio-Political Scenario; A Christian Response, in A Vision of Mission in the New Millennium, Malipurathu, Thomas and Stanislaus, L, SVD (Ed), Mumbai: St. Paul's Press, 2001, 59-61.

progress on two fronts, high productivity and equitable distribution. Accordingly, reforms of the land were visualized as important pillars for a strong and prosperous country. If these projects are reconsidered and we join the people, these realities could come true for the people and there should be progress among the Santals.

Land, forest and animals alone do not complete human life. Humans have to be cared for and well treated. Herbal medicines are not enough to meet the needs of the people in the villages. They need health care centres with doctors and nurses. This is an area of grave concern. In fact, there are projects and provisions from the government but due to lack of attention and initiative from the Santals these facilities do not reach the people. This is an area to which we need to pay attention. Several people die in the village every day due to lack of medical care. Many of the tribal girls get married by the time they attain puberty and many of the pregnant women do not receive ante-natal medical care. Circumstances compel these women to deliver their babies at home, unattended and unaided by anyone. This is only one area, there are also several other cases of disease. There could be several factors responsible for this. Even if one survives an illness, it only leaves him or her more vulnerable to another, with the body's defences dwindling because of poverty and malnourishment. The situation sometimes is so intense that they have also stopped blaming the authorities for the deaths as they know it does not help any more. Haunted by poverty and illnesses that follow each other in quick succession, the tribal people seem resigned to a slow, agonising death. I know from experience that it is a wretched life to live through constant sickness without proper treatment. There is no quality to it. Illness has become almost their second nature (my own personal experience in the village). It is this situation that we want to address.

Having access to healthcare facilities is a basic expectation for any society. Various disease prevention methods can help reduce overall costs for healthcare. We have to meet the needs of people in this field by giving proper instructions and expert advice. People often do not have the means to go to city hospitals as they are either far away or too expensive. We should be able to contact the authorities concerned so as to meet the needs of people in the villages. There are also voluntary agencies, NGOs and trained health workers who are ready to help in such situations. Our duty is to contact them and make them available to the people. They support healthcare projects and provide free medical relief, health check-ups and perform medical procedures such as eye surgery to all patients, irrespective of their caste, religion or gender. They will focus on preventing diseases, which means providing appropriate vaccinations to all the people who live in a particular area. They also help the people and address varieties of issues such as emergency aid, or humanitarian affairs as well as health.

Since many of the tribal people are steeped in legal battles (land disputes and disputes with non-tribal people) they need direct legal aid. This is very crucial for marginalised communities fighting for their rights because often help is inaccessible to them. Inability to understand the laws or approach the judiciary on their own makes local communities and small organisations working with them vulnerable to exploitation by the state and other forces. We are expected to provide direct legal services to these people by helping in legal problems like false criminal cases, illegal custodies, getting bails, harassment and human rights violations, land alienation, either through writ petitions or public interest litigation. We have to take up legal action on these issues which are related to tribal life, resources, and we have to struggle against displacement by industries because such cases are violations of the Constitution of India.

Non-Formal and Adult Education

Literacy is universally recognized as the most powerful instrument of social change and this instrument plays a vital role in the social, cultural and health development of a country. In the context of Santals, literacy is important for their development and for adolescent girls amongst them because of correlations with the survival of their children later on. Therefore, we should take special efforts to advise the people to learn to read and achieve a better literacy rate among the Santals. The Constitution of India provides the facility for free education: "The State shall provide free and compulsory education to all children of the age of six to fourteen years in such manner as the State may, by law, determine."[571]

Only through literacy people can change their standard and situation of life. Unfortunately for India in general and among the Santals in particular literacy is a persistent problem. One reason why so many Santals are oppressed and marginalised is because they are illiterate. They are unable to read and write and so the people could easily be made victims in unwanted problems and situations. The rich and mighty people in the area do make use of this weakness of the Santals (Cf. Chapter 1). Despite government's many efforts, many Santal children are out of school or never go to school. Illiteracy affects not only the individual's life, but society as well. Because the vast majority of the grown-up Santals are illiterate, they could have non-formal and adult education. Together with leaning to read and write they could also learn skills for personal development. Educating adults differs from educating children in several ways. One of the most important differences is that adults have accumulated knowledge and experience that can add to or hinder the learning experience. Another difference is that most adult education is voluntary; therefore, the participants are generally better motivated. In the villages, people have enough time to learn if the volunteers who help can find time for them.

Technical Expertise and Cottage Industry

There are possibilities of aiming to upgrading the skills of tribal youths in various traditional/modern vocations depending upon their educational qualifications,

571 The Constitution of India, Part III, Fundamental rights, No. 21A.

present economic trends and the market potential; this would enable them to gain suitable employment or enable them to become self-employed. One of the goals of this project is to encourage the Santals to learn skills that enable them to help other tribal people. This is done by training qualified Santals so that they may become practitioners, skilled labourers, and/or volunteers who go back to work in their communities.

We should also plan and support small organisations and communities with technical expertise in seeking alternative sustainable development designs which can be managed by the communities. This includes harnessing locally available natural resources for meeting the basic needs of drinking water, electricity, irrigation, housing, etc appropriate to the area. With the help of technical experts, we can promote socially enduring and balanced development policies of the government. In this context we could think of a cottage industry which was very strongly supported by Mahatma Gandhi. Cottage industry is where created products and services are home-based, rather than factory-based. The products and services created by cottage industry are often unique and distinctive, given the fact that they are usually not mass-produced. Cottage industries provide economic opportunities for the poor or the middle-income section of people through employment and income generation schemes all over the world, and especially in low income and technologically underdeveloped countries. The cottage industry cannot compete with the industrial system of today.

Cottage industries can be very functional given the Indian reality; the vast majority of India's population lives in villages and many people are engaged in agriculture. They have ample time to earn additional income part of the year, when there is little farming work to do. Some of the products that could be produced in the villages are: straw baskets, mud toys, woollen shawls, wooden toys, handmade show pieces, khadi (Indian hand spun and hand-woven cloth) clothes, embroidering, leaf plates and so on, to mention only a few items. The Tribal Cooperative Marketing Development is another great support for the tribal people as it helps in providing marketing assistance and remunerative prices to tribal people. This cooperative is helpful for their minor forest produce and surplus agricultural produce and thus keeps exploitative private traders and middlemen away.

Many Santals keep domestic animals in their houses. Milk production has a big market in India. Each house can keep a few cows and/or buffaloes primarily for milk and milk products. The domesticated water buffalo is of great benefit to farmers. The dairy sector offers a good opportunity and as such there is an opportunity for new and expanding markets. Growth prospects in the dairy sector are very bright. If the Santals are trained to keep them and care for them properly they should be able to maintain a better life. Cows and buffaloes are income-generating means and the people can only make gains. Adding to these they could start poultry farms and fisheries as there are small ponds in villages. These are small items which any family could do if there is the will and desire to keep themselves going.

Self-help Group (SHG): Model for Self-sufficiency

Self-help groups are very functional in villages as they are often managed by women; but there are also mixed groups. SHG is a group of rural poor who have volunteered to organise themselves into groups to eradicate poverty in the villages. They decided to save regularly and convert their savings into a common fund. The members of the group agreed to use this common fund and such other funds that they may receive as a group through common management.

These groups generally consist of about 10 to 20 persons. The group should devise a code of conduct (group management norms) to bind itself. This should be in the form of regular meetings (weekly or fortnightly), functioning in a democratic manner, allowing free exchange of views, participation by the members in the decision-making process. They also draw up an agenda for each meeting and take up discussions pertaining to the agenda. The members should build their corpus through regular savings. The group should be able to collect the minimum voluntary saving amount from all the members regularly at the group meetings. The savings so collected will be the group fund. This fund should be used to advance loans to the members. The group should develop financial management norms covering the loan sanction procedure, repayment schedule and interest rates. The members at the group meetings should take all decisions concerning loans through a participatory decision-making process. The group should be able to prioritise loan applications, fix repayment schedules, fix appropriate rate of interest for the loans advanced and closely monitor the repayment of the loan instalments from the loan taker. Some of the activities are related to community actions. They are: improving community services including water supply, education, health care, veterinary care, village road, trying to stop sale and consumption of alcohol, protecting natural resources and acts of charity (to non-members). The promotion and operation of self-help groups, how members relate to one another, how groups interact with their communities, as well as the effect groups had on their social, political, and economic environments, have been very good in some Santal villages, as I have experienced. If they are able to function well in all the villages of India the result will be a rich profile, both quantitative and qualitative, of rural self-help in India.

Media Advocacy for Up to Date Information

Media advocacy is aimed at spreading policy-related information through the communications media so that there could be a change of policy, or to alter the public's view of an issue or problem. This can also create public awareness about the existing problem and thus influence policy makers or decision makers. It is thus one of the best ways to gain the attention of decision-makers, from local elected officials to top government officers. Media being the most powerful instrument of publishing information, gathering information, creating public awareness and acting as a pressure on the government to follow transparency and objectivity in its policies and programmes. Decisions to support legislative initiatives are frequently influenced by the media coverage. Getting media coverage can be at times very easy for people who can write articles. We can write about the difficulties, problems and draw the attention of the people concerned. Our advocacy efforts will affirmatively address the needs of traditionally under-served and under-represented communities through partnership with such communities. Though we may live in villages with illiterate people we should be up-to-date with the latest information in the world media. We need to get help and support from government agencies and campaign for the protection of peoples' rights. Small local groups need to come out of their isolated struggles as issues affecting people are based on policies of the state. We, with our experience and access to other people's networks should help local struggles by providing links to larger movements so as to build up a strong lobby support for the issues in the region.

Education for Life: Empowerment and Identity

The need for funds to educate the young in many developing countries is a big issue. The problem is the same among the Santals. The literacy rate among the tribal people is at a very low rate; According to the 1991 census, it is only 26.78%. The male literacy rate is 38.40% and female is only 14.75%.[572] That is the reason why the situation of the trial people is grim. Without education young people stand little chance of escaping the poverty trap into which so many are born. In turn the impact is on wider issues; protection of the environment is of little interest when basic necessities of life are hard to come by. We need to back the development of schools, both in terms of buildings and equipment, and also need to help individuals' education where appropriate.

Land and nature form an important part of Santal life. They learn from nature for their life as they know it is a great teacher from their past experiences. At present they need to learn to exist in harmony with nature. But this education alone is inadequate today because the Santals are in contact with other groups who are the so-called educated of society. To face the challenges, dangers and risks, the Santals have to be equipped with formal education and technical skills for life. To solve this problem, parents have to be given incentives and encouragement to send the children to school.

As long as power is not in Santal hands, they cannot revolt against the oppressors and the oppressive system. They need to have the will as well, to change. They are aware that they have neither economic, nor social, nor political power. They are robbed of their own wealth by the powerful minority. Power

572 Puthuparambil, Chacko SJ, Jharkhand me Visthapan evam Manavathikar, Dumka: Lakshmi Press, 2008, 153.

from this ruling minority has to be given to the tribal people. It would mean that they would be able to read and write; they would be properly fed; they could decide about their lives. How are they going to put into effect the changes in society? There should be scales of values and guidelines and principles. We can say that human destiny is the highest value; it is their right to rule their own life. They have to organise themselves to join the struggle for identity. That means they will say no to exploitation, under-development and marginalisation. Thus, they should find their identity as Santals. The time has come when the Santals can say that they are no longer worthless. They are directed to their destiny with our help and support.

In order to be effective and achieve this destiny we ourselves have to stabilize our life. We may need to stabilize our lives in a way that leaves us time and energy to devote to our life purpose project. We need to give emotional support to social issues. Only then will we be totally involved in what we are committed to doing. It is empowering to envision a positive future, imagining a changed society and the social process that might lead to it. This provides specific goals to work for, mobilizes energy and excitement, and also encourages a hopeful attitude about the impact we can have on the world.

5.3.2. Basic Human Communities: Model of Kingdom Communities

"They devoted themselves to the apostles' instruction and the communal life, to the breaking of bread and the prayers" (Acts 2:42). The post Easter perspective of the early Church is deeply rooted in Jesus. Their mission is stamped with the character of Jesus' own ministry. They were a community of people without much power and influence, having varying amounts of possessions. They were ready to share them with others. The believers in Jesus were quiet, religious people who gladly called themselves poor and treasured the sayings of Jesus. They devoted themselves to prayer and to the breaking of bread. "And all who believed were together and had all things in common; and sold their possessions and goods and distributed them to all, as any had need. And day by day attending the temple together and breaking the bread in their homes, they partook of food with glad and generous hearts" (Acts 2:42-46). No one lived in poverty and misfortune because there was no exploitation. This Church, which is the model of the Kingdom of God, is called the Church of the poor.[573]

This is the same mission we are called to propagate. If we follow the three symbols of Jesus (prophet, teacher and healer) used by the theologian, Roger Haight, the message becomes clearer to us. Jesus proclaimed that the kingdom of God was about to begin and would involve radical change. This would take place by the mighty deeds of the prophet Jesus. Jesus as the eschatological prophet envisages the coming of the kingdom of God in the concrete terms

573 De Santo Ana, Julio, Good News to the Poor, Madras: The Christian Literature Society, 1978, 39.

of social transformation within the towns and villages of Palestine. Jesus had disciples and they learned from him. Jesus taught with the authority of a teacher of the wisdom of God. Justice is transformed within the framework of God's transcendent wisdom that is disclosed in parables: the kingdom of God relativizes justice; the kingdom of God turns the orderly structure of society on its head. Jesus referred to himself as the embodiment of Wisdom in the flesh. There are plenty of evidences that Jesus performed exorcisms, healings, and mighty deeds (Matt 4:23; Matt 12:15; Mark 1:21-28; Mark 6:7-11) that transcended normal explanation. Jesus was a healer and exorcist. He displayed such a power that people had to judge whether it was from God or from the devil. The gospel message is that Jesus worked by the power of God.[574] The mission of the Jesuits is the same; to be prophet, teacher and healer to the Santals.

The Basic/Small Christian Community (BCC) is the new way of being the Church and the aim of BCCs is the aim of the Church itself. Church is the continuation of the life and ministry of Jesus Christ in history. The presence of Jesus Christ in history and the Emmanuel experience, i.e., 'God with us experience' in the world are the most important factors of Christian life. In the course of history, the 'God with us experience' was lost in the Church, as the Church community became large crowds, incapable of relating to each other. To experience this Church concretely we need to have local, small communities, which we may call basic/small Christian communities. We think of such communities because we see that such communities had functioned well according to the Bible. The early Christian communities had benefited from such a community life. We find the basis for small Christian communities in the Bible. This approach was based on the vision of a "New way of being Church", a church that witnesses to the Risen Lord.[575]

The importance of the laity became more accepted and the need for a lay organization was realized. They wanted to discover a more contextualised pastoral approach that would take into consideration the cultures and needs of the local churches. This model would incorporate the basic principles of life, respect for the experience of the participants and be open to the real situation and needs of the local community. It is a process of realizing the vision of a participatory Church. It addresses the entire people of God. This pastoral approach is Christ and community centred.[576]

Leadership is a very important factor in any growth whether it is a family, community or government. A new way of being Church needs collaborative leadership. The leadership is not thrust upon one person. It is something similar to the first Christian community in the New Testament. They were prophets and

574 Cf. Haight, Roger, Jesus Symbol of God, Maryknoll: Orbis Books, 1999, 60-73.

575 Cf. Eilers, Franz-Josef, SVD, For all the Peoples of Asia Vol. 2, Manila: Claretian Publications, 107-10.

576 Cf. Eilers, Franz-Josef, SVD, For all the Peoples of Asia Vol. 2, 107-10.

teachers; they even did the servile work (Acts 6:1), which shows they had learned the lesson that leaders of the church must be servants (John 13:1-17; Luke 22:24-27). The primary activity of the church leaders, however, is found in Acts 6:4 (We will turn this responsibility over to them and will give our attention to prayer and the ministry of the word). All pastoral leaders are called upon to actively involve and renew themselves through participation in the life of SCCs.[577]

The leader is expected to have the vision of God's plan for the community. The community unites with other communities, the parish, diocese, and universal Church. The gifts and talents of each member of the community should be recognised and responsibilities should be delegated to inspire zeal to evangelise and serve in the community. There should be unity in the community, praying for God's grace and fostering a continual interaction among the members of the community. The leader is not a person who would impose his ideas and views on others. The group members exhibit equality in their behaviour. No one is expected to speak with authority as teacher of the group. All need to listen to each other patiently whether one is a leader or no leader. Thus, this community is built up where each one is treated as an equal and expected to make a contribution to the group in his or her own way.[578]

Small/Basic Human Communities

In this context it is worth saying something about the SHCs (small human communities) of the Santal community where I have worked. There are basic Christian communities under different parishes. But, my work was among the small human communities. I say human communities because the majority of the people I have worked with were non-Christians. Since the group had Christians and non-Christians, we always had to be careful not to hurt the feelings of the non-Christians. However, many of the non-Christians also came regularly to the Eucharistic celebration.

We used to have the celebration of the Eucharist and after the reading of the Gospel we spent some time reflecting about it. Some important words or sentences were repeated. The group was then asked to comment on the Gospel to say what it meant to them, in their own context. At times it could be a very painful experience because some of them broke down, narrating their sad stories. After the gospel sharing many people made their own spontaneous prayers, very concrete to their life situations. Some of them prayed with tears. I still remember a very poor woman once praying for my good health and well-being. At such moments we were wonder-struck at their love and concern for others in spite of their poverty.

---

577 Cf. AsIPA, available from, www.ishwanikendra.org/docs/articles_asipa, accessed on 11.12.2008.

578 Nazareth, Ashley, Adult Faith Formation through SCCs, in Vidyajyoti Journal Vol. 65, No. 6, June 2001, 412.

Gospel sharing is one of the main parts of the SCCs. This is done in seven steps. 1) Inviting the Lord. We make a prayer inviting the Lord to be present to the group. 2) The text is read by someone from the group. The same text may be read from different versions or languages. 3) Words or phrases are picked out and read aloud and then we meditate on them. The text is read again. 4) Then there is silence for some time allowing God to speak to us. 5) Then we share with one another what they have heard in their hearts. What struck the Santals: they share very briefly without discussing or preaching. 6) Here it is business: They discuss any task which the group is expected to do; it may be the report on the previous task or the new task they have to carry out. 7) They pray spontaneously from the heart. Then the session is ended with a prayer or a hymn which we all know.[579]

This is not the end of the Gospel sharing. After the Eucharistic celebration we sit around in a group and share the day-to-day experiences. Family problems, financial difficulties, legal problems, social problems and so on are shared in the group. The sincerity and openness with which they share, is incredible. Several of the group members share their views and understanding of Jesus in their life and pray aloud in the group. We try to see everything in the light of the Gospel and try to find out what Jesus is telling us today in such situations. In this context we discuss social justice issues and make action plans. It may involve going to government offices and meeting the officers concerned; we may need to write applications to officers regarding certain problems; we may need to help the people meet lawyers regarding legal problems, etc. Thus, the Gospel becomes more meaningful to all of us in our day-to-day life.

During the Bible study several of the group members pray for different needs and reasons. Their spontaneous prayers are often heart-rending. The Bible study is concluded with a song which most of the people know by heart. After the prayers are over there is what is called the business talk to plan out for the coming activities; who would do what and who would go where, etc. Many would have to go to visit the villages regarding some problem or other, go to offices to meet officers or lawyers, and so on. By then most of the group members would disperse. Then the core group sits together to write reports or applications which have to be submitted to the offices. It is usually a long session. But the people never complain about the time spent because they are never in a hurry. They have allotted the whole day for this task on that particular day.

Some of the other activities of the group are the following: The group members, visit the Santal families two by two (Christian and non-Christian) to inquire about the health of the family members, about the children if they go regularly to school, about the cultivation of crops depending on the season, whether non-Santals oppress them in any way. The members come back after a week and report their experiences to the whole group in the weekly meeting after the Eucharistic celebration. We also conduct an overall evaluation of the activities

579 AsIPA Desk, FABC, Taiwan, 7 steps Gospel Sharing Method, taken from the Lumko Institute.

at least once a month. This is the time when we realize the process of action – reflection – action really taking place in the context. Twice a year the regular members have training programmes which make them more conscious of their responsibilities and commitment. It is the task of everyone to proclaim the Gospel and more so to live the Gospel; not always will we succeed. But it is wonderful to realize that God can still use us in spite of weaknesses and lethargy. So, we should share the Good News as meaningfully as possible in a way pleasing to God and beneficial to humanity. It is real surprise for us to see how the Christian Santals and the non-Christian Santals work together when they are in this group. No one asks each other whether they are Christians or non-Christians. No one is asked to be converted.

The basic Christian/human communities are therefore signs of the Kingdom of God where the people of God are on Exodus, a people following the footsteps of a God who invites them to journey towards their ultimate and definitive liberation. It is a lofty and demanding journey; the struggle is arduous but God's people are assured of victory. I believe that "the earth is to be truly a home for humanity, caring, consoling, providing. God is a God of plenty and of just distribution, of rejoicing and celebration."[580]

Total Liberation as Salvation

We need to interpret salvation in the present historical context as a single yet complex process of historical liberation which encompasses the totality of human existence, i.e., involving the whole person. If we carefully analyse the context of Jesus, we know that the centre of Jesus' preaching was the kingdom of God, and this referred to the historical, social and political sphere, or an arrangement of life in history that was also religious. The kingdom of God had its grounding in the will of God; it would be established by God; but it would exist in the world, consist in social-political arrangements among human beings, and not be established apart from human agents. The Kingdom of God Jesus preached was thus a movement in history. Therefore, the Kingdom of God Jesus preached was not to be merely a kingdom of religious virtues instead it consists in a social-political situation in which humanity, whose essence is freedom or liberty, flourishes. The kingdom is a hoped-for utopia in the midst of the sufferings of history.[581]

The kingdom of God is also proclaimed as a God whose love, freely given, frees human beings to love (Gal 5:1, 13). The appropriate human response to God's self-communication, love itself, requires the freedom made possible by God's love. Freedom is the basis for the meeting of divine and human persons in a communion of love. Such freedom becomes historically concrete through the creation of a just and humane socio-economic and political order, the emancipation of human consciousness from self-concern to solidarity with others, and our redemption

580 Balasurya, Tissa, Planetary Theology, London: SCM Press, 1984, 160.

581 Haight, Roger, Jesus Symbol of God, Maryknoll: Orbis Books, 1999, 76.

from sin for a communion of love. If by the history of salvation we mean not only those actions that are properly divine - creation, incarnation, redemption - but the actions of human beings as they respond to divine initiatives. There is liberation from social situations of oppression and marginalization that force many, in fact all people in some way, to live in conditions contrary to God's will for their life. But it is not enough that we be liberated from oppressive socio-economic structures; also needed is a personal transformation by which we live with profound inner freedom in the face of every kind of servitude. There is liberation from sin, which attacks the deepest root of all servitude; for sin is the breaking of friendship with God and with other human beings, and therefore cannot be eradicated except by the unmerited redemptive love of the Lord whom we receive by faith and in communion with one another. Salvation is God's unmerited action in history, which God leads beyond itself. It is God's gift of definitive life to God's children, given in a history in which we must build fellowship. Filiation and fellowship are both a grace and a task to be carried out; these two aspects must be distinguished without being separated in accordance with the faith of the church.[582]

5.3.3. Liturgical Inculturation in Praxis for the Santals

Jesus rejected the ritualised religion of the Jews though he himself had to undergo certain practices like: circumcision (Lk 2:21), his presence in the temple (Lk 2:39-52; Lk 19:45-48), his attendance at the synagogue (Mt 4:23; Lk 4:16, 33) and his observance of Passover (Mt 26:17 ff). He clashed with the legalists, "Look, it is against our law for your disciples to do this (picking heads of wheat and eat the grain) on the Sabbath" (Mt 12:12); "they watched him very closely to see whether he would cure him on the Sabbath" (Mk 3:2); he did not care about washing his hands before eating (Mt 15:2). These are not matters of great offence according to Jesus. He wants to save and not destroy life (Mk 3: 4). He is against those who claim to hold the keys of the kingdom but refuse entrance to others (Lk 11:52). He denounces the religious and social power structures: the scribes and Pharisees and usurpers. The Pharisees scoffed at him as he spoke against them (Lk 16:4). He condemns wealth that makes many people poor and praises poverty.[583] If we understand the context of Jesus in this way, we need to think seriously about the praxis of inculturation in the context of Santals. As we proceed in this path, we need to be aware of certain elements which affect the whole Church.

To prepare an inculturation of the liturgy, Episcopal conferences should call upon people who are competent both in the liturgical tradition of the Roman rite and in the appreciation of local cultural values. Preliminary studies of a historical, anthropological, exegetical and theological character are necessary. But these need to be examined in the light of the pastoral experience of the local clergy, especially those born in the country. The advice of "wise people" of the country, whose

582 Cf. Gutiérrez, Gustavo, A Theology of Liberation, New York: Orbis Books, 1993, xxxvii-xxxix.

583 Ellacuria, Ignacio, Freedom Made Flesh, New York: Orbis Books, 1976, 33.

human wisdom is enriched by the light of the Gospel, would also be valuable. Liturgical inculturation should try to satisfy the needs of traditional culture and at the same time take account of the needs of those affected by an urban and industrial culture.[584]

The Second Vatican Council has laid down the goal which should guide the inculturation of the Roman rite (cf. Fifth Instruction "For the right Implementation of the Constitution on the Sacred Liturgy of the Second Vatican Council", *Sacrosanctum Concilium,* art. 36, *Liturgiam authenticam*, on the use of vernacular languages in the publication of the books of the Roman liturgy). It is to restore the liturgy so that the texts and the rite express clearly the holy things they signify and so that Christian people, as far as possible, may be able to understand them with ease and to take part in the rites fully, actively and as befits a community.[585] One of the first things to do in this direction is translating liturgical books into the language of the people. The completion of translations and their revision, where necessary, should be effected according to the directives given by the Holy See onthis subject. Different literary genres are to be respected, and the content of the texts of the Latin typical edition is to be preserved; at the same time the translations must be understandable to participants, suitable for proclamation and singing, with appropriate responses and acclamations by the assembly.[586] All peoples, even the most primitive, have a religious language which is suitable for expressing prayer, but liturgical language has its own special characteristics. It is deeply impregnated by the Bible. It is to be seen that without losing the spirit of the Bible, changes could be made to facilitate the people.[587]

The vernacular, unlike Latin, is a living language and is thus a sure vehicle of culture. It expresses the people's thought and behavioural patterns and is an established bearer of their values and institutions. So, the use of the vernacular in the liturgy is in itself a sign that inculturation has taken place. This method offers a wide range of possibilities. With effort one can discover similarities between the liturgical rites and those of one's own culture, between liturgical symbolism and the local system of symbols, and between liturgical language and the ritual language of people.

For example, for the rites of Christian initiation, Episcopal conferences are to examine with care and prudence what can properly be admitted from the traditions and character of each people and in mission countries to judge whether initiation ceremonies practiced among the people can be adapted into the rite of Christian initiation and to decide whether they should be used. In order to adapt the sacrament of marriage to the customs of different regions and peoples, each

584 Varietates Legitimae, Instruction: Inculturation and the Roman Liturgy, Congregation for Divine Worship and the Discipline of the Sacraments on March 29, 1994, No. 30.

585 Varietates Legitimae, No. 35.

586 Varietates Legitimae, No. 53.

587 Varietates Legitimae, No. 53.

Episcopal conference has the faculty to prepare its own proper marriage rite, which must always conform to the law which requires that the ordained minister or the assisting layperson, according to the case, must ask for and obtain the consent of the contracting parties and give them the nuptial blessing. The proper rite must obviously bring out clearly the Christian meaning of marriage, emphasize the grace of the sacrament and underline the duties of the spouses. These elements are to be kept intact. Among all peoples, funerals are always surrounded with special rites, often of great expressive value. Episcopal conferences must choose those which correspond best to local customs. They may preserve all that is good in family traditions and local customs, and ensure that funeral rites manifest the Christian faith in the resurrection and bear witness to the true values of the Gospel. It is in this perspective that funeral rituals can incorporate the customs of different cultures and respond as best they can to the needs and traditions of each region.[588]

Deen Sewa Dal (Servants of the poor, in Hazaribagh district of Jharkhand state) is a movement that is kept alive among the Santals. There is less theory here and more practice in terms of awareness of a new consciousness of a distinctive culture. In this forum they seek to remedy some of the mistakes of the previous approaches, namely evangelising, which seems to have under-valued the Santal culture. At present the efforts of inculturation are a way of Santalisation of traditional Christian feasts and rituals. For example, baptism, marriage and funerals are performed almost totally according to Santal customs without diluting the Christian faith.[589]

The Santals celebrate *Sohrae* and Christmas as one feast; also, Easter and *Baha Porob*. Marriage too is celebrated with the Mass in the village. The understanding behind such celebrations is that such feasts have much in common both in the time of celebration and in their themes. The Baha Porob (flower festival) is the feast of the Resurrection of Jesus and the new flowers of the *sal* and *mahua* tree. The Baha Porob and Easter fall more or less at the same time. As the leaves of the forest fall, then new leaves begin to blossom. Jesus died and was buried and then rose again to new life. The Santals also remember their ancestors during the Baha Porob. So, the Santals understand this theme very well. In fact, the revival of some of these customs disturbs the older Catholics who no longer practise them. We need to instruct them adequately before we implement them. Thus, there are possibilities of making not only changes in liturgy but also in the life situation of people. Then the hope for a new humanity is not merely a dream but a reality.[590]

588 Varietates Legitimae, Instruction: Inculturation and the Roman Liturgy, 56, 57, 58.

589 Valamkunnel, Joseph, SJ, Deena Sewa Dal: An Ecclesial Movement in the Jungles of Jharkhand, in Emerging Indian Missiology, Mattam, Joseph and Valiamangalam Joseph (eds), Delhi: ISPCK, 2006, 113.

590 Cf. Deen Sewa Dal, Hor ari-cali ar Porobko (Santal Rites and Feasts), Ranchi: Catholic Press, 1996, 6-8.

Conclusion: Towards a New Humanity

Hope is the one human emotion, the one virtue that keeps humankind afloat, diverting tragedy, healing the sick, comforting the desperate, deciding with certainty that there is a way out. Hope is different from optimism and wishful thinking. It means placing a desired object or goal in one's mind, and waiting for a favourable outcome. Hope is the lived conviction that God's power permeates the universe and that in the end, love will win.

It should be understood that both poverty and wealth can either enslave or liberate, either keep people away from or unite them with God's salvific action. A new society, permeated with a kind of sisterhood and brotherhood, where the gap between the rich and the poor is bridged (Cf. Acts 4:32-34), should be begun. It emerged during the time of Jesus. Even the murder of Jesus did not destroy what he started. In that way, we can understand why God through Jesus has chosen the poor and given preference to them. In the orientation to and solidarity with the poor, God's salvation is present. Thus, our preferential option is rooted in God himself. God is the one who has chosen and saved us; it is not worldly wealth, human power, authority or achievement. Therefore, if we ignore the poor, we ignore God. This is practical atheism. The struggle to overcome poverty is a way to participate in God's plan through Jesus; it is the way of Jesus' disciples. We need to understand well that Jesus brought alternatives for new life so that all forms of poverty can be eradicated (Lk 4:18-19; Mat 19:16-30; Lk 18:18-30; Mat 25:31-46). As a result, the old world, specifically represented by the religious and political authorities who wanted to maintain their status quo, rejected and killed him. As Jesus took a definite stand in favour of the poor, he died as the poorest among the poor. However, God resurrected him from the dead and the murder of Jesus did not destroy what he had begun. This is the hope we hold on to. If Jesus was raised from the dead it is a clear sign that all that Jesus suffered and lived was approved by God the Father. All our suffering and pain is not end in themselves. We need to see beyond the dark clouds for the silver lining.

We believe as Christians that God is a God of justice: in the Bible, God acted on behalf of the poor and through the poor. The Church, in turn, must be in solidarity with the poor, the oppressed, and the suffering. Our preferential option for the poor and life with them bring the poor into the heart of the Church, inviting them to become subjects in their faith journey by reflecting on their own experiences of life, faith, and the church. The poor are often considered by others (rich and powerful) as "non-people" (people who are not taken into account). They become, in the Church, "God's people" (I Pet 1:10). The members of the Church, as members of society, have the same right and duty to promote the common good as do other citizens. Christians ought to fulfil their temporal obligations with fidelity and competence. They should act as leaven in the world, in their family, professional, social, cultural and political life.[591] The longing to follow Jesus and search for and discover God is authentic for the Church and the disciples of Jesus, only when the commitment is manifested in preferential option for the poor and the neglected.

What is remarkable about primitive Christianity is that it had a revolutionary nature, not in terms of war but in terms of ideology. Jew and Roman, Greek and Barbarian, free and slave, rich and poor, woman and man, accepted one another as brothers and sisters. It was indeed a sociological impossibility but the small Christian community caused the wonder.[592] The Church chose preferential option for the poor as her hallmark.

Love for the poor has formed a major part of the witness of the Church universal throughout all times and places. Love for those who are poor is one of the "practices" through which, by the power of the Holy Spirit, the Church has proclaimed the apostolic faith, first articulated in the kerygmatic preaching (Jesus' ministry to preach or proclaim (*Kerygma*), Good News to the poor and the blind and the captive) on the resurrection of the Lord. It is an integral element of the tradition of the Gospel that goes back to those who knew Jesus himself. Jesus of Nazareth is described by the writers of the New Testament as one who cared deeply for the poor and, indeed, shared their condition.

The Good News of Jesus has the power to recreate human beings and their society. It has strengthening, challenging, consoling and purifying effect because Jesus spoke and lived with compassion for the people. Purified of all shortcomings, Jesus is epitomised as Gods message because the time is fulfilled and the reign of God is at hand (Mk 1:15). This message of Jesus is to draw everyone to him. Our experience of Jesus should enable us to look into Jesus' events, all that Jesus said and did. We should then assert that authentic faith and religion must be converted into practice, a practice designed to liberate the people (Santals). The meaning of believing in God is, serving the needy Santals and thus fashioning the Kingdom of God through the Church.

A new humanity transforms people's fear into hope. In the hope of a new generation, the promise to reinterpret the human condition becomes possible. Millions of people seek alternatives to today's fearful world. New humanity communities are now developing as a result, with promise for generating many options to create communities. A new humanity is a vision that inspires a new respect for life and the earth and realizes that all human experiences are created out of our own internal beliefs. One of the most distinctive aspects of the Santal community is the hopeful and yet pragmatic way in which they face the future. Far from fearing it, they are dedicated to creating a new and peaceful society based on principles of justice, prosperity, and continuing advancement. This vision reflects not only an appreciation for humanity's historic longing for peace

591 Catholic Social Teaching, Justice in the World, 38.

592 Soares-Prabhu, George, SJ., Theology of Liberation: An Indian Biblical Perspective, 48.

and collective well-being, but also our understanding that humanity as a whole (we need to hope) has now reached a new level of maturity. That it is possible to create societies founded upon cooperation, trust, and genuine concern for others is at the heart of Santal belief and action.

Hope in the coming kingdom is already beginning to take root in the hearts of people, even among the Santals. The radical transformation of the world in the Paschal Mystery of the Lord gives full meaning to the efforts of people, and in particular of the young, to lessen injustice, violence and hatred and to advance all together in justice, freedom, kinship and love. At the same time as it proclaims the Gospel of the Lord, its Redeemer and Saviour, the Church calls on all, especially the poor, the oppressed and the afflicted, to cooperate with God to bring about liberation from every sin and to build a world which will reach the fullness of creation only when it becomes the work of people for people.[593]

"For now, I create new heavens and a new earth and the past will not be remembered... No more will the sound of weeping or the sound of cries be heard" (Isa 65:17ff).

593 Cf. Catholic Social Teaching, Justice in the World, 76, 77.

Personal Epilogue

I have lived in Europe for nearly five years. Life here has been very different from my situation in India. Without hesitation I should say that I have enjoyed my life in Europe. In many ways life has been different and luxurious compared to my life in North India among the tribal people. However, there was always something that I missed, I thought. This was the first time in my life in the Society of Jesus that I spent time only doing my studies. During my study days in India I always had some involvement with the poor people in the village, slum or some social activities. Here I found no opportunity for such activities.

What I enjoyed was my parish ministry in Europe. It was a very good opportunity to come to know the culture, life style and practices (religious and social) of people in Europe. Since I had the opportunity occasionally to stay with families, the experience was better as I could experience the day-to-day life pattern of families, people. I was also exposed to (at least partially) the realities of people. Though the majority of people have money to carry on with their day-to-day life there are many people who live alone and lonely. No denying the fact that all of us are in some measure lonely creatures. At the very core of our human nature is our need to love with great passion, and our need to be loved unconditionally. Our happiness, it seems, depends on loving and being loved. And so, we go on longing, hungering, thirsting and searching for the source of this happiness, the object of love that will satisfy this need. What strikes me is what St. Augustine once said: our hearts are restless until they find rest in God. I found that it is really very true in the life of many people who have some religious motivation in their hearts. Our restless longings, our unfulfilled desires, our loneliness, or that sense of emptiness that we feel in our life, even if we are in the midst of a community, or in relationship with others, all these things, painful as they are sometimes, they are, nevertheless, sacramental, because they can lead us back to God.

Many have no one to talk to, share their life with. There are many wounded people longing eagerly for comfort and community. But in the fast running and changing world it is not all that easy to find comfort and consolation of the heart. Talking to these people was for me a real experience of sharing the Good News.

These are also occasions for me to realise my own vocation as a religious priest as they have confidence and trust in us as we are priests. If the Church is the *corpus Christi*, Christ's Body on earth, then we must continue and extend to all people the human and divine communion that is revealed to us in the incarnation. We, the Church, we as a religious community, we are all called to establishing such communion in this world full of people who have lost their way to God but struggling to connect with God, people who are lonely for deep and authentic intimacy with others, people who are looking for contacts and community where they will find recognition.

I should also say that these years here in Europe have helped me to read several books, reflect personally on the life and situation of Santals from a distance. I know that it might help me some time after all. I do not deny that the intellectual world has its own attractions but it has also its futility by keeping away from activities of social action. If the ideas are fleshed out in real action there is definitely meaning and fulfilment.

What has disturbed me is also the situation in India today. Now we are at a time when tribal communities in India are used to grabbing headlines for all the unflattering reasons: starvation deaths, disease and displacement. In recent times there has been additional news. Death and persecution on the basis of religious conversion became the headlines. The latest flashpoint is the tribal dominated district of Kandhamal in Orissa, one of the very poor states of India.

When we weave our lives with our needy neighbours, we are engaged on emotional, spiritual and material levels. We are drawn out of our cocoons, our introversion, and our own needy selves. We learn faith lessons. We learn diligence in prayer. We learn to be givers of self and of resources. We become active participants with the Holy Spirit, like a hand in a glove. We learn to hear the voice of God and we see him work. We learn what cannot be learned otherwise. All in all, we need the poor, the fatherless, the widows, and the homeless because this is how we walk with Jesus. I need to be reminded of those who yearn for a better life.

We should never become discouraged. We must remember that we are about a holy purpose in building up the Kingdom to redeem all humanity; or, at least those on our regions. If the whole Church would take more seriously the high calling, we might come closer to fulfilling Jesus' great commission to reach all people everywhere with the Gospel of the Cross. If the churches everywhere would somehow open our doors to all seekers, then people everywhere would stop a minute to consider the message of the Cross.

I think the myth of phoenix is a good example to conclude the dissertation. The phoenix was a mythological bird able to consume itself in flame. Nothing remained but an ashen seed from which the Phoenix would rise again in a new beginning. Like the phoenix rising, a new humanity has entered the world, holding the belief that life is sacred and unconditional love, the covenant for a new human being. The phoenix symbolizes immortality, resurrection and life after death. The world has entered a new cycle, requiring each person to choose their next, best evolutionary step. Some people want to create a new direction for a new humanity.

"The wolf will live with the lamb, the leopard will lie down with the goat, the calf and the lion and the yearling together; and a little child will lead them" (Isaiah 11: 6).

Bibliography

Ad Gentes, Vatican II, Decree on the Mission Activity of the Church, promulgated by Pope Paul VI on December 7, 1965.

Ahmed, Syed Khalique, Rape of the Tribal, in *Indian Express* Monday, December 14, 1998.

AISWACS, Santal Festival, New Delhi: AISWACS, 2004.

Amaladoss, Michael SJ, "Theologising in a Tribal Context: Some Methodological Observations", Sevartham Vol. 4, 1984.

Amalorpavadass, Duraiswami Simon, Gospel and Culture, Bangalore: National Biblical Catechetical and Liturgical Centre, 1978.

Archer, William George, The Hill of the Flutes, London: George Allen & Unwin Ltd, 1946.

_______, Tribal Law and Justice, New Delhi: Concept Publishing Company, 1985.

Areeparambil, Mathew, Struggle for Swaraj: A History of Adivasi Movements in Jharkhand, Tribal Training Centre: Chaibasa, 2002.

_______, Tribals of Jharkhand: Victims of Development, New Delhi: Indian Social Institute, 1998.

Aril, James SJ, The Missionary Approach of Fr. Lievens, Ranchi: Catholic Press, 2001.

Arrupe, Pedro SJ, "Letter on Inculturation" in *Jesuit Formation and Inculturation in India Today*, Aixila, Jerome (ed), Delhi, 1978.

Arulsamy, Santiago, Liberation Theology in Asia, in *Indian Theological Studies*, 22 (3), September 1985.

Ashmore, Harry S. (Chief Editor), Encyclopaedia Britanica Vol 19, Chicago: William Benton, 1962, 958-60).

AsIPA Desk, FABC, Taiwan, 7 Steps Gospel Sharing Method, Taken from the Lumko Institute.

Balasundaram, Franklyn J, Contemporary Asian Christian Theology, Bangalore: ISPCK, 1998.

Balasurya, Tissa, Planetary Theology, London: SCM Press, 1984.

Bell, Daniel M, Liberation Theology after the end of History, London: Routledge, 2003.

Bergmann, Sigurd, God in Context: A Survey on Contextual Theology, Burlington: Ashgate Publishing Company, 2003.

Bevans, Stephen B., Models of Contextual Theology, New York: Orbis Books, 1994.

Biswas, Prabhat Chandra, Santals of the Santal Parganas, Delhi: Bharatiya Adimjati Sevak Sangh, 1956.

Bodding, Paul Olaf, A Santali Dictionary *(5 volumes).* Oslo: I Kommisjon Hos Jacob Dybwab (Norwegian Academy of Science and Letters), 1936.

Bodding, Paul Olaf, Santal Folk Tales, New Delhi: Gyan Publishing House, 1997.

_______, Studies in Santal Medicine and Connected Folklore Parts I, II & III, Kolkata: The Asiatic Society, 2001.

_______, Traditions and Institutions of the Santals, New Delhi: Gyan Publishing House, 2001.

Boff, Leonardo and Elizondo, Virgil (eds), Any Room for Christ in Asia?, Maryknoll: Orbis Books, 1993.

Bosch, David J, Transforming Mission, New York: Orbis Books, 1993.

Bradley-Birt, Francis, The Story of an Indian Upland, London: Smith, Elder & Co, 1905.

Campbell, Alexander, Santal Folktales, West Bengal: Pokhuria Santal Mission Press, 1891.

Catalogue of the Dumak-Raiganj Province of the Society of Jesus, 2007.

Chatterji, Patralekha, Kandhamal and horrors of state-in-retreat syndrome, in *Asian Age,* New Delhi, October 27, 2008.

Chaudhury, Arnab, The Santals: Religion and Rituals, New Delhi: Ashish Publishing House, 1987, 15.

Chethimattam, John B (ed), Inculturating Our Theological Thinking, in *Jeevadhara Vol. XXX No. 179,* Sep. 2000.

Chiromba, Frederick E, Evangelization and Inculturation, Gweru (Zimbabwe): Mambo Press, 1989.

Choudhury, Sahu, The Santhal Women: A Social Profile, New Delhi: Sarup & Sons, 1996.

Chupungco, Anscar J, O.S.B, Liturgical Inculturation: Sacramentals, Religiosity, and Catechesis, Minnesota: The Liturgical Press, 1992.

Comblin, Jose`, The Meaning of Mission, New York: Orbis Books, 1978.

Cone, James M., Asian Theology Today: Searching for Definitions, in *Christian Century,* New York: Orbis Books, May 23, 1979.

Cordaro, Guiseppe, SJ, Ai Nostri Amici (Diario 1938), Palermo: Rettoria Casaprofessa, 1938.

Culshaw, Wesley J, Tribal Heritage: A Study of the Santals, London: Lutterworth Press, 1949.

Datta-Majumdar, The Santal: A Study in Culture – Change, Delhi: Dept. of Anthropology, Govt. Oof India, 1956.

De Santo Ana, Julio, Good News to the Poor, Madras: The Christian Literature Society.

De Steenhault, Yves SJ, History of the Jesuits in West Bengal Part I, Ranchi: Catholic Press, 2003.

_______, History of the Jesuits in West Bengal Part II, Ranchi: Catholic Press, 2003.

Dei Verbum, Vatican II, Promulgated by Pope Paul VI on November 18, 1965.

Devalle, Susanna, Discourses of Ethnicity, New Delhi: Sage Publications: 1982.

Dodge, John V, (Executive Editor), Britannica World Language Dictionary Vol. 2, Chicago: Encyclopaedia Britannica Inc., 1962.

Dodge, John V. (Executive Editor), Britannica World Language Dictionary Vol. 19, Chicago: Encyclopaedia Britannica Inc., 1962.

_______, Britannica World Language Dictionary Vol. 4, Chicago: Encyclopaedia Britannica Inc., 1962.

Dorr, Donal, Mission in Today's World, New York: Orbis Books, 2002.

Dubey, S. N. & Mirdha, Rahia (Ed), Land Alienation and Restoration in *Tribal Communities in India*, Bombay: Himalaya Publishing House, 1977.

Ecclesia in Asia, Post-Synodal Apostolic Exhortation, Addressed to the bishops, priests and deacons, men and women in the consecrated life and all the lay faithful on Jesus Christ the Saviour and His mission of love and service in Asia by Pope John Paul II on November 6, 1999.

Eilers, Franz-Josef, SVD, For all the Peoples of Asia Vol. 2, Manila: Claretian Publications, 107-10.

Ellacuria, Ignacio, Freedom Made Flesh, New York: Orbis Books, 1976.

Evangelii Nuntiandi, Apostolic Exhortation to the Episcopate, to the clergy and to all the faithful of the entire world by Pope Paul VI on December 8, 1975.

Ferm, Deane William, Outlining Rice-Roots Theology, in *Christian Century* January 25, 1984.

Fox, Thomas C, Pentecost, in *Asia: A New Way of Being Church*, New York: Orbis Books, 2002.

Franz Weber, Option für die Armen, Innsbruck, 1998.

Gaudium et Spes Pastoral Constitution on the Church in the Modern World, promulgated by Pope Paul VI on December 7, 1965.

General Congregation 32, Decree 4, Our Mission Today: The Service of Faith and the Promotion of Justice, Rome: December 2nd, 1974 - March 7th, 1975.

General Congregation 34, Decree 3, Our Mission and Justice, Rome: January 5th – March 22nd, 1995.

General Congregation 35, Decree 3, Challenges to Our Mission Today: Sent to the Frontiers, Rome: January 7th – 6th March 2008.

Gill, Kenneth D., Toward a Contextualized Theology for the Third World, Frankfurt: Peter Lang, 1994.

Guru Kolean (dictated), Horkoren Mare Haprakkoreak' Katha (Ţhe Traditions and Institutions of the Santals – English translation), Benagraia (West Bengal): Benegaria Mission Press, 2000.

Gutierrez, Gustavo, A Theology of Liberation, Maryknoll: Orbis Books, 1993.

Haight, Roger, Jesus Symbol of God, Maryknoll: Orbis Books, 1999.

Holiday, Holiday Publications limited, Dhaka, Friday, March, 2005.

Horari-caliar Porobko (Santal Rites and Feasts), Ranchi: Catholic Press, 1996, 6-8.

Justice in the world, Catholic Social Teaching, World Synod of Catholic Bishops (America), 1971.

Kappen, Sebastian, SJ, Jesus and Culture, Delhi: ISPCK, 2002.

Kavunkal, Jacob, SVD, The "Abba" Experience of Jesus: Model and Motive for Mission in Asia, Indore: Satprachar Press, 1995.

Kocherry, Thomas, My Vision of Mission in India: From a Personal Mission to a Global Vision, in *The Church in Mission,* Malipurathu, Thomas and L. Stanislaus (eds), Gujarat: Gujarat Sahitya Prakash, 2002.

Kujur, Jacob, SJ, Liberative Aspects in Tribal Theology, in *Sevartham Vol. 22*, 1997.

Kujur, Marianus, SJ, Sent to the Frontiers – Decree on Mission, in *Jivan: News and Views of Jesuits in India*, August 2008.

Kujur, Raphael, "Tribal Church in Chotanagpur: Identity and Mission", *Sevartham Vol. 23*, 1998.

Kullu, Paulus, SJ, Theology in Tribal Religio-Cultural Context, in *Sevartham Vol. 28*, 2003.

Kumar, Arbind, Tribal Participation, Jharkhand: Lok Jagriti Kendra, 2002.

Lakra, Christopher SJ, Theologizing in the Jharkhand context, in *Sevartham Vol. 22*, 1997.

Letter from the Curia Praepositi Generalis Societatis Jesu, Decree of the Establishment of the Province of Dumka-Raiganj, Rome: 21 December 1988.

Letter of erection of the Diocese of Dumka and the appointment of the First Bishop of Dumka: Sub Secreto Sancti Officcii, August 30, 1962.

Letter of Johannes B. Janssen SJ (Superior General), Praepositus Generalis SocietatisIesu, Febraury 4, 1956.

_______, On the Silver Jubilee of the Mission, October 10, 1950.

Lumen Gentium Vatican II, Dogmatic Constitution of the Church, Promulgated by Pope Paul VI on November 21, 1965.

M. Hillar and H. R. Leuchtag, eds, Liberation Theology, in *Humanism and Social Issues. Anthology of Essays*, Houston: American Humanist Association, 1993.

Mammen, Mathew (ed), Manorama Yearbook 2008, Kottayam: Malayala Manorama Press, 2008.

Massey, James, Socio-Political Scenario; A Christian Response, in *A Vision of Mission in the New Millennium*, Malipurathu, Thomas and Stanislaus, L, SVD (Ed), Mumbai: St. Paul's Press, 2001.

Mejia, Rodrigo, SJ, Pastoral Theology and the Pastoral Circle, This paper is an extract from IMBISA Occasional Paper, No. 5 entitled "The Pastoral Circle, Harare-Zimbabwe, 2000.

Mukherje, Charulal, The Santals, Calcutta: A Mukherjee & Co. Pr. Ltd, 1939.

Mulla, Elder, SJ, (Translator), Spiritual Exercises of St. Ignatius, Oregon: Published by the Jesuits of Oregon Province, 2009.

Mundu, John B., Tribal and Indigenous Peoples in India, Media House, Delhi: 2003.

Narrain, Siddharth, Justice for Dalits still a Dream, in *The Hindu* (Indian Newspaper) Thursday, May 11, 2006.

Nazareth, Ashley, Adult Faith Formation through SCCs, in *Vidyajyoti Journal Vol. 65, No. 6*, June 2001.

Nida, Eugene A., Customs, Culture and Christianity, London: The Tyndale Press, 1963.

Nita, Mathur, Santal Worldview, New Delhi: Concept Publishing Company, 2001.

Nolan, Albert, Jesus Before Christianity, New York: Orbis Books, 1978.

Nostra Aetate, Vatican II, The Relation of the Church to Non-Christian Religions, Proclaimed by Pope Paul VI on October 28, 1965.

O`Malley, Lewis Sydney Steward, Bengal District Gazetteers: Santal Parganas, Calcutta: The Bengal Secretariat, Book Department, 1910.

OptatamTotius, Vatican II, Decree on Priestly Training, Proclaimed by Pope Paul VI on October 28, 1965.

Orans, Martin, The Santal: A Tribe in Search of a Great Tradition, Detroit: Wayne State University Press, 1965.

Orientale Lumen. Apostolic Letter Pope John Paul II to the bishops, clergy and faithful to mark the centenary of Orientalum Dignitas of Pope Leo XIII on May 2, 1995.

Our Field (Calcutta Jesuit Mission Newsletter), Jan - Feb 1945.

_______, June, 1939.

_______, March, 1939.

_______, March, 1943.

Pacem in Terris, Encyclical of Pope John XXIII on establishing universal peace in truth, justice, charity and liberty, on April 11, 1963.

Padinjarekuttu, Isaac, "George Soares-Prabhu S.J. and the Quest for a Contextual Theology" in *Biblical Themes for a Contextual Theology*, Soares-Prabhu George S.J., Pune: Jnana-Deepa Vidyapeeth Theology Series, 1999.

Parapullil, Anthony SJ, "Tribal Theology," *Sevartham Vol. 2*, 1977.

Perez-Esclarin, Antonio, Atheism and Liberation, London: SCM Press, 1980.

Petrella, Ivan, The Future of Liberation Theology, London: SCM Press, 2006.

Pieris, Aloysius SJ, An Asian Theology of Liberation, Edinburgh: T&T Clark, 1988.

Pope John Paul II, Slavorum Apostoli (Encyclical Epistle), given in Rome at Saint Peter's by Pope John Paul II on 2 June, 1985.

Pope Pius XII, Evangelii Praecone. Encyclical on promotion of Catholic missions to our venerable brethren, patriarchs, primates, archbishops, bishops and other local ordinaries enjoying peace and communion with the apostolic see by Pope Pius XII on June 2, 1951.

Poupard, Paul (Cardinal), Towards a Pastoral Approach to Culture, Vatican City, May 23, 1999.

Prasad, Narmadeshwan, Land and People of Tribal Bihar, Ranchi: Bihar Tribal Research Institute, 1961.

Puthuparambil, Chacko SJ, Jharkhand me Visthapanevam Manavathikar (Displacement and Human Rights in Jharkhand – English translation), Dumka: Lakshmi Press, 2008.

Randeep, Ramesh, Mumbai terror attacks: India fury at Pakistan as bloody siege is crushed, in *The Observer*, UK, Sunday 30 November 2008.

Ray, Praful Chandra, Socio-Cultural Process and Psychological Adaptation of the Santal, Calcutta: Reliance Printing Works, 1975.

Roth, Cecil (Editor in Chief), The Standard Jewish Encyclopedia, Tel-Aviv: Massadah Publishing Company Ltd, 1958/9.

Sahay, K. N., Dynamics and Democracies of Tribal Societies: Regional and Indian Perspectives, New Delhi: Commonwealth Publishers, 1998.

Sahu, Chaturbhay, The Santal Women: A Social Profile, New Delhi: Sarup & Sons, 1996.

Schineller, Peter, SJ, A Handbook on Inculturation, New York: Paulist Press, 1990.

Scicluna, John SJ, "The Pioneer of the Santal Mission" in *Jesuit Profiles (Some Eminent Jesuits of South Asia)*, Sundaram, Lawrence V (Ed), Gujarat: Gujarat Sahitya Prakash, 1991.

_______, Can You face a Challenge?, Madras: St. Joseph's Technical School, 1961.

Senior, Donald and Stuhlmueller, Carroll, Biblical Foundations for Mission, London: SCM Press Ltd, 1983.

Shorter, Aylward, Toward a Theology of Inculturation, London: Geoffrey Chapman, 1988.

Siggmund, Paul E., Oxford: Liberation Theology at the Crossroads: Democracy or Revolution? Oxford: Oxford University Press, 1990.

Singh, Sunil Kumar, Inside Jharkhand, Ranchi: Crown Publications, 2003.

Singh, Virendra, The Indian Forest Act – 1927, Allahabad (India): Law Publishers, 1976.

Snyder, Graydon F., Inculturation of the Jesus Tradition, Pennsylvania: Trinity Press International, 1999.

Soares-Prabhu, George SJ, Expanding the Horizon of Christian Mission, in Jnana-Deepa Vidyapeeth, Theology Series Vol - I, Pune: 1999.

_______, Theology of Liberation: An Indian Biblical Perspective, in *Collected Writings of George M.Soares-Prabhu, SJ, Vol 4*, D'Sa, Francis X., SJ (ed), Pune: Jnana-Deepa Vidyapeeth Theology Series, 2001.

Sobrino, Jon, Christology at the Crossroads, New York: Orbis Books, 1985.

Sobrino, Jon, The Church and the Poor, London: SCM Press, 1985.

Sublimus Die, Papal Encyclical on the enslavement and evangelization of Indians by Pope Paul III, May 29, 1537.

Synod Document, Diocese of Dumka, Ranchi: Catholic Press, 2000.

Tirkey, Amrit, SJ, Tribal Land: A Theological Reflection, in *Sevartham Vol. 30*, 2005.

Troisi, Joseph, Tribal Religion: Religious Beliefs and Practices among the Santals, New Delhi: Manohar, 1978.

Valamkunnel, Joseph SJ, Deena Sewa Dal: An Ecclesial Movement in the Jungles of Jharkhand, in *Emerging Indian Missiology*, Mattam, Joseph and Valiamangalam Joseph (eds), Delhi: ISPCK, 2006.

Varietates Legitimae, Instruction: Inculturation and the Roman Liturgy, Congregation for Divine Worship and the Discipline of the Sacraments on March 29, 1994.

Vidyarthi, Lalita Prasad & Rai, Brajesh. Kumar, Tribal India: A Dimension of Indian Civilization, New Delhi: Concept Publishing Company, 1985.

W.C.C. (World Council of Churches), Land Rights for Indigenous People, Geneva: W.C.C., 1983.

Waliggo, John Mary, Making a Church that is truly African, in *Inculturation: Its Meaning and Emergency*, Africa: St. Paul's Publications, 1986.

Wilfred, Felix, On the Banks of Ganges (Doing Contextual Theology), Delhi: ISPCK, 2002.

Wilfred, Felix, Sunset in the East, Madras: Siga, 1991.

Web Sites

Adivasi, "Library of Congress Studies", available from: www.wikipediaencyclopedia.com, accessed on 09.05.2008.

Akbar, available from: http://en.wikipedia.org/wiki/Akbar, accessed on 24.04.2008.

Aryans, available from: http://adaniel.tripod.com/aryans.htm, accessed on 09.05.2008.

Asipa, available: www.ishwanikendra.org/docs/articles_asipa, accessed on 12.10.2008.

Asoka, accessed on 24.04.2008, available from: http://en.wikipedia.org/wiki/Akbar.

Beyond Inculturation, (Amaladoss, Michael SJ), available from: http://www.google.com/search?q=beyond+inculturation%2C+Amaladoss&sourceid=navclient-ff&ie=UTF-8&rlz=1B3GGGL_enAT209AT209&aq=t, accessed on 04.11.2008.

Christian Aggression, available from: http://www.christianaggression.org/about_need.php, accessed on 13.05.2008.

Christian Heritage, available from: http://freetruth.50webs.org/A4a.htm, accessed on 08.01.2009.

Christian Mission History, available from: http://home.snu.edu/~HCULBERT/400.htm, accessed on 19.01.2009.

Church Councils, Catholic Encyclopaedia, available from: http://www.newadvent.org/cathen/15030c.htm, accessed on 16.01.2009.

Constitution of India, available from: http://indiacode.nic.in/coiweb/welcome.html, accessed on 09.05.2008.

Contextual Theologizing, (José M. de Mesa), available from: http://eapi.admu.edu.ph/eapr003/mesa.htm, accessed on 17.05.2008.

Culture, available from: http://en.wikipedia.org/wiki/Culture, accessed on 04.11.2008.

District Commissioner, National Informatics Centre, District Profile. "A Land of Vibrant People and Black Stone", Pakur, available from: http://pakur.nic.in/, accessed on 09.05.2008,.

Dumka Diocese, available from: http://www.cbcisite.com/Dumka.htm, accessed on 13.05.2008.

Education and the World Bank, available from: http://web.worldbank.org/Wbsite/External/Topics/Exteducation/0,,Contentmdk:20606691~menuP

K:1463878~pagePK:148956~piPK:216618~theSitePK:282386,00.html, accessed on 13.05.2008,

Evangelisation in a Culture of Pluralism, Challenges and opportunities, (Phan, Peter C), available from: http://dlibrary.acu.edu.au/research/theology/ejournal/aejt_9/phan.htm, accessed on 11.01.2009.

Excommunication, available from: http://www.thefreedictionary.com/anathema, accessed on 02.02.2009.

Hermeneutic circle: available from: http://atheism.about.com/library/glossary/aesthetics/bldef_hermeneuticcircle.htm, accessed on 10.03.2009.

Hindu atrocities against Christians in India, available from: http://www.christian-faith.com/forjesus/hindu-atrocities-against-christians-in-india, accessed on 28.08.2008.

History of the Christian Church, (Schaff, Philip), available from: http://www.ccel.org/s/schaff/history/1__gen.htm, accessed on 22.02.2008.

Inculturation and Ecclesia in Oceania: Pearls in the Deep, (Gibbs, Philip SVD), in Australian EJournal of Theology, ISSUE 3 - ISSN 1448 – 632, August 2004, available from: http://dlibrary.acu.edu.au/research/theology/ejournal/aejt_3/Gibbs.htm, accessed on 02.11.2008.

Inculturation and the Roman Liturgy, available from: http://www.adoremus.org/doc_inculturation.html#anchor819363, accessed on 14.01.2009.

Inculturation as a Missionary/Evangelical Presence in a Religiously Plural Society (Pieris, Aloysius SJ), available from: http://eapi.admu.edu.ph/eapr95/pieris.htm, accessed on 08.01.2009.

Inculturation FABC, available from: http://eapi.admu.edu.ph/eapr94/nemet.htm, accessed on 06.01.2009.

Inculturation, available from http://www.ewtn.com/library/Montfort/Handbook/Incult.htm, accessed on 07.01.2009.

Inculturation, available from: http://eapi.admu.edu.ph/eapr94/nemet.htm, accessed on 04.11.2008.

Inculturation, Enculturation, the soft method, available from: http://ssubbanna.sulekha.com/blog/post/2008/05/inculturation-enculturation-the-soft-method.htm, accessed on 07.12.2008.

Inculturation, Varietates Legitimae 19, 20, available from: http://www.adoremus.org/doc_inculturation.html, accessed on 06.01.2009.

India - Land and People, High Commission of India, London, available from: http://www.hcilondon.net/india-overview/land-people/index.html, accessed on 22.02.2008.

Latin American Christians Reshape Liberation Theology, (Smith, Alex), available from: http://www.villagelife.org/church/archives/pres_latinamerican.html, accessed on 10.04.2008.

Local Churches, (Rayan, Samuel SJ), available from: http://www.sedos.org/english/rayan1.htm, accessed on 10.01.2009.

Mahajans, available from: http://en.wikipedia.org/wiki/Mahajan, accessed on 15.05.2008.

Maps of India, available from: http://www.mapsofindia.com/maps/india/india-political-map.htm, accessed on 22.03.2008.

Matteo Ricci, available from: http://en.wikipedia.org/wiki/Matteo_Ricci, accessed on 09.11.2008.

Melville Jean Herskovits, available from: http://en.wikipedia.org/wiki/Melville_Herskovits, accessed on 04.11.2008.

Mission Today: "Aware we are sent." (FABC Document No. 61), James H. Kroeger, available from: http://www.ucanews.com/html/fabc-papers/fabc-61.htm, accessed on 08.01.2009.

Mughals: available from, http://www.britannica.com/eb/article-9054153/Mughal-Dynasty), accessed on 15.05.2008.

Mysterium Ecclesia, available from: http://www.saint-mike.org/library/Curia/Congregations/Faith/Mysterium_Ecclesiae.html accessed on 17.05.2008.

On a Struggle against communalism, available from: http://www.questia.com/, accessed on 06.03.2008,

Propaganda Fide: available from, http://mv.vatican.va/3_EN/pages/x-Schede/METs/METs_Main_06.html, accessed on 19.01.2009.

Purnea Diocese, available from: http://www.cbcisite.com/Purnea.htm, accessed on 13.05.2008.

Raiganj Diocese, available from: http://www.cbcisite.com/Raiganj.htm, accessed on 13.05.2008.

Ram Mohan Roy, available from: http://en.wikipedia.org/wiki/Ram_Mohan_Roy, accessed on 24.04.2008.

Restoring The Fundamental Human Rights of Indigenous Peoples, available from: http://www.aaanativearts.com/article1543.html, accessed on 16.01.2009.

Roberto de Nobili, available from: http://www.jesuit.org.uk/inter-faith/whowasdenobili.htm, accessed on 09.11.2008.

Ryot, A peasant or cultivator of the soil, available from: http://www.thefreedictionary.com/Ryot, accessed on 29.05.2008.

Sanskritization, available from: ttp://en.wikipedia.org/wiki/Sanskritization, accessed on 25.02.2008.

Sebastian Kappen, available from: http://en.wikipedia.org/wiki/Sebastian_Kappen, accessed on 26.02.08.

Sir Edward Tylor, available from: http://en.wikipedia.org/wiki/Edward_Tylor, accessed on 29.12.2008.

Sri Ramakrishna Paramahamsa, available from: http://en.wikipedia.org/wiki/Ramakrishna, accessed on 24.04.2008.

Syncretism, available from: http://en.wikipedia.org/wiki/Syncretism, accessed on 21.01.2009.

The Inculturation of the Christian Gospel, (Pruitt, Richard A), available from: http://edt.missouri.edu/Fall2007/Thesis/PruittR-121207-T9136/research.pdf, accessed on 11.12.2008.

The Tribes of India, (Krishnanand Laxman Kamat), available from: http://www.culturopedia.com/, accessed on 09.05.2008,

Theologies: Liberation Vs Submission, (Jean-Pierre Cloutier), accessed on 08.04.2008, available from: http://www.cyberie.qc.ca/jpc/haiti/theology.html.

Theologizing at the Service of Life: The Contextual Theological Methodology of FABC, FABC Papers No. 108, (Yun-Ka Tan, Jonathan), available from: http://www.ucanews.com/html/fabc-papers/fabc-0.htm, accessed on 08.03.2008.

Towards Asian Liturgical Inculturation FABC Paper No. 89, (Jonathan Yun-Ka Tan), available from: http://www.ucanews.com/html/fabc-papers/fabc-89.htm, accessed on 05.11.2008.

Tribes of India – The Origin of Races in India, available from: www.culturopedia.com, accessed on 09.05.2005.

Why India? Indians Against Missionaries, available from: http://home.ntelos.net/~userper/religion/why_india.htm, accessed on 25.03.2008.

World Christian Database, available from: http://www.christianaggression.com/item_display.php?type=NEWS&id=1114450073, accessed on, 25.02.2008.